RUSSIA SINCE 1980

Russia Since 1980 recounts the epochal political, economic, and social changes that destroyed the Soviet Union, ushering in a perplexing new order. Two decades after Mikhail Gorbachev initiated his regime-wrecking radical reforms, Russia has reemerged as a superpower. It has survived a hyperdepression, modernized, restored private property and business, adopted a liberal democratic persona, and asserted claims to global leadership. Many in the West perceive these developments as proof of a better globalized tomorrow, while others foresee a new cold war. Globalizers contend that Russia is speedily democratizing, marketizing, and humanizing, creating a regime based on the rule of law and respect for civil rights. Opponents counterclaim that Russia before and during the Soviet period was similarly misportrayed and insist that Dmitri Medvedev's Russia is just another variation of an authoritarian "Muscovite" model that has prevailed for more than five centuries. The cases for both positions are explored while chronicling events since 1980, and a verdict is rendered in favor of Muscovite continuity. Russia will continue to challenge the West until it breaks with its cultural legacy.

Steven Rosefielde is Professor of Economics at the University of North Carolina, Chapel Hill; former Adjunct Professor of National Security Affairs, U.S. Naval Post-graduate School; and Adjunct Professor of Defense and Strategic Studies, Center for Defense and Strategic Studies, Missouri State University, Springfield. The author or editor of thirteen books on Russia and the Soviet Union, he has also published more than a hundred articles in journals such as the *American Economic Review, European Economic Review, Economica, Soviet Studies,* and *Europe-Asia Studies.* Professor Rosefielde is a member of the Russian Academy of Natural Sciences and was a Fellow of the Carnegie Corporation of New York from 2000 to 2003. He has served as a consultant to the Office of the Secretary of Defense. He has also advised several directors of the U.S. Central Intelligence Agency; the Central Economics and Mathematics Institute, Moscow, for more than a quarter-century; and the Center for Defense and Foreign Policy, Moscow, for more than a decade.

Stefan Hedlund is Professor of East European Studies at Uppsala University, Sweden. Before 1991, his research was centered on the Soviet economic system. Since then, he has been focusing on Russia's adaptation to post-Soviet realities. This has included research on the multiple challenges of economic transition as well as the importance of Russia's historical legacy for the reforms. His latest book, among sixteen authored and coauthored titles in English and Swedish, is *Russian Path Dependence* (2005). Professor Hedlund received a master's degree in economics from the University of California, Santa Barbara, and his doctorate in economics from the University of Lund, Sweden.

THE WORLD SINCE 1980

This new series is designed to examine politics, economics, and social change in important countries and regions over the past two and a half decades. No prior background knowledge of a given country will be required by readers. The books are written by leading social scientists.

Volumes published

Brazil Since 1980; Francisco Vidal Luna and Herbert S. Klein

Israel Since 1980; Guy Ben-Porat, Yagil Levy, Shlomo Mizrahi, Ayre Naor, and Erez Tzfadia

Japan Since 1980; Thomas Cargill and Takayuki Sakamoto

Mexico Since 1980; Stephen Haber, Herbert S. Klein, Noel Maurer, and Kevin J. Middlebrook

Russia Since 1980; Steven Rosefielde and Stefan Hedlund

The United States Since 1980; Dean Baker

Volumes in preparation

Britain Since 1980; Roger Middleton

China Since 1980; Ross Garnaut

France Since 1980; Timothy Smith

India Since 1980; Sumit Ganguly

RUSSIA SINCE 1980

Wrestling with Westernization

Steven Rosefielde

University of North Carolina, Chapel Hill

Stefan Hedlund

Uppsala University, Sweden

CAMBRIDGE
UNIVERSITY PRESS

CAMBRIDGE UNIVERSITY PRESS
Cambridge, New York, Melbourne, Madrid, Cape Town, Singapore, São Paulo, Delhi

Cambridge University Press
32 Avenue of the Americas, New York, NY 10013-2473, USA

www.cambridge.org
Information on this title: www.cambridge.org/9780521613842

First published 2009

Printed in the United States of America

A catalog record for this publication is available from the British Library.

Library of Congress Cataloging in Publication Data
Rosefielde, Steven.
Russia since 1980 / Steven Rosefielde, Stefan Hedlund.
    p.   cm. – (The world since 1980)
Includes bibliographical references and index.
ISBN 978-0-521-84913-5 (hdbk.) – ISBN 978-0-521-61384-2 (pbk.)
1. Russia (Federation) – Politics and government – 1991–   2. Soviet Union – Politics and
government – 1985–1991.   3. Russia (Federation) – Economic conditions – 1991–
4. Soviet Union – Economic conditions – 1985–1991.   5. Russia (Federation) – Social
conditions – 1991–   6. Soviet Union – Social conditions – 1970–1991.   I. Hedlund, Stefan,
1953–   II. Title.   III. Series.
DK510.763.R664   2008
947.085′4–dc22   2008033627

ISBN   978-0-521-84913-5 hardback
ISBN   978-0-521-61384-2 paperback

In memory of my beloved son David Rosefielde

Contents

List of Figures, Tables, and Boxes

Figures

Tables

Boxes

Acronyms

ASUP	Automatic System of Management and Planning
CIA	American Central Intelligence Agency
CIS	Commonwealth of Independent States (former Soviet Republics)
CPSU	Communist Party of the Soviet Union (KPSS)
EU	European Union
FSB	*Federal'naia sluzhba bezopasnosti Rossiiskoi Federatsii*
GDP	Gross Domestic Product
Genshtab	Soviet Armed Forces General Staff
glavk	Main Sub-ministerial Department
Gosarbitrazh	State Arbitration Agency
Gosbank	State Bank
Goskomstat	State Statistics Committee
Goskomtsen	State Price Committee
Gosplan	State Planning Agency
Gossnabsbyt	State Committee for Material–Technical Supply (wholesale procurement and distribution agency)
Gosstandart	State Standards Committee
Gosstroi	State Construction Agency
GosTekhnika	State Committee for New Technology
GRU	Main Intelligence Administration of the General Staff of the Russian Armed Forces
Gulag	State Concentration Camp System
IMF	International Monetary Fund
KGB	State Security Committee (secret police)
khrozraschyot	economic cost accounting (self-financing state enterprises)
kolkhoz	collective farm
METI	Ministry of Economics Trade and Industry (Japan)

MFT	Ministry of Foreign Trade
NEP	New Economic Policy
nepmen	private businessmen without property ownership right
NMP	Net Material Product
OECD	Organization for Economic Cooperation and Development
OPK	Defense Industrial Complex (alternative name for VPK)
perestroika	radical economic market reform
piatiletki	five year plans
Politburo	Political Bureau (Highest State Political Body)
predpriatie	enterprises
prodrazverstka	product requisitioning (without compensation)
RDT&E	Research Development Testing and Evaluation
Sovkhoz	State farm
tekhpromfinplan	enterprise technical, industrial, financial plan
USSR	Union of Soviet Socialist Republics
VPK	Military Industrial Complex
WTO	World Trade Organization

Timeline

882	Oleg first Grand Prince of Kiev
1054	Death of Yaroslav the Wise
1147	First mention of Moscow
1169	Sack of Kiev by Andrei Bogolyubsky
1237–40	Mongol Storm
1240	Kiev destroyed by the Mongols
1385	Dynastic union between Poland and Lithuania
1389	Dmitry Donskoi defeats the Mongols at Kulikovo
1462	Ivan the Great becomes Grand Prince of Muscovy
1471	First war between Muscovy and Novgorod
1480	End of Mongol Yoke
1494	Defeat of Novgorod by Muscovy, closure of the Hansa Yard and arrest of German merchants
1547	Ivan the Terrible becomes first tsar
1558–82	Livonian war
1565–72	Oprichnina, partition of the land
1569	Commonwealth of Poland-Lithuania
1598	Death of Fyodor II, start of the *time of trouble*
1613	Mikhail Romanov elected tsar, end of the *time of trouble*
1645	Mikhail dead, succeeded by Alexei
1649	Ulozhenie law code, de facto recognizes serfdom
1682	Alexei dead, Peter the Great shares throne with Sophia
1689	Peter the Great becomes tsar in his own right
1700	Start of Great Northern War, defeat against Sweden at Narva
1703	Founding of St. Petersburg
1709	Defeat of Swedish King Charles XII at Poltava
1712	Government moves to St. Petersburg
1721	Peace with Sweden at Nystad, Peter the Great proclaimed Emperor

1725	Death of Peter the Great, Catherine I Empress
1762	Peter III Emperor for six months, mandatory service abolished for the gentry
1762	Catherine the Great Empress
1767	Legislative commission
1773–75	Pugachev rebellion
1785	Charter of the Nobility, introduction of property rights
1796	Death of Catherine the Great, Paul emperor
1801	Alexander I becomes emperor, following murder of Paul
1812	Napoleon invades Russia
1825	Nicholas I becomes emperor, Decembrist coup
1853–57	Crimean War
1855	Death of Nicholas I, Alexander II becomes emperor
1861	Emancipation of the serfs
1864	Judicial reform
1881	Alexander II dead in terrorist bombing, Alexander III emperor
1884	Criminal code, repression
1894	Nicholas II emperor, last of the Romanovs
1904	War against Japan
1905	Defeat by Japan, Bloody Sunday in St. Petersburg, October Manifesto
1906	Basic law, elections to a duma
1914–18	Great War
1917	February Revolution, October coup d'etat
1921	Introduction of NEP
1924	Lenin dies
1928	First Five Year Plan
1930	Mass collectivization
1934	Victors' Congress
1936	Stalin Constitution
1936–38	Purges, show trials
1939	Molotov-Ribbentrop Pact
1941	Nazi Germany invades the USSR
1945	Victory over Germany
1953	Death of Stalin
1961	Cuban Missile Crisis
1964	Khrushchev ousted, Brezhnev becomes general secretary
1979	Soviet invasion of Afghanistan
1980	Olympic Games in Moscow
1982	Brezhnev dies, succeeded by Yurii Andropov

1984	Andropov dies, succeeded by Konstantin Chernenko
1985	Chernenko dies, succeeded by Mikhail Gorbachev
1986	Chernobyl nuclear disaster, first summit meeting with Ronald Reagan
1987	Central Committee Plenum on radical reform
1989	Velvet revolutions in Central Europe, end of war in Afghanistan
1990	War of laws, USSR on brink of disintegration
1991	Boris Yeltsin president, failed coup, dissolution of USSR
1992	Russian reform
1994	First war in Chechnya
1996	Yeltsin reelected
1998	Financial meltdown in Moscow
1999	Apartment bombings, Putin prime minister, second war in Chechnya, Yeltsin resigns, designates Vladimir Putin as acting president
2000	Putin elected president
2004	Putin reelected president
2007	Putin designates Medvedev heir apparent, Medvedev designates Putin his future prime minister
2008	Medvedev elected president, Putin appointed prime minister

Preface

Soviet civilization failed.[1] This was the verdict of its leaders, and the judgment of history. Whatever its merits may have been, they were eclipsed by the system's material and spiritual defects. What went wrong? Was Bolshevism a degenerate form of the Russian idea?[2] Is the Russian inferior? Or did the fault lie with socialism? Regardless of the answers, where should Russia be heading: toward American democratic free enterprise,[3] European Union social democracy, Muscovy,[4] slavophil anarcho-populism, or some Chinese-type fifth way?

---

[1] Peter Baker and Susan Glasser, *Kremlin Rising: Vladimir Putin's Russia and the End of Revolution*, Scribner, New York, 2005; John Lewis Gaddis, *The Cold War*, Allen Lane, London, 2005.

[2] Tim McDaniel, *The Agony of the Russian Idea*, Princeton University Press, Princeton, NJ, 1996; Igor Chubais, "From the Russian Idea to the Idea of a New Russia: How We Must Overcome the Crisis of Ideas," http://www.aconet.org/wps/chi01. Fyodor Dostoyevsky coined the term *the Russian idea*.

[3] The term *democratic free enterprise* here and throughout the text refers to an ideal system in which consumer sovereignty prevails in competitively efficient markets and popular sovereignty determines public choice through fair ballots and other forms of democratic participation. The concept has been formalized by Abram Bergson in his works on welfare economics and coincides closely with what Paul Samuelson and others consider neoclassical economics. The terms *EU social democracy, slavophilism,* and *anarcho-populism* are used in the same ideal senses. America embraces democratic free enterprise as its credo but doesn't adhere strictly to it. Similar lapses between theory and practice apply to other systems. See Steven Rosefielde, *American Democracy: Icon and Mirage*, 2008, unpublished manuscript; Abram Bergson, "The Concept of Social Welfare," *Quarterly Journal of Economics*, 68, 2(May 1954): 233–52, Bergson, "Social Choice and Welfare Economics under Representative Government," *Journal of Public Economics*, 6, 3(1967): 171–90.

[4] Authoritarian rent-granting governance regime established in the fifteenth century by Ivan the Great, Grand Duke of Muscovy. See chapter 1.

Choosing the right course has been the burning question of Russian history since Peter the Great flirted with westernization in the late seventeenth century, succinctly expressed by Nikolai Chernyshevsky's rallying cry "*Chto delat?*" (What is to be done?).[5] Should Russia westernize in a libertarian or socialist mode, trust in anarcho-populism, or, as slavophiles argued, follow a more spiritual trajectory?[6]

Westernizing intellectuals from the eighteenth century onward, such as Mikhail Tugan-Baranovsky, championed democracy and markets running the gamut from Smithian small government libertarianism to Meadean social democracy.[7] The common denominators connecting these ideas were individual empowerment, happiness, sovereignty, and social justice. The good society for westernizers was one in which people were free to maximize their utility, constrained only by a Lockean social contract, including the rule of law and the democratic provision of collectivist public services.

Anarcho-populists shared similar goals, but distrusted capitalist markets, while slavophiles saw unbridled individual self-seeking as an Enlightenment anathema. They advocated communalist principles of social organization and mutual support instead. Slavophiles might concede that westernizers could accommodate communalism under their tent but were convinced nonetheless that the selfishness of westernizers would triumph over altruism.

However, most westernizers, anarcho-populists, and slavophiles concurred on one point. Bolshevism was reprehensible. Liberal westernizers in particular condemned communist criminalization of business, entrepreneurship, and private property. They rejected one-party authoritarianism, the curtailment of civil and religious freedoms, secret

---

[5] Nikolai Gavrilovich Chernyshevsky (1828–89) was a Russian revolutionary democrat, socialist, and founder of Narodism (Russian populism). He wrote "Chto Delat?" (What is to be Done?) in the St. Peter and Paul Fortress after his arrest in 1862.

[6] Slavophilism, sometimes called Russophilism, affirms the uniqueness of Russian culture, founded on Eastern Orthodoxy, stressing spiritual universalism, the Russian search for the City of God, not Russian provincialism. See Nikolai Berdyaev, "Slavophilism and the Slavic Idea," in *The Fate of Russia*, 1915, www.beryaev.com/berdiaev/berd_lib/1915_202.html. Resistance to modernization is common in most traditional cultures, and the concerns raised are often valid.

[7] M. I. Tugan Baranovsky, *The Russian Factory in the 19th Century*, Richard D. Irwin, Homewood, IL, 1970; James Meade, *The Just Economy*, George Allen and Unwin, London, 1978.

police repression, and structural militarization. Anarcho-populists and slavophiles cared little about state suppression of democratic free enterprise but bemoaned Soviet oppression of communality, mutual support, and orthodoxy.[8]

These criticisms weren't the whole story. Many liberals and socialists who acknowledged Bolshevism's flaws still found redeeming value, holding out hope that the system's vices would eventually be purged. However, this wishful thinking is no longer persuasive. Most who once maintained that Soviet communism might ultimately be better than democratic free enterprise accept the verdict of history.

Discrediting Soviet communism however has not settled the question of *Chto delat*. Russia's leaders remain ambivalent. They desire the advantages of western industrial modernization as they did during the Soviet era and seek the benefits of partial marketization but still cling to the Muscovite authoritarian martial police state (the other dominant face of the Russian idea). They embrace the rhetoric of liberalism and popular self-determination, while acting like autocrats. They know what should be done to achieve the ideas of the West and East, but what will they do? The answer for the last half-millennium has been to profess western, populist, or slavophil ideals but act as apostles of the authoritarian martial police state, despite its instability, vulnerability, and inferior economic potential. This still seems the most likely course, but the die isn't cast. For centuries, Muscovite engagement with modernity and the West has been a fitful tug of war between ruler self-interest and statesmanship, glossed with idealist rhetoric. The result at every critical juncture has been inferior, or even catastrophic, but the haphazard quest for a better system, incorporating successful elements from the outside world, goes on and could ultimately yield satisfactory results. Perhaps Russia can outgrow its addiction to rent-granting and emulate a more dynamic, commercially oriented authoritarian model like China's. This volume accepts Russia's multipotentiality without cosmetic gloss. It elaborates the ingredients of the Russian drama, documenting the state of play and highlighting the gap between Kremlin claims and contemporary realities and trends pointing toward the perpetuation of Muscovy. It characterizes the events since 1980, including Leonid Brezhnev's reforms, Mikhail Gorbachev's Market Communism, Boris Yeltsin's Market Muscovy, and

---

[8] A.V. Chayanov, *The Theory of Peasant Economy*, Richard D. Irwin, Homewood, IL, 1966.

Vladimir Putin's imperial martial police state as a missed historical opportunity to westernize,[9] permanently end the cold war, and foster prosperity with all Russia's neighbors. Perhaps Dmitri Medvedev or some other ruler will achieve better results after Putin vacates the stage, but progress won't be easy.

---

[9] Putin has embraced Anatoly Chubais's advocacy of liberal imperialism. The state is autocratic. Russia may well have the world's largest army. The *Federal'naia sluzhba bezopasnosti Rossiiskoi Federatsii* or FSB (secret police) disciplines opposition and society.

Acknowledgments

Scholars always stand on the shoulders of their predecessors. We owe a debt of gratitude to a vast array of Soviet and Russian specialists throughout the globe. Several institutions supported this undertaking in various ways, including the Institute for Arts and Humanities (University of North Carolina) and Trento University. We thank them and their directors, John McGowan and Bruno Dallago. In addition, we express our deep-felt appreciation to Nancy Kocher, who typed and corrected endless manuscript drafts, and to Susan and Justine Rosefielde for their steadfast support.

Introduction

The collapse of the Soviet Union was "the greatest geopolitical catastrophe of the 20th century."

Vladimir Putin, April 24, 2005

The year 1980 can be viewed as the beginning both of the end of Soviet communism and a time of turbulent Russian transformation.[1] The era that ensued began on a humdrum note with Soviet declarations of socialist superiority, tempered by concerns about the changing *correlation of forces*, and western expectations of Kremlin *muddling through* with no appreciation that the economy might have entered a period of protracted stagnation. And it continued through what can be called Vladimir Putin's imperial authoritarian restoration. In between, the Communist Party of the Soviet Union, which oversaw a *socialist* centrally planned, authoritarian martial police state, tried to liberalize, modernize, and partly westernize by adopting Mikhail Gorbachev's ambitious program of *glasnost* (political candor), *demokratizatsia* (democratization), *uskorenie* (GDP growth acceleration), *perestroika* (radical economic reform), and *novoe myslennie* (new thinking to end the cold war). Although widely heralded at home and abroad, these programs contributed variously to an acute economic depression, the destruction of communist power, and the dissolution of the USSR into fifteen independent republics, culminating in the Kremlin's loss of 30 percent of its territories and 48 percent of its population.[2]

---

[1] This treatise is part of a Cambridge University Press nation studies series covering the period 1980 to the present.

[2] Steven Rosefielde, *Russian Economics from Lenin to Putin*, Blackwell, London, 2006, chapter 8.

1

The post-Soviet years were similarly convulsive. Boris Yeltsin, Russia's first postcommunist president, undaunted by the results of Gorbachev's Muscovite liberalization,[3] chose an even more extreme course mislabeled *perekhod* (radical market transition), which purportedly sought to expand the scope of late Soviet era business, entrepreneurship, and private property with *shock* therapeutic methods, to open the economy to globalization, and forge a multiparty democracy. In the process, Yeltsin restored media freedom, drastically cut military expenditures, and curbed the powers of the secret police. Had these liberalizing, modernizing, and westernizing policies reflected the government's primary motive they would have been more beneficial. But they were mostly secondary policies abetting or concealing the asset-grabbing and revenue misappropriation that immiserized much of the population.[4] Democracy too was honored more in word than in deed, leading to a palace coup d'etat orchestrated by the *Federal'naia sluzhba bezopasnosti Rossiiskoi Federatsii* (FSB) that installed secret police head Vladimir Putin as Yeltsin's successor in 2000.[5]

Putin's presidency marked the end of the first phase of post-Soviet regime change. Under his aegis, multiparty democracy, which survives in name only, all but vanished in practice. Power was consolidated in his hands, despite the facade of balloting, much like arrangements during Soviet times. The secret police was revitalized, military spending revived, civil liberties curtailed, the press muzzled, and the independence of large corporations restricted.[6] Although Putin proclaimed an ambitious program to end mass poverty, his first initiative drastically pared Soviet era social welfare programs,[7] pauperizing many and further widening the gulf between rich and poor, despite an oil boom. This action, together with the disintegration of the Russian Communist Party led some analysts to declare 2004 as the real start

---

[3] Muscovite refers to autocratic governance strategies characteristic of Ivan the Great, founder of the Russian state in the fifteenth century. See Chapter 1.

[4] Ibid., chapter 11.

[5] Stephen Blank, "The 18th Brumaire of Vladimir Putin," in Uri Ra'anan (ed.), *Flawed Succession: Russia's Power Transfer Crisis*, Lexington Books for Rowman and Littlefield, Lanham, MD, 2005, pp. 133–70.

[6] Steven Rosefielde, *Russia in the 21st Century: The Prodigal Superpower*, Cambridge University Press, London, 2005.

[7] Irina Skliarova and Ksenia Veretennikova, "The Social Pyramid," *Johnson's Russia List*, No. 8281, Article 2, July 5, 2004. "There will be no 'monetization of benefits.' Essentially, the previous system will be replaced by a hybrid of in-kind benefits and monetary compensation. Benefits will be retained only by disabled persons and World War II veterans. Other pensioners will lose everything."

of the postcommunist epoch, the year the social contract between Russia's rulers and masses became null and void, replaced by a new form of Muscovite rent-granting beholden to neither aristocrats nor the proletariat.[8] As Yevgeny Yasin, Russia's former economics minister expressed it, "Russia still has no property rights other than the Tsar's – the rest is merely a brief given in return for service."[9]

Of course, Yasin may be mistaken. Putin, now prime minister, and newly elected president Dmitri Medvedev still sometimes insist that their goal is to westernize, to transform Russia into a democratic free enterprise system founded on the rule of law and social justice.[10] And the Kremlin occasionally contends that Russia wants to reduce its military to the bare minimum and integrate into the global economy.[11] The epic therefore continues to unfold. Is Russia heading forward to a new model putting the Muscovite authoritarian police state behind it or back to the future?[12] The situation is murkier than before, and even the G-7 is having second thoughts about the inevitability of the democratic free enterprise transition it desires.[13]

This shouldn't be surprising. Western scholars for centuries have misappraised Russian prospects for liberalization, democratization, westernization, and even a better authoritarianism through the prism

---

[8] Peter Lavelle, "Putin Ends the 'Old Regime.'" *Johnson's Russia List*, No. 8283, Article 11, July 6, 2004.

[9] "Privatization Was Economically Ineffective – Audit Chamber," *Johnson's Russia List*, No. 8279, Article 12, July 3, 2004.

[10] Alan Cullison and Andrew Osborn, "Russia Shuffle Keeps Putin in Play: Medvedev Offers His Backer Prime Minister Position," *Johnson's Russia List*, No. 254, Article 4, December 12, 2007.

[11] But as usual the signals are contradictory. See "Russia's Ivanov Calls for Parity between Russian, US Nuclear Forces," *Johnson's Russia List*, No. 253, Article 425, December 12, 2007.

[12] Andrew Kuchins, "Alternative Futures for Russia to 2017," *Johnson's Russia List*, No. 256, Article 4, December 4, 2007; Anders Aslund, "Putin's Three Ring Circus, "*Johnson's Russia List*, No. 256, Article 24, December 14, 2007.

[13] *World Bank Report, From Transition to Development: Poverty Reduction and Economic Management Unit Europe and Central Asia Region*, April, 2004, www.worldbank. org.ru; Oleh Havrylyshyn, "Unchartered Waters, Pirate Raids, and Safe Havens: A Parsimonious Model and Transition Progress," paper presented at the BOFIT/CEFIR Workshop on Transition Economics, Helsinki, Finland, April 2–3, 2004, Havrylyshyn, *Divergent Paths in Post-Communist Transformation*, Palgrave Macmillan, Basingstoke, UK, 2006. George Tenet, Director of Central Intelligence, "The Worldwide Threat 2004: Challenges in a Changing Global Context," testimony before the Senate Select Committee on Intelligence, February 24, 2004, excerpted in *Johnson's Russia List*, No. 8089, Article 1, February 27, 2004.

of their Enlightenment premises.[14] At least since the time of Catherine the Great (1729–96), they have predicted that Russia would emulate and catch up with its west European peers, but the path has never been straight or certain. The dominant motif for nearly a half-millennium has been best described by Alexander Gerschenkron's concept of continuity and change.[15] Russia since Ivan III, called Ivan the Great (1440–1501), grand duke of Muscovy has survived a series of crises, where leaders recognize the nation's backwardness, partially adapt causing a growth spurt, followed by a protracted period of stagnation before resuming a forward course without ever overtaking Europe, or embracing westernization (including democratic socialism). This pattern, and the accompanying persistent backwardness are a consequence of Russia's protean Muscovite culture, which adapts in its own fashion without assimilating the Enlightenment ideal of socially just, democratic free enterprise (consumer sovereignty in the private sector and popular sovereignty over public programs), or shedding its reliance on rent-granting as the preferred form of government control. Instead of making individual welfare the centerpiece of its worldview, Muscovite regimes place the tsar (subsequently the general secretary of the Communist Party, and more recently the president) at the apex of an authoritarian hierarchy. Whether explicit or implicit, the autocrat owns the realm, delegating the management of his assets to rent-seekers who generate incomes for themselves in return for taxes and service. Few restrictions are placed on these *servitors* who are usually permitted to oppress those under their control. Russian serfs were more slaves than feudal peasants. They could be bought and sold and forced to work in industrial factories, without the customary protections of western Europe. There were edicts but no rule of law.[16]

As a consequence, pre-Soviet Russia was astonishingly unjust from the perspective of contemporaneous western norms. A small segment

[14] David Engerman, *Modernization from The Other Shore: American Intellectuals and the Romance of Russian Development, Article 1*, Harvard University Press, Cambridge, MA, 2003.
[15] Alexander Gerschenkron, "Russia: Patterns and Problems of Economics Development, 1861–1958," in Alexander Gerschenkron (ed.), *Economic Backwardness in Historical Perspective*, Harvard University Press, Cambridge, MA, 1962, pp.119–51.
[16] Mikhail Tugan-Baranovsky, *The Russian Factory in the 19th Century*, Richard D. Irwin, Homewood, IL, 1970.

of society lived lavishly off the land, resources, and people, while the vast majority was pauperized without civil rights, legal recourse, or democratic process. These grievances sparked mass movements for political change and social justice during the late nineteenth century. Although political parties had little power, their struggle for social liberation seemed to have borne fruit in the Bolshevik coup d'etat of 1917. Many social romantics claimed that *revolutionary* Soviet Russia embodied superior principles of socialist enlightenment. People not only received the right to vote, to assemble, to protest, to think freely, and to express their views publicly but also were granted equal opportunity regardless of gender, race, ethnicity, and religion. Whereas western democratic free enterprise in practice only provided the illusion of a fair social contract, some contended that Bolshevism eradicated injustice.

This wishful thinking however was soon shattered. By 1922, Emma Goldman fully detailed in *My Disillusionment in Russia* how Lenin had snuffed out political pluralism, creating a one-party police state.[17] There were triumphal claims of empowerment, equality, and social justice, but they had little substance. The state modernized, fostering universal education and employment after 1928 in effort to overcome economic backwardness. Incomes also became more egalitarian because of the *liquidation* of the tsar, nobles, and capitalists as a class, but throughout, the state's primary interest was what the people could do for the party, not how the regime could enhance the people's welfare. Nowhere was this more apparent than in Lenin's nationalization of private property and business. In free enterprise societies, people have the right to run businesses, start new companies (entrepreneurship), and own productive property and financial assets. Each of these rights provides expanded channels for maximizing individual utility, including the right of self-employment. The Bolsheviks by contrast preferred to reserve these rights to the state by criminalizing business, entrepreneurship, and private property. With some small exceptions, almost everyone was prohibited from working for himself under these ground rules. The state became the sole source employer, placing everyone's livelihood and personal freedom at its mercy. Instead of liberating the people, Soviet economic relations, combined with an omnipresent police state, kept most of the population servile. Where

---

[17] Emma Goldman, *My Disillusionment in Russia*, Thomas Y. Crowell, New York, 1970.

socialist romanticism dreamed of utopia, reality was transmuted into dystopia (cacatopia), especially under Stalin.[18]

The social upheaval wrought first by Gorbachev's destruction of the Soviet Union and Yeltsin's heady promises of radical westernization have revived Russian aspirations for freedom and social justice. This motif will be used throughout to guide our narrative. The promises of the past few decades will be contrasted with the reality of persistent authoritarianism, rent-granting, inequity, injustice, and repressed civil liberties. At the end of the day, it will be shown that while the struggle for economic, political, and social justice; affluence and national power has yielded some post-Soviet successes, and better outcomes are possible by borrowing from other authoritarian martial police states such as China, Muscovy remains, without a virtuous Russian idea to navigate a superior future.

---

[18] Steven Rosefielde, *Red Holocaust*, Routledge 2009. Dystopia is the antithesis of utopia, a realm where everything that is supposed to be perfectly good turns out perfectly bad. If utopia is heaven, dystopia is hell. The term was first used by John Stuart Mill in the nineteenth century. Jeremy Bentham coined the synonym *cacatopia*, often spelled *kakatopia*.

PART I

RUSSIA BEFORE 1980

1

Muscovy and the West

Russians dislike westerners portraying them as European cultural outsiders and attribute the stereotype to Russophobia.[1] However, they acknowledge and even celebrate their exceptionalism among themselves.[2] As Alexander Gerschenkron phrased it, Russia might have been just like Europe if Tartar domination (1237–1480) and its malign legacy hadn't prevented it from assimilating three great cultural movements: humanism, the Renaissance (fourteenth to seventeenth centuries), and the Reformation (1517).[3] Even this formulation is too generous. Russia also lacked any practical acquaintance with Roman law, which underlay the Magna Carta and the foundations of western economic, political, and civic institutions. For at least a millennium, the land of Russia has been different, even though it has modernized and borrowed western institutions in its own fashion over the centuries.

A deep appreciation of Russia's special characteristics and potential is indispensable for any serious assessment of the post-Soviet epoch, its immediate antecedents, and its prospects. Without it, analysts tend to assume that the economic, political, and societal foundations of Russia and the West are identical, that the only factor dividing them is

---

[1] "Triumphant Vengeance: Philosopher Zinoviev Considers That the West Regained Its Power Thanks to Russia's Defeat," *Pravda*, June 30, 2004, reprinted in *Johnson's Russia List*, No. 8276, Article 15, July 1, 2004.

[2] Alexander Yakovlev, *A Century of Violence in Soviet Russia*, Yale University Press. New Haven, CT, 2002; cf. Richard Pipes, "Flight from Freedom: What Russians Think and Want," *Foreign Affairs*, May–June 2004; James Billington, *Russia in Search of Itself*, Woodrow Wilson Center, Washington DC, 2004.

[3] Alexander Gerschenkron, *Europe in the Russian Mirror: Four Lectures in Economic History*, Cambridge University Press, London, 1970.

relative backwardness, and that any unfinished business will be speedily completed, culminating in Russia's full westernization. Where there once was a gulf separating East and West in the tsarist and Soviet eras, the East now is expected to dissolve seamlessly into the West. Indeed, this was the dominant view until the spring of 2004, when Vladimir Putin's growing authoritarianism and economic illiberalism gave pause to both the World Bank and the American Central Intelligence Agency (CIA).[4] Since then, talk of imminent transition by government institutions and specialists has ceased.[5]

Why did Russia disappoint them? It is easy to blame Putin, but his personal priorities and ethics are only part of the story. More than anything else, his actions and those of his predecessors Mikhail Gorbachev and Boris Yeltsin were forged in the matrix of Muscovite

[4] World Bank Report, *From Transition to Development, Poverty Reduction and Economic Management Unit Europe and Central Asia Region*, April, 2004, www.worldbank.org.ru; CIA, *Global Trends 2015 on Russia*, reprinted in *Johnson's Russia List,* No. 8192, Article 3, May 2, 2004; George Tenet, Director of Central Intelligence, "The Worldwide Threat 2004: Challenges in a Changing Global Context," testimony before the Senate Select Committee on Intelligence, February 24, 2004, excerpted in *Johnson's Russia List*, No. 8089, Article 10, February 27, 2004. For a contrary view, see Stanley Fisher and Ratna Sahay, "Transition Economies: The Role of Institutions and Initial Conditions," in *Festschrift in Honor of Guillermo A. Calvo*, April 15–16, 2004. These authors argue that "the accusation that the IFIs lost Russia, and the charge that shock treatment and too rapid privatization produced unnecessary output losses, disorganization, corruption and misery have been familiar parts of the indictment of the approach recommended by western officials and other advisers. In our earlier work (Fischer, Sahay and Vegh, 1996a, 1996b, and 1998) we concluded that the transition experience confirmed the view that both macroeconomic stabilization and structural reforms contribute to growth, and that the more structural reform that took place, the more rapidly the economy grew. In this paper we . . . argue that the charge that the IFIs did not take account of the importance of institutional development, especially the rule of law, is without merit" (p. 3). A similar position is developed in Andrei Shleifer and Daniel Treisman, "A Normal Country," *Foreign Affairs*, 83, 2(March/April 2004). Cf. Steven Rosefielde, "An Abnormal Country," *European Journal of Comparative Economics*, 2, 1(2005): 3–16. Institute for Economies in Transition Discussion Paper, No. 6, 2004. www.bof.fi/BOFIT/.
[5] Marshall Goldman, "Putin and the Oligarchs," *Foreign Affairs*, 83, 6(November/December 2004): 33–44; Michael McFaul, Nikolai Petrov, and Andrei Ryabov, *Between Dictatorship and Democracy: Russian Post-Communist Political Reform*, Carnegie Endowment, Washington, DC, 2004; Jakob H. Hedenskog, Vilhelm Konnander, Bertil Nygren, Ingmar Oldberg, and Christer Pursiainen, *Russia as a Great Power*, Routledge, New York, 2005; Anders Aslund, *Policy Brief No. 41*, Carnegie Endowment for International Peace, August 2005.

culture, traceable to Ivan III Vasilevich, known as Ivan the Great, Grand Prince of Muscovy (1440–1505). The Muscovite idea is that the ruler, whether he is called grand duke, tsar, *vozhd* (leader), general secretary, or president, is an autocrat who, de facto or de jure, owns all of the country's productive assets and governs for himself in the name of the nation.[6] He is the law and rules by edict absolutely or behind a facade of parliamentary constitutionalism. Everyone else is a *rab* (slave of the ruler). Individuals of other stations may have private lives and may seek to maximize their happiness, but they are always subject to commands, edicts, and rules imposed from above by their supreme lord, without protection of the rule of law. They have no inviolable human, property, economic, political, or social rights. Whatever has been given can be rescinded, regardless of custom or precedent. Social welfare in this cultural framework is synonymous with the autocrat's welfare, given whatever allotment he chooses to share with his people.

On its face, universal autocratic ownership and governance seem intrinsically totalitarian.[7] It is easy to imagine Ivan the Terrible (Ivan IV Vasilevich, 1530–84, first tsar of Russia) assigning his servitors detailed economic, administrative, police, martial, and diplomatic tasks and meticulously monitoring their performance. However, comprehensive control was never feasible, even during Joseph Stalin's reign.[8] Autocrats had only sketchy knowledge of their realm, its potentials, and the requirements for efficient utilization and were never successful at devising an honest and effective bureaucracy to do the job for them. Consequently, they were compelled by circumstances to grant servitors substantial independence in operating the autocrat's

---

[6] Stefan Hedlund, *Russian Path Dependence*, Routledge, London, 2005; Richard Pipes, *Property and Freedom*, Alfred A. Knopf, New York, 1999; Alexander Gerschenkron, *Economic Backwardness in Historical Perspective*, Harvard University Press, Cambridge, MA, 1961; Edward Keenan, "Muscovite Political Folkways," *Russian Review*, 45, 2(1986).

[7] Hannah Arendt, *The Origins of Totalitarianism,* Harcourt, Brace, New York, 1951, C. J. Friedrich and Z. K. Brzezinski, *Totalitarian Dictatorship and Autocracy*, Harvard University Press, Cambridge, 1956. A. Gleason, *Totalitarianism: The inner history of the Cold War*, Oxford University Press, New York, 1995. Hans Maier, *Totalitarianism and Political Religions: Concepts for the Comparison of Dictatorships – Theory and History of Interpretations,* Vol. 111, Routledge, Abingdon, 2008. While the USSR was variously dictatorial or despotic, the system wasn't totalitarian because it permitted significant autonomy.

[8] Steven Rosefielde, *Russian Economics from Lenin to Putin*, Blackwell, London, 2006.

properties for their own benefit (*pomestie*) in return for tax and service obligations, while tolerating bureaucratic corruption and inefficiency. Autocrats were rent-grantors, and servitors were rent-seekers.[9] As long as rulers received what they needed, they didn't concern themselves with overpaying or with their deputies' exploitation of the peasantry. This attitude, optimizing where possible and satisficing where circumstances dictated, was coercive, not totalitarian, even though in principle the scope of the tsar's authority was unbounded. It was a callous mechanism for squeezing taxes from a servile population, but not an instrument of comprehensive nano control. Russia's autocrats didn't systematically oppress the people or bother themselves about their plight. They simply permitted their servitors to get the job done whatever that entailed.

The arrangement was paradoxical. On paper, the tsar and the state were all powerful, but they often were weak in practice. In times of crisis, pressure could be exerted to mobilize resources for defense or industrialization, but even then, outcomes depended more on the vagaries of rent-granting in a natural economy with underdeveloped markets, making Russia a colossus with clay feet. The Kremlin could struggle to keep up with the West but remained forever backward.

History, of course, isn't static. Servitors conspired to transform rent-granting into private property. Like paramours scheming for marriage, some of these *stationary bandits* (in Mancur Olson's terminology) were successful.[10] However, a critical mass needed to achieve free enterprise under the rule of contract law or democracy was never reached, even though Catherine the Great relieved the nobility of lifetime service and Tsar Nicholas II's premier Piotr Stolypin (1862–1911) tried to create peasant landownership in the *ukaz* of November 9,

---

[9] *Rent* here and throughout the text is an income acquired from the noncompetitive institutional control of assets rather than competitive labor, management, land, or capital value added. It is not used in the sense of a house or lease payment. On rent-granting and rent-seeking, see Anne Krueger, "The Political Economy of Rent-Seeking Society," *American Economic Review*, 64, 3(1974): 291–303; Peter Boone and D. Rodionov, "Rent Seeking in Russia and the CIS," paper presented at the 10th Anniversary Conference of the EBRD, London, December 2001; Joel Hellman, "Winners Take All: The Politics of Partial Reform in Post-Communist Nations," *World Politics*, 50, 2(1998): 203–34. Leonid Polischuk and Alexei Savvatev, "Spontaneous (non) Emergence of Property Rights," *Economics of Transition*, 12, 1(2004): 103–27.

[10] Mancur Olson, *Power and Prosperity: Outgrowing Capitalist and Communist Dictatorships*, Basic Books, New York, 2000.

1906. Patrimonialist Muscovy was always able to keep rent-granting in command through political intrigue, the secret police, and the army. It refused to serve Douglass North's role of credible enforcer for an autonomous, self-regulating society because sovereigns preferred autocracy to economic and political liberty.[11]

Although the attributes of Muscovy varied from epoch to epoch, its footprint has remained unmistakable, the key traits being patrimonial rent-granting, based on the rule of men rather than the rule of law, where the ruler's optimization is narrowly circumscribed by a short span of control.[12] These characteristics have made Russia a nation extraordinarily dependent on the machinations of the privileged and the tight supervision of the secret police. Effort is primarily mobilized through coercion rather than entrepreneurial initiative and market

[11]   Douglass North and Robert Thomas, *The Rise of the Western World*, Cambridge University Press, London, 1972. There is considerable controversy regarding the persistent domination of Muscovite culture. Numerous reforms have been undertaken that superficially seemed to erode the tradition and persuaded catch-up theorists that Russia was on the high road to westernization. The mainstay of this belief is the notion that Russian culture has evolved, embracing Enlightenment norms, and is only distinguished by its relative backwardness. Perhaps their faith will be validated someday, but it hasn't happened yet. For example, although Catherine the Great introduced a Charter of the Nobility in 1785 formally conferring property rights and due process to the aristocracy, in practice the service nobility preferred to remain within the old framework of serving the tsar and accepting whatever privilege and handout might be granted in return for their service. Even during the heyday of judicial reform under Alexander II, the most prominent of all liberal tsars, the culture of autocracy remained so firmly entrenched that constitutional constraints could not even be seriously discussed. Although the tsar had ministers, he would never allow them to form and meet as a government led by a prime minister. The only exception to this rule was played out in the years 1906–17. Following a series of disasters in the Russo-Japanese war, Tsar Nicholas II was forced into such a retreat that for a few short years Russia really appeared to be on her way toward Europe. There was a constitution providing both for free elections and for a full catalogue of rights. But even if the movement were genuine, the Bolsheviks soon reversed the clock.

[12]   Richard Pipes, *Russia under the Old Regime*, Charles Scribner's Sons, New York 1974; p. 113; cf. David Engerman, *Modernization from the Other Shore*, Harvard University Press, Cambridge, MA, 2004; W. E. Mosse, *Perestroika under the Tsars*, I. B. Taurus & Co., London, 1992; Ester Kingston-Mann, *In Search of the True West: Culture, Economics and Problems of Russian Development*, Princeton University Press, Princeton, NJ, 1998; James Billington, *Icon and Axe*, Random House, New York, 1970. Russian autocrats use legislation and judicial procedures as a means of managing affairs in their interest, but this is the rule of men, not the independent rule of law required by free enterprise. See Ron Childress, "Legal Discourse in Post-Soviet Russia," draft, June, 2007.

discipline,[13] hindering catch-up with the western high-productivity frontier. Conquest has often proven to be more gratifying to rulers than competitive national economic rivalry. They frequently have been content to live lavishly from natural resource–financed foreign imports rather than nurturing high value-added mass production. It is always possible that these cultural proclivities are teething problems and that the Kremlin will soon mature; however, until it does, the model will remain pre-enlightened.

The best way to appreciate the intrinsic defects of the Russian method is to contrast it with what Samuel Huntington calls the *idea of the West*,[14] especially its democratic, libertarian, and social justice components. Unlike the tsar-centered universe of Muscovy, the welfare of each and every individual is primary in the western Enlightenment ideal.[15] People are assumed to be autonomous, rational, and effective in discovering and seizing opportunities to enhance their well-being (utility) efficiently. They are able to perceive and evaluate alternatives in terms of their consistently ordered preferences and choose accordingly. Of course, people aren't fully informed, but they can and do learn. Likewise, the concept isn't inherently selfish. The humanist, Renaissance, Reformation, and Enlightenment traditions encourage everyone to deal with others compassionately, justly, and altruistically, including family, friends, and the larger community. Individuals therefore are thought to be self-reliant and the best judge of what is required for their happiness. Their worth doesn't depend on their servility and service to the tsar. It depends only on how they actualize their human potential.

---

[13] Peter the Great built the first command economy, with the possible exception of Ptolemaic Egypt. His growth strategy rested on forced mobilization of resources, supporting a powerful military-industrial complex. All subjects were drafted into his *Blockian* project for total war. They were required to perform lifelong service to the tsar and were listed in Peter's Table of Ranks. New industries were run by nobles with serf labor, not unlike Stalin's Gulag economy. The *Tabel o rangakh* survived to the end of the empire and was resurrected thereafter in Soviet time as the *nomenklatura system*. There were two lists. One contained all subjects, party members, and others considered for important appointments and the other posts that could not be filled without prior party consent.

[14] Samuel Huntington, *The Clash of Civilizations and the Remaking of World Order*, Simon & Schuster, New York, 1996; Huntington, "The West: Unique, Not Universal," *Foreign Affairs*, 75, 6(1996): 28–46.

[15] The Enlightenment incorporates the heritage of humanism, the Renaissance, and Reformation and is used throughout the text in this sense.

Economists describe the outcome of effective individual utility seeking as consumer sovereignty.[16] The schooling, training, careers, incomes, consumption, investment, and charitable transfers individuals select are the ones they desire, subject to natural and competitive constraints. We can't have everything we want in a resource-scarce world, but we can induce the supply mechanism to provide us with the things we prefer rather than those imposed by tsars and servitors. The idea of the West that everyone should and can be consumer empowered isn't wishful thinking. Vilfredo Pareto (1848–1923) was the first to demonstrate mathematically, using simple and plausible axioms, that people who desire to maximize their utility across all domains of choice can do so if they have well-ordered preference fields and are rational in the sense that their choices correspond with their preferences. In addition, he showed that if these transactions are fairly and voluntarily negotiated, then each individual can achieve a just optimum without the intervention of external authorities.[17]

The preeminence of people's individual wills moreover applies to public goods. In an imperfect world, the social contract and golden rule of fair play assumed by Pareto require enforcement by the rule of contract and criminal law.[18] Similarly, there are many infrastructural, defense, and transfer activities widely believed to be better provided by governments than markets. The idea of the West requires that these programs be designed and implemented in accordance with democratic preferences. Just as with the supply of private goods in the marketplace, democracy offers a mechanism for the establishment of consumer sovereignty in the delivery of public services. Tsars are not needed. The people can govern themselves better than others ruling on their behalf or claiming to serve the nation, although it cannot be proven that they will always do so.

Democracy isn't synonymous with balloting. The rule of the *demos* (people) requires popular sovereignty over public programs, including social justice achieved through participatory consensus, majoritarian ballots, or representation. Officials must not only be elected. They

---

[16] Utility seeking doesn't have to be enlightened to achieve an optimum, but superior ethics improve the quality of consumer sovereignty.

[17] Vilfredo Pareto, *Manuel d'economie politique*, Paris, 1909.

[18] The golden rule is "do unto others as you would have them do unto you." This norm is found both in Christian and Confucian thought. See Steven Rosefielde, *Comparative Economic Systems: Culture, Wealth and Power in the 21st Century*, Blackwell, London, 2002.

also must act as faithful agents of the electorate. Kenneth Arrow has shown that balloting is less effective than market negotiation in ensuring that individuals receive the services they demand.[19] Nonetheless, Abram Bergson and Paul Samuelson have argued that representational democracy is likely to be better than other political alternatives.[20] Representative democracy, it turns out, isn't as ideal as Enlightenment advocates hoped, but it is probably the next best thing.[21] This judgment only applies to the Pareto standard. Bergson has formally demonstrated that competitive outcomes may not be to everyone's taste. Tsars and social activists may disesteem popular choices. The privileged demand to be indulged, and advocates of affirmative action for women, homosexuals, and racial and ethnic minorities may feel that the public isn't doing all that it should. Conflicts of this sort could be irreconcilable. The idea of the West doesn't provide a unique social welfare ideal. The best that can be achieved is to vet and openly debate grievances in an effort to achieve national consensus.

This lacuna provides a wedge for autocrats such as Vladimir Lenin who claimed to speak not for the proletariat of today but for the socially enlightened workers of tomorrow. To Lenin, Bolshevik socialism seemed to be better than Paretian democratic free enterprise because it embodied the progressive, democratic desires of the masses as he imagined them, purged of degenerate contemporary attitudes. Lenin spoke the language of democracy and human liberation but

---

[19] Kenneth Arrow, *Social Choice and Individual Values*, Wiley, New York, 2nd edition, 1963; Arrow, "Optimal and Voluntary Income Distribution," in Steven Rosefielde, ed., *Economic Welfare and the Economics of Soviet Socialism*, Cambridge University Press, Cambridge, 1981, pp. 267–88.

[20] Abram Bergson, "A Reformulation of Certain Aspects of Welfare Economics," *Quarterly Journal of Economics*, 52, 1(February 1938): 310–34; Bergson, "Socialist Economics," in H. Ellis (ed.), *A Survey of Contemporary Economics*, Richard D. Irwin, Homewood, IL, 1948, pp. 412–48; Bergson, "The Concept of Social Welfare," *Quarterly Journal of Economics*, 68, 2(May 1954): 233–52; Bergson, *Essays in Normative Economics*, Harvard University Press, Cambridge, MA, 1966; Bergson, "Market Socialism Revisited," *Journal of Political Economy*, 75, 4(October 1967): 655–73; and Bergson, "Social Choice and Welfare Economics under Representative Government," *Journal of Public Economics*, 6, 3(October 1976): 171–90. Paul Samuelson, "Reaffirming the Existence of a 'Reasonable' Bergson-Samuelson Social Welfare Function," *Economica*, 44(1977): 81–88; Samuelson, "Bergsonian Welfare Economics," in Steven Rosefielde (ed.), *Economic Welfare and the Economics of Soviet Socialism*, pp. 223–66.

[21] R. G. Lipsey and Kelvin Lancaster, "The General Theory of the Second Best," *The Review of Economic Studies*, 24, 1(1956–57): 11–32.

acted like a Muscovite autocrat, ruling in an authoritarian fashion from above on the *paternalist* pretext that the people weren't ready to rule themselves. This propensity to feign adherence to democracy and human liberation while suppressing political, economic, and social competition has made it difficult for westerners to grasp Russian behavior and potential. There is a powerful temptation to accept the Leninist Enlightenment rhetoric and the claims of tsarist autocrats before him at face value and then infer that, if the system is rough around the edges, these blemishes will be swiftly rectified. This optimism has never been validated. Muscovy has remained Muscovy, even though it has had numerous opportunities to do better.

Russia's perpetual economic, political, and social backwardness are entirely explicable. Muscovite autocrats cannot plausibly satisfy consumer sovereign demands, nor pretend they can improve on Pareto. The system was designed to enrich the few at the expense of the many, to coerce compliance, to repress dissidence, and to maintain large armies for defense or conquest. Therefore, it can do some things well. It can provide an opulent lifestyle for the privileged, an impressive public facade, and a powerful martial police state. However, it has not provided general prosperity nor allowed the majority to realize even a fraction of their human potential. These deficiencies manifest themselves in low physical factor productivity, low value added, inefficient distribution and transfer, a feeble capacity to export industrial manufactures to the West, and widespread forced substitution. If the system were consumer sovereign, people would have expanded choices in all economic domains and be correspondingly better off. Likewise, their political, social, and spiritual lives would be enhanced by augmenting their personal freedom.

The same logic applies to growth. The driving force behind optimal development is science and technological progress attuned to consumer sovereignty. Since the Muscovite system is primarily responsive to ruler's and servitors' preferences, technological choice is dominated by their needs, and not those of the population, even if rent-granting were efficient. But rent-granting in all its forms, including the Soviet version of central planning, is anticompetitive. Technological development and transfer tend to be parochially and adversely selected. While they usually increase physical productivity, the resulting value added judged from a global perspective is scant. This causes cognitive dissonance. On paper, tsars, commissars, and Putin have often reported impressive rates of industrial and aggregate economic growth. Some

of this was statistical make-believe,[22] but even the real component
was qualitatively low in two senses. First, products were adversely
selected substitutes with low and rapidly diminishing utility. Second,
their characteristics were sub global standard, accounting in part for
the grayness of Soviet reality. These defects are best appreciated with
a historical example. During the cold war, official Soviet and CIA
statistics showed Russia catching up with American living standards.
Both suggested that Russian per capita gross domestic product (GDP)
was 68 percent of the United States' in 1989 (valued in dollars). Yet,
just two years later the figure had dropped to 14.7 percent computed
at the market rate of exchange.[23] In a blink of an eye, seven decades
of catch-up had been erased, and the illusion of progress dispelled.
Russia's relative backwardness on the competitive market measure had
widened, not diminished.

This perplexing outcome can be called the paradox of Muscovite
modernization. Rejecting democratic free enterprise or European
social democracy doesn't preclude growth. The Kremlin has repeatedly
demonstrated that it can mobilize resources and borrow technology
from abroad to enhance aggregate productivity. But, despite the economic advantages of backwardness, it has failed to recover lost ground
because of the low quality of its modernization. Russia has been able
to achieve the statistical illusion of progress but not the substance. It
could conceivably do better. Rapid growth for the ruler and his min-
ions is possible at least for a while, as China's recent development surge
makes plain, if a way can be found to make technological choice and
diffusion efficient. But westernization – that is, the adoption of democratic free enterprise or European Union social democracy – seems
more promising. It holds out hope not only for general prosperity but
also for high-quality, sustained growth and development.

Muscovite rulers and servitors have resisted the benefits of westernization, other forms of populist control, and alternative authoritarian

---

[22] Girsh Itsykovich Khanin, "Ekonomicheskoe razvite Rossii 1999–2004 gody:
predvaritel'naia alternativnaia otsenka sostoiania rossiiskoi ekonomiki i ee analiz,"
paper presented at the VI World Congress of the International Council for Central
and East European Studies," Europe-Our Common Home?" Berlin, Germany,
July 25–30, 2005. Also see Khanin, "Economic Growth and the Mobilization
Model," in Michael Ellman (ed.), *Russia's Oil and Natural Gas-Bonanza or Curse*,
Anthem Press, London, 2006, chapter 7.
[23] Steven Rosefielde, *Efficiency and Russia's Economic Recovery Potential to the Year
2000 and Beyond*, Ashgate, Aldershot, 1998, table S1, p. xxii.

market models while feigning to share their goals because they don't want and are afraid to surrender their privileges. Although the population should prosper under democratic free enterprise and might do better by borrowing aspects of the Chinese model, those in control are apt to suffer. In self-defense, Muscovite spokesmen often argue that the reality of the West is far less than the ideal promises. Of course, in this regard, they are right. Humans are never as rational as many models presume. People's judgments are impaired by intellectual, existential, and psychological shortcomings, including addictions and manias, and as Adam Smith observed, they conspire in restraint of trade. But these same shortcomings apply to Muscovy. Even in those areas where it tries to optimize, results often are disappointing. It may therefore be fairly concluded, as human rights activists have consistently maintained, that expanding social, political, and economic freedoms, combined with a strong dose of compassion, is the wisest path to prosperity and Pareto's optimal social welfare.

Box 1.1 Prisoner of Distrust

Francis Fukuyama has argued that trust is the foundation stone of democracy. Without it, there can be no Lockean social contract. Muscovy exemplifies the corollary that distrust generated by the rule of men helps perpetuate the system. Tsars, Lenin, Stalin, Yeltsin, and Putin knew in their bones that there were rivals intriguing to depose them and that they would exploit any effort to forge an authentic social contract to seize the reins, as Yeltsin did to Gorbachev. Successions do occur, of course, because no one is immortal, but Russian distrust and intrigue keep them largely within the Muscovite mold.

Russia is governed by a nonwestern Muscovite culture.

The core characteristics of Muscovy are autocracy, rent-granting, servitor intrigue, an imperial military, secret police–enforced social discipline, and the absence of the rule of law, making it the antithesis of the *idea of the West* exemplified by democratic free enterprise and European social democracy.

Russia professes Enlightenment, and many in the West are beguiled, but Muscovy is intrinsically antidemocratic and socially exploitive.

Muscovy is less economically efficient than the West. It misallocates resources and ineffectively harnesses transferred technologies and domestic innovations for commercial purposes.

2

Soviet Reform Communism

The Soviet Union was a Muscovite authoritarian martial police state ruled by the Bolshevik Party under the banner of revolutionary Marxism. It claimed to be a proletarian democracy (leaders heeded the workers' will), committed to eradicating economic and social injustice, and the creation of a tranquil communist paradise where everyone harmoniously fulfilled his or her full human potential.[1] The writings and actions of important Bolsheviks convincingly demonstrated that most were enthralled by Leninist liberationism, while rationalizing Soviet despotic deeds. Cynicism gradually eroded Bolshevik zealotry, buffeted by the traumas of War Communism, collectivization, industrialization, repression, terror, Gulag, forced labor, World War II, Soviet imperialism, and the bleakness of postwar reality, but Russian intellectuals remained wedded to Marxist ideology. Most were convinced Leninists until Mikhail Gorbachev shattered their faith. The Soviet intelligentsia, like its western brethren, acknowledged some of the regime's warts but believed that communism would evolve progressively. Until that fine day, it thought the dictatorship of the proletariat (Communist Party) should dedicate itself to proving the merit of Soviet economic planning, promoting the liberation of oppressed peoples everywhere (except in the USSR), and peacefully fostering postcapitalist globalization.

Western attitudes were more diverse. Some were swept off their feet by Marxist revolutionary rhetoric, while others, focusing on deeds, were swayed by the Bolsheviks' suppression of political opposition; subordination of independent trade unions to communist domination;

---

[1] The term *authoritarian martial police state* describes the system's defining attributes without implying an immutable ideal type or the impossibility of transition.

criminalization of private property, business, and entrepreneurship; secret police repression of civil liberties; terror, Gulag, and forced labor; fomenting of global class war; promotion of communist insurrections in Europe, Asia, and the Third World; and proxy wars, military expansionism, arms racing, and imperialism. Like Ronald Reagan, they perceived the Soviet Union as an *evil empire*.[2] And, of course, there was a middle ground, populated by observers who believed that even if Stalinism were reprehensible, the "thaw," which followed his death,[3] Nikita Khrushchev's *peaceful coexistence*,[4] Brezhnev's *détente*,[5] Kosygin's economic reforms,[6] the arms control and disarmament process,[7] and limited toleration for political dissidence,[8] all pointed toward liberalization that would eventually lead either to capitalist and socialist *convergence*,[9] or the universal triumph of democratic free enterprise. Most commentators expected Soviet communism to endure, and no western specialist predicted the USSR's self-destruction before 1987,[10] even though now it is often taken for granted that the Soviet Union was marked for death. All concepts of Bolshevism used by western analysts to appraise the Soviet Union's and Russia's destiny were inadequate because they paid insufficient attention to the Muscovite dimension. They treated the USSR's authoritarian martial police state variously as

---

[2] Ronald Reagan, Speech to the House of Commons, June 8, 1982.

[3] Ilya Ehrenburg, *The Thaw*, Alfred Knopf, New York, 1962.

[4] A doctrine promoted by Khrushchev repudiating the idea that socialist class war would necessarily triumph through the force of arms.

[5] A term for softening adversarial relationships.

[6] The Kosygin reforms were a series of initiatives granting more formal discretionary authority to red directors (enterprise managers) over productive operations within the core Stalinist natural economy model that criminalized private ownership, business, and entrepreneurship, including consumer negotiations with state-owned firms. See Alexei Kosgyin, "Ob uluchshenii upraveleniia promyshlennostiu sovershenstvovanii planirovania i usileniia ekonomiheskovo stimulirovanii promyshlennovo proizvodstva" ("On Improving Industrial Management, Perfect Planning, and Increasing Economic Incentives for Industrial Production"), *Pravda*, September 28, 1965.

[7] The primary East-West arms-control agreement during this period was the Strategic Arms Limitation Treaty (SALT I) covering nuclear weapons.

[8] The Soviets agreed to uphold basic civil rights in the 1977 Helsinki Accord.

[9] A hypothesis that the world's disparate political and economic systems are destined to converge to a common type. In the context of the cold war, this system was construed as a mixture of markets and plans, either mostly socialist or capitalist, whichever proved best. See Steven Rosefielde, "Convergence Theory," *International Encyclopedia of the Social Sciences*, 2nd ed., 2007.

[10] Steven Rosefielde, "The Soviet Economy in Crisis: Birman's Cumulative Disequilibrium Hypothesis," *Soviet Studies*, X2, 1(April 1988): 222–44.

beneficent, malevolent, or a system transitioning to something better, as if Russia's failed half-millennial struggle for civic empowerment against Muscovite authoritarianism was extraneous.

This myopia is doubly misleading. First, it erroneously mis-suggests that Russia was ripe for westernization absent Bolshevism and second that the Soviet Union's collapse is attributable entirely to communism's faulty economic institutions, rather than its volatile Muscovite foundations. Despite a great deal of western socialist literature and the claims of Kremlin leaders to the contrary, the Soviet command economy (physical systems management), shorn of Stalin's terror, Gulag, and mass killings,[11] was indeed inferior to democratic free enterprise as an engine of social prosperity. But this doesn't imply that post-Stalin Reform Communism had to self-destruct of its own accord. Gorbachev and his circle scrapped the USSR's liberal physical systems management regime in a fit of opportunism and inadvertence, hoping to find a Muscovite course that better served their private desires. Had Gorbachev and his servitors been more temperate, Russia still would be on the post-Stalin treadmill of liberal Soviet economic reform. The leadership would have continued tinkering with physical systems management, published cosmetically enhanced statistics verifying its success, and muddled through.

Box 2.1 Treadmill of Economic Reform

The Soviet physical management system in its core Leninist/Stalinist form was founded on the administrative command planning approach to factor allocation, production, and goods distribution. It criminalized private ownership, business, and entrepreneurship and rested on the false premise that requisitioning and rationing were superior to competitive markets. Soviet leaders failing to see the error of their misplaced faith ceaselessly strove to improve the system by reforming planning, administration, spatial authority, management, laws, and incentives. Although, it can be shown that there is a correspondence between perfect planning and perfect competition in theory, neither ideal nor good outcomes were achievable in practice. The result, as Gertrude Schroeder phrased it, was that the Soviet Union from Khrushchev through Gorbachev was on a "treadmill of perpetual economic reform," where grandiose promises were repeatedly made, none of which came to fruition.

---

[11] Steven Rosefielde, *Russian Economics from Lenin to Putin,* Blackwell, London, 2007; (Gulag chapter) Anne Applebaum, *GULAG: A History*, Doubleday, New York, 2003; Robert Conquest, *The Great Terror: Stalin's Purge of the Thirties,*

It is therefore essential to approach Russia's postcommunist experience without historicist prejudgment to appreciate that what has transpired wasn't inevitable, or entirely the result of communism's inner contradictions, but was a manifestation of Russia's susceptibility to *smuta* (Times of Trouble)[12] and a centuries-long process of Muscovite adaptive experimentation. This requires some familiarity with Muscovy and the limitations of Soviet Reform Communism, which Gorbachev inherited from his predecessors. Chapter 1 provided the Muscovite background. A concise review of the theory and practice of Reform Communism and its Muscovite essence is elaborated next to complete the preliminaries, enabling readers to grasp what might have been, why it wasn't to be, and why the neo-Muscovite regime that emerged thereafter hasn't confirmed Francis Fukuyama's musing about the "end of history."[13]

The touchstone of the Soviet economic model from its inception under Stalin (1929) through Konstantin Chernenko's brief reign (1984) was the deep-seated conviction that physical systems management (planning, assignment, requisitioning, and distribution disconnected from consumer demand) was superior to all market alternatives, including worker-managed market socialism (syndicalism).[14] For a half-century, Kremlin leaders believed that commands and directives gave them more control, faster development, and greater military power, while protecting the proletariat from capitalist exploitation. This was accomplished by criminalizing private business, entrepreneurship, and property and suppressing market forces, complemented by the erection of a state economic administrative apparatus, including five-year planning (*piatiletki*).[15] Planned natural economy (an

---

Macmillan, New York, 1980; Stephane Coutois, Nicolas Worth, et al., *Black Book of Communism*, Harvard University Press, Cambridge, MA, 1999.

[12] The term *smuta* refers to the interregnum between death of Fyodor II (ending the Rurik dynasty in 1598) and the ascension of the first Romanov tsar in 1613, known as the Time of Troubles (*Smutnoe Vremya*). It was a period of intrigue and chaos, which appears to recur periodically in Russia in various guises. See Stefan Hedlund, *Russian Path Dependence*, Routledge, London, 2005.

[13] Francis Fukuyama, *The End of History and the Last Man*, Free Press, New York, 1992.

[14] Lyubo Sirc, *The Yugoslav Economy under Self-Management*, St. Martin's Press, New York, 1979; Branko Horvat, "Yugoslav Economic Policy in the Post-War Period: Problems, Ideas, Institutional Development," *American Economic Review*, June Supplement, 1971. Steven Rosefielde and R. W. Pfouts, "The Firm in Illyria: Market Syndicalism Revisited," *Journal of Comparative Economics*, 10, 2(June 1986): 160–70.

[15] Rosefielde, *Russian Economics from Lenin to Putin*.

economy based on engineering principles rather than value-seeking negotiated exchange) not only was equated with scientific social-ism but also anyone advocating the legalization of private ownership, business, and entrepreneurship was vulnerable to denunciation as an enemy of the people (*vrag naroda*).[16]

To the astonishment of many western economists such Lionel Rob-bins, Ludwig von Mises, and Fredrich von Hayek,[17] the Soviet com-mand model not only survived but also for a time appeared to flourish, giving rise to now dimly remembered claims of socialist superiority and heated debates about the comparative merit of capitalist and com-munist systems.[18] Even allowing for statistical exaggeration, the evi-dence shows that physical systems management worked well enough to sustain Soviet power, allowing Moscow to challenge the West for decades.[19] But then, just when western socialist economists persuaded themselves in the late 1960s that the future really was theirs,[20] the Soviet natural economy lost its vigor. Official statistics revealed that aggregate economic growth was gradually decelerating, and many, including Gorbachev, concluded that the real situation was more dire than the data disclosed.

The problem wasn't the impossibility of planning. After decades of debate,[21] and the development of input–output tables, linear program-ming, and mathematical optimization theory,[22] western and Soviet

[16] Ibid.
[17] Lionel Robbins, *An Essay on the Nature and Significance of Economic Science*, Macmil-lan, London, 1935. Ludwig von Mises, *Socialism; An economic and sociological ana-lysis*, J. Cape, London, 1936. Fredrich von Hayek (ed.), *Collectivist Economic Plan-ning: Critical studies on the possibilities of socialism*, G. Routledge, London, 1935.
[18] Abram Bergson, *Productivity and the Social System: The USSR and the West*, Harvard University Press, Cambridge, MA, 1978.
[19] Rosefielde, "The Riddle of Postwar Russian Economic Growth: Statistics Lied and Were Misconstrued," *Europe-Asia Studies*, 55, 3(2003): 469–81. Rosefielde, *Russian Economics from Lenin to Putin*; G. L. Khanin, *Dinamika ekonomicheskovo razvitiya*, Nauka, Novosibirsk, 1991.
[20] Maurice Dobb, *Soviet Development since 1917*, International Publishers, 1948. Dobb, *Welfare Economics and the Economics of Socialism*, Cambridge University Press, Cambridge, 1969.
[21] Abram Bergson, "Socialist Economics," in H. Ellis (ed.), *A Survey of Contemporary Economics*, Richard D. Irwin, Homewood, IL, 1958, pp. 412–48.
[22] Robert Dorfman, Paul Samuelson, and Robert Solow, *Linear Programming and Economic Analysis*, McGraw-Hill, New York, 1958; Michael Ellman, *Soviet Plan-ning Today: Proposals for an Optimally Functioning Economic System*, Cambridge University Press, Cambridge, 1971; Steven Rosefielde, *The Transformation of the*

economists discovered the *duality theorem*, the formal equivalence of perfect planning and perfect markets for which Leonid Kontorovich and Tjalling Koopmans were co-recipients of the 1975 Nobel Prize in Economics.[23] Given a set of seemingly plausible assumptions, the primary technical distinctions between plans and markets appeared to be reducible to timely data acquisition, processing, and computability,[24] setting aside the further complexities of incentives and moral hazards. Therefore, the comparative merit of these rival systems was claimed to hinge on the efficiency of planning and market practice, with the Soviets wagering that even if the advantage temporarily lay with the West, the tables could be turned by improved planning,

1966 Soviet Input-Output Table from Producers to Adjusted Factor Cost Values, G. E. Tempo, Washington, DC, 1975.

[23] Leonid Kontorovich, *The Best Use of Resources*, 1958; Tjalling Koopmans and Michael Montias, "On the Description and Comparison of Economic Systems," in A. Eckstein (ed.), *Comparison of Economic Systems*, University of California Press, Berkeley, 1971, pp. 27–78; Martin Weitzman famously argued in the sixties that optimization with prices and quantities gave the same result. This was a restatement of the well-known systems *duality* principle claiming the equivalence of optimal plans and markets. But in retrospect, the concept should have been restated as an impossibility theorem: That Soviet practice precluded the achievement of optimality by any means. See Martin Weitzman, "Prices versus Quantities," *Review of Economic Studies*, 41 4(October 1974): 477–91. Cf. Mark Harrison, "Command and Collapse: The Fundamental Problem of Command in a Partially Centralized Economy," *Comparative Economic Studies*, 472(June 2005): 296–314.

[24] Richard Judy, "Information, Control, and Soviet Economic Management," in John Hardt, et al. (eds.), *Mathematics and Computers in Soviet Economic Planning*, Yale University Press, New Haven, CT, 1967, pp. 1–67. Late in 1963, a special commission of the Chief Administration on the Introduction of Computer Technology to the National Economy of the USSR reported that the purpose would be to perform computations related to formulating optional national economic plans, recomputations of state prices, operational control, banking, finance, and statistics (p. 36). See also, G. Popov, *Elektronnye mashiny i upravlenie ekonomiki*, Moscow, 1963, p. 142; V. F. Pugachev, "Voprosy optimal'novo planirovanniia narodnovo khoziaistvo s pomoshch'iu edinoi gosudarstvennoi seti vychislet'nykh tsentrov, *Voprosy ekonomiki*, No. 7, 1964; Nikolai Fedorenko, *Optimal Functioning System for a Socialist Economy*, Progress, Moscow, 1974. Martin Weitzman, "Iterative Multi-Level Planning with Production Targets," *Econometrica* (1970): 50–65. Martin Cave, *Computers and Economic Planning: The Soviet Experience*, Cambridge University Press, Cambridge, 1980. Martin Cave and Paul Hare, *Alternative Approaches to Economic Planning*, St. Martin's Press, New York, 1981. David Conn, "A Comparison of Alternative Incentive Structures for Centrally Planned Economic Systems," *Journal of Comparative Economics*, 3, 3(1979): 235–53.

incentives, and discipline. Hence, Reform Communism, the search for better methods of physical systems management begun in 1956 with *Libermanism* (introduction of managerial bonuses linked to *profitability* instead of physical output),[25] continued unabated until the midpoint of Gorbachev's rule.

The conceptual capstone of the Reform Communist effort was an ambitious program called the automatic system of planning and management, which aspired to combine enhanced computer-based five-year national economic planning with a set of real-time indicators and incentives assisting decision makers to optimally choose when events disrupted plan fulfillment.[26] The Central Planning Agency (*Gosplan*) and associated research institutes acquired and compiled data from all sources, including the State Statistical Agency (*Goskomstat*)

[25] Martin Weitzman, "The New Soviet Incentive Model," *Bell Journal of Economics*, 7 (1976): 251–57. Evsei Liberman, *Ekonomicheskie metody povysheniya effektivnosti proisvodstva*, 1970. English translation, *Economic Methods and the Effectiveness of Production*, New York, 1972. Evsei Domar, "On the Optimal Compensation of a Socialist Manager," *Quarterly Journal of Economics*, 88, 1 (February 1974): 1–19. David Granick, "The Ministry as a Maximizing Unit in Soviet Industry," *Journal of Comparative Economics*, 4, 3(September 1980): 255–73; Bengt Holmstrom, "Design of Incentive Schemes and the New Soviet Incentive Model," *European Economic Review*, 17, 2(February 1982): 188–248. N. Ireland and Peter Law, "Incentive and Efficiency in the Kosygin Reforms," *Journal of Comparative Economics*, 4, 1(March 1980): 33–39; Michael Keren, I. Miller, and J. Thornton, "The Ratchet Effect: A Dynamic Managerial Incentive Model of the Soviet Enterprise," *Journal of Comparative Economics*, 7, 4(December 1982): 347–67. Heidi Kroll, "Decentralization and Pre-Contract Dispute in Soviet Industry," *Soviet Economy*, 2 (January–March 1986): 51–71. M. Loeb and W. Magat, "Success Indicators in the Soviet Union: The Problem of Incentives and Efficient Allocation, *American Economic Review*, 68, 1(March 1978): 173–181; V. I. Danilin, C. A. K. Lovell, I. S. Materov, and S. Rosefielde, "Measuring and Improving Enterprise Efficiency in the Soviet Union," *Economica*, 52, 206(1984): 225–34. John Bonin, "On the Design of Managerial Incentive Structures in a Decentralized Planning Environment," *American Economic Review*, 66, 4(September 1976): 682–87. John Bonin and Wataru Fukuda, "Controlling a Risk-Averse, Effort-Selecting Manager in the Soviet Incentive Model," *Journal of Comparative Economics*, 11, 2(1987): 221–34; David Conn, "A Comparison of Alternative Incentive Structures for Centrally Planned Economic Systems," *Journal of Comparative Economics*, 3, 3(September 1979): 235–53; Conn, "Effort, Efficiency and Incentives in Economic Organizations," *Journal of Comparative Economics*, 6, 3(September 1982): 223–34.

[26] S. A. Kuznetsov, V. L. Makarov, and V. D. Marshak, *Informatsionnaia Baza, Perspektivnovo Planirovannia v OASU*, Ekonomika, Moscow 1982; K. A. Bagrinovsky and V. S. Prokopova, *Imitatsionnye Sistemy Priniatia Ekonomicheskikh Planovykh Proizvodstvennykh Ob"edinii i Modeli Planirovannia ikh Deiatel'nosti*, Nauka, 1984.

and enterprises on past and current potentials. The information was used to compute preliminary production targets for subaggregates (branches, sectors, and subsectors) and then adjusted and reconciled through a process called *material balancing*.[27] Next, the interbranch and interindustrial supplies required to achieve targets were compared and rebalanced ad hoc.

The main computing center of *Gosplan* strove to compute 25 million balances, one for each product in the official nomenclature, but could not do it. The best they accomplished was the preparation of 150 aggregate control plans, linearly disaggregated into 7,000 material subbalances and 750,000 micromaterial balances (some evaluated with linear programs),[28] few of which reflected achievable equilibrium, compelling buyers to content themselves with whatever was supplied through forced substitution, not the voluntary meetings of minds. Managers were incentivized to do their best with what they were given but seldom if ever received what was needed to truly optimize.

Countless rules and indicators were concocted and calculated to assist them in coping with perpetual shortages, buttressed with complementary material incentives. Managers were rewarded for saving inputs, maximizing physical production and profit, adopting advanced technologies, and introducing new goods, subject to quotas, assortments, and line-item budgetary constraints.[29] In addition, there was much talk but little reality to programs for the interactive revision and transmission of indicators, linked with central and enterprise linear programs. The *computopic* (sci-fi) intent was laudable, but the

---

[27] Rosefielde, *Russian Economics from Lenin to Putin*.

[28] Vladimir Popov and Nikolai Shmelev, *The Turning Point: Revitalizing the Soviet Economy*, Doubleday, New York, 1989. See the reference to M. Yun in *Turning Point*. Gosplan was responsible for 2,000 material balances, Gossnab for 15,000. Industrial branch ministries compiled 50,000 material balances, paired with 50,000 contracts that were then disaggregated by a factor ranging from 10 to 15. Personal communication with Vladimir Popov, June 2004.

[29] Steven Rosefielde and R. W. Pfouts, "Economic Optimization and Technical Efficiency in Soviet Enterprises Jointly Regulated by Plans and Incentives," *European Economic Review*, 32, 6(1988): 1285–1299. Also see A. Kosygin, "Ob uluchshenii upravleniia promyshlennostiu sovershentvovanii planirovania i usilennia ekonomicheskovo stimulirovanii promyshennovo proisvodsta" (On Improving Industrial Management, Perfect Planning and Increasing Economic Incentives for Industrial Production), *Pravda*, September 28, 1965. Joseph Berliner, *The Innovation Decision in Soviet Industry*, MIT Press, Cambridge, MA, 1976.

task was insuperable because the data were unreliable, obsolete, and incomplete; planners and household demand functions could not be accurately quantified; the requirements of optimal computing were beyond Soviet capabilities; incentives were contradictory; and resources could be preemptorily commandeered by commissars, the secret police (KGB), and the military industrial complex (VPK), which caused further losses by hoarding prolonged warfighting resources reserves as an aspect of what Vitaly Shlykov has termed *structural militarization*.[30] And these problems were compounded by a stream of disruptive administrative reforms like Khrushchev's Regional Economic Councils (*Sovet Narodnovo Khoziaistvo*, more popularly known as *sovnarkhozy*), shifting supervisory authority from the center and republics to 105 newly formed regional jurisdictions, for which Khrushchev was dubbed a hare-brained schemer.[31]

Try as the leadership might, it could not overcome what Hayek aptly labeled *planned chaos*,[32] that is, the regime's inability to create a computable, administrative, and enterprise incentivized surrogate for competitive markets capable of optimally equilibrating supply and demand in terms of either consumers' or planners' preferences. Planning on close inspection, despite its Nobel advocates east and west, proved merely to be a framework for allocating resources in-kind to large ministerial administrative units and a cudgel for holding enterprises and ministries responsible for targets devised by *Gosplan* even if they were infeasible. It was little more than monkey business camouflaging the real motor of Soviet physical systems management – Muscovite rent-granting.

As in tsarist times, the ruler (general secretary of the Communist Party) commanded his rent-grantees (commissars, ministers, enterprise managers called *red directors*, the heads of the VPK and KGB)

[30] Vitaly Shlykov, "Nazad v budushchee, ili Ekonomicheskie uroki kholodnoi voiny," *Rossia v Global'noi Politike*, 4, 2(March–April 2006): 26–40. Steven Rosefielde, *Russian Economics from Lenin to Putin*, chapter 9, pp. 141–44.

[31] Rosefielde, *Russian Economics from Lenin to Putin*; Abram Bergson, *The Economics of Soviet Planning*, Yale University Press, New Haven, CT, 1964. Gertrude Schroeder, "The Soviet Economy on a Treadmill of Reforms," in *Soviet Economy in a Time of Change*, Joint Economic Committee of Congress, Washington, D.C. October 10, 1979, pp. 312–366.

[32] Fredrich von Hayek, "Socialist Calculation: The Competitive Solution," *Economica*, May 1940. Jan Winiecki, *The Distorted World of Soviet-Type Economies*, University of Pittsburgh Press, Pittsburgh, 1988.

to get the job done (fulfill plan directives) anyway they could unencumbered by the rule of law, and without private property rights, in return for informally reserving some revenues for personal use and other insider privileges.[33] No one cared whether the micro and macro aspects of annual and five-year plans were really met beneath the paper facade. Eugene Zaleski has shown that even official results often fell short of targets by more than 50 percent.[34] Moreover, the Communist Party tolerated a spectrum of gray market activities, including *tolkachy* (enterprise procurement personnel tasked to bartering informally for supplies with other firms) commonly known as the second economy,[35] which often served the purposes of the Kremlin's rent-grantees. What mattered for the regime was mobilizing servitor effort and resources with all available methods to assure that production exceeded prior achieved levels and served the primary superpower purposes of the Soviet authoritarian martial police state. Muscovite bullying and rent-granting, not optimal planning, were the orders of the day and were effective in the same limited ways they were in the precommunist era. Commodities were produced and aggregate output grew, but most people lived in proletarian squalor, with something approaching prosperity accessible only to a few.

Although this communist version of the Muscovite knout was unsophisticated, the Kremlin demonstrated that it sufficed for dragooning the population into the labor force, investing, transferring technology from abroad, expanding production, modernizing, developing, and

[33] Rosefielde, *Russian Economics from Lenin to Putin*; Saul Estrin and Mike Wright, "Corporate Governance in the Former Soviet Union: An Overview," *Journal of Comparative Economics*, 27, 3(1999): 398–421; Paul Gregory (ed.), *Behind the Facade of Stalin's Command Economy*, Princeton University Press, Princeton, NJ, 2002; Gregory, *The Political Economy of Stalinism: Evidence from the Soviet Secret Archives*, Cambridge University Press, London, 2003. Alec Nove, *An Economic History of the USSR*, Pelican, London, 1972.

[34] Eugene Zaleski, *Planning Reforms in the Soviet Union 1962–1966*. University of North Carolina Press, Chapel Hill, 1967, pp. 141–83.

[35] Gur Ofer and Aron Vinokur, *The Soviet Household under the Old Regime: Economic Conditions and Behavior in the 1970s*, Cambridge: Cambridge University Press, 1992. Gregory Grossman, "Notes on the Illegal Private Economy and Corruption," in Joint Economic Committee of Congress, *Soviet Economy in a Time of Change*, October 10, 1979, Washington DC, pp. 834–55, Paul Gregory (ed.), *Behind the Façade of Stalin's Command Economy*, Princeton University Press, Princeton, NJ, 2002; Gregory, *The Political Economy of Stalinism: Evidence from the Soviet Secret Archives*, Cambridge University Press, London, 2003.

maintaining immense structurally militarized armed forces.[36] However, the leadership could not construct a competitive Muscovite
physical systems management mechanism. Western markets surpassed
Soviet planning and Muscovy. Despite numerous deficiencies, experience confirmed that free competition satisfied consumer demand
better and fostered faster rates of material growth than Muscovite
Reform Communism,[37] without constraining individual liberty or
popular democratic sovereignty over the provision of public goods.

By the early 1980s, segments of Soviet society began to accept this
doleful message and pondered how to play out the string. During the
Reform Communist era, every conceivable physical systems management remedy had been considered and tried without noticeable benefit. Indeed, growth steadily fell as Soviet planning and management
became more sophisticated, causing some insiders to acknowledge
publicly that the *correlation of forces* (economic, political, strategic factors determining relative superpower) was turning against the USSR.
And others even suggested that the economy was stagnating (*zastoi*)
behind the official statistical smokescreen,[38] posing the familiar Russia
question *chto delat*? (What was to be done?)[39]

---

[36]   Vitaly Shlykov, *Chto Pogubilo Sovetskii Soiuz? Amerikanskaia Razvedka i Sovetskikh
Voennykh Raskhodakh* (What Destroyed the Soviet Union? American Intelligence
Estimates of Soviet Military Expenditures). *Voennyi Vestnik*, No. 8, Moscow,
April 2001. Steven Rosefielde, *Russia in the 21st Century: The Prodigal Superpower*,
Cambridge University Press, Cambridge, 2005. David Epstein, "The Economic
Cost of Soviet Security and Empire," in Charles Wolf, Jr., and Henry Rowan
(eds.), *The Impoverished Superpower: Perestroika and the Soviet Military Burden*, Insti-
tute of Contemporary Studies, San Francisco, CA, 1990, pp. 155–84.

[37]   Steven Rosefielde, "Tea Leaves and Productivity: Bergsonian Norms for Gauging
the Soviet Union," *Comparative Economic Studies*, 47, 2(June 2005): 259–73;
Rosefielde, "Comparative Production Potential in the USSR and the West:
Pre-transition Assessments," in Rosefielde (ed.), *Efficiency and Russia's Economic
Recovery Potential to the Year 2000 and Beyond*, Ashgate, Aldershot, 1998, pp. 101–
35. Abram Bergson, *Planning and Productivity under Soviet Socialism*, Columbia
University Press, New York, 1968; Bergson, *Productivity and the Social System*;
Bergson, "Comparative Productivity: The USSR, Eastern Europe and the West,"
American Economic Review, 77, 3(1987): 342–57.

[38]   Abel Aganbegyan, *The Economic Challenge of Perestroika*, Indiana University Press,
Bloomington, 1998; Mikhail Gorbachev, *Perestroika i Novoe Myshlenie*, Politicheskie Literatury, Moscow, 1987.

[39]   The title of a book written by the socialist revolutionary Nikolai Chernyshevsky
in 1863 that became the rallying cry for Russian modernization. Many western scholars nonetheless remain hopeful about the superiority of some form of

Inertia inclined the leadership to round up the usual suspects, to sing its own praises, and to persevere. While life was drab and material prospects dim for most, ordinary people found consolation in the system's barebones job security,[40] and Kremlin insiders were solaced by the benefits of communist rent-seeking and their retention of power.

Reversing Stalin and returning to Lenin's New Economic Policy (1921–28) of market leasing socialism offered another solution[41] for those brave enough to risk denunciation as *vrag naroda*. The Kremlin didn't have to abandon Reform Communism if its leaders decided that better performance was indispensable. It only had to circumscribe the scope of physical systems management, while retaining prohibitions against private property and some forms of business and entrepreneurship. This could have been accomplished by relaxing restrictions on private business and entrepreneurship and allowing productive entities of all descriptions to lease state assets. As during the 1920s, market liberalization could be restricted to small enterprises, preserving state planning control over the "commanding heights," or could have been broadened as the leadership preferred. No one knew with certainty that Muscovite market socialism was inferior to western free enterprise or European Union social democracy,[42] and ideological taboos aside, the possibilities, as Deng Xiaoping realized in the Chinese context, seemed worth exploring, even if it took another fifty years to determine whether authoritarian Market Communism or democratic free enterprise was best.

The market option had another advantage. It provided a venue for exploring more radical solutions. As the state reduced its dependence on physical systems management, the Kremlin could retain authoritarian communism as China did but shed Muscovite rent-granting in favor a more efficient Weberian bureaucratic order. It could retain authoritarianism but discard Muscovite rent-granting and

socialism. See Alec Nove, *The Economics of Feasible Socialism*, A. A. Balkema, London, 1983.

[40] David Granick, "Soviet Use of Fixed Prices: Hypothesis for a Job-Right Constraint," in Steven Rosefielde, *Economic Welfare and the Economics of Soviet Socialism*, Cambridge University Press, Cambridge, 1981.

[41] Rosefielde, *Russian Economics from Lenin to Putin*.

[42] Bergson, "Market Socialism Revisited," *Journal of Political Economy*, 75, 4(1967): 655–73.

communism. It could dispense with Muscovite communism and embrace the Slavophil or Russian idea. Or it could transition to democratic free enterprise.

Box 2.2 Second Economy

The Soviet Union always had an official and a shadow economy. Its *first economy* was based on physical systems management (requisitioning, rationing planning, administration, and management) during War Communism (1917–21), Command Communism (1929–55), and Reform Communism (1956–87), with some market admixtures during New Economic Policy, or NEP (1921–29), and Market Communism (1987–91). All coexisted with a *second economy*, which diverted some official resources for illegal private processing and market sale. Most analysts include other informal market activities such as *tolkachi* services in the second economy, but they are excluded here because they are considered an aspect of physical systems management. The definition is a matter of taste. More importantly, it should be appreciated that second economy *colored markets*, as Aron Katsenelinboigen called them, didn't suffice to make the Soviet system globally competitive, prevent Soviet disunion, or serve as a platform for smooth transition to democratic free enterprise. The second economy didn't displace Muscovy.

As Gorbachev's fateful accession to the Communist Party general secretaryship neared, it was difficult to imagine the *Politburo* adopting a radical course. The Soviet Union had the world's largest nuclear and conventional military forces, the KGB was omnipresent, the CIA thought the USSR's economy was growing faster than America's,[43] and the Russian population showed no serious signs of restiveness. Trashing authoritarianism, communism, or Muscovite rent-granting for any reason, including the pursuit of Slavophilism or democratic free enterprise, didn't seem in the cards. Gorbachev's mentor, KGB chairman Yuri Andropov, thought by some to have been a liberal, didn't display any enthusiasm for Market Communism, and none for Slavophilism or democratic free enterprise during his brief fifteen-month term as Soviet ruler. Konstantin Chernenko, his successor, was chosen as a counterforce to Andropov's tepid liberalism, and his

---

[43] CIA, *Measures of Soviet Gross National Product in 1982 Prices*, Joint Economic Committee of Congress, Washington, DC, November 1990. Steven Rosefielde, *False Science: Underestimating the Soviet Arms Buildup*, Transactions Press, Brunswick NJ, 1979. Rosefielde, *Russia in the 21st Century*.

most probable replacement, Grigory Romanov, first secretary of the Leningrad regional Communist Party was said by some to be a fervent Stalinist. Had he seemed less menacing to his Politburo colleagues, Gorbachev might never have come to power.[44]

The most that could have been expected, ignoring the role of hare-brained schemers, rent-grantee opportunism, *smuta* (times of trouble), and extremism in Muscovite history, seemed to be a limited decriminalization of private ownership, business, and entrepreneurship in the service of the Kremlin's authoritarian goals. That this nearly universal judgment was so far off the mark speaks volumes about the deficiencies of Marxist and cold war intellectual frameworks. The potential for Soviet self-destruction was there; scholars simply didn't pay adequate attention and still have great difficulty comprehending what actually transpired. They speak as if the economic failings of communism destroyed the *evil empire*, when it was Muscovite deference for Gorbachev's harebrained schemes[45] and his rent-grantees' opportunism that destabilized the physical management system. The destabilization created a pretext for Boris Yeltsin's coup d'etat and his installation of a new postcommunist market Muscovite rent-granting regime that failed to advance either Slavophil idea or westernized democratic free enterprise.

- The Soviet Union was a Muscovite authoritarian martial police state ruled by the Bolshevik party under the banner of revolutionary Marxism.
- Communist ideology blinded many east and west to the real nature of the system.
- Most commentators expected Soviet communism to endure almost to the bitter end, even though now it is assumed that the USSR was marked for death.
- Soviet communism softened after Stalin, but made little real headway toward westernization. Its modernization was a treadmill of economic reform.
- The majority were right about the technical sustainability of the Soviet economic system, but failed to factor in forces of internal opportunism.

[44] Arnold Beichman and Mikhail Bernshtam, *Andropov, New Challenge to the West: A Political Biography*, Stein and Day, New York, 1983.
[45] Dale Herspring, *The Kremlin and the High Command*, University of Kansas Press, Lawrence, 2006.

- The touchstone of the Soviet economic model was a belief in the superiority of physical systems management over all competitors including market socialism.
- It was implemented by criminalizing private business, entrepreneurship and property, suppressing market forces, and erecting a state economic administrative apparatus, including five year planning to direct productive activity.
- Western theorists predicted instantaneous collapse, but this didn't occur because Russian engineering was sound. The system hardly produced anything people wanted, but it did produce the basics.
- Defective technological progress was physical systems management's long term Achilles' heel. The state spent lavishly on science, without satisfactory results.
- Central planning failed here and elsewhere because it was comparatively inefficient in practice.
- All attempts to improve planning efficiency yielded meager results. Indeed, GDP growth was inversely correlated with advances in planning.
- By the early eighties, segments of Soviet society began to accept this doleful message, leading Gorbachev to relax prohibitions on Market Communism imposed in 1929.

PART II

GORBACHEV

Gorbachev Timeline

1985

March	Gorbachev appointed general secretary
April	Central Committee plenum launches program on restructuring and acceleration, Boris Yeltsin brought to Moscow as Central Committee secretary for construction
May	Launch of antialcohol campaign
November	First summit meeting with Ronald Reagan in Geneva
December	Yeltsin appointed First Secretary of Moscow Party Committee, becomes candidate member of Politburo

1986

February	Twenty-Seventh Communist Party Congress
April	Chernobyl nuclear disaster
May	Law on unearned incomes
July	Speech in Vladivostok on opening a window on the Pacific
October	Summit meeting with Ronald Reagan in Reykjavik
November	Decree on individual labor activities
December	Sakharov released from internal exile in Gorky

1987

January	Central Committee Plenum launches program on democratization
June	Central Committee Plenum launches program on *radical economic reform,* including law on state enterprises
October	Speech in Murmansk on human factor and brake mechanism
November	Seventieth anniversary of October Revolution, Yeltsin fired from position as Moscow party boss

December   Summit meeting with Reagan in Washington, INF treaty

1988
February   Yeltsin dropped from Politburo
June   Nineteenth Party Conference, lively debates, support for democratization
October   Popular fronts formed in the Baltics
December   Constitutional amendment to create a new Congress of People's Deputies, safeguards to secure seats for the elite

1989
February   Last Soviet troops leave Afghanistan
March   Elections to Congress of People's Deputies, Yeltsin elected
May   Gorbachev elected president of the Supreme Soviet, Summit meeting in Beijing
May/June   First session of Congress of People's Deputies, lively televised debates
September   Yeltsin's first visit to the United States, surrounded by reports of heavy drinking
December   Summit meeting with Reagan in Malta

1990
March   Congress of People's Deputies, constitution amended to remove clause on the leading role of the party, Gorbachev elected president of the USSR, Yeltsin elected to Russian Federation Supreme Soviet, Lithuania declares independence
May   Yeltsin elected chairman of Russian Federation Supreme Soviet
July   Last session of the Communist Party of the Soviet Union, Gorbachev reelected general secretary, Yeltsin leaves the party
August   Shatalin Plan on transition to market economy in 500 days
September   Wrangling over Shatalin plan, finally rejected by Gorbachev

1991
January   Hard-line crackdown in Lithuania and Latvia, Yeltsin speaks of the need to create a Russian army in defense against the Soviet Union
February   Yeltsin calls on Gorbachev to resign
March   Mass demonstrations calling on Gorbachev to resign, referendum on new union treaty

April   Yeltsin narrowly survives vote of no confidence in Russian
               parliament
June   Yeltsin wins first popular election as Russian president
August   Hard-line coup against Gorbachev, Yeltsin triumphant
September   Supreme Soviet votes to dissolve USSR
October   Yeltsin receives special powers to rule Russia by decree
November   Yeltsin bans all Communist Party activity and nationalizes
               party assets
December   Gorbachev resigns

3

Pandora's Box

The West's panacea for Stalinism and the inefficiency of the Soviet planned natural economy was liberalization, which many were convinced would steer the Kremlin to democratic socialism and perhaps free enterprise. Moscow for whatever reasons liberalized, as described in Chapter 2, but didn't reach the promised land. Democratic socialism, free enterprise, and multiparty democracy remained forever on the bright, shining horizon, until Mikhail Gorbachev initiated his destructive reforms.

It is difficult to judge whether he had a coherent agenda. Like his predecessors, Gorbachev was prone to making grandiose gestures that committed him to little. In this spirit, Stalin had constitutionally proscribed inhumane punishments in 1936, the year before the NKVD (Stalin era Soviet secret police) archive indicates 353,000 people were executed as enemies of the people.[1] Democratic Market Communism also may have been mainly for show,[2] with one crucial difference. Gorbachev and his entourage seem to have had a venal hidden agenda that caused things to get out of hand quickly. They talked prudently about supplementing Lenin's natural economy with *yarmaki* (bazaars),

---

[1] Steven Rosefielde, "Stalinism in Post-Communist Perspective: New Evidence on Killings, Forced Labour and Economic Growth in the 1930s," *Europe-Asia Studies*, 48, 6(1996), Table A.1, p. 986.

[2] Mikhail Gorbachev, *Perestroika i Novoe Myshlenie*, Politicheskie Literatury, Moscow, 1987. Most contemporary commentators took Gorbachev's idealism at face value. See Marshall Goldman, *What Went Wrong with Perestroika*, Norton, New York, 1992; Padma Desai, *Perestroika in Perspective: The Design and Dilemmas of Soviet Reform,* Princeton University Press, Princeton, NJ, 1989; Abel Aganbegyan, *The Economic Challenge of Perestroika*, Indiana University Press, Bloomington, 1988; Aganbegyan, *Inside Perestroika: The Future of the Soviet Economy*, Harper and Row, New York, 1989.

cooperatives, leasing (*arenda*), enterprise worker councils (*trudovye kollektivy*), increased managerial autonomy, entrepreneurship, foreign joint ventures, and better prices but knowingly allowed this to become a vehicle for insiders to seize control over enterprise revenues, materials, and assets.

For many economists, this was a necessary evil. They argued that private property was essential for market efficiency and didn't fret about how it was acquired because assets would eventually pass into honest hands.[3] Similarly, while they knew that the welfare properties of markets depended on the rule of law and democracy, they turned a blind eye toward Muscovy, assuming that once marketization had begun it would culminate in Pareto efficient democratic socialism, or democratic free enterprise. Precedent didn't give them pause. Neither the tsarist, nor NEP (New Economic Policy 1921–29) episodes mattered because this time things would be different.

Not all markets are ideal, nor can it be shown that they are predestined to be so. A market is merely a transactionary space, real or virtual, where two or more individuals can enhance their utility by entering into mutually advantageous business relationships, including education, training, employment, exchange, finance, and investment. It does not require private property, the rule of law, or symmetric bargaining power, and may be immoral. Slave markets, for example, may have been competitive for masters, but this didn't redeem their inhumanity. Markets may be purely economic, or their character may be mediated by politics and culture. In general, only Pareto-efficient markets can be proven to improve the social welfare, under a plausible set of assumptions. Markets that closely approximate this norm are also likely to be beneficial. The rest, however, must be evaluated case by case.

The Reform Communist Soviet Union provides a good example. Although the state monopolized production, entrepreneurship, and property, it tolerated inter-enterprise bartering (asset redistribution markets) through agents called *tolkachi* (pushers) and looked the other way at kickbacks and bribes (*blat*). It can be reasonably assumed that these exchanges had some beneficial effect but not enough to deduce whether the virtues of *market colors*,[4] or expanded opportunities for

---

[3] Anders Aslund, "Amnesty the Oligarchs," *Moscow Times*, March 14, 2003.
[4] Aron Katsenlinboigen, *Studies in Soviet Planning*, M. E. Sharpe, White Plains, NY, 1978, chapter 7 (Market Colors and the Soviet Economy), pp. 165–202.

managerial misappropriation of government revenues, materials, and assets motivated Gorbachev to marketize.

Box 3.1 Mikhail Gorbachev

Mikhail Sergeyevich Gorbachev was born March 2, 1931, in the southwest Russian town of Stavropol, one month after his archrival Boris Yeltsin. His father was a collective farmer, who served nine years in Gulag for withholding grain. He joined the Komsomol (Young Communist League) in 1946 and entered Moscow State University's law school in 1952, graduating in 1955. Fifteen years later, he became first secretary of the Stavropol Regional Party Committee, and a Communist Party Central Committee of the Soviet Union member in 1971, rising to party secretary for agriculture in 1978. He became a candidate member of the Politburo in 1979 and a full member in 1980. Much of his rise was owed to the patronage of Mikhail Suslov, the leading party ideologue. Gorbachev was a highly active and visible Politburo member under Yuri Andropov and Konstantin Chernenko, despite being its youngest member, and was selected general secretary of the Communist Party of the Soviet Union when Chernenko died on March 10, 1985. His primary failure and accomplishment, depending on one's viewpoint, was to oversee the destruction of the Soviet Union. For this reason, he is held in low esteem in Russia and is highly regarded in some circles in the West.

Therefore, it shouldn't be surprising that Market Communism turned out to be something different than Gorbachev pretended, a search for a revised Muscovite compact, rather than free enterprise. History reveals that the grandsons of the Bolshevik coup d'etat didn't destroy the Soviet Union in a valiant effort to advance the cause of communist prosperity or even to return to their common European home; instead, it transformed Soviet managers and ministers into roving bandits(asset-grabbing privateers) with a tacit presidential charter to privatize the people's assets and revenues to themselves under the new Muscovite rule of men.[5]

The conditions for this initiative were ripe. As the fateful Orwellian year 1984 approached, the state statistical agency (*Goskomstat*) curtailed publication of vital health and demographic indicators, as well as the size of the grain harvest, suggesting that the environment and

---

[5] Mancur Olson, *Power and Prosperity: Outgrowing Capitalist and Communists Dictatorships*, Basic Books, New York, 2000, elaborates the concept of roving bandits.

economy were deteriorating.[6] In 1982, the government launched a
food program to alleviate an undisclosed shortage within a decade,
which provided an eerie contrast to the dust-laden shelves in the state
stores,[7] despite the importation of tens of millions of tons of grain
from the United States. Many derided the Soviet Union as an "Upper
Volta with nuclear missiles," or a "banana republic without bananas."[8]
Others portrayed it as system trapped on a treadmill of reform,[9] and
Andrei Amalrik alone in the USSR foresaw its impending demise.[10]

[6] During these years of increasing information darkness, Murray Feshbach served
as something of a caretaker of Soviet statistics on health and demography, com-
piling and publishing a range of estimates that subsequently would turn out to
have been highly accurate. For the environmental angle, see Murray Feshbach,
"Environmental Calamities: Widespread and Costly," in *The Former Soviet Union
in Transition*, Vol. 2, Joint Economic Committee of Congress, Washington, DC,
May 1993, pp. 577–96.

[7] *Prodovolstvennaya programma SSSR na period do 1990 goda i mery po ee realisatsiya*,
Moscow, 1982. Bare shelves it should be noted weren't an infallible measure
of crisis because produce was directly distributed in factory canteens, and other
foodstuffs vanished into the second economy. Cf. Allan Mustard and Christopher
Goldthwait, "Food Availability in the former Soviet Union: A Summary Report
of Three Missions Led by the U.S. Department of Agriculture," in *The Former
Soviet Union in Transition*, Vol. 2, Joint Economic Committee of Congress, Washington, DC, May 1993, pp. 506–13. "Three missions to the Soviet Union in May,
September, and October 1991 at the joint request of the Soviet government and
the White House made four critical determinations . . . first, the Soviet Union
did not face a threat of widespread famine but did face deterioration in food
availability . . . second the root of most difficulties in supplying foodstuffs to the
population was inefficiency in the food distribution system . . . third, the keys to
improvements in food availability are movement away from the collapsed command system . . . , fourth, the Soviet Union needs extension of credit to maintain
something approaching the historical level of food and feed imports" (p. 506). A
new superministry *Gosagroprom* was inaugurated in November 1985 to marshal
agrarian effort but as could easily have been predicted was scrapped as a failure
in 1989.

[8] The expression "banana republic without bananas" was allegedly coined by the
German Chancellor Helmut Schmidt, during a visit to the USSR in the late
seventies, an image that challenged the official Soviet and CIA characterizations
but was nonetheless apt. Over time, it became something of a household phrase
to be used even by Mikhail Gorbachev.

[9] Gertrude Schroeder, "Soviet Economy on a Treadmill of Reforms," in *Soviet
Economy in a Time of Change*, Joint Economic Committee of Congress, Washington, DC, 1979, pp. 312–40.

[10] Andrei Amalrik, *Will the Soviet Union Survive Until 1984?*, Harper and Row, New
York, 1970. Cf. Steven Rosefielde, "The Soviet Economy in Crisis: Birman's
Cumulative Disequilibrium Hypothesis," *Soviet Studies*, 40, 2(April 1988): 222–
44.

Certainly, the political leadership seemed paralytic. In the early years of the 1980s, the Soviet superpower was ruled by an ailing Leonid Brezhnev, whose grasp on reality was slipping fast. In November 1982, only days after the annual November 7 Politburo lineup on top of the Lenin mausoleum, he died and was succeeded by the long-standing chairman of the dreaded KGB, Yuri Andropov, who in turn died after a mere fifteen months in power.[11] Andropov's successor as general secretary, Konstantin Chernenko, was ill already at his accession. His thirteen months in power was to prove something of a golden age for Soviet anecdotes, ascribed to the ubiquitous Radio Yerevan. The old guard of the Communist Party of the Soviet Union no longer inspired fear but rather ridicule. When the torch passed to Mikhail Gorbachev, who assumed power as general secretary in March 1985, the political system of the Soviet Union came close to what Max Weber once called a *gerontocracy*, or the French Kremlinologist Michel Tatu called *le marxisme-senilisme*.[12]

There was ferment for a mover and shaker, and Gorbachev filled the bill. He was a man of many faces, appealing to a cross section of constituencies desiring reform. He convinced the KGB and the military that he could improve the correlation of forces by resolute liberalization,[13] the people that he was a champion of better living standards, and his entourage that they could enrich themselves.

Gorbachev's first appearance as (the last) general secretary of the Communist Party of the Soviet Union took place at a plenum of the Central Committee in April 1985. He used the occasion to draw up the principles of a program for socialist renewal. The time had now come to accelerate economic growth (*uskorenie tempov rosta*). It was time to restructure (*perestroit*) both management and planning

---

[11] Arnold Beichman and Mikhail Bernstam, *Andropov: New Challenge to the West*, New York, Stein and Day, 1983.

[12] Max Weber, *Wirtschaft und Gesellschaft*, Vol. I, Mohr, Tubingen, p. 133.

[13] Abraham Becker, "Gorbachev's Program for Economic Modernization and Reform: Some Important Political-Military Implications," in *Economic Reforms in the U.S.S.R.*, Joint Economic Committee of Congress, Washington DC, September/October 1987, pp. 95–106. "Ogarkov is no longer the center of the policymaking process, but he may well believe that Gorbachev's economic program, at long last, has the potential for coping with this most important military challenge. That is, in setting out to modernize Soviet industry by concentrating on the development of machinery and particularly its high technology branches, the Gorbachev regime is also creating the foundation for advanced military technology as well" (p. 102).

functions, and it was seen as particularly important to speed up scientific and technological development (*kardinalnoe uskorenie nauchnotekhnicheskovo progressa*).[14]

However, there was no talk here of abandoning the planned economy and physical systems management.[15] Nor was there any form

---

[14] *Kommunist*, no. 7, 1985, pp. 6–7. Cf. Marshall Goldman, "Gorbachev and Perestroika," in *Economic Reforms in the U.S.S.R.*, Joint Economic Committee of Congress, Washington, DC, September/October 1987, pp. 47–58. Murray Feshbach, "Crisis Call by Gorbachev," in *Economic Reforms in the U.S.S.R.*, Joint Economic Committee of Congress, Washington, DC, September/October 1987, pp. 63–89.

[15] The U.S. government and consulting scholars scoured every aspect of Gorbachev reforms. In the initial phases (1985–86), the general tone was *old wine in new bottles*, leading to continued devitalization, but with the standard and obligatory nod toward the possibility of creeping marketization. The main exception here was defense, where Gorbachev's reforms were initially seen as bolstering the Soviet Union's weapons technology, but the emphasis shifted later to disarmament and military industrial conversion. See Stanley Cohn, "Soviet Intensive Economic Development Strategy in Perspective," in *Gorbachev's Economic Plans*, Vol. 1, Joint Economic Committee of Congress, Washington, DC, November 1987, pp. 10–26. Ed Hewett, Bryan Roberts, and Jan Vanous, "On the Feasibility of Key Targets in the Soviet Twelfth Five Year Plan (1986–90)," in *Gorbachev's Economic Plans*, Vol. 1, Joint Economic Committee of Congress, Washington, DC, November 1987, pp. 27–53. Douglas Kreshover, "Gorbachev and the Economy: The Developing Gameplan," in *Gorbachev's Economic Plans*, Vol. 1, Joint Economic Committee of Congress, Washington, DC, November 1987, pp. 54–69. Joseph Berliner, "Organizational Restructuring of the Soviet Economy," in *Gorbachev's Economic Plans*, Vol. 1, Joint Economic Committee of Congress, Washington, DC, November 1987, pp. 70–83. Lawrence Klein and Daniel Bond, "The Soviet Bloc in the World Economy," in *Gorbachev's Economic Plans*, Vol. 1, Joint Economic Committee of Congress, Washington, DC, November 1987, pp. 84–99. Lawrence Brainard, "Soviet International Financial Policy: Traditional Formulas or New Innovations?" in *Gorbachev's Economic Plans*, Vol. 1, Joint Economic Committee of Congress, Washington, DC, November 1987, pp. 100–115. Laurie Kurtzweg, "Trends in Soviet Gross National Product," in *Gorbachev's Economic Plans*, Vol. 1, Joint Economic Committee of Congress, Washington, DC, November 1987, pp. 126–65. W. Ward Kingkade, "Demographic Trends in the Soviet Union," in *Gorbachev's Economic Plans*, Vol. 1, Joint Economic Committee of Congress, Washington, DC, November 1987, pp. 166–86. Stephen Rapawy, "Labor Force and Employment in the U.S.S.R.," in *Gorbachev's Economic Plans*, Vol. 1, Joint Economic Committee of Congress, Washington, DC, November 1987, pp. 187–212. Gregory Grossman, "Roots of Gorbachev's Problems: Private Income and Outlay in the Late 1970s," in *Gorbachev's Economic Plans*, Vol. 1, Joint Economic Committee of Congress, Washington, DC, November 1987, pp. 213–30. Robert Leggett, "Soviet Investment Policy: The Key to Gorbachev's Program for Revitalizing the Soviet Economy," in *Gorbachev's Economic Plans*,

of criticism of the system as such. In Gorbachev's view, all that was needed was a substantial shake-up to tap the human factor, and on that count, the new party leader would display considerable energy. Old party stalwarts were retired in rapid succession, and younger men

Vol. 1, Joint Economic Committee of Congress, Washington, DC, November 1987, pp. 236–56. F. I. Kushnirsky, "The Role of Industrial Modernization in Soviet Economic Planning," in *Gorbachev's Economic Plans*, Vol. 1, Joint Economic Committee of Congress, Washington, DC, November 1987, pp. 257–73. Abraham Becker, "Gorbachev's Defense-Economic Dilemma," in *Gorbachev's Economic Plans*, Vol. 1, Joint Economic Committee of Congress, Washington, DC, November 1987, pp. 388–404. Bonnie Matosich, "Estimating Soviet Military Hardware Purchases: The 'Residual' Approach," in *Gorbachev's Economic Plans*, Vol. 1, Joint Economic Committee of Congress, Washington, DC, November 1987, pp. 404–30. Murray Feshbach, "Soviet Military Health Issues," in *Gorbachev's Economic Plans*, Vol. 1, Joint Economic Committee of Congress, Washington, DC, November 1987, pp. 462–80. Jonathan Stern, "Soviet Oil and Gas Production and Exports to the West: A Framework for Analysis and Forecasting," in *Gorbachev's Economic Plans*, Vol. 1, Joint Economic Committee of Congress, Washington, DC, November 1987, pp. 500–13. Kenneth Gray, "Reform and Resource Allocation in Soviet Agriculture," in *Gorbachev's Economic Plans*, Vol. 2, Joint Economic Committee of Congress, Washington, DC, November 23, 1987, pp. 9–25. Penelope Doolittle and Margaret Hughes, "Gorbachev's Agricultural Policy: Building on the Brezhnev Food Program," in *Gorbachev's Economic Plans*, Vol. 2, Joint Economic Committee of Congress, Washington, DC, November 23, 1987, pp. 26–44. Ann Goodman, Margaret Hughes, and Gertrude Schroeder, "Raising the Efficiency of Soviet Farm Labor: Problems and Prospects," in *Gorbachev's Economic Plans*, Vol. 2, Joint Economic Committee of Congress, Washington, DC, November 23, 1987, pp. 100–25. Paul Cocks, "Soviet Science and Technology Strategy: Borrowing from the Defense Sector," in *Gorbachev's Economic Plans*, Vol. 2, Joint Economic Committee of Congress, Washington, DC, November 23, 1987, pp. 145–60. Richard Judy, "The Soviet Information Revolution: Some Prospects and Comparisons," in *Gorbachev's Economic Plans*, Vol. 2, Joint Economic Committee of Congress, Washington, DC, November 23, 1987, pp. 161–75. S. E. Goodman, "The Prospective Impacts of Computing: Selected Economic-Industrial-Strategic Issues," in *Gorbachev's Economic Plans*, Vol. 2, Joint Economic Committee of Congress, Washington, DC, November 23, 1987, pp. 176–84. William McHenry, "The Integration of Management Information Systems in Soviet Enterprises," in *Gorbachev's Economic Plans*, Joint Economic Committee of Congress, Washington, DC, November 23, 1987, pp. 185–99. Gertrude Schroeder, "U.S.S.R.: Toward the Service Economy at a Snail's Pace," in *Gorbachev's Economic Plans*, Vol. 2, Joint Economic Committee of Congress, Washington, DC, November 23, 1987, pp. 240–60. Joan McIntyre, "Soviet Efforts to Revamp the Foreign Trade Sector," in *Gorbachev's Economic Plans*, Vol. 2, Joint Economic Committee of Congress, Washington, DC, November 23, 1987, pp. 489–503. Gary Bertsch, "U.S. Policy Governing Economic and Technological Relations with the U.S.S.R.," in *Gorbachev's Economic Plans*, Vol. 2, Joint Economic Committee of Congress, Washington, DC, November 23, 1987, pp. 433–47.

took their places.[16] To western observers who wanted to see the Soviet Union transformed, this radical rejuvenation of the Soviet power elite was bound to be taken as a sign of better times.

During Gorbachev's first two years in power, he mainly indulged himself in scapegoating. He initiated an antialcohol campaign to bolster worker discipline, earning himself the sobriquet *mineralny sekretar* (from the mineral water that was served in lieu of vodka) instead of *generalny sekretar*.[17] He issued a decree in May 1986 attacking nonlabor incomes (*netrudovye dohkody*),[18] which adversely affected the supply of private produce to urban food markets through the second economy.[19] He created a product quality improvement agency called *Gospriemka*, which played havoc with managerial bonuses.[20] Moreover, in an important speech in Murmansk, he blamed the country's 18 million

[16] In 1985 alone, three out of ten voting members of the mighty Politburo were removed, and the purge did not stop with this august body. When the Communist Party convened for its twenty-sixth congress, in 1986, no less than 38 percent of the living voting members of the Central Committee had been either retired or seriously demoted, and the important cadre of oblast first secretaries had gone through a similar turnover: 32 percent were Gorbachev appointees (Jerry Hough, *Opening up the Soviet Economy*, Brookings Institution, Washington, DC, 1988, pp. 29, 31). Ominously for Gorbachev, one of the first of the younger men who was thus recruited to the very highest places of power was a party first secretary from Stavropol by the name of Boris Nikolaevich Yeltsin. On the *human factor*, see Elizabeth Teague, "Gorbachev's 'Human Factor' Policies," in *Gorbachev's Economic Plans*, Vol. 2, Joint Economic Committee of Congress, Washington, DC, November 23, 1987, pp. 224–39.

[17] Stephen White, *Russia Goes Dry: Alcohol, State and Society*, Cambridge University Press, Cambridge, 1996. Vladimir Treml, "Gorbachev's Anti-Drinking Campaign: A 'Noble Experiment' or a Costly Exercise in Futility?" in *Gorbachev's Economic Plans*, Vol. 2, Joint Economic Committee of Congress, Washington, DC, November 23, 1987, pp. 297–311. Restaurants were prohibited from serving any form of alcohol before 2 p.m. Stores could begin selling wine and beer at that same time, but hard spirits could only be bought between 4 p.m. and 8 p.m. As the number of licensed outlets was also drastically curtailed, the first hot summer antialcohol campaigning was marked by huge lines and numerous disturbances.

[18] *Pravda*, May 28, 1986.

[19] *Pravda*, November 21, 1986. Cf. Roger Blough, Jennifer Muratore, and Steve Berk, "Gorbachev's Policy on the Private Sector: Two Steps Forward, One Step Backward," in *Gorbachev's Economic Plans*, Vol. 2, Joint Economic Committee of Congress, Washington, DC, November 23, 1987, pp. 261–71.

[20] The full name was *Gosudarstvennaya priemnaya kommissiya*, or *State Reception Committee*. It would be known by its diminutive *Gospriemka* because the more logical *Gospriem* would bring to mind state receptions where food and drinks are served. It was a rather curious confusion of words for a rather curious reform.

bureaucrats for acting as a braking mechanism (*mekhanism tor-mozheniya*) on his reforms.[21] Each of these impediments was real, but they were only symptoms, not the primary cause. Inefficiency and a myriad of absurdities were endemic in command natural economies and could not be extirpated piecemeal.

Predictably, Gorbachev's mobilization initiative 1985–86 yielded paltry results, providing either a pretext, or justification, for a heretical, market-oriented path known as *perestroika* (radical economic reform). At a Central Committee plenum in June 1987, a package of decrees was presented, which were centered on a new law on the operation of state enterprises.[22] The law stated that the mandatory nature of planning would cease and that enterprises would henceforth be allowed to draw up their own plans. This seemed more novel than it was. Enterprises had been preparing *tekhpromfinplans* (enterprise technical, industrial, and financial plans) for decades, which were approved by their administrative supervisors (*glavki*), subject to overall resource constraints mandated by *Gosplan*. They were hemmed in further by contracts and party, military, and KGB intervention. Their behavior was guided by state-mandated managerial bonus incentives, an obligation to sell all noncontracted goods solely to the state wholesale monopoly (*Gossnabsbyt*), and state banking controls over finance and the use of enterprise revenues. This wasn't lost on the reformers, who also voted to adopt nearly a dozen decrees that called for parallel changes in the behavior of a range of government agencies, but whatever liberalization may have been intended was partly offset by a new provision for a system of state orders, known as *goszakaz*. Managers would be granted greater autonomy over nonpriority goods, but strategic products were still subject to state requisitioning.

The banking reforms of 1987–88, which created a number of specialized banks known as *spetsbanki*, off-shoots of established institutions, were also largely perfunctory. The old *Stroibank* (Construction Bank), for example, was broken up into three different investment banks. The *Promstroibank* supported industrial construction. The *Agroprombank* was in charge of agricultural investment, and the *Zhilsotsbank* concentrated on housing and public facilities. The foreign trade bank,

[21] *Ekonomicheskaya Gazeta*, Vol. 41, 1987, p. 3.
[22] Gertrude Schroeder, "Anatomy of Gorbachev's Economic Reforms," *Soviet Economy*, 3, 3 (1987).

the *Vneshtorgbank*, also was given more independence and was renamed *Vneshekonombank*.

Cooperatives, another strand in Gorbachev's "tiptoe" marketization, seemed to be more of the same. In 1988, he introduced a decree permitting small groups of entrepreneurs to lease state facilities (*arenda*) collectively and form cooperative businesses. The experiment started with cooperative cafés (*kooperativnoe kafe*). It soon mushroomed, encompassing foreign joint ventures such as McDonald's, improving the quality of life in Soviet cities at no public cost.

It seemed at the time that Gorbachev's enterprise and banking reform, supplemented by cooperative services, were positive, albeit baby steps toward NEP-type Langean market socialism, social democracy, or even democratic free enterprise. He could have pressed these stem cells into the service of Leninist Market Communism by retaining the criminalization of big business, entrepreneurship, and private property; moved forward with an orderly and equitable transition to free enterprise; or permitted a helter-skelter return to a new form of pre-Soviet market Muscovy. His declaratory position expounded in *Perestroika: Radical Reform for My Country and the World* was emphatic. The Bolsheviks were on the march back to the Leninist Market Communism that Stalin repressed in 1929. But this was belied by his inaction. Instead of displaying due diligence over personal use of state revenues, materials, and property inculcated into every Bolshevik since 1917, Gorbachev winked at a counterrevolution from below opening Pandora's Box. He allowed enterprise managers and others not only to profit maximize for the state in various market-like ways, which was beneficial, but also to misappropriate state revenues, divert production for personal use, spontaneously privatize state assets, and export the proceeds abroad. In the process, red directors disregarded state contracts and obligations, disorganizing interindustrial intermediate input flows, and triggering a depression from which the Soviet Union never recovered and Russia has barely emerged.

Box 3.2 Langean Market Socialism

Oscar Lange was the first economist to demonstrate with neoclassical theory that markets could be effectively employed as alternatives to requisitioning and rationing for socialist purposes in economies that criminalized private property, business, and entrepreneurship. In "On the Economic Theory of Socialism," published in 1936, he claimed that this could be accomplished by instructing state managers to produce to the point at which marginal revenue equaled marginal cost, instead of managers maximizing their own private benefit, with the assistance of a state price board that adjusted prices until gluts and shortages were cleared. Although Lange's proofs were seriously flawed, and the optimization proposed was second-best, the concept revealed nonetheless how state ownership and competitive market efficiency could be partly reconciled. Gorbachev's market reforms were Langean because they didn't require or envision widespread privatization.

Red directors who were supposed to be transformed into Langean managers became pre-Muscovite privateers without secure property rights and the rule of law. Some, perhaps most, were opportunistic. But others it seems were prepared. According to various sources, well-placed actors within the KGB and the party began using their international networks to move capital assets out of the country before 1985. This provided them with the experience needed to inveigle or entice Gorbachev into crafting corruptible reforms.

By 1987, privateers were diligently building the new infrastructure of banks, trading companies, stock and currency exchanges, and corporate shells needed for this purpose, including joint ventures linking them with foreign investors and business partners. An estimated 80 percent of all joint ventures included KGB officers.[23]

A key element of this plunder machine was hundreds of commercial banks that were growing like mushrooms in the rain. Having little interest in traditional banking operations, they focused on short-term speculation and capital flight. This also was the time when Russian oligarchs (politically influential, superrich, insider businessmen) began to emerge as serious players. Some came out of the shadow economy; others were government ministers proceeding to lay private claims on their fiefdoms. The archetype was Yeltsin's future Prime Minister Viktor Chernomyrdin, who would transform himself from minister of the Soviet gas industry into the main stakeholder in privatized *Gazprom* (gas industry).

---

[23] "Russia 2000," Stratfor.com, November 2, 1999. Cited from *Johnson's Russia List*, November 3, 1999, p. 13.

Given all the heated debates that would later ensue about how
Yeltsin and his shock therapy engendered mass plunder. It should be
noted that the looting began under Gorbachev's watch. It was his
malign neglect that transformed the rhetoric of Market Communism
into the pillage of the nation's assets.

The scale of this plunder was astounding. It not only bankrupted
the Soviet Union, forcing Russian President Boris Yeltsin to appeal
to the G-7 for $6 billion of assistance on December 6, 1991,[24] but
triggered a free fall in aggregate production commencing in 1990,
aptly known as *catastroika*.

In retrospect, the Soviet Union didn't collapse because the liberalized command economy devised after 1953 was marked for death.
The system was inefficient, corrupt, and reprehensible in a myriad of
ways, but sustainable just as the CIA and most Sovietologists maintained. It was destroyed by Gorbachev's tolerance and complicity in
allowing privateers to misappropriate state revenues, pilfer materials, spontaneously privatize, and hotwire their ill-gotten gains abroad,
all of which disorganized production. This may not have been his
intention. The economic mobilization policies adopted during the
first phase of Gorbachev's reforms (1985–86), were mostly traditional
and ineffective.[25] They neither accelerated NMP (net material product) growth (Table 3.1)[26] nor alleviated the hidden stagnation (*zastoi*)
acknowledged by Abel Aganbegyan.[27]

Official data show that the second phase of the reform, *perestroika*
(1987–89) was worse. Enterprise reform, including *trudovye kollektivy*

---

[24] Citing Russian investigators, Stratfor analysts claim that in 1989–91, the KGB's
first chief directorate alone succeeded in funneling at least 60 metric tons of gold,
150 metric tons of silver, 8 metric tons of platinum, and $15 to $50 billion in
hard currency abroad." Ibid. On the Soviet Union's external debt, see Patricia
Wertman, "The External Financial Position of the Former Soviet Union: From
Riches to Rags?, in *The Former Soviet Union in Transition*, Vol. 1, Joint Economic
Committee of Congress, Washington, DC, February 1993, pp. 389–404. "The
debt of the former Soviet Union (FSU) was approximately $65.9 billion at the
end of October 1991" (p. 389). Soviet external bank and nonbank trade-related
debt rose from 31.3 in 1985 to $56.9 billion by the end of 1990 (p. 391). For
a review of the Soviet Union's internal finances, see James Duran, Jr., "Russian
Fiscal and Monetary Stabilization: A Tough Road Ahead," in *The Former Soviet
Union in Transition*, Joint Economic Committee of Congress, Washington, DC,
February 1993, pp. 196–217.
[25] Goldman, *What Went Wrong with Perestroika*.
[26] *Narodnoe khoziaistvo SSSR*.
[27] Aganbegyan, *Inside Perestroika*.

Table 3.1. *Soviet net material product growth, 1981–91 (indexed to the preceding year)*

Year	Initial	Revised
1981	103.2	
1982	103.4	
1983	104.2	
1984	103.3	
1985	103.6	102.4
1986	104.3	103.3
1987	102.9	102.6
1988		103.5
1989		101.9
1990		98.0
1991		91.7

Notes: The initial series was reported in *Narodnoe khoziaistvo SSSR*, 1987. The revised figures (provided without explanation) were reported in *Narodnoe khoziaistvo SSSR*, 1990. They presumably were adjusted to reflect Gorbachev's views about stagnation (*zastoi*). The Soviet Union was dissolved before the 1991 edition of *Narodnoe khoziaistvo* could be prepared. The figure for 1991 therefore was extrapolated using corresponding series for the Russian Federation.

Sources: Narodnoe khoziastvo SSSR, 1987, Finansy i statistika, Moscow, 1987, p. 8; *Narodnoe khoziaistvo SSSR*, 1990, Finansy i statistika, Moscow, 1990, p. 7; and *Narodnoe khoziaistvo Rossiiskoi Federderatsii*, 1992, Moscow, 1992, p. 14.

(worker councils)[28] and experiments in cooperatives, leasing, *yarmaki*, commodity auctions, banking, and foreign joint ventures, which were supposed to have demonstrated the superiority of Market Communism,[29] caused NMP growth to decelerate.

[28] Steven Rosefielde and R. W. Pfouts, "Reform and the Defense Sector," *Kommunist*, 15(October 1989): 6566.

[29] Steven Rosefielde, "Regulated Market Socialism: The Semi-Competitive Soviet Solution," *Soviet Union/Union Sovietique*, 13, Pt. 1 (Spring 1986), pp. 1–21. Rosefielde, "State Directed Market Socialism: The Enigma of Gorbachev's Radical Industrial Reforms," *Soviet Union/Union Sovietique*, 16, 1(1989): 1–22. Rosefielde, "Ruble Convertibility: Promise or Threat," in Simon Serfaty (ed.), *The Future of U.S.-Soviet Relations: Twenty American Initiatives for a New Agenda*, Johns Hopkins University Press, Baltimore, 1989. Rosefielde, "Market Communism at the Brink," *Global Affairs*, 5, 2(Spring 1990): 95–108. Rosefielde, "Democratic Market Communism: Gorbachev's Design for Utopia," *Shogaku-Ronshu*

This setback may have been offset in Gorbachev's eyes by improved supplies for those with spare change, but it also set the stage for the disorganization of the physical systems control mechanism when asset-grabbing, revenue misappropriation, and materials diversion accelerated with managerial empowerment in the third phase of his reform. The 10 percent drop in NMP officially reported (1990–91) dramatically confirms that when Gorbachev winked at this malfeasance, red directors and commissars seized the moment. They pressed Gorbachev to expand privateers–friendly reforms and rapidly intensified their plunder. In an instant, monies earmarked for intermediate inputs were diverted to luxury consumption goods, while production, taxes, and other state payments plummeted. The wild rumpus had begun and swiftly degenerated into free-for-all *catastroika* after the Soviet Union crashed and burned.

It can be argued using official statistics (1985–88) that Gorbachev had no hard evidence to suggest that his Market Communist reforms would become *catastroikic* and therefore should not be suspected of conspiring with the privateers. But alarm bells should have sounded when Soviet GNP slowed below 2 percent in 1989 and turned negative in 1990 for the first time since 1921. Gorbachev may have been in denial, but he wasn't a fool. He had little to gain as a responsible guardian of the people's welfare, and everything to lose by opening Pandora's Box wide, and he should have retrenched. That he accelerated his *catastroikic* reforms, including the abolition of directive planning in the spring of 1991,[30] amid the emergence of significant open inflation and a frenzied scramble for private control of state revenues, materials, and assets, suggests that he was under the thrall of, and

---

(*Fukushima Journal of Commerce, Economics and Economic History*), 59, 3(March 1991): 15–23. Rosefielde, "Gorbachev's Transition Plan: Strategy for Disaster," *Global Affairs*, 6, 2(Spring 1991): 1–21. Rosefielde, "Les limites du liberalisme economique sovietique: la perestroika va-t-elle passer a la trappe?" ("The Limits of Soviet Economic Liberalism: Perestroika in Limbo"), *Revue D'Etudes Comparatives Est-Ouest*, 22, 2(October 1991): 59–70. Rosefielde, "Soviet Market Socialism: An Evolutionary Perspective," *Research on the Soviet Union and Eastern Europe*, 1 (1990): 23–43. Rosefielde, "The New Soviet Foreign Trade Mechanism: East West Trade Expansion Possibilities under Perestroika," in Eric Stubbs (ed.), *Soviet Foreign Economic Policy and International Security*, M. E. Sharpe, Armonk, NY, pp. 75–86.

[30] Gosplan ceased preparing annual directive plans. Enterprises were obligated thereafter only to fulfill five-year plan targets, greatly increasing their room for maneuver.

perhaps in league with, the misappropriators. He claimed throughout that he was a communist but didn't lift a finger to protect the people from the ravages of his policies.

Most western observers likewise were unperturbed. They had supported Gorbachev from the start, first as a ray of hope to oppose Ronald Reagan's anti–evil empire policies, and then for the Soviet president's westernizing rhetoric. This not only included economic liberalization with its promised convergence, but Gorbachev's political programs of *demokratizatsia* (democratization), *novoe myshlenie* (new thinking, including Russia's return to its common European home), deep arms reductions, and even the cessation of the cold war. Although official economic statistics didn't support the claim judged from the standard of contemporaneous western economic performance,[31] opinion makers had no difficulty portraying Reform Communism as a system in trouble, which could benefit from better incentives, prices, and augmented enterprise autonomy. *Perestoika* was a blueprint for paring bureaucracy, substituting economic regulation for directive planning, and curbing military outlays to stimulate growth and improve consumption. Many were optimistic,[32] and like Gorbachev weren't chastened when things started to fall apart because they failed to consider the possibility that insiders would hijack official reform legislation, abetted by presidential inattentiveness. They didn't imagine that the Communist Party, the KGB, and *genshtab* would permit economic ministerial, regional, and managerial cadre to destroy the Soviet Union and Bolshevik power. Some like Charles Bettleheim had raised the issue in a different context, but the idea wasn't taken seriously outside Marxist circles.[33]

Plummeting production (1989–91) instead was attributed to the side effects of arms reductions,[34] ascribed to political events such as

[31] Steven Rosefielde, "Is the Economy as Bad as the Soviets Say?" *Orbis*, 34, 4(Fall 1990): 509–527. Cf. Rosefielde, "The Riddle of Postwar Russian Economic Growth: Statistics Lied and Were Misconstrued," *Europe-Asia Studies*, 55, 3(2003): 469–81.

[32] Desai, *Perestroika in Perspective*.

[33] Charles Bettleheim, *Class Struggles in the USSR, Second Period: 923–1930*, Monthly Review Press, New York, 1978.

[34] Donald Firth and James Noren, *Soviet Defense Spending: A History of the CIA Estimates 1950–1990*, Texas A&M University Press, College Station, 1998. James Noren and Laurie Kurtzweg, "The Soviet Union Unravels: 1985–91," in *The Former Soviet Union in Transition*, Joint Economic Committee of Congress, Washington, DC, February 1993.

the secession of the Baltic States and the failed August 19, 1991 coup d'etat[35] or was viewed as a mystery because in western eyes liberalization could only be beneficial. In any event, few were worried because if *catastroika* did bring about the collapse of Soviet power, so much the better. Then Russia would be free to westernize comprehensively, without the excess baggage of communism.[36] *Perestroika*, it seemed to many, was a win–win situation. It would either make the Soviet Union prosperous and benign or set the stage for Russian democratic free enterprise and enlightenment. There was no middle way because *perekhod* (market transition) was said to be ineluctable. Other outcomes were unthinkable, except the bogeyman of communist restoration. Culture might matter but not enough to fret about market Muscovy, making it plausible to suppose that the best course for those who wrecked the Soviet Union would have been to secure their wealth by westernizing under the rule of law. That they didn't confirms the power of Russian culture and provides a framework for comprehending the post–Soviet experience.

Box 3.3 Abortive Coup of 1991

On August 19, 1991, high-ranking CPSU and government members formed a State Emergency Committee and removed Mikhail Gorbachev as General Party secretary and head of state, citing his poor health. They had intended to arrest Boris Yeltsin as well but were disorganized. Although popular support for Gorbachev was nearly invisible, and there was widespread sympathy for the conspirators' actions, the operation was poorly planned and lacked iron-willed leadership. Lenin would not have failed. Western writers usually credit the coup d'etat's collapse on August 21 to Boris Yeltsin's heroism, valiant popular resistance, the media, and international pressure. Yeltsin's showmanship was clearly important, but the other factors were subsidiary.

Was the dissolution of the Soviet Union economically inevitable? Strange as it may seem today, this wasn't the consensus yesterday. The

---

[35] Goldman, *What Went Wrong with Perestroika*. Judy Shelton, *The Coming Soviet Crash: Gorbachev's Desperate Pursuit of Credit in Western Financial Markets*, Free Press, New York, 1989. Shelton blames the collapse on a monetary crisis, with little justification.

[36] Anders Aslund, "Heritage of the Gorbachev Era," in the *Former Soviet Union in Transition*, Joint Economic Committee of Congress, Washington, DC, February 1993, pp. 184–95.

CIA and most Sovietologists expected Gorbachev to scrape by. They were confident that liberalization in all its forms would improve the quality of Soviet life, and when *catastroika* reared its ugly head, they believed that the security services and the Communist Party could restore the status quo ante. Both the agency and the pundits were probably wrong about its resilience because they hadn't factored in the cancer of spontaneous revenue, materials, and asset seizing. But they were probably right about the sustainability of Lenin's natural economy had the leadership retained control of the commanding heights, suppressing revenue misappropriation, pilfering, and spontaneous privatization. Privateers could not have privatized the Soviet Union and destroyed communism under Stalin's watch and would not have been able to do so in 1991 if the security services, *genshtab*, and party reached a consensus on how to depose Gorbachev and eliminate Yeltsin.[37] The economics of reform, or even Market Communism, didn't have to bring down the Bolshevik house of cards. It was the avaricious and vacillatory vanguard of the proletariat that betrayed Lenin by allowing privateers to hijack liberalization.

- After being appointed general secretary of the Communist Party in 1985, Mikhail Gorbachev tried to accelerate economic growth with traditional Reform Communist mobilization campaigns.
- In 1987, he changed course, embarking on radical economic reform (*perestroika*). He didn't repudiate communism, physical systems management, or preponderant state ownership of the means of production, seeking instead to bolster them with the selective introduction of market forces.
- He introduced *yarmaki* (bazaar), cooperatives, *arenda* (leasing), enterprise worker councils (*trudovye kollektivy*), augmented managerial autonomy, entrepreneurship, foreign joint ventures, and permitted some expanded negotiated pricing.
- The rhetoric was radical but not the practice. State rather than consumer sovereignty prevailed.
- The excitement surrounding these reforms and parallel initiatives in democracy, civil rights, and foreign policy centered more on people's fears than on the reforms' immediate impact.

---

[37] One of the chief conspirators in the abortive August 1991 coup d'etat against Gorbachev revealed that there were plans to arrest Yeltsin too. See Yuri Stroganov, "Oleg Shenin: It's a Pity Yeltsin Wasn't Arrested," *Johnson's Russia List*, No. 8333, Article 9, August 19, 2004.

- Many argued that Gorbachev's radical reforms were path dependent, without considering Muscovy.
- This was a fatal error because it prevented Gorbachev and well-wishers from being vigilant to the danger of co-option.
- A group of insiders and their supporters quickly grasped how Gorbachev's posturing could be exploited, allowing them to prosper by asset-grabbing, rent-seeking, and misappropriation to the detriment of society and Soviet power.
- The scale of plundering was astonishing, as insiders grabbed assets, misappropriated funds, and disregarded production and intermediate input distribution plans in pursuit of their personal interests.
- The mayhem caused a double-digit GDP fall in 1991, which spiraled into a hyperdepression, often called *catastroika* (catastrophic reform).
- *Catastroika* and the power struggle between Gorbachev and Boris Yeltsin were primarily responsible for Soviet disunion.
- Gorbachev was in a position to understand that the licentious aspects of *perestroika* threatened the welfare of the Russian people and the existence of the Soviet Union, but he failed to take countermeasures, suggesting the possibility of his complicity.
- Physical systems management and Market Communism were both feasible. The Soviet Union would still exist today if Gorbachev had been a responsible communist.

4

Blindman's Bluff

Wishful Thinking

As memories of Sovietology fade,[1] many scholars prefer to forget that they misappraised the motives of those pressing for Soviet regime change and portrayed the Gorbachev years as a time of high hopes. Socialists who kept the faith continued to believe that the future was theirs,[2] that the USSR would eventually realize its ideals. Western optimists of various persuasions likewise were encouraged by Gorbachev's post-1986 democratic and humanistic rhetoric, tiptoe marketization, and most of all by gestures of rapprochement.[3] Although, they grasped many of the Soviet Union's economic shortcomings, most preferred not to consider the possibility that warmer relations might be a subterfuge or sabotaged by stagnation, depression, or collapse. The *glasnost* (openness) years for them were perceived in accordance with western harmonist public culture as the dawning of a new enlightened age of westernization, arms control, disarmament, peace,

---

[1] Sovietology was a postwar western discipline devoted to the study of all aspects of the Soviet Union. Kremlinology, focused on Soviet politics, was a subcomponent of the field.

[2] *Narodnoe Khoziaistvo SSSR za 70 Let, Yubileinyi Statisticheskii Ezhegodnik*, Finansy i Statistika, 1987, p. 12.

[3] Padma Desai, *Perestroika in Perspective: The Design and Dilemmas of Soviet Reform*, Princeton University Press, Princeton, NJ, 1989; Ed Hewett, *Reforming the Soviet Economy: Equality vs. Efficiency*, Brookings Institution, Washington, DC, 1987.

and global prosperity.[4] Privateers and *catastroika* were invisible on their radar screens (see appendix), and even today, the myth of Ronald Reagan's and Gorbachev's epochal, cold war–ending statesmanship distorts reality and overshadows the real drama.[5]

---

[4] Patchwork of beliefs, platitudes, and attitudes akin to a collective mind that allows policymakers to build consensus on bipartisan or nonpartisan wishful thinking. American public culture approves partisan debate; tolerates distortion and attitude management by the media, business, and government; and conceals latent conflicts to promote tranquility, and forge consensus on the basis of shared wishful thinking. American public culture has the virtue of protecting its representational political governance system but the defect of making us purblind, especially concerning national security and foreign relations. It is akin to ideology but far more subtle.

[5] Jack F. Matlock, Jr., *Reagan and Gorbachev: How the Cold War Ended,* Random House, New York, 2004. Joyce Barnathan, "Inside the Great Thaw," *Business Week,* August 9, 2004, reprinted in *Johnson's Russia List,* No. 8320, Article 9, August 7, 2004. Richard Pipes, "Inside Reagan's Bid for Detente," *Johnson's Russia List,* No. 8337, Article 12, August 22, 2004. Pipes (former Soviet specialist in the National Security Council, while Matlock was briefly in charge of the Moscow embassy in the early 1980s before moving on to Prague) reports that Jack Matlock has a master's degree from Columbia University and was U.S. ambassador to Russia from 1987 to 1991, a period discussed in his book, *Autopsy of an Empire: The American Ambassador's Account of the Collapse of the Soviet Union,* Random House, New York, 1997. In his latest book, Matlock addresses the years 1983 to 1987 when he occupied the post of director for European and Soviet Affairs in President Reagan's National Security Council. Pipes observes that Matlock's stint in Prague prevented him from appreciating Reagan's visceral hostility toward communism and the USSR. Reagan, during the first two years of his presidency, wasn't consumed with a desire to negotiate with Moscow. Just the opposite. Reagan was convinced that America made all the concessions in past negotiations and was reluctant to engage unless he was assured of a positive outcome. "Friction between the White House and Foggy Bottom in the early phases of Reagan's presidency was constant. The State Department resembles a gigantic firm of international lawyers who perceive their mission to be the elimination of all conflicts through negotiation. Refusal to engage in talks, let alone resorting to force, is to them a mark of failure. Viewing themselves as consummate pragmatists, they intensely dislike anything that smacks of ideology. Now, negotiations are a fine thing, provided that the parties to them agree on fundamentals, the most basic of which is recognition of one another's right to exist. Where this recognition is absent, negotiations are an exercise in futility. Such is the case in the Middle East, where the Arabs continue to reject Israel on grounds that it occupies Palestinian territory and hence has no right to be. Since seizing power in 1917, the Soviet government

The period of heady optimism began abruptly in 1987 with Gorbachev's declaration of *novoe myslenie* (new thinking), symbolizing his
desire to bury the hatchet with Europe and America on a host of ideological, security, trade, investment, political, and human rights issues.
Before 1987, western specialists fretted that *uskorenie* (GDP growth

> proceeded on the premise that all capitalist regimes were doomed. Every treaty
> with these regimes was, therefore, an armistice in force only as long as Moscow
> found it convenient. Reagan sensed this and felt that it was his duty, by word
> and deed, to convince Moscow it had no chance of relegating the United States
> to the 'dustbin of history.'" Matlock's account improves after mid-1983 when
> he returned to the White House from Prague. The ice between Moscow and
> Washington had started to melt. (Pipes surmises due to the NATO war exercise
> code-named Able Archer, which the Russians misinterpreted as preparation for
> a nuclear strike on their territory.) William Lee, "The ABM Treaty Charade:
> A Study in Elite Illusion and Delusion," *Journal of Social, Political and Economic
> Studies*, Monograph 25, Washington, DC, 1997, pp. 97–105. SNIE (Special
> National Intelligence Estimate), 11-10-84/JX, "Implication of Recent Soviet
> Military-Political Activities." The scare persuaded Reagan to soften somewhat
> his anticommunist rhetoric but not to suspend aid to Polish Solidarity or to
> cease pressuring the Saudis to increase their oil output, which lowered world oil
> prices with devastating consequences for Soviet hard-currency earnings. Pipes
> continues, "The real break came in March 1985 with the election of Gorbachev
> as head of the Soviet Communist Party and thus, de facto chief executive of the
> Soviet Union and its bloc. Reagan at first reacted cautiously to this change but,
> trusting his impressions of the new leader following several personal encounters,
> gradually gained confidence in him. The most engrossing sections of Matlock's
> book deal with the summit in Reykjavik, Iceland, in October 1986. Reagan was
> widely blamed for rejecting Gorbachev's offer to eliminate all strategic nuclear
> weapons in exchange for the United States' giving up testing missile defenses,
> Reagan's pet project. Although Western scientists ridiculed Reagan's Strategic
> Defense Initiative as 'Star Wars' and continue to dismiss President Bush's efforts
> in the same direction, the Russians, with their unbounded faith in American
> technology, took them very seriously, so seriously that they were willing to
> surrender their vast strategic nuclear arsenal if SDI testing was abandoned. Reagan
> refused to accept the deal, so the summit broke up without result. Matlock defends
> the president on this issue. An active participant in these events, he insists that
> Reagan was fully cognizant of what was at stake and then goes on to explain how
> tenuous Gorbachev's offer really was." In Matlock's words, "Those who have
> accused Reagan of passing up a unique opportunity to rid the world of nuclear
> weapons must assume that, once there had been broad agreement in principle,
> a treaty would have been forthcoming – automatically as it were – and that this
> treaty would have been ratified by the legislatures of both countries and then
> faithfully implemented. . . . Nothing in the history of U.S.-Soviet relations up
> to then would have provided any encouragement for such expectations. . . . The
> program in its entirety was too ambitious to be practical."

acceleration) would modernize Soviet weapons technology,[6] intensi-
fying the arms race[7] or that such fears would preclude the Kremlin
from gaining the financial assistance it needed to westernize.[8] After
the June 1987 Communist Party plenum, the consensus, including the
American Central Intelligence Agency (CIA), State Department, and
Arms Control and Disarmament Agency, but excluding the Defense
Intelligence Agency (DIA) and the Office of the Secretary of Defense
(OSD), turned 180 degrees.[9] Gorbachev was portrayed as a man of

---

[6] Stanley Cohn, "Soviet Intensive Economic Development Strategy in Perspec-
tive," in *Gorbachev's Economic Plans*, Vol. 1, Joint Economic Committee of
Congress, Washington, DC, November 23, 1987, pp. 10–26. Douglas Kreshover,
"Gorbachev and the Economy: The Developing Gameplan," in *Gorbachev's
Economic Plans*, Vol. 1, Joint Economic Committee of Congress, Washington,
DC, November 23, 1987, pp. 54–69. Abraham Becker, "Gorbachev's Defense-
Economic Dilemma," in *Gorbachev's Economic Plans*, Vol. 1, Joint Economic
Committee of Congress, Washington, DC, November 23, 1987, pp. 372–87.
Shelley Deutch, "The Soviet Weapons Industry: An Overview," in *Gorbachev's
Economic Plans*, Vol. 1, Joint Economic Committee of Congress, Washington,
DC, November 23, 1987, pp. 405–30. Bonnie Matosich, "Estimating Soviet
Hardware Purchases: The 'Residual' Approach," in *Gorbachev's Economic Plans*,
Vol. 1, Joint Economic Committee of Congress, Washington, DC, November
23, 1987, pp. 431–61. Murray Feshbach, "Soviet Military Health Issues," in
Gorbachev's Economic Plans, Vol. 1, November 23, 1987, pp. 462–80. Andrew
Marshall, "Commentary," in *Gorbachev's Economic Plans*, Vol. 1, Joint Economic
Committee of Congress, Washington, DC, November 23, 1987, pp. 481–84.
Joseph Berliner, "Prepared Statement," in *Economic Reforms in the U.S.S.R., Joint
Economic Committee of Congress*, Washington, DC, September/October 1987,
pp. 274–85. Ed Hewett, "The June 1987 Plenum and Economic Reform in
the USSR," in *Economic Reforms in the U.S.S.R.*, Joint Economic Committee of
Congress, Washington, DC, September/October 1987, pp. 290–302. Gertrude
Schroeder, "Prepared Statement," in *Economic Reforms in the U.S.S.R.*, Joint Economic Committee of Congress, Washington, DC, September/October 1987,
pp. 307–26.

[7] Albert Wohlstetter, "Racing Forward or Ambling Back," in *Defending America*,
Basic Books, New York, 1977, pp. 110–68. The Soviet Union steadily built
up its arms forces through the postwar period regardless of whether American defense spending was rising or falling. Hence, the term arms "race" was a
misnomer.

[8] Jerry Hough, "Prepared Statement," in *Economic Reforms in the U.S.S.R.*, Joint
Economic Committee of Congress, Washington, DC, September/October 1987,
pp. 426–44.

[9] "Prepared Statement of the Defense Intelligence Agency," in *Economic Reforms in
the U.S.S.R.*, Joint Economic Committee of Congress, Washington DC, Septem-
ber/October 1987, pp. 242–50.

peace, prodded in part by an exorbitant burden of defense (share of GDP devoted to military activities), who sincerely desired to improve living standards[10] and forge a better global order.[11]

Although many understood that Gorbachev's charm offensive might not have been anything more than a ploy to *Finlandize* Europe,[12] like

[10] One strategy that gathered headlines was the Ryzhkov plan to augment resources devoted to civilian production with the military industrial complex. Nikolai Ryzhkov, "O gosudarstvennom plane ekonomicheskovo i sotsial'novo razvitiia SSSR na 1986-1990 gody" (On the State Plan of the Economic and Social Development of the USSR during 1986–90), *Pravda*, June 19, 1986, pp. 1–3. Julian Cooper, "Technology Transfer between Military and Civilian Ministries," in *Gorbachev's Economic Plans*, Vol. 1, Joint Economic Committee of Congress, Washington, DC, November 23, 1987, pp. 388–405. Paul Cocks, "Soviet Science and Technology Strategy: Borrowing from the Defense Sector," in *Gorbachev's Economic Plans*, Vol. 2, Washington, DC, November 23, 1987, pp. 145–60. Gary Bertsch, "U.S. Policy Governing Economic and Technological Relations with the U.S.S.R.," in *Gorbachev's Economic Plans*, Vol. 2, Joint Economic Committee of Congress, Washington, DC, November 23, 1987, pp. 433–47. David Wigg, Deputy Assistant Secretary of Defense Policy Analysis, "Prepared Statement," in *Economic Reforms in the U.S.S.R.*, Joint Economic Committee of Congress, Washington, DC, September/October 1987, pp. 15–30. Murray Feshbach, "Prepared Statement," in *Economic Reforms in the U.S.S.R.*, Joint Economic Committee of Congress, Washington, DC, September/October 1987, pp. 63–90. Abraham Becker, "Gorbachev's Program for Economic Modernization and Reform: Some Important Political-Military Implications," in *Economic Reforms in the U.S.S.R.*, Joint Economic Committee of Congress, Washington, DC, September/October 1987, pp. 95–106. Condoleezza Rice, "Soviet Foreign and Defense Policy under Gorbachev," in *Economic Reforms in the U.S.S.R.*, Joint Economic Committee of Congress, Washington, DC, September/October 1987, pp. 135–44.

[11] William Colby, Former Director of Central Intelligence Agency, "Statement," in *Economic Reforms in the U.S.S.R.*, Joint Economic Committee of Congress, Washington, DC, September/October 1987, pp. 173–81. Robert Blackwill, NIO/U.S.S.S.R., Central Intelligence Agency, Accompanied by Douglas White-house, Chief, Economic Performance Division, "Gorbachev's Program: Motives and Prospects," in *Economic Reforms in the U.S.S.R.*, Joint Economic Committee of Congress, Washington, DC, September/October 1987, pp. 213–39. Thomas Simons, Jr., Deputy Assistant Secretary of State for Europe, "Prepared Statement" in *Economic Reforms in the U.S.S.R.*, Joint Economic Committee of Congress, Washington, DC, September/October 1987, pp. 351–69. Joseph Nye, Jr., and Whitney MacMillan, *How Should America Respond to Gorbachev's Challenge? A Report of the Task Force on Soviet New Thinking,* Institute for East-West Security Studies, New York, 1987. James Noren and Laurie Kurtzweg, "The Soviet Economy Unravels," in the *Former Soviet Union in Transition*, Vol. 1, Joint Economic Committee of Congress, Washington, DC, February 1993, pp. 8–33.

[12] During the postwar period, Finland was particularly deferential to Soviet foreign policy concerns. In the view of some western analysts, but not the Finns themselves, Finland was a de facto Soviet protectorate. Anatoly Golitsyn, a KGB defector elaborated this hypothesis in *New Lies for Old*, Dodd, Mead & Company, New

Nikita Khrushchev's *mirovoe sosushchestvovanie* (peaceful coexistence) and Leonid Brezhnev's *détente*, the CIA and the State Department, coaxed by America's NATO allies, swiftly interpreted *glasnost* according to their own wishful thinking. The starting point was familiar. The Russians had been on a westernizing fast track since the late seventeenth century but were waylaid by the Bolshevik coup d'etat. Jerry Hough put the matter this way in testimony before the Subcommittee on National Security Economics, October 15, 1987:

> Russia in the 19th century was very open to the West, dominated by the Westernized lead Peter the Great had created.

Lenin temporarily derailed this process.

> I think that . . . the Communist revolution in 1917 is the Khomeini revolution of Russian history . . .

But the forces of anti-westernism, as Gorbachev understands them, are spent.[13]

> He is going to lead the Peter the Great reopening of Russia to the West . . . [14]

And Russia is likely to westernize and de-structurally militarize because

> the so-called bureaucrats want more change than Gorbachev, . . . (and the) liberal middle class . . . has grown enormously, (and the) Russians are scared because . . . they're not even equal with South Korea . . . (and don't seek world domination).

> As a consequence, Russia agreed to the zero option whereby the Kremlin withdrew its SS-20 intermediate range ballistic missiles in exchange for America's Pershing missile withdrawals, and will press for substantial reductions in conventional forces as the best way to court European assistance and save money.[15]

York, 1984, and *The Perestroika Deception: The World's Slide Towards the 'Second October Revolution'*, Edward Harle, London & New York, 1995. His conspiracy theory was rejected by the CIA, but the merchandising of *perestroika* for political advantage seems indisputable. For a detailed examination of the evidence, see Romana Hlouskova, "Golitsyn, KGB, and the Velvet Revolution," unpublished paper December 2003.

[13] Jerry Hough, "Statement," before the Subcommittee on National Security Economics, Joint Economic Committee of Congress, Washington, DC, September/October 1987, pp. 420–21.

[14] Ibid., p. 421.

[15] Ibid., pp. 423–25.

Gorbachev, in other words, although still a product of Kremlin fears and complexes, irreversibly returned Russia to its historic westernizing glide path after being blown off course for nearly seventy years. Having discovered that Leninism was a blind alley, he had no choice other than to move forward, spurred by economic stagnation and the futility of the Soviet authoritarian martial police state. Foolish western policy could slow but not forestall the process, and the West could afford to be magnanimous because the *genshtab*'s military intentions were benign. That Gorbachev's rhetoric and arms control proposals undermined NATO and exposed Europe to Moscow's superior conventional armies in Hough's view was coincidental and provided no compelling grounds for portraying Gorbachev as Machiavellian or quixotic.

This vintage "as you like it" expression of American public cultural wishful thinking was also embraced in 1987 by the CIA, which guardedly described Gorbachev as a pragmatic visionary. On the one hand, the agency ascribed Soviet motivation to economic and defensive military necessity. Gorbachev was beset by too many objective pressures to concern himself with seizing targets of opportunity as Brezhnev had done in Afghanistan or shifting the correlation of forces in the Kremlin's direction (even though secret Soviet military doctrinal documents said this was precisely what was being done).[16] On the other hand, he was said to believe " . . . that both the system and society require modernization and invigoration, if the U.S.S.R. is to remain competitive in the next century . . . He has hitched his star to the effort of achieving this kind of reform and shown, to an extent few thought possible 2 years ago, that he is willing to use his power to push the country and the party where he thinks it should go."[17]

Gorbachev was placed between a rock and a hard place because, in accordance with the American credo, Leninist natural economy (physical systems management) was uncompetitive and could not sustain Soviet superpower without beggaring the nation. He grasped the predicament and fortunately seemed to be a sufficiently astute statesman and visionary to acquiesce to necessity by leading the USSR toward managed democratic free enterprise instead of Armageddon. The modeling was not wholly determinist because the CIA conceded

---

[16] *Voennaya Mysl'*.

[17] "Statement of Robert Blackwill, NIO/U.S.S.R., Central Intelligence Agency, before the Subcommittee on National Security Economics, Joint Economic Committee of Congress, Washington, DC, September/October 1987, p. 208.

that "the reform/modernization could cause serious economic disarray . . . depressing economic growth during the rest of the 1980s to an average annual rate of less than two percent," but none of its scenarios envisioned *catastroika* torpedoing westernization.[18]

Instead, the agency's analytic construct drove it to envision a future in which the inferiority of Reform Communist physical systems management, or any market-assisted variant thereof, pressured the Soviet Union to curry favor with the West through arms control and disarmament, good neighborliness, incipient democratization, improved human rights, and economic liberalization. *Perestroika*, understood as a halfway house, might alleviate some material hardships, but as the West's harmonist credo taught, it couldn't be fruitful enough to compete with America or dysfunctional enough to destabilize international security.[19] Although economics in the CIA's paradigm was the prime catalyst, improved economic outcomes were secondary to the peaceful, free, open, humanitarian, and just world order emerging from Gorbachev's new thinking.

This idealization, as his Nobel Peace Prize attests, made Gorbachev seem heroic. The meager results of *perestroika* through 1989 and the depression that ensued were easily discounted and construed as the price for cleansing the Soviet Union of its pre-Enlightenment vices. The relaxation of secret police harassment, expanded emigration of Jews and other minorities, fringe penetration of western commerce, greater toleration of free speech and media expression, the introduction of contested elections within the party and state institutions, reductions in intermediate nuclear forces, rearward deployment of conventional arms, as well as professions of east-west reconciliation all captured headlines, not so much for what they accomplished but for what pundits claimed they portended.

Box 4.1 Arms Race

Political commentators sometimes portray the post–Second World War conflict between the Soviet Union and the West (cold war) as an ideological and geostrategic rivalry propelled by an arms race disconnected from cost/benefit analysis. Stopping the arms race from this perspective meant more than reducing military forces. It signified a return to sanity.

---

[18] "Prepared Statement of the Central Intelligence Agency," 1987, p. 23.
[19] Ibid., pp. 213–39.

> The facts don't support the hypothesis. The Soviets overarmed, but
> the United States didn't. Mikhail Gorbachev's arms control initiatives,
> therefore, may be partially construed as an effort to contain what Vitaly
> Shlykov calls structural militarization or as a gambit to improve the cor-
> relations of forces, rather than an initiative to end force as a instrument
> of geostrategic rivalry.

However, Gorbachev's deeds everywhere were less than met the
eye. Recall that, for the most part, despite all the hoopla, business,
entrepreneurship, and private property remained formally criminalized. The Communist Party preserved its political monopoly. Elected
officials weren't obligated to their constituents. Gorbachev called himself *president* but was *elected* by the Congress of People's Deputies of
the USSR, not directly by the people. The secret police were only
accountable to Gorbachev. The influence of the military was pervasive,
and there was no rule of law. In short Gorbachev's Soviet, Muscovite
authoritarian, martial police state had adorned itself with the trappings
of liberalization and had become less harsh, without ever establishing
popular economic, political, and civic sovereignty. Aspects of life,
especially civil liberties, had improved, but the prospects of Russia's
oppressed for an enlightened society remained no better than under
Tsar Nicholas II.

The CIA and Sovietologists more broadly knew but disregarded
this because they insisted on analyzing the economics, politics, and
foreign relations of Gorbachev's Soviet Union through rose-colored
filters. Soviet economic potential was gauged by a western consensus
on the deficiencies of central planning,[20] instead of post-tsarist rent-
granting. Specialists accurately claimed that Soviet planning was more
cumbersome than western markets in practice, that it was unrespon-
sive to consumer demand. However, they failed to penetrate more
deeply into the root of Soviet underperformance, giving the false

---

[20] Abram Bergson, "*Socialist Economics,*" in Abram Bergson, *Essays in Normative Eco-
    nomics*, Belknap Press, Cambridge, MA, 1966, pp. 234–36; Bergson, "Technolog-
    ical Progress," in Abram Bergson and Herbert Levine, eds., *The Soviet Economy
    toward the Year 2000*, Allen and Unwin, London, 1983, pp. 34–78; Bergson, "The
    U.S.S.R. before the Fall: How Poor and Why?" *Journal of Economic Perspective*,
    5, 4(1991): 29–44. Steven Rosefielde, "Tea Leaves and Productivity: Bergsonian
    Norms for Gauging the Soviet Union," *Comparative Economic Studies*, 47, 2(June
    2005): 259–73.

impression that Soviet economic woes would vanish if planning were abandoned. Had the CIA appreciated that tiptoe marketization was as likely to culminate in insider spontaneous privatization, enterprise revenue misappropriation, and materials theft rather than enhanced efficiency under the rule of law, its worst-case scenario would have been *catastroika*, not something short of 2 percent GDP growth.

Box 4.2   Soviet Satellites

The Molotov-Ribbentrop nonaggression pact signed August 23, 1939, between Russia and Germany contained a secret protocol sanctioning the conquest, division, and annexation of Finland, Latvia, Estonia, Lithuania, Poland, and Romania. This treaty, together with agreements reached between Joseph Stalin, Franklin Roosevelt, and Winston Churchill at Yalta February 6–11, 1945, constituted the Soviet Union's basis for claiming a sphere of postwar influence in eastern and central Europe commonly described as Soviet satellites, including East Germany, Czechoslavakia, Hungary, Poland, Romania and Bulgaria. Estonia, Latvia, and Lithuania, were made Soviet republics, and Finland managed to achieve a neutral status, although it ceded substantial territory to the USSR. All the satellite nations were governed by communist parties, replicated Soviet political economy, and formed economic (CMEA) and military (Warsaw) pacts with Moscow. The unraveling of this empire (together with Cuba) was an epochal aspect of the Gorbachev years. All eastern and central European satellites withdrew from their economic and military pacts, and subsequently joined the European Union, together with the former Soviet Baltic republics. Some claim with justification that 1991 marked the real conclusion of the Second World War, culminating in the liberation of eastern and central Europe from the dead hands of Adolf Hitler and Stalin.

The CIA and European conception of electoral politics as a vehicle for popular sovereignty rather than a device for veiling authoritarianism also beguiled many western observers. The West wanted to believe that democracy was path dependent, that once Gorbachev democratized the party, popular sovereign democracy would follow. Most seemed certain that democratization couldn't be co-opted because the people wouldn't permit it. This Spartacus syndrome didn't save Greek slaves, or Lenin's victims, and didn't prevent Boris Yeltsin from usurping power once Gorbachev signaled that he wouldn't vigorously defend himself.

Muscovite Regime Change

Gorbachev, for his part, shared neither the West's desire for popular sovereign democracy, nor its faith in democratic path dependence, believing instead, like his predecessors, that he could talk the talk, indulge servitors, and vanquish rivals without having to surrender authoritarian control. But he lacked Lenin's and Stalin's cunning, resulting in a seesaw political battle with Yeltsin, which he not only gradually lost but delegitimatized communist rule. Gorbachev may have fancied himself a master of illusion, but he was merely playing blindman's bluff.

The origins of his twin defeats as the leader of Market Communism and defender of Soviet power can be traced to an extraordinary party conference June 1988, where speaker after speaker in the spirit of *glasnost* transgressed the invisible lines of managed candor. Courageous editors then probed further and found that the censors and party control organs were too disorganized to impose the intended restrictions on public discourse. Although it wasn't de-Stalinization because no one was held to account, it was indeed a time of great revelations. Mass graves were identified and opened. Witnesses were allowed to tell their tales, and the public at large awoke to the fact that they had been forced to live amid lies and deception.

As the traditional basis of Soviet authority eroded, the general secretary began looking for ways to shore up his power. In March 1989, he inaugurated the Congress of People's Deputies, imbuing it with some democratic elements. Designed to meet only twice yearly, it was to have 2,250 members, one-third reserved for important groups, including 100 seats for the power elite, with the remainder up for grabs.[21] The first session was held in June and drove home what many had suspected, that the party's general secretary would never willingly share power.

The next fall central Europe was shaken by the revolutionary upheavals that would end in breakdown for the German Democratic

---

[21] The design of these partly rigged elections was similar to the grand compromise that was struck between the Polish Communist Party and the independent labor union Solidarity. In that case, the era of communist rule could be ended via an election where the party was guaranteed half of the seats in the Sejm, leaving the rest for open competition, which in practice meant Solidarity. In Poland, this marked a first step toward democratic multiparty politics. In the Soviet Union, the charade would have a number of unintended consequences.

Republic, the GDR, collapse for the Warsaw Pact, and eventually German unification. Although Gorbachev chose to refrain from military intervention, accepting these counterrevolutionary developments in the Soviet empire, he continued to resist abandoning communist rule at home. In November 1989, against the backdrop of the ongoing "velvet revolution" in Czechoslovakia, a Soviet Reform Commission led by academician Leonid Abalkin presented a package of suggested programs touting the strength of the socialist economic system. Nor was Gorbachev swayed by agitation aimed at legitimizing open multi-factional competition within the Communist Party or even multiparty democracy at the Communist Party Congress held the following summer. Mustering his political skills, Gorbachev managed to have himself reelected general secretary, and the delegates reaffirmed the party's monolithic character. However, the victory was Pyrrhic because he failed to subdue Boris Yeltsin who, after his election as president of the Russian Federation, used that position as a battering ram to destroy the Soviet Union and rid himself of the general secretary. Whether Yeltsin really believed that he could reconstitute the union under his own leadership after dislodging Gorbachev is unimportant. What is essential is that for all the talk of westernizing reform, in 1990–91, the Soviet Union was devoid of any institutions permitting the people to choose their own form of government and representatives. Popular sovereignty was irrelevant. The internecine battle between Tsar Gorbachev and his Muscovite vassal Boris Yeltsin was resolved the traditional way, through factional intrigue, despite the West's abiding faith in democratic path dependence.

The origin of their personal animosity can be traced to the days when Yeltsin was first party secretary for Moscow. He seized the spotlight at the Communist Party's festivities celebrating the seventieth anniversary of the Bolshevik Revolution in November 1987 by announcing his desire to resign from the Politburo, a defiant gesture that called attention to him as a prospective independent political force. Gorbachev retaliated by publicly humiliating his former protégé and then sending him into internal exile where he was barred from meeting with foreigners.

What made the case extraordinary was Yeltsin's ability to stage a comeback. The first step on this road was taken at the June 1988 party conference, where he managed to push his way to the rostrum and raise the issue of his own political rehabilitation. Gorbachev curtly rebuffed him, and Yeltsin chose to bide his time, a tactic that proved successful when he won a landslide (89 percent) of the vote for an independent seat at the new Congress of People's Deputies.

The Kremlin soon retaliated by excluding Yeltsin from the list of appointees to the Supreme Soviet, a smaller body responsible for day-to-day legislative activities. However, once again Yeltsin successfully counterpunched when one of the appointed delegates ceded his seat in favor of Gorbachev's rival, making it clear to everyone that Yeltsin might prove to be a viable challenger.

Yeltsin tried to capitalize on his growing stature in the spring of 1990. Following a round of elections to the local soviets, which brought victory to a number of well-known radicals, Yeltsin decided to run for a seat in the parallel Congress of People's Deputies in the Russian Federation. Winning another landslide victory for a seat representing his hometown Sverdlovsk/Yekaterinburg, he also proceeded to win a seat in the Russian Supreme Soviet, leading to a showdown with Gorbachev when the time came for electing a chairman.

Determined to stop Yeltsin in his tracks, the general secretary not only called and addressed a special session of the Russian Party Congress but he also went as far as to back a candidate of his own for chairman, Ivan Polozkov, a hard-line conservative who would go on to found the Russian Communist Party and even involve himself in the 1991 coup d'etat against Gorbachev.[22] Yeltsin however, was unstoppable.

---

[22] "Plots of August: 13 Years Later," *Johnson's Russia List*, Vol. 8342, Article 15, August 25, 2004. "Political observer Leonid Radzikhovsky noted in the *Russkii Kurier* newspaper that Yeltsin has never sought to celebrate the anniversary of August 1991: "Evidently, Tsar Boris didn't like being reminded of direct democracy and the 'taste of freedom.'" "45% of respondents now regard the events of August 1991 as an episode in power-struggles between various political clans, rather than a victory for democratic forces," according to VTsIOM director Vladimir Petukhov. Cf. Georgy Ilyichev, "A Bit of Turmoil on Red Square," *Johnson's Russia List*, Vol. 8335, Article 1, August 20, 2004. Again according to Vladimir Petukhov "a great deal about the 1991 events remains undiscussed and unexplained. Few people are now satisfied with the theory that the GKChP (State Emergency Committee) broke up the Soviet Union; there is growing awareness that the Soviet Union came to an end not due to the actions of Gorbachev, Yeltsin, or the GKChP, but due to fundamental economic and social causes. Also see Yuri Stroganov, "Oleg Shenin: It's A Pity Yeltsin Wasn't Arrested," *Johnson's Russia List*, Vol. 8333, Article 9, August 19, 2004. Oleg Shenin was one of the masterminds of the GKChP's plot against Gorbachev. He now claims that "one of the Committee's key errors was that it did not dissociate itself from Gorbachev. The goals declared by Gorbachev at the dawn of perestroika sounded correct. . . .

Having won the election as chairman of the Supreme Soviet, a post then known as president, he proceeded in June 1990 to have that body issue a declaration of sovereignty for the Russian Federation that inter alia declared Russian law superior to Soviet law. This swiftly led to a war of laws culminating in the breakup of the Soviet Union into its constituent republics.

When the Communist Party of the Soviet Union met for its last congress, Yeltsin was ready to throw down the gauntlet. Because of the ferment caused by *glasnost*, the congress opened in an atmosphere of great expectations for the emergence of a multiparty system. As it became obvious that Gorbachev would prevail, Yeltsin seized his opportunity. Rising in the midst of a session, he declared from the floor that he no longer saw any possibility of being associated with the Communist Party, and then he marched out, proceeding by limousine to a factory where he told workers and television cameras of his decision.

Although by now the confrontation was very much like a traditional chicken race, where there could be only one winner (or two losers), shortly after the party congress, there would be a final chance for rapprochement preserving the Soviet Union. In August, Moscow was rife with rumors about a pending deal on a major initiative for economic reform known as the *Shatalin plan* or simply as the *500-day program*.[23]

Box 4.3 The 500-Day Program

The 500-day program was a blueprint for the Soviet Union rapidly transitioning from planning to the market, published in August 1990 as a report entitled *Transition to the Market*. It was the brainchild of Grigory Yavlinsky but was prepared at Gorbachev's behest under the direction of Stanislav Shatalin. Other eminent participants included Nikolai Petrakov, Sergei Aleksashenko, Boris Fyodorov, and Yevgeny Yasin.

But words were at variance with his deeds and it became clear that if the situation persisted, the Soviet Union would collapse." Also, Shenin contends that the coup failed because the GKChP didn't use its military forces. And he goes on to assert that Yeltsin should have been arrested. "We should have detained him in Kazakhstan, where he had been the day before. We should have also isolated Popov, Luzhkov, Gdlyan, Ivanov and others. I don't understand why it was not done. This was stupid."

23 Stanislav Shatalin, et al., *Transition to the Market: 500 Days*, pt. 1, Arkhangelskoe, Moscow, August 1990. Cf. Ed Hewett, "The New Soviet Plan," *Foreign Affairs*, 69, 5 (1990).

The document was rejected by Nikolai Ryzhkov, the Soviet premier, given tepid approval by Gorbachev, and embraced by Yeltsin. The term *perekhod* (transition) soon distinguished his agenda from Gorbachev's *perestroika* (radical reform). The document was a textbook encomium to perfectly competitive markets, written by scholars with no direct experience and should not have been taken seriously.

Led by Stanislav Shatalin, the group of economists that stood behind the initiative also included a young Harvard-trained economist, Grigorii Yavlinsky, the future head of Russia's Yabloko Party. Although, the program did present a detailed timetable for how the Soviet command economy could be transformed in a mere 500 days into a functioning market economy, it was not the economics but rather the ideological challenge that should be remembered. The opening lines presented a tribute to liberal market economy that was oceans away from the Abalkin plan:

> Mankind has still not succeeded in finding anything more efficient than a market economy. The market creates a strong stimulant for mankind's self-fulfillment, for an increase in the economic activity and for rapid technological progress. Its self-regulating mechanisms guarantee the best co-ordination of all the activities of the economic actors, a rational use of the materials, financial and work resources and a balance of the national economy.[24]

Nor did Shatalin take his timetable seriously, quipping in response to Rosefielde at Duke University on November 1991 that it didn't matter whether transition was achieved in 500 days or 500 years as long as it rid Russia of communism.

As it turned out, Gorbachev would shy away from the deal. Following some wrangling with rewrites and counterproposals, he simply declared that he could not support an economic reform plan that looked like a train schedule. The rift between Yeltsin's Russia and Gorbachev's USSR was now complete. The Soviet leader oriented ever closer to the hardliners, exemplified by the January 1991 crackdown on Riga and Vilnius, while contradictorily pressing forward with his destructive economic program. Apparently convinced that NATO and the West had their hands full in the 1991 Gulf War, the Kremlin believed it could repress the increasingly rebellious Baltic

---

[24] *Komsomolskaya Pravda*, September 29, 1990.

republics with impunity; at the same time, it sanctioned asset–grabbing, revenue misappropriation, and materials diversion at home.

Box 4.4 Satellite and Baltic Events

Boris Yeltsin wasn't the only force testing Gorbachev's mettle. In the fall of 1989, civil unrest in East Germany led to the destruction of the Berlin Wall, the resignation of Communist Party boss Erich Honnecker, and German reunification. The election of Solidarity leader Lech Walesa as president of Poland in December 1989 continued the pattern, which was then extended beyond the Kremlin's satellites to its constituent republics. A sequence of protests and concessions began in the Baltic republics on August 23, 1989, culminating in their independence. At every stage, Gorbachev could have forcibly quelled rebellion, but he didn't, and Yeltsin learned by watching.

Exactly how Gorbachev was involved in the Baltic crackdown may never be known. What we do know is that Yeltsin again seized opportunity when it knocked on his door. Learning about the activities of Soviet paratroops in Vilnius and of Soviet OMON special forces in Riga, he at once flew to Tallinn, the capital of Estonia, where he not only met with the Baltic leaders but also called on the world to intervene and even suggested that it might be necessary to form a Russian army to protect the country against Soviet aggression.

In March, Gorbachev came close to having Yeltsin removed from his post in the Russian Supreme Soviet, but he shied away from repressing mass demonstrations supporting Yeltsin in Moscow. In June, Yeltsin became the first popularly elected Russian president, and in August, he emerged victorious from the failed coup against Gorbachev.

No other image would have such a profound impact on western views of Russia as that of a defiant Yeltsin speaking atop an armored car parked in front of the Moscow White House, at the time home to the Supreme Soviet of the Russian Federation. Calling on Russians to resist the putschists, he assumed the role of a true Russian hero. While the organizers of the coup d'etat may have tried to depose Gorbachev for his liberalism,[25] the general secretary emerged from the episode looking ineffectual, allowing Yeltsin to posture as the nation's only

---

[25] Anders Aslund attributes the botched coup d'etat to the "Novo-Ogaryovo" process developing a new union treaty effectively dissolving the Soviet Union. See Aslund, "Purge or Coup?" *Johnson's Russia List*, Vol. 6, Article 9, January 9, 2008.

3

viable anticommunist and pro-western leader. He became commonly depicted as the guarantor of Russia's transformation to democratic free enterprise.

Behind the scenes, however, different games were being played. Meeting in a government dacha in the Moscow suburb of Arkhangel-skoe, a small group of young economists were laying plans for the introduction of an economic reform policy that would be known as shock therapy. There they were joined by an even smaller group of western economists, who would proceed to assume the role of advisors to the Russian government. It was in these days that Russia's economic future was being determined, and it was done in a traditionally clandestine manner.

As will be shown in subsequent chapters, once Yeltsin had deposed Gorbachev, he would display no more interest in a popular sovereign society, with free markets operating under the rule of law than his predecessor. He did not call elections for a democratic parliament. He eschewed public discussions of post-Soviet policies and excluded the country's democratic forces from his government. He assumed the post of prime minister for himself and compelled the Congress of People's Deputies to grant him rights to rule the country by decree.

Given these developments, it is important not to be taken in by western public cultural biases.[26] Gorbachev's blindman's bluff reforms and epic struggle with Yeltsin were always about reconfiguring Muscovy and never about path-dependent westernization. Ideology and central planning, which preoccupied most earnest experts, were just sideshows, camouflaging the quest by various insiders to narrowly privatize wealth and power and rid themselves of constraints on public ostentation.[27]

What Should Have Been Done

Western policymakers aren't bashful about claiming that they contributed significantly to cleansing the world of Bolshevism and setting Russia on the path of democratic free enterprise during the

---

[26] Leon Aron, *Russia's Revolution Essays 1989–2006*, American Enterprise Institute, Washington, DC, 2007. Leon Aron, *Yeltsin: A Revolutionary Life*, American Enterprise Institute, Washington, DC, 2000.

[27] By the early 1990s, many bodyguards escorting *new* Russian women could be seen flaunting jewels and fur on the streets of Moscow.

Gorbachev years. Insofar as any western policy initiatives from General Daniel Graham's (director of the Defense Intelligence Agency) high-technology frontier competitive "star wars" strategy to Ronald Reagan's cooperative approach to arms control and disarmament, significantly effected the reconfiguration of Muscovy, it can be fairly said in their favor that they weakened autocracy and partially reincorporated markets into the Muscovite economic mechanism. However, these advances didn't mean that Russia achieved popular democratic or consumer economic sovereignty. The patrimonial, rent-granting system was merely rejiggered. Whatever was done by the West was clearly insufficient to accomplish its professed Enlightenment goals, and the shock therapy it advocated harmed Russian welfare in the short, intermediate, and perhaps long run.

Could the West have done better if it had properly conceptualized Russia in Muscovite terms? Certainly its intelligence agencies could have provided government leaders and private citizens alike with more realistic models of Russia's democratic and economic prospects. Moreover, the West could have alerted Soviet liberals to the pitfalls of co-opted westernization. This cautionary advice couldn't have prevented insiders from hijacking *perestroika* and *demokratizatsia* (with Gorbachev's complicity or gullibility) because the liberals were no match for the pillagers, but it could have contributed toward limiting abuses and thereby hastening the possibilities of attaining democratic free enterprise in the distant future. Western leaders at a minimum should have warned Russian liberals (and Gorbachev) that it was essential to avoid having the nation's wealth misappropriated and concentrated unproductively in the hands of a few insiders. Liberals should have been urged to resist the shock therapeutic, blindman's bluff indulgences that subsequently culminated in *catastroika*, that is, a hyperdepression that ultimately caused 3.4 million excess deaths,[28] instead of being told that this was the necessary cost of progress. They should have been tutored that the rule of law was indispensable to effective westernization. They should have been encouraged to hold Yeltsin to his promises of popular sovereign democracy instead of being counseled to believe that a strong state was essential for a successful transition. Proper conceptualization thus really mattered, and although the West remains steadfastly in denial, it got almost everything wrong.

[28] Steven Rosefielde, "Premature Deaths: Russia's Radical Transition," *Europe-Asia Studies*, 53, 8 (2001): 1159–76.

APPENDIX: CIA List of Gorbachev Era Milestones

James Noren and Laurie Kurtzweg, "The Soviet Economy Unravels: 1985–91," in *The Former Soviet Union in Transition*, Vol. 1, Joint Economic Committee of Congress, Washington, DC, February 1993, pp. 31–33.

Noren and Kurtzweg's Time Line

Milestones in Economic Policy and Performance during the Gorbachev Era

March 1985	Gorbachev becomes general secretary, makes economic revitalization a top priority.
1985	Gorbachev outlines initial strategy: short-run reliance on human factor to improve productivity and weed out incompetents; longer-term counts on organizational changes and modernization.
November 1985	Draft guideline for 1986–90 plan feature acceleration in industrial and agricultural growth, give special prominence to machinery sector as prime mover in modernization campaign; plan depends on unrealistic assumptions about conservation and productivity.
February 1986	At Communist Party Congress, Gorbachev proclaims *reasonable sufficiency* guideline for defense programs.
1986	Leadership reorganizes foreign trade apparatus, establishes guidelines for setting up joint ventures between Soviet enterprise and foreign partners.
June 1987	Supreme Soviet and Central Committee approve guidelines for *new economic mechanism* to include enterprise self-financing, narrower scope of state plans, price and wage revisions, greater freedom to engage in international trade.
October 1987	Ryzhkov sets out program for expanding defense industry involvement in civil production.
October 1987	1988 plan reflects new emphasis on consumer. New quality control program disrupts industry. Investment program falls far behind because of confusion in construction and machinery shortages.
January 1988	Broad implementation of reforms approved in 1987 begins.

Fall 1988	Gorbachev raises 1989 targets for production of consumer goods, announces cuts in defense outlays and state investment, tasks for defense sector with greatly increased support for civilian economy, stretches out reform process.
1988	State budget deficit continues to climb, January 1989. Implementation of 1987 reforms expands to entire economy, contributes to disruption of traditional supply relationships.
October 1989	Abalkin reform program calls for gradual transition from state to other forms of ownership, development of market-oriented financial system.
December 1989	Supreme Soviet approves Ryzhkov reform and stabilization program – watering down of Abalkin program.
1989	Economy sputters as production of energy and basic materials falls: transportation and distribution problems, exacerbated by strikes and ethnic tensions, interfere with supplies. Investment program stalls as unfinished construction rises. Spending on defense declines, led by cuts in weapons procurement. Open and repressed inflation evident: shortages intensify, leading to rationing in many localities international financial position deteriorates as USSR borrows to pay for increased imports of consumer goods and industrial equipment.
August 1990	Shatalin reform program calls for market determination of output and prices, increase in republic authority over economic policy and reforms.
October 1990	Gorbachev reform program is adopted, providing for gradual elimination of state controls over output and prices, sale or transfer of property to owners other than state, eventual convertibility of ruble to hard currency.
1990	Central and republic governments at loggerheads over wide range of economic issues, including reforms. Regional autarky disrupts economies. Soviet economy passes from stagnation to decline. Investment and defense spending continue to fall. Inflation accelerates, shoppers sweep store shelves clean, shortages of energy and industrial materials worsen, barter proliferates.

Noren and Kurtzweg

1. miss spontaneous privatization
2. conflate public declarations with actions
3. statistics don't correspond with narrative
4. accept declaratory defense spending cuts as real

- Claims that Ronald Reagan's and Mikhail Gorbachev's statesman-
  ship ended the cold war, and westernized Russia are spurious.
- Until June 1987, the western security establishment considered
  Gorbachev's programs threatening.
- After June, sentiment rapidly changed, and Gorbachev was viewed
  as a liberal man of peace who desired Russia to return to its common
  western home.
- The CIA straddled the fence, calling him a pragmatic visionary.
  This meant that he was driven by necessity to liberalize but was also
  wise enough to accelerate the transition.
- The CIA expected the Soviet Union to flourish eventually as it
  liberalized, without causing a loss of American leverage in pressing
  arms control, human rights, and western commercial penetration
  because GNP growth was forecast to decelerate to 2 percent in the
  late 1980s.
- Its assessment was too hopeful because the agency failed to appreciate that Market Communist rhetoric didn't reflect Muscovite
  motives.
- Nonetheless, Gorbachev's blindman's bluff liberal posturing em-
  boldened some to push the boundaries of permitted dissent, and
  deviance.
- Boris Yeltsin capitalized on the opportunity in his capacity as first
  elected president of the Soviet Russian Federation, to launch a war
  of laws challenging the supremacy of Soviet authority.
- Soon thereafter, he became the popular hero of the abortive 1991
  coup d'etat after appearing atop an armored car urging democratic liberalization. According to Oleg Shenin, an organizer of
  the GKChP (extraordinary Commission), Yeltsin was supposed to
  be arrested at the airport in Kazakhstan, but the operation was
  botched.
- The economic pandemonium precipitated by *perestroika* and the
  political rivalry between Gorbachev and Yeltsin best co-explain the

fall of the USSR, not the visionary gloss of participants east and west.

- The West gave Gorbachev a great deal of bad advice because cultural blinders prevented it from grasping Soviet communism's Muscovite essence.

5

Squalid Superpower

Muscovite tsars and communist leaders always promised that their martial police states would promote the greater social good. Autocratic rent-granting was presented not as a curse but as a blessing that would empower Russia to catch up with and overtake the developed West. It might be supposed that those taking the long view would summarily dismiss such posturing, but this wasn't the case. Economic historians tend to accept Muscovite claims of extraordinarily rapid industrial growth spurts both before and after the Bolshevik epoch. Table 5.1 presents Angus Maddison's comparative GDP (gross domestic product) and per capita GDP growth estimate for the tsarist period valued in 1990 U.S. dollars. Although, Russia's performance was subpar on both measures, its industrial component was much better.[1]

---

[1] Russia's GNP growth rate (1860–1917) was below the west European norm, even taking into consideration Paul Gregory's upward revision of Prokopovich's estimates. The drag was agriculture. Industry grew rapidly in spurts, punctuated by revolution and depression. There is room for debate about the structural exceptionalism of the tsarist growth pattern, and of course the statistics should be taken with an ample dash of salt. Angus Maddison's historical GDP growth series show the USSR (territorially defined) outpacing western Europe (1500–1820, 1820–70, and 1870–1913), but substantially underperforming America. The USSR's per capita GDP growth throughout however was unfavorable. See Angus Maddison, *The World Economy, Historical Series*, OECD, Paris, 2003, pp. 261–263. See the literature cited below for the nuances. Olga Crisp, *Studies in the Russian Economy before 1914*, Macmillan Press, London, 1976; Raymond Goldsmith, "The Economic Growth of Tsarist Russia 1860–1913," in *Economic Development and Cultural Change*, 9, Pt. 2(1961): 441–75; Paul Gregory, "Economic Growth and Structural Change in Tsarist Russia: A Case of Modern Economic Growth," *Soviet Studies*, Vol. 3, 1972; Gregory "Russian National Income in 1913 – Some Insights into Russian Economic Development," *Quarterly Journal of Economics*, August 1976; Gregory, "Russian Industrialization: A Survey of the Western

Table 5.1. *Russian GDP and per capita GDP*
1820–1913 (1990 international Geary-Khamis dollars)

	GDP (millions)	GDP per capita
1820	37,678	688
1870	83,646	943
1900	154,049	1,237
1913	232,351	1,488
Growth rate	2.0	0.8

Note: Maddison defines Russia for the geographical territory of the USSR.

Source: Angus Maddison, *The World Economy: Historical
Statistic*, OECD, Paris, 2003, pp. 98, 100. The corresponding growth rates for twelve western nations were 1.9 and
1.2. Maddison, pp. 47, 49, 59, 61.

The consensus of the CIA, academics, and the Communist Party of
the Soviet Union was that despite the Bolsheviks' criminalization of
business, entrepreneurship, and private property, and Hitler's occupa-
tion, the USSR more than held its own vis-à-vis the developed West
(1921–89).

Was this Soviet era consensus correct? And if so, does it imply that
post-Yeltsin Muscovy may prosper and westernize?

Comparative Size: The Soviet Era Consensus

Economic historians estimate that tsarist GNP (gross national product)
on the eve of the Bolshevik coup d'etat was approximately 30 percent

Literature," *Jahrbucher fur die Geschichte Osteuropas*, December 1976; Gregory,
"Russian Living Standards during the Industrialization Era," *Review of Income and
Wealth*, 1980; Gregory, *Russian National Income, 1885–1913*, Cambridge University Press, Cambridge, 1983; Gregory, *Before Command: The Russian Economy from
Emancipation to Stalin*, Princeton University Press, Princeton, NJ, 1994; Alexander Gershenkron, "The Rate of Growth of Industrial Production in Russia Since
1885," *Journal of Economic History*, VII-S, 1947; Gershenkron, *Economic Backwardness in Historical Perspective*, Belknap Press, Harvard University, Cambridge, MA.,
1962; Yasushi Toda, "Catching-up and Convergence: The Standard of Living
and the Consumption Pattern of the Russians and the Japanese in 1913 and
1975–1976," paper presented at the 10th World Congress of the International
Economic History Association, Leuven, 1990. William Blackwell, *The Beginnings
of Russian Industrialization 1800–1860*, Princeton University Press, Princeton, NJ,
1968.

of America's.[2] Seventy-two years later, after tumultuous wars, and depressions both the CIA and official Soviet statistics reported that the gap had been dramatically reduced. Soviet GNP in 1989 had risen to 67 percent of the American level.[3] The comparative size estimates can be challenged on a variety of technical grounds. The territory of the tsarist empire and the Soviet Union weren't identical and purchasing power parity estimates are sensitive to judgments about comparative worth. Nonetheless, the direction of change seems unmistakable. The growth of the Soviet Union's natural economy outstripped the American system.

This finding is confirmed by Abram Bergson's calculations for the post-tsarist subperiod, 1955–70, which shows the Soviet Union's comparative economic size rising from 45.2 to 62.7 percent of America's,[4] suggesting rapid catch-up before 1955, followed by nineteen years of glacial advance. Although this performance was said to be lackluster, given the advantages of economic backwardness, and suggested that the Soviet Union might remain permanently stuck at a level 33 percent below the American benchmark, the costs of criminalizing business, entrepreneurship, and private property seem negligible compared with the dire predictions of democratic free marketeers.[5]

Guns And Margarine

Data on defense activities and trends are similarly perplexing. Bergson's estimates indicate that defense spending was low before 1935, rising

---

[2] See note 15.

[3] CIA, *Handbook of International Economic Statistics*, CPAS92, September 1992, Tables 7 and 21, pp. 25 and 39.

[4] Abram Bergson, "The Comparative National Incomes of the Soviet Union and the United States," in Bergson, *Productivity and the Social System – The USSR and the West*, Harvard University Press, Cambridge, MA, 1978, pp. 47–67. The figure for 1955 is from Table 5.1, p. 49; for 1970 from Table 5.7, p. 67.

[5] Fredrich von Hayek, "Socialist Calculation: The Competitive Solution," *Economica*, Vol. 7, May 1940, pp. 125–49; Hayek, *Collectivist Economic Planning: Critical Studies on the Possibilities of Socialism*, George Routledge & Sons, London, 1935; Ludwig von Mises, *Socialism,* Jonathan Cape, London, 1936; Lionel, Robbins, *An Essay on the Nature and Significance of Economic Science*, Macmillan, London, 1932. This inference holds even if Angus Maddison's far less favorable alternative results apply, especially since few nations on his calculations made substantial headway in catching up with America. See note 15, and Steven Rosefielde and Quinn Mills, *Masters of Illusion: American Leadership in a New Age*, Cambridge University Press, Cambridge, 2007.

Table 5.2. *Soviet defense burden 1928–90; defense spending as a percentage of GNP*

	Bergson	CIA
1928	1.0	
1937	6.2	
1940	13.8	
1944	38.8	
1950	10.3	
1951		24.2
1955	10.2	19.5
1960		14.5
1965		16
1970		15.4
1975		15.5
1980		15.3
1985		14.9
1990		13.8
2000		13.2

Note: Bergson's estimates are derived from the official Soviet defense budget and are valued in established 1937 ruble prices. The CIA's numbers are valued in established 1982 ruble prices. The estimate for 2000 was computed by Rosefielde in 2000 dollars using CIA methods.

Source: Abram Bergson, *The Real National Income of the Soviet Union since 1928*, Harvard University Press, Cambridge, MA, 1961, p. 46, table 3; p. 48, table 4; pp. 61, 364. Noel Firth and James Noren, *Soviet Defense Spending: A History of CIA Estimates 1950–1990*, Texas A&M University, College Station, 1998, pp. 129–30, table 5.10 (table 6.4, Steven Rosefielde, *Russia in the 21st Century: The Prodigal Superpower*, London, Cambridge University Press, 2005).

rapidly to 10 percent of GNP on the brink of World War II and hovering in this vicinity during the 1950s. CIA estimates thereafter are closer to 15 percent (see Table 5.2). Both sets of estimates are based on careful and comprehensive calculations, suggesting that the Soviet Union can be legitimately classified as a martial state (1935–1991). This characterization was heatedly disputed before 1989. Official statistics and adjustments thereof by Franklyn Holzman indicated that the Soviet defense burden was much smaller,[6] in a range between 2.5 and 5 percent.

---

[6] Franklyn Holzman, "Are the Soviets Really Outspending the U.S. on Defense?" *International Security*, 4, 4(1982): 78–101.

Table 5.3. *CIA estimates of Soviet weapons procurement's 1980–89 (1982 ruble prices: billions)*

1980	50
1981	48
1982	50
1983	49
1984	50
1985	51
1986	52
1987	55
1988	54
1989	50

Source: Central Intelligence Agency and Defense Intelligence Agency, *The Soviet Economy Stumbles Badly in 1989*, presented to the Technology and National Security Subcommittee of the Joint Economic Committee, Congress of the United States, April 20, 1990, published in *Allocation of Resources in the Soviet Union and China*, Joint Economic Committee, April 20, 1990, p. 4, fig. 4.

But this counterevidence was discredited by Gorbachev himself when he acknowledged that *Goskomstat's* defense spending statistics excluded weapons! As a consequence, whether Bergson's and the CIA's estimates are precise, they convey a better impression of the scale of the Soviet defense effort, a judgment supported by the USSR's 5-million-strong standing army and 52,000 nuclear weapons.[7]

Most western analysts who accepted the Kremlin's martial orientation considered it a fading relic of a bygone age. The CIA, for example, citing its own statistics, contended that the defense burden was steadily diminishing after 1970 due to low or even no weapons growth (Table 5.3), while living standards steadily improved (Table 5.4). The shoddy quality of Soviet consumer goods and empty retail shelves were duly noted, but this didn't deter the agency from stressing the USSR's gradual westernization, especially after the onset of Gorbachev's liberalizing reforms.

Most analysts asserted that these trends were the harbingers of the shape of things to come. The prognosis was for better times and

[7] Steven Rosefielde, *Russia in the 21st Century: The Prodigal Superpower*, Cambridge University Press, London, 2005.

Table 5.4. *Soviet consumption 1950–87 CIA estimates in 1982 established prices (billions of rubles)*

	Consumption	Consumer goods	Consumer services
1950	90.8	71.0	19.8
1955	123.1	97.5	25.6
1960	162.9	130.1	32.8
1965	198.4	154.3	44.0
1970	266.8	210.3	56.5
1975	323.5	255.1	68.3
1980	372.7	293.9	78.8
1985	405.7	315.2	89.5
1987	411.7	316.5	95.2

Compound annual rates of growth percent

	4.0	4.0	4.0

Source: Central Intelligence Agency, *Measures of Soviet Gross National Product in 1982 Prices,* Joint Economic Committee of Congress, Washington, DC, November 1990, table A-11, pp. 84–87.

improved east–west accommodation, with or without the decriminalization of business, entrepreneurship, and private property, and presumably conditions should have been even brighter once Gorbachev's roving bandits were transformed into stationary rent-seekers or even western-style free enterprisers.

However, these forecasts and the statistics supporting them were misleading. First, Bergson's and the CIA's GNP growth estimates were contradicted by Gorbachev's admission that the Soviet economy ceased growing throughout the 1980s[8] and the subsequent Soviet collapse. Second, the CIA made a grave technical error in estimating Soviet weapons production that drastically understated arms growth and the regime's commitment to what Vitaly Shlykov has called Soviet *structural militarization.*[9] Hayek was right. Lenin's natural economy didn't prove its mettle, and Muscovy never changed its martial stripes under communism.

[8] Abel Aganbegyan, *The Economic Challenge of Perestroika,* Indiana University Press, Bloomington, 1988.
[9] Vitaly Shlykov, *Chto Pogubilo Sovetskii Soiuz? Amerikanskaia Razvedka o Sovetskikh Voennykh Raskhodakh (What Destroyed the Soviet Union? American Intelligence Estimates of Soviet Military Expenditures). Voenny Vestnik,* No. 8, Moscow, April 2001.

Box 5.1 Structural Militarization

Structural militarization, a term coined by Vitaly Shlykov, former deputy
chairman of the Russian Defense Council, asserted that excessive Soviet
defense spending was systemically ingrained. Even if leaders sought to
curtail military activities, Muscovite culture conditioned rulers and the
military industrial complex to plan for the worst case and then add
funds to guard against the unforeseeable. Military industries had priority access to scarce materials, especially natural resources, and managers were rewarded for output rather than profit maximizing. The
more they produced, the more they earned. They couldn't produce
too many weapons. Nor were managers wholly dependent on the state
budget because communities were compelled to provide supplies free of
cost, partly to conceal the true level of defense from hostiles. Moreover, civilian production facilities were militarized. All Soviet civilian
factories were designed to allow rapid military conversion and required
to maintain material reserves in case of a war emergency. During the
Yeltsin years, the military industrial complex was starved for funds, and
there was substantial privatization, but this wasn't sufficient to eliminate
structural militarization. Capacities and rules were maintained, privatization was reversed, defense was being reprioritized, and incentives
were designed to bolster the production of fifth-generation weapons
systems, deemphasizing research, development testing, and evaluation.

The overestimation of Soviet GNP growth was caused by padded
production reports, overvaluation of new and improved goods, biased
index weighting, and unabashed political tampering.[10] Lenin considered statistics a weapon in the arsenal of class war, which made crafting
favorable numbers a socialist duty. The magnitude and source of this
statistical corruption varied with circumstances. When the 1937 census disclosed the carnage of forced industrialization and terror, Stalin
didn't hesitate to suppress it, order a recount, and literally shoot the
demographers. But he adopted a more temperate attitude on other
occasions. Limitations on some types of statistical corruption had to
be imposed to ensure that factors were mobilized and to provide
objective measures of accomplishment on important investment and
defense programs. Soviet leaders unsurprisingly wanted to have their
cake and eat it. They insisted on accuracy and the *right* results, leaving

---

[10] Steven Rosefielde, "The Riddle of Postwar Russian Economic Growth: Statistics
Lied and Were Misconstrued," *Europe-Asia Studies*, 55, 3(2003): 469–81.

the tug of war of events to determine how irreconcilable imperatives would play themselves out.

Bergson and the CIA, however, refused to see matters this way.[11] While acknowledging doubts about the scrupulousness of those providing and processing data, they nonetheless took the position that Soviet statistics were reliable enough to usefully access aggregate performance, corrected here and there for hidden inflation, that is, any technique or phenomenon that overstated the price component of value-added growth. The practical consequence of this protocol in Bergson's case was to take most official series at face value, while the CIA felt free to adjust specific subseries downward, such as machinery (including weapons), when it suspected *Goskomstat's* numbers were distorted by hidden inflation.[12] Accordingly, Bergson's series closely tracked *Goskomstat's*, especially after 1955, while the CIA's estimates grew more slowly, particularly in the defense sector, where the *residual* military component of *Goskomstat's* machinery subsector grew at double-digit rates, while the CIA's didn't grow at all.[13]

Since corruption in martial police states is opaque, no one will ever know how much aggregate economic growth was exaggerated. However, realistic discounts, neutrally applied across all sectors make Soviet GNP growth subpar, despite a rapid military arms buildup. The real Soviet Union behind the benevolent mask, as Shlykov assures us, was a structurally militarized police state, a guns and margarine slumscape that allowed the Kremlin to be a military superpower at the expense of the people's short- and long-term welfare. It was what Muscovy was best suited to do but failed to keep its gratuitous promise of general prosperity, just as democratic free enterprise theory predicted.[14] This seems to be becoming the new accepted wisdom. Recent OECD purchasing power parity dollar estimates compiled by Maddison, reported in Tables 5.5, 5.6, and 5.7 and graphed in Figures 5.1, 5.2, and 5.3,

---

[11] Steven Rosefielde, "Tea Leaves and Productivity: Bergsonian Norms for Gauging the Soviet Future," *Comparative Economic Studies*, 47, 2(June 2005): 259–73.

[12] Rosefielde, *Russia in the 21st Century*.

[13] Ibid.

[14] Estimates with unadjusted Goskomstat data still show Soviet consumption in a favorable light. See Elizabeth Brainard, "Reassessing the Standard of Living in the Soviet Union: An Analysis Using Archival and Anthropometric Data," paper presented to the Abram Bergson Memorial Conference, Harvard University, Davis Center, Cambridge, MA, November 23–24, 2003. Irwin Collier, "The 'Welfare Standard; and Soviet Consumers," *Comparative Economic Studies*, 47, 2(June 2005): 333–45.

Table 5.5. *USSR and Russia GDP 1913–2002*
(billion 1990 international Geary-Khamis dollars)

	USSR	Russia
1913	232.8	–
1928	231.9	–
1929	238.4	–
1938	405.2	–
1940	420.3	–
1945	333.7	–
1950	510.2	–
1973	1,513.1	872.5
1989	2,037.3	–
1991	1,863.5	1,094.1
1998	1,124.9	655.4
2001	1,343.2	790.6
2002	1,405.6	825.3

Note: Maddison defines Russia in 1913 for the territory of the USSR. The series labeled Russia refers to post–Soviet boundaries.

Source: Angus Maddison, *The World Economy: Historical Statistics*, OECD, Paris, 2003, pp. 98–99, 111.

Table 5.6. *USSR and Russia per capita GDP 1913–2002 (1990 international Geary-Khamis dollars)*

	USSR	Russia
1913	1,448	
1929	1,386	
1938	2,150	
1940	2,234	
1946	1,913	
1950	2,841	
1973	6,059	6,582
1989	7,098	
1991	6,409	7,370
1998	3,861	4,459
2001	4,626	5,435
2002	4,844	5,693

Note: Maddison defines Russia in 1913 for the territory of the USSR. The series labeled Russia refers to post-Soviet boundaries.

Source: Angus Maddison, *The World Economy: Historical Statistics*, OECD, Paris, 2003, pp. 100, 101, 111.

Table 5.7 *Comparative size estimates USSR and the United States 1917–2001 (billion 1990 international Geary-Khamis dollars and percent)*

	GDP			Per capita GDP		
	US	USSR	USSR/US	US	USSR	USSR/US
1917	544.8	232.4	42.6	5,248	1,458	28.4
1928	794.7	231.9	29.9	6,569	1,370	20.9
1955	1,898.1	648.0	35.8	10,897	2,841	26.1
1970	3,801.9	1,351.8	43.9	15,030	5,575	37.1
1989	5,703.5	2,037.5	35.7	23,059	7,098	30.8
1991	5,775.9	1,863.5	32.3	22,785	6,409	28.1
1998	7,349.9	1,124.9	15.3	26,619	3,861	14.5
2001	7,965.8	1,343.2	16.9	27,948	4,626	16.6

Note: The Geary-Khamis approach (named for R. S. Geary and S. H. Khamis) is a method for multilateralizing (multinational index weighting) that exhibits transitivity and other desirable properties. It was used by Kravis, Heston, and Summers as a method for aggregating ICP results available at the basic heading level. Maddison uses PPPs of this type for seventy countries, representing 93.7 percent of world GDP in 1990. His procedure for the United States and USSR boils down to a Paasche index because the GDPs of these countries should not require the aggregation technique Maddison stipulates. Also, the figure for USSR per capita GDP for 1917, actually refers to 1913, and figures 1992–2001 pertain as indicated to the former USSR. Data on Russia are also available but don't alter the big picture.

Sources: Angus Maddison, *The World Economy: Historical Statistics*, OECD, Paris, 2003, pp. 84–89, 98–101.

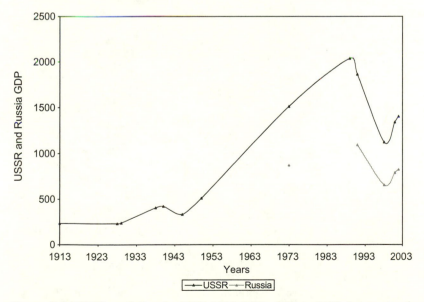

Figure 5.1. USSR and Russia GDP 1913–2002 (billion 1990 international Geary-Khamis dollars).

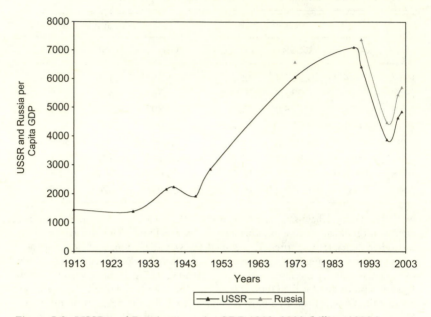

Figure 5.2. USSR and Russia per capita GDP 1913–2002 (billion 1990 international Geary-Khamis dollars).

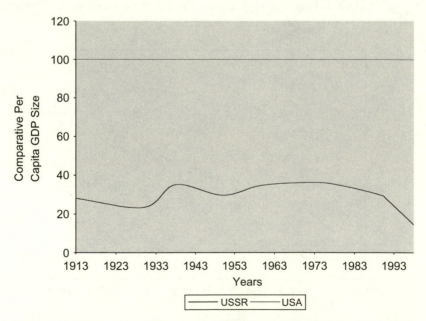

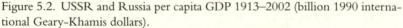

Figure 5.3. Comparative size estimates: USSR and United States 1917–2001 (billion 1990 international Geary-Khamis dollars and percent). *Source:* Angus Maddison, The World Economy: Historical Statistics, OECD, Paris, 2003.

confirm Russia's (defined on a Soviet territorial basis) inferior performance and demonstrate that it lost ground to America during the twentieth century, despite the advantages of economic backwardness. The Muscovite system provided an ample supply of weapons, but otherwise was gravely inferior. Goods were basic, services rude, the environment ravaged, and forced substitution ubiquitous without any prospect for meaningful improvement, compounded by labor coercion and civic repression.

The Soviet experience stripped of Bergson's and the CIA's wishful thinking thus doesn't justify the supposition that neo-Muscovite arrangements crafted by Gorbachev and successors are compatible with convergence and westernizing prosperity. When the dust settled in the mid-1990s, new purchasing power parity comparative GNP size estimates, confirmed with market exchange rate figures showed that Russia had made no headway from 1917 to 1991 in overtaking America and that the gap had probably significantly widened.[15] Allowance

---

[15] There is no definitive purchasing power parity comparative size estimate of American and Soviet GNP in 1917. Changes in Soviet territorial and population size 1917–1991 are additional complications. Nonetheless ballpark estimates can be computed using Abram Bergson's net national product calculations for America and the Soviet Union, and appropriate interpolations. The essential data are as follows:

Table 5.1n. *USSR and United States national product*

USSR Measure	1917	1926	1928	1937	1950	1955	1958
1937 ruble factor cost	(61.4)	(61.4)	67.1	100	132.7	(184.8)	225.5
composite 1937 base	(38.7)	(38.7)	38.1	100	129.9	(181.1)	221.0
United States Measure	1999/08	1917	1928	1929	1948	1955	1957
1929 dollars	43	(67.2)	(96.7)	100			
1954 dollars				100	162.5	209.5	225.3

Method: Bracketed figures are interpolated using intraperiod compound annual growth rates. Soviet economists contended that GNP recovered from the "War Communist" hyperdepression by 1926 (see Alec Nove, *An Economic History of the U.S.S.R.*, Penguin, London, 1982, p. 94). It is assumed accordingly that Soviet GNP was roughly the same in 1917 and 1926.

Source: Abram Bergson, *Productivity and the Social System – The USSR and the West*, Harvard University Press, Cambridge, MA, 1978, Table 8.1, pp. 120–21.

for forced substitution and related restrictions on economic and social freedom compound the failure.

This ultimately may be the fate of post-Soviet Russia too unless it breaks decisively Muscovy.

* Soviet economic growth outpaced the west from 1921 to 1989 according to most authoritative but erroneous estimates, despite the Bolshevik's criminalization of business, entrepreneurship, and private property.

Table 5.2n. *Comparative size estimates USSR and the United States 1917–1991*

(Dollar Purchasing Power Parities) Measure	1917	1928	1955	1970	1989
1937 ruble factor cost for USSR	46.8	35.6	45.2		
composite base for USSR					
1955	30.1	20.6	35.6		
1970				62.7	
1989					67
1995 ppp					40.7
1995 exchange rate					14.5

Method: Ratios of Soviet and American NNP for the years 1928/1955 and 1917/1955 are formed from Table 5.1 and multiplied by Bergson's estimate of comparative GNP size for 1955 (45.2). This yields the comparative size estimates for 1917 and 1928. The figure for 1970 is Bergson's. The CIA estimated Soviet comparative size in 1989 at 67 percent of America's. This is recalculated using post-Soviet purchasing power parities for 1995, and the corresponding market exchange rate provided in the Rosefielde source above.

The various estimates for 1917 and 1928, when compared with the 1995 market exchange rate estimate of comparative Soviet GNP size in 1989 suggest a significant decline. The Soviet Union lost ground, rather than made headway catching up with the United States. Counterpart productivity statistics would undoubtedly show the same results. The 1995 purchasing power parity, ppp, estimate for comparative Soviet GNP size in 1989 is mixed, displaying some catch up using the early 1928 base, and a sharp decline otherwise. On balance it appears that despite the advantages of relative backwardness, the Soviet Union fell further behind America during the communist era.

Source: Table 5.1n. Bergson, Ibid., Table 5.1, p. 49, and Table 5.7, p. 67. Steven Rosefielde, *Efficiency and the Economic Recovery Potential of Russia*, Ashgate, Aldershot, 1998, Table S.1, and Method section (CIA), pp. xxii–xxiii.

- These statistics show that Soviet GNP rose from 30 percent of America's in 1917 to 67 percent in 1989.
- The Soviet living standard closely approximated the west European mean in 1989.
- Soviet economic growth decelerated steadily after the late 1960s.
- Although, economic growth remained respectable on the official ledger, Soviet insiders and the CIA believed that the economy was stagnant or moving in that direction.
- Their explanations differed. Many Soviet economists insisted that consumer goods growth was exaggerated by managers improperly raising prices to reflect imaginary product improvements. The CIA claimed that hidden inflation was concentrated in Soviet military machine building (weapons) statistics.
- The Soviet interpretation suggested that planning was consumer-goods unfriendly, while the agency's hypothesis implied that vast sums were wasted on imaginary weapons improvements.
- The CIA's interpretation was wrong on both counts. Its weapons growth estimates were marred by a serious cost-estimating error, and its consumer goods estimates failed to adequately account for hidden inflation.
- Proper adjustment for both factors reveals that the Soviet GNP diverged from, rather than converged toward, the American norm. It also shows that living standards in the USSR were meager.
- The Soviet Union behind the statistical fluff was a squalid super-power. Its goods were basic, services rude, the environment rav-aged, and forced substitution ubiquitous without any prospect for meaningful improvement, compounded by labor coercion and civic repression.
- Leninism failed. Soviet socialism wasn't superior as Kremlin rulers repeatedly claimed. In the final analysis, the criminalization of private property, business, and entrepreneurship impaired Soviet economic performance, despite the benefits of relative economic backwardness.

PART III

YELTSIN

Yeltsin Timeline

1992

January	Introduction of economic *shock therapy*, deregulation of prices
June	Yegor Gaidar appointed acting prime minister
November	Viktor Gerashchenko appointed head of the Central Bank
December	Showdown with Russian parliament, Gaidar replaced by Viktor Chernomyrdin

1993

January	Summit meeting with George Bush, START II Treaty
March	Renewed conflict with Russian parliament on pace of reform, Yeltsin narrowly survives vote of no confidence
April	Yeltsin wins nationwide referendum on reform
September	Yeltsin disbands Supreme Soviet, vice president Alexander Rutskoi sworn in as new president, armed standoff
October	Tank assault on parliament building, parliamentarians surrender
December	Simultaneous elections to a new Duma and referendum on new constitution

1994

June	Formal partnership with NATO
October	Black Tuesday, ruble drops more than 20 percent against dollar, Gerashchenko forced to resign
December	First war in Chechnya

1995

October   Summit meeting with Bill Clinton, Yeltsin hospitalized with
             heart problems
December   Duma election, victory for communists and nationalists

1996

June   Yeltsin wins first round of presidential election, suffers heart
             attack
July   Yeltsin wins reelection in second round, makes deal with
             Alexander Lebed to become national security chief
August   Lebed brokers a cease fire in Chechnya
October   Lebed is fired
November   Yeltsin has successful quintuple heart bypass surgery

1997

January   Yeltsin hospitalized with double pneumonia
March   Yeltsin returns to the Kremlin, appoints economic *dream
             team*

1998

March   Entire government fired, including Prime Minister Viktor
             Chernomyrdin
June   Turmoil on financial markets
July   Bailout package arranged by the IMF
August   Financial meltdown in Moscow, ruble collapses, Yevgeny
             Primakov becomes prime minister

1999

May   Primakov fired, replaced by Sergei Stepashin
August   Islamic republic proclaimed in Dagestan by Chechen insur-
             gents, Vladimir Putin appointed prime minister
September   Apartment bombings in Moscow and Volgodonsk, launch
             of second war in Chechnya
December   Duma election, victory for pro-Kremlin party, Yeltsin steps
             down, appoints Putin as acting president

6

Demolition and Systems Building

Bonfire of the Privateers

The Soviet Union's death was startling. No one knew the fate that awaited. State-dependent workers, peasants, bureaucrats, administrators, red directors, communists, liberal democrats, and privateers were bewildered. Each placed its hopes on the government. Some couldn't believe that Boris Yeltsin intended to scuttle planning. Liberals expected the state to foster democratic free enterprise, while privateers considered the regime to be a partner in crime. As might be expected, the Yeltsin administration found it expedient to pose as all things to all people, while pursuing its own hidden agenda, namely, constructing a new Muscovite system based on the rule of men and enriching Yeltsin's family circle and crony servitors.

Box 6.1 Boris Yeltsin

Boris Nikolaievich Yeltsin, first president of the Russian Federation, was born February 1, 1931, in the village of Butka, Sverdlovsk Oblast, and died April 23, 2007. His grandfather was exiled for being a kulak, and his father spent three years in Gulag for anti-Soviet agitation in 1934–37. Boris was a construction major at the Ural Polytechnic Institute in Sverdlovsk, graduating at the start of Nikita Khrushchev's reign in 1955. He became the head of the Sverdlovsk House-Building Combine in 1965, joining the CPSU *nomenklatura* in 1968 at age thirty-seven, when he was appointed head of construction by the Sverdlovsk Regional Party Committee. In 1975, he became secretary of the Regional Committee on Industrial Development, and the next year, he was promoted to first secretary of the CPSU Committee of the Sverdlovsk Oblast, remaining

---

in this powerful post until 1985, when Mikhail Gorbachev and Yegor Ligachev appointed him first secretary of the Moscow Communist Party Committee and a member of the Politburo. He posed as a man of the people during this period, taking the tram to work, instead of a private limousine. But he soon fell afoul of Gorbachev. He was exiled from Moscow and attempted suicide in 1987, before staging a remarkable political comeback resulting in the USSR's dismemberment and his reign as Russia's first president. Most scholars recognize that Yeltsin's actions weren't wholly motivated by the ideals he espoused and blame him in varying degrees for *catastroika* and for suppressing parliamentary democracy, which led to the restoration of Muscovite authoritarianism under Vladimir Putin. In rendering summary verdicts, both liberal and conservative westerners, assuming that any step toward democracy was path dependent, concluded that the destruction of the USSR in the name of liberalization made him an epochal statesman. See the *Economist*, "It was messy, but he gave Russia a future that Putin is now putting in jeopardy," *Johnson's Russia List*, Article 14, Vol. 97, April 27, 2007. This editorial creates a hagiology positioning Putin as Yeltsin's disciple, instead of the victor in a palace coup d'etat and mystically attributes today's recovery to timbers cunningly laid by Yeltsin. Cf. Anne Applebaum, "Boris Yeltsin, 1931–2007: A Genuine Man of Transition," *Washington Post*, April 24, 2007. Masha Lipman correctly observes that Putin forced Yeltsin to resign, and recognizes that the defeat of communism was mostly the result of a power struggle at the top, but still reduces his reign to the claim that "he turned Russia into a free nation." See Lipman, "Yeltsin the Revolutionary," *Washington Post*, April 25, 2007. Andrei Illarionov claims that Yeltsin ruled autocratically so that he could do more for Russia. See Andrei Illarionov, "In the End, Yeltsin Went the Way of Freedom," *Johnson's Russia List*, Article 16, Vol. 99, April 30, 2007. The reality behind the tinsel is that Yeltsin was a closet autocrat before 1991 and an open one thereafter, who caused *catastroika* by indulging roving bandits when the Chinese example proves that he could have done better. It is true that he became the first directly elected president of the Russian Federation on June 12, 1991, but the symbolism of this event surpasses its substance because the election was dimly understood by the electorate and was primarily a tactical maneuver to delegitimatize Gorbachev's rule as the Soviet Union's president. Cf. Leon Aron, *Yeltsin: A Revolutionary Life*, St. Martin's Press, New York, 2000. Aron, *Russia's Revolution: Essays 1989–2006*, AEI Press, Washington, DC, 2007.

This was accomplished by pretending to carry out a disciplined shock therapeutic privatization program designed to create a loyal group of rent-seeking servitors from among the ranks of post-Soviet privateers. Gorbachev had established the precedent by tolerating spontaneous privatization in the late 1980s and had created conditions for accelerating the process by rescinding *Gosplan's* directive authority. *Gosplan's* five-year and annual plans ceased being compulsory in 1991, effectively transferring authority to the economic ministries, their administrative departments (*glavki*), the ad hoc intervention of the Communist Party, secret police, military, and regional potentates, as well as bonus-seeking managers governed by profit- and output-based incentives and guaranteed state purchase.

Yeltsin's strategy was to remove swiftly these remaining supervisory and state-incentive-regulated layers on behalf of his supporters. He launched a two-pronged administrative civilian sector decontrol initiative in 1992. First, the state cancelled 60 percent of its contracts, and ceased paying managerial bonuses. Guaranteed state purchase was rescinded, and incentives became a discretionary internal matter for enterprise managers. Second, ministries and *glavks* lost their directive powers. They had oversight responsibilities, but little effective control, making managers administratively independent without any external incentive to maximize output or profit maximize on the state's behalf.

These actions were complemented by terminating communist control activities and curtailing secret police civilian surveillance. Military and secret police authorities continued to play a critical role in defense industrial firms, but otherwise, the only sources of discipline were regional officials, and new government agencies with the power to issue state contracts.

The rationale given for this shock therapy offered by the Yeltsin administration and its G-7 advisers was to transform state managers into capitalist entrepreneurs even before they acquired de jure ownership rights, buttressed by the rule of law. The explanation was widely applauded and would have been justifiable, if Muscovite culture had been eradicated. But, in practice, it cloaked the regime's propensity to shunt the burden of adaptation onto the people's shoulders, and its pro-privateer (later pro-oligarch) hidden agenda. Civilian managers who in theory were hired by majority worker owners were unchecked. They could divert enterprise revenues and dispose of state assets for their personal benefit with impunity, which often seemed the

best course for companies with undesirable products and no marketing skills. During the Soviet era, product characteristics, marketing,
and finance were the state's concern. Managers earned rewards solely
for production. Under the new order, these same managers were told
to fend for themselves. They had to redesign products, establish marketing strategies, and acquire the credit to do so from nonexistent
financial institutions. The task wasn't impossible, but prospects for
efficient profit seeking were sufficiently bleak that many managers
focused on cannibalizing their firms until property/control rights and
credible enforcement mechanisms materialized.

Box 6.2 Ownership

The means of production, including all land, natural resources, structures, and equipment belonged to the people in the Soviet Union, held
in trust by the state. Individuals could hold some precious metals and
gems for adornment but not for business purposes. The only exception
was some limited consumer cooperative assets.

Gorbachev loosened these restrictions by selectively permitting producer cooperative leasing *arenda*, raising the possibility of extending
the principle to workers in large factories, and winking at spontaneous
privatization where audacious individuals tested the waters by asserting
ownership claims.

Soon after assuming power, Yeltsin endorsed fuller privatization,
with the state retaining ownership of natural resources, together with
industrial, administrative, and commercial land. Industrial structures and
equipment were to be divided in principle into three types of shares
reserved for: managers, workers, and the state. Initially, the state would
retain approximately half the shares, with workers receiving 80 percent
of the other half and managers receiving the residual. This division
suggested that worker ownership would be a powerful force in shap-
ing Russian economic activity and wealth. But this was misleading
because control rights were vested with managers, including the power
to set and distribute dividends. They had the upper hand. Additionally,
Yeltsin gave vouchers to all citizens allowing them to bid for a part of
the state's ownership share. This permitted state administrative workers,
peasants, and others to acquire a stake in the people's industrial assets.
The program was mismanaged by private mutual funds, and the initiative ended badly with most voucher-holders receiving nothing and
insiders of various kinds acquiring huge stakes in lucrative assets. The
law permits the state to issue new shares, diluting ownership and thereby

renationalizing, but this option has remained dormant. Agricultural land over the years has been partially privatized but is subject to strict control to prevent it from being put to alternative use. The net result of these disparate aspects of the privatization process has been the concentration of ownership and control of lucrative industrial assets (especially natural resource processing and media properties) in relatively few hands and a more mixed picture in agriculture where there are some large oligarchic private holdings, increasing numbers of private farms, communal farming, and land diversion to urban use. Worker ownership is significant in some firms, and the state is rapidly renationalizing ownership in the natural resource sector and defense. On balance, the people's patrimony was stolen by a few scoundrels; selected workers and peasants benefited; and in the Muscovite tradition, everything is reappropriable by the ruler without limitation.

It is not known whether the Yeltsin administration contemplated using the same tactics in the military industrial complex. Discipline certainly declined here as well but mostly took the form of stealing prolonged war fighting reserves worth tens of billions of dollars, rather than the flagrant misappropriation of revenues, and enterprise asset stripping.[1]

The interests of civilian sector privateers and oligarchs, however, weren't ignored. Yeltsin's *liberals* helped emerging oligarchic natural resource processors maximize unearned rents by curtailing subsidized sales to the military industrial complex. Defense spending was cut 90 percent,[2] allowing processors to increase resource deliveries elsewhere at global market prices. The reduction was portrayed as a bold arms control and disarmament initiative and eliminating the hidden subsidy was economically justified, but its primary purpose seems to have been the enrichment of civilian cronies in Yeltsin's court.

The demolition of social institutions and the social safety net followed a parallel course.[3] The workplace had been a primary provider of social services during the communist era. Workers received housing, recreation, vacation, and medical and communal dining services free or

---

[1] Vitaly Shlykov, various FOI conferences.

[2] Julian Cooper, "The Economics of Russian Defense Policy," paper presented at the conference on Russia under President Vladimir Putin: Towards the Second Term, European University Institute, Florence, April 22–23, 2004.

[3] Mark Field and Judyth Twigg, *Russia's Torn Safety Nets: Health and Social Welfare during the Transition*, St. Martin's Press, New York, 2000.

at nominal cost and had the opportunity to buy products unavailable in ordinary state retail outlets. Decontrol and state contract cancellations compelled managers to drastically prune, or abolish, these activities, problems compounded by mass dismissals (which underscored the ineffectuality of worker ownership). Living standards plummeted as hyperinflation reduced pensions to a pittance and wage arrears ravaged purchasing power. The state, which had assured the population an adequate spartan existence, suddenly vanished into the woodwork, leaving a destitute army of proletarians to fend for themselves. As in the case of industrial enterprises, it was conveniently assumed that these shock methods would encourage the emergence of alternative service providers, while the primary impact was asset and resource diversion to privateers and oligarchs.

Politics was the exception that proved the rule. Had Yeltsin desired, he could have easily transferred power to the electorate by calling for free, multiparty elections and a popular constitutional convention. Demolition in the political area however took the opposite form. Instead of capitalizing on the opportunity to forge popular democracy after rescinding the Communist Party's monopoly on state power, Yeltsin chose to demolish the incipient democratization he helped initiate, ruling in his own right without any political party, and suppressing democratic opposition. Nor did he take any action to create an effective rule of law, preferring to operate as an edict-wielding autocrat, with the implicit power to subject privateers and oligarchs to his will as circumstances dictated.

This impression, however, was qualified by his contradictory policy of diminishing the size, scope, and power of the security services, including both the Committee on State Security (KGB), renamed the Federal Security Service (FSB), the Ministry of Internal Affairs (MVD), and the military. The KGB was broken up into five separate agencies, including the Federal Border Service and the Federal Agency for Government Communications and Information (FAPSI), but was neither disbanded, nor subordinated to the rule of law. It was FAPSI's job to not only encode and secure government communications but also to intercept e-mails, faxes, and other private communications, as well as to record telephone and radio conversations in Russia and abroad. The FSB acted similarly clinging to traditional methods, while maintaining a lower profile. Although it and the other new intelligence agencies weren't the omnipresent force they had been during Stalin's time, or the Reform Communist period before Gorbachev, they continued to have enormous coercive potential. By the end of the 1990s, fourteen agencies possessed armed troops, including a hundred thousand border guard soldiers equipped with armor, an air force, and a navy.[4] Similarly, while weapons production plummeted, and military personnel were cut by more than 50 percent, the military industrial complex (VPK) and the general staff (*genshtab*) remained intact.[5]

The prerequisites for a full-fledged struggle between a post-Soviet Muscovite order and democratic free enterprise thus were quickly laid in the economic, security, social, and political arenas. A Muscovite outcome entailed a gradual recentralization of autocratic authority in all spheres, the transformation of privateers and oligarchs into servitors, and the reconstruction of a martial police state under the rule of men. Democratic free enterprise necessitated the converse path, transferring economic sovereignty to consumers, and political sovereignty to the people, as well as returning stolen assets to the nation. Westernizers pressed an agenda of privatization, liberalization, and stabilization believing that it would do the trick, while Muscovites were intent on harnessing the same principles for their traditional purposes.

It was characteristic of the era that scant attention was paid to the particularities of demolition. Westerners preferred not to fret about equitable privatization and social justice, evaluating Russia's prospects instead in terms of abstractions like shock therapy versus gradualism, which presupposed that Yeltsin was resolutely heading fast forward toward Gorbachev's "common European home" or, at worst, at a snail's pace. And the rhetoric of Yeltsin's liberal young Turks suggested that they too may have been befuddled by the dual potentiality of their policies, sometimes believing that it was possible to start with a clean slate. Their program of destructive creation was a classic case of what Russian cultural historians have called Russian *maximalism*. For whatever complex of reasons, the pendulum must be pushed to the opposite extreme. Every victory must be unconditional. The past must be eradicated. Yuri Lotman would have been amused.

---

[4] Pavel Felgenhauer, "KGB: Big, Bad and Back?" *Moscow Times*, March 12, 2003. Amy Knight, *Spies without Cloaks: The KGB's Successors*, Princeton University Press, Princeton, NJ, 1996; Knight "A Modern Crime and Punishment: Who Killed Russia's Leading Liberal?" *The Globe and Mail*, April 23, 2003, reprinted in *Johnson's Russia List*, No. 7153, Article 12, April 24, 2003.

[5] Vitaly Shlykov, "Russian Defense Industrial Complex after 9–11," paper presented at the Russian Security Policy and the War on Terrorism Conference, U.S. Naval Postgraduate School, Monterey, CA, June 2003.

It is small wonder that the debacle of demolition would be compared with Lenin's tactics or be branded *market Bolshevism*.[6] Just as under communism, while the initial results were catastrophic, segments of the population deluded themselves that Russia was on the express lane to utopia. They were persuaded with metaphors like extracting teeth, sawing off legs, and turning fish soup into aquaria that declarations of good intentions were enough, that the details were irrelevant.

Again, in good Russian tradition, it all boiled down to an expedient belief in miracles. Following a few years of demolition and rapacious privateering, many deluded Russians imagined that they would awaken to find themselves in a smoothly functioning market economy, based on consumer sovereignty and the rule of law, giving fresh irony to the nineteenth-century tsarist poet Fyodor Tiutchev's mystic judgment, "with the mind alone, Russia cannot be understood. No ordinary yardstick spans her greatness. She stands alone, unique – In Russia one can only believe."[7]

Authoritarian Renewal

The belief however was misplaced because, although the autocrat demolished the communist control apparatus in plundering state assets, Yeltsin never ceded authority to privateers and oligarchs. State power remained vested in the tsar's hands, and no adventurer dared usurp it, despite his vulnerability. This deference was crucial. Had privateers and oligarchs seized the reins of power they might have become an effective vehicle for promoting the rule of law and democracy, which bolstered their property rights, but the autocrat had a different agenda. Yeltsin required a postcommunist system that preserved the concept of Muscovite authoritarianism on a modern institutionalist basis. Lacking both vision and plan, he set about the task haphazardly responding to events. The first challenge came in the political arena when Ruslan Khasbulatov, the head of the Duma, tried to assert limited parliamentary checks over Yeltsin's autocratic governance. The president responded resolutely by treating popular sovereignty as a usurpation of power and forcibly repressed it with tanks and machine

---

[6] Peter Reddaway and Dimitri Glinski, *The Tragedy of Russia's Reforms: Market Bolshevism against Democracy*, United States Institute of Peace, Washington, DC, 2001.

[7] James Billington, *The Icon and the Axe: An Interpretive History of Russian Culture*, Vintage, New York, 1970, p. 320.

guns. For those who failed to grasp the distinction between popular parliamentary sovereignty and autocratic rule in the name of the people, Yeltsin's assault may have been construed as an intragovernmental usurpation of power, but its significance was deeper. It extinguished the hope that Yeltsin's democratic rhetoric would be swiftly translated into Enlightenment deeds.

The lesson of 1993 was soon confirmed by subsequent presidential contests. Yeltsin handily won reelection in 1996 with financial support and media control provided by his cronies Boris Berezovsky and Vladimir Gusinsky, benefactors of the president's rent-granting. The contest was a mockery of the democratic process but preserved the appearance of a viable multiparty contest. The ascendancy of political rule over the people was complemented by a parallel process of reempowering the martial police state and bureaucracy. During the heyday of profligate rent-granting, communist-era structures of governance and control were drastically curtailed on behalf of roving banditry. The process, however, was self-limiting. Yeltsin gradually recognized that extravagant rent-granting nurtured potential rivals, was superfluous, and contributed to hyperdepression. His best interest lay in reining pandemonium by creating a bureaucratic martial secret police counterweight to oligarchy, enabling him to avoid capture by either faction. After a period of curtailment, secret police officials were posted to head and staff the tax department and were strategically placed in state resource processing companies like Gazprom. The central bank gradually shifted from financing state expenditures with excess money emission (hyperinflation) to reliance on direct flat-rate income taxation favoring the wealthy. It slowly curbed an epidemic of Ponzi schemes and weaned itself from shifting the adjustment burden entirely to institutions and the public. Gorbachev's and Yeltsin's initial impulse was to disregard the state's obligation to promote full employment, price stability, and steady growth by managing aggregate effective demand. This forced everyone, including government service providers, the police, soldiers, educators, researchers, and workers to fend for themselves without efficient market mechanisms and the rule of law, while insiders received state contracts and assets. As the years passed, however, the Yeltsin administration began paying wage arrears to state workers, increasing government employment, curbing some mafia crime, and providing some responsible macroeconomic management after the financial crisis of August 1998. The stabilization, liberalization, and privatization achieved in these ways wasn't the Pareto ideal the G-7 had in mind, but it did partially restore the state's ability to bureaucratically manage and govern in conjunction with Muscovite autocracy.

The Yeltsin administration's attitude toward society evolved similarly. From 1992 through 1998, the Kremlin tolerated all aspects of social liberality, except Duma encroachment on autocracy. People could read, write, and speak freely about the Soviet past and contemporary issues. They could associate and organize, behaving as they chose with few restrictions. Almost anything went. Products were adulterated, pornography flourished, and prostitutes lined up in a disorderly queue in front of the hotel Moskva favored by Duma politicians to be shuttled into passing cars until the wee hours of snowy mornings. There was an epidemic of child abuse and abandonment, drug abuse, and HIV infection. But as the *siloviki* gathered strength, symbolized by Vladimir Putin's appointment to the directorship of the FSB just before the August/September 1998 financial crisis, attitudes began to harden against promiscuousness. Street vendors and streetwalkers vanished from public view, faint portents of pervasive restraints that ensued later.

The importance of these systems-building events have gone largely unrecognized. They were overshadowed by *catastroika* and construed as political, economic, and social disciplinary measures needed for overcoming the chaos of the times. In retrospect, however, this was myopic. During Yeltsin's watch, the power services not only kept democracy and ambitious privateers and oligarchs at bay, they became key players in the manipulation, exploitation, management, and control of the market, ballot, and social order for their private benefit at the president's behest. Their boss in Muscovite fashion seldom commanded or macro managed the *siloviki*. They learned their trade from the inside through trial and error, beginning with networks of ex-convicts, Gulag trustees, local police, and mafia godfathers, then graduating to tax supervisors, board members of lucrative state corporations, and assassins. Military officers discovered the cornucopia of *Rosvooruzhenie* (Russian Arms Export Agency), the pilfering of prolonged warfighting natural resource reserves, including diamonds, and when caught were rewarded with other sinecures such as a monopoly on foreign auto imports. Officials in *Minatom* (Ministry of Atomic Energy) grew rich selling nuclear technologies and reactors to China and Iran.

In the process, the *siloviki* discovered two crucial things. A market economy offered greater opportunities for their self-enrichment than loyal security service in the Soviet-planned order without killing the goose that laid the golden egg, and that they were better positioned than oligarchs and other rent-seekers to defend their privileges with armed force for themselves and the autocrat. Postcommunist systems building during Yeltsin's reign in this way was a learning-by-doing process where power service rent-seekers gradually figured out how to wrest control of natural resources and other lucrative assets from civilian cronies to themselves. As in the early Bolshevik era, they didn't have to dominate all aspects of economy, polity, and society. Controlling the commanding heights was sufficient. And, of course, the *siloviki* didn't do much more during the Yeltsin years than learn the ropes and lay the foundation for advances in the next phase under Putin's (a *silovik* himself) rejuvenated autocracy, the military, and the secret police.

None of this should have been surprising, given Yeltsin's original sin, the repression of parliamentary democracy. Once popular sovereignty is suppressed, sustainable power predictably shifts to the security services defending autocracy. Systems building then becomes an interactive exercise in finding the appropriate balance between the tsar and his praetorians. The process was neither elegant nor quick, but it was decisive. By the start of the new millennium, Russia had built the foundations for a repressive neoimperial authoritarian martial police state. It only would be a matter of a few years before martial values would return to vogue and natural resources would be diverted to full-spectrum military modernization.

Western Perceptions

Yeltsin's veiled authoritarianism was interpreted by many as proof that Russia had rejected its past and was irreversibly transitioning to democratic free enterprise, a judgment that appeared to be trebly confirmed by the demolition of the communist physical systems management mechanism, the introduction of markets, and the downsizing of the security services. It was easy to believe that the decriminalization of business would blossom into free enterprise and that the normalization of relations between the state and citizens would culminate in popularly sovereign democracy. Military spending fell 90 percent from 1988 to 1999, while the FSB was reorganized and curtailed. The West's only worry was the increasingly remote possibility of a communist revanche, otherwise, it seemed like smooth sailing because liberalization and authoritarianism were supposed to be mutually exclusive.

The fact that tsarist Russia had managed to combine markets with its liberal authoritarian martial police states under Catherine the Great, Alexander II, and Alexander III didn't register. When tsarism wasn't being romanticized as democratizing capitalism, it was dismissed as ancient history. Nor did anyone pay attention to the Bolshevik market experiment (1921–28) known as NEP (the New Economic Policy), where Lenin combined private business, entrepreneurship, and market leasing with a liberalizing authoritarian martial police state. G-7 assessments during the Gorbachev-Yeltsin phase would have been more guarded if it had. It would have been apparent that Gorbachev and Yeltsin didn't have to westernize even though this is what they said because they wanted to have their cake and eat it, which meant, in this instance, that they wished to promote privateering, oligarchy, authoritarianism, and state power without ceding control to new wealth and popular democracy. Privateers and oligarchs could live luxuriously but couldn't serve as a transmission belt from Muscovite authoritarianism to democratic free enterprise, sometimes referred to as the *Novgorod model*.[8] They could acquire provisional property rights, achieving a position akin to temporary wives in a sultan's harem, but couldn't become an independent political force for full westernization.

- The dissolution of the Soviet Union was unexpected and bewildering. The Yeltsin administration and most of the population were compelled to improvise.
- Yeltsin decided to stick with his political demolition strategy. It had destroyed the Soviet Union and was the course of least resistance.
- Since Gorbachev had already abolished coercive planning and unofficially sanctioned asset-grabbing and enterprise revenue misappropriation, demolition meant extending these processes by further

[8] Vladimir Kovalev, "Group Says to Restore Novgorod Republic," *Johnson's Russia List*, No. 9107, March 30, 2005. A group of people formed by writer and publisher Alexander Vertyachikh have declared themselves "citizens of the free Novgorod Republic that was illegally annexed by Moscow tsars in 1471–1479." The merchant town (and region of) Novgorod had a chaotic form of democracy from the twelfth to the fifteenth centuries rooted in a popular assembly called the *veche*, which elected *posadniki* (governors as spokesmen in relations with Kiev, Vladimir, and even Moscow). The *veche* was an anarchistic institution, without constitutional provisions or rules of orderly procedure. Disputed issues were settled in fistfights on the Volkhov River Bridge. It was the elected *veche* governors, not Novgorod citizenry, who oligarchically governed Russia's northwestern democracy.

curtailing administrative supervision, canceling guaranteed state production purchases, rescinding procurement contracts, and abolishing state managerial incentives in the civilian sector.

- Communist Party control was eliminated, KGB activities circumscribed, and military spending cut 90 percent.
- Controls in the defense sector remained mostly in force.
- This demolition process was the essence of *shock therapy*.
- Demolition also meant state abandonment. Everyone was left to fend for himself or herself, as if abnegation of state responsibility was the best course.
- Abandonment included the elimination of social services provided by Soviet factories, including housing, recreation, vacation, and medical and communal dining benefits.
- It also meant that nearly a quarter of the labor force was unemployed, without job retraining programs and benefits.
- And Yeltsin abandoned the incipient democratization he had championed in the late 1980s by dissolving parliament and arresting those who opposed him.
- Success in this environment went to the ruthless and best connected, with the largest fortunes accrued by those who gained control of natural resource–processing activities.
- The diversion of natural resources from defense to civilian oligarchs altered Russia's economic orientation.
- The corollary of Yeltsin's abandonment of incipient democratization was the resurgence of authoritarianism.
- The first evidence of this intent was his suppression of parliament in 1993.
- The gradual reempowerment of the security services, including the military followed soon thereafter.
- Then the administrative bureaucracy as an instrument of autocratic power was strengthened, including placing the FSB in charge of tax collection.
- These actions can be given a liberal interpretation, but in Muscovy they had different implications. They meant the empowerment of the *siloviki* within Yeltsin's administration.
- Russia began to modernize during the Yeltsin years but didn't westernize.

7

Crisis Management

Order of Economic Liberalization

Russia's post–1986 odyssey is the saga of the Kremlin's passage from an authoritarian Reform Communist physical management system to authoritarian Market Muscovy, with many seemingly portentous subplots that aren't. Most analysts for diverse reasons wanted to believe that Mikhail Gorbachev, Boris Yeltsin, and Vladimir Putin were engaged in a struggle to construct democratic free enterprise or social democracy in the land of Rus and scripted their narratives accordingly. Their stories were studded with wicked communists, the VPK, secret police, and reactionary chauvinists conspiring to restore autocracy and central planning and valiant democrats such as Gorbachev and Yeltsin determined not to let this happen. The battlefield was liberalization and transition. Villains strove to preserve the old order by urging gradual marketization, while westernizers insisted on shock therapy as the only sure way of breaking with communism. They demanded the immediate dissolution of the Communist Party and the termination of central planning, ministerial directives, guaranteed enterprise sales, state contracts, state-funded managerial bonuses, state ownership, price and exchange rate fixing, the monopoly of foreign trade and banking, as well as VPK and KGB economic oversight, arguing that dislocations would be surmounted by the invisible hand and expert western advice and assistance. Academician Stanislav Shatalin envisioned full transition in 500 hundred days,[1] while others forecast a shallow recession

---

[1] Stanislav Shatalin, et al., *Transition to the Market: 500 Days*, pt. 1, Arkhangelskoe, Moscow, August 1990.

swiftly reversed by ascending the J curve.[2] But this wasn't essential. The shock therapists default position was to apply the accumulated wisdom of the World Bank and International Monetary Fund (IMF), which subsequently became associated with what John Williamson dubbed the Washington Consensus.[3] Transition, Ronald McKinnon asserted, could be secured by calming and nurturing patchwork markets with a staged crisis management program known as the order of economic liberalization.[4] The strategy called for monetary restraint to discipline recently decontrolled state prices, followed by market-building measures to spur recovery and growth. Inflation fighting was primary in the first stage, recovery, full employment, growth, and optimal fiscal regulation in the second.

Box 7.1 Shock Therapy

Free enterprise theory teaches that anticompetitive restrictions prevent individuals from maximizing their utility and social welfare. Most advocates appreciate that a case can be made for some state economic governance but reject claims based on the duality theorem (equivalence of perfect planning and perfect competition) that planning and pervasive controls are as good as or better than the market. They believe that planning and controls have little redeeming value and should be abolished, not phased out to cut losses and raise efficiency. The transition strategy inspired by this attitude is called shock therapy, borrowing from the psychotherapeutic lexicon, where patients are roused to action with electric prods. Pragmatists satirize the dogma as *shock without therapy*. Jeffrey Sachs was the apostle of shock therapy in Gorbachev's Russia. He argued in the late 1980s that it caused West Germany's postwar success and refused to believe that a more gradual approach suited Muscovy better. His confidence was misplaced, and he cannot escape some responsibility for *catastroika* and Russia's 3.4 million excess deaths. Relatedly, many believe that western transition assistance was tainted by corruption, which contributed to *catastoika*. Harvard economist Andrei Shleifer for example was convicted in U.S. federal court of fraudulent dealings for personal gain with the Yeltsin administration while leading

---

[2] Josef Brada and Arthur King, "Is There a J-Curve for Economic Transition from Socialism to Capitalism?" *Economics of Planning*, 25, 1(1992): 37–53.

[3] John Williamson, "Democracy and the 'Washington Consensus,'" *World Development*, 21, 8(1993): 1329–36.

[4] Ronald McKinnon, *The Order of Economic Liberalization: Financial Control in the Transition to a Market Economy*, Johns Hopkins University Press, Baltimore, 1991.

a U.S. Agency for International Development–funded Harvard Institute for Economic Development advising team.* The only mitigating factor both in Sachs's and Shleifer's cases is that Gorbachev and Yeltsin undoubtedly would have acted much as they did under insider pressure.

*   David McClintick, "How Harvard Lost Russia," *Institutional Investors Magazine*, January 2006; Janine Wedel, *Collision and Collusion*, Palgrave Macmillan, New York, 2001.

Box 7.2 Washington Consensus

The Washington Consensus is a set of ten development policies that the World Bank, International Monetary Fund, and other Washington-based institutions believed in the 1990s should be used to manage third world economic crises. The term, coined by John Williamson, was subsequently broadened to encompass a wider gamut of neoliberal policies, including those designed to foster transition. Shock therapy, the order of economic liberalization, voucher privatization, and democratization were aspects of this orthodoxy. The Washington Consensus's axioms were sound but not always appropriate and in many instances counterproductive.* They had little bearing on Muscovite reality.

*   Howard Stein, *Beyond the World Bank Agenda: An Institutional Approach to Development*, University of Chicago Press, Chicago, 2008.

The wisdom of this sequencing was debated on the false premise that Russia was like Mexico or Argentina,[5] nations said to be on the high road to democratic free enterprise.[6] Some contended that full employment and growth could not be achieved without first establishing monetary stability, while others argued that it was better to proceed vice versa, judged from the Latin American experience. But this macroeconomic strategizing was misplaced. Russia needed to do more than just master the lessons of Latin America in combating hyperinflation and hyperdepression to transition efficiently. It had to rid itself of contingent property rights, the rule of men, and Muscovite autocracy.

[5] Joseph Stiglitz, *Globalization and Its Discontents*, W. W. Norton & Company, Allen Lane, New York, 2002.
[6] Andrei Shleifer and Daniel Treisman, "A Normal Country," *Foreign Affairs*, 83, 2(March/April 2004): 20–38. Andrei Shleifer, *A Normal Country: Russia after Communism*, Harvard University Press, Cambridge, MA, 2005.

Hyperinflation

Gorbachev's and Yeltsin's mishandling of Soviet and postcommunist runaway inflation illustrates the point. There should have been no place for inflation during the Soviet era because wages, prices, and exchange rates were fixed by the State Price Committee in accordance with Marxist labor value theory. Most goods could not be legally exchanged on any other terms among enterprises, wholesalers, and retailers. Nonetheless, inflationary pressures existed, and prices did sometimes rise. During the Brezhnev years, consumer goods inflation was less than 1 percent per annum.[7] This was negligible by market economy standards, but Igor Birman argued that this masked the intensity of Russia's real monetary disequilibrium. Reasoning that the Soviet Union was an economy of shortages, where goods were always in deficit relative to household purchasing power, he claimed that repressed inflation menaced Soviet economic stability.[8] The theme was echoed by the Central Intelligence Agency, and sensationalized in Judy Shelton's book *The Coming Soviet Crash*.[9]

All argued that the Soviet Union was beset by a ruble overhang,[10] that is, rapidly rising idle cash balances deposited in Gosbank for want of anything to buy. They could not prove that this was so because depositors earned modest interest on their money, and people might have had legitimate reasons for preferring augmented future to

[7] *Narodnoe khoziaistvo SSSR za 70 Let*, Finansy i statistika, Moscow, p. 480. There may also have been some hidden inflation in the retail price indexes, perhaps 1 percent per annum. See Steven Rosefielde, *False Science: Underestimating the Soviet Arms Buildup*, 2nd edition, Transaction Press, New Brunswick, NJ, 1987, chapter 11; and David Howard, The *Disequilibrium Model in a Controlled Economy*, Lexington Books, Lexington MA, 1979. pp. 139–48; Steven Rosefielde, "Cumulative Disequilibrium," *Soviet Studies*; Rosefielde, "The Soviet Economy in Crisis: Birman's Cumulative Disequilibrium Hypotheses," *Soviet Studies*, 40, 1(April 1988): 222–44.

[8] Igor Birman, *Ekonomika Nedostach* (*The Economy of Shortages*), Chalidze Publishing, New York, 1983; Birman, *Secret Incomes of the Soviet State Budget*, Martinus Nijhoff Publishers, Boston, 1981; Birman and Roger Clarke, "Inflation and the Money Supply in the Soviet Economy," *Soviet Studies*, 37, 4(October 1985): 501–2. Steven Rosefielde, "Book Review of Birman, Secret Incomes of the Soviet State Budget," *Journal of Economic Literature*, 21 (1983): 1018–19.

[9] Judy Shelton, *The Coming Soviet Crash: Gorbachev's Desperate Pursuit of Credit in Western Financial Markets*, Free Press, New York, 1989.

[10] Patrick Conway, "Ruble Overhang and Ruble Shortage: Were They the Same Thing," *Journal of Comparative Economics*, 24 (1998): 1–24.

present expenditures, including the purchase of big-ticket items such as automobiles in a financial system that offered no consumer credit. Nonetheless, authorities east and west should have been alerted to the potential monetary disequilibrium and have considered the merit of various correctives.[11] Soviet planners directly controlled enterprise wage funds and could have restricted the growth of wages by ordering Gosbank to limit enterprise wage payment growth to a rate less than retail inflation. Goskomtsen could have increased retail prices sufficiently to absorb the ruble overhang or adopted a mixed strategy. And, most important of all, specialists should have recognized that any liberalization of the banking system, which increased the income velocity of money by permitting loans on a fractional reserve basis had the potential for destabilizing monetary equilibrium.[12] The volume of cash in circulation when nations switch from controlled to fractional reserve systems can increase tenfold, supplemented further by M1 in a short period of time unless banking reforms are introduced gradually. Of course, matters easily can be aggravated if authorities irresponsibly resort to printing money.

The data reveal that Gorbachev's banking reforms, combined with unregulated bazaars (*yarmaki*), and the relaxation of state price discipline caused a low-triple-digit inflationary surge (1988–91) that authorities largely disregarded (Table 7.1). The regime appeared indifferent to the looming crisis, even though the state had all the tools it required to shut down the printing press and adopt rules for an orderly transition. Worse still, those including complicitous monetary officials who profited by borrowing ahead of the inflationary spiral, repaying in depreciated coin, and shifting purchasing power from ordinary people to themselves, mastered the game of self-enrichment. When the Soviet Union dissolved, they were ready to pounce, together with a government willing to emit money in lieu of direct taxation.

The Yeltsin administration's notion of optimal transition policy was to abnegate its proprietary, regulatory, contractual, fiscal, and monetary responsibilities under the guise of liberalization. Enterprise managers and workers were told to fend for themselves, while the

---

[11] Rudiger Dornbusch, "Lessons from Experiences with High Inflation," *World Bank Economic Review*, 6 (1992): 13–32.

[12] Patrick Conway, "Sustain Inflation in Response to Price Liberalization," World Bank Policy Research Working Paper 1368, 1994; Padma, Desai, "Perestroika, Prices and the Ruble Problem," *Harriman Institute Forum*, 2 (1989):11.

Table 7.1. *Russian consumer and producer prices*
1990–2004 (percentage change over preceding year)

	Consumer Prices	Producer Prices
1990	5.2	3.9
1991	160.0	240.0
1992	2,510.0	3,280.0
1993	840.0	900.0
1994	220.0	230.0
1995	197.4	237.6
1996	47.8	50.8
1997	14.7	15.0
1998	27.8	7.0
1999	85.7	59.1
2000	20.8	46.5
2001	21.6	19.1
2002	16.0	11.8
2003	13.6	15.6
2004	11.1	11.1

Source: National Statistics. United Nations, *Economic Survey of Europe*, 2005, No. 1, New York, Appendix Table B.8, Table 5.2.5, p. 68, and Chart 5.2.2, p. 69.

government met its budgetary needs by emitting money and dis-
cretely monetizing the state debt. These phenomena, burden shifting and deficit spending, were closely connected. The government's
shock therapeutic decision to repudiate its Soviet-era commitment
to purchase everything firms produced and cancel its procurement
contracts without compensation left former red directors in the lurch.
Managers found themselves without orders and unable to finance
operations with bank credit from any source. With little room for
maneuver, industrial production, and turnover tax (value-added tax)
payments plummeted 60 to 70 percent in tandem, leaving producers
impecunious, and the government underfunded. High double-digit
unemployment rates, massive wage arrears, and the dearth of consumer credit meant that workers and peasants were in no position
to bid up retail prices out of personal disposable income, despite the
drastically diminished supplies of household goods. People at the outset retained bank savings and used some of these funds to cope with
unemployment and wage arrears, but savings weren't the primary

source of excess demand driven inflation. The culprits were the government and speculators inside or closely connected with state and private banks.

The eruption was spectacular. Ruble emission exploded, spewing a continuous torrent of currency from the moment Yeltsin assumed power, triggering an inflationary surge rate in excess of 2,500 percent. Emil Ershov, who headed Goskomstat's audit division, has disclosed that Russia's price sample size and sampling techniques were too primitive to estimate accurately the full intensity of the phenomenon, but it can be confidently said that the hyperinflationary spiral, which ravaged the people's bank savings, was caused by the government. *Sberbank* (state savings bank) depositors received interest but only enough to offset 3 percent of the depreciation.[13]

The Yeltsin administration used its share of the implicit inflation tax to finance operations, while insiders of various descriptions went on a spending spree for tangible assets readily convertible into dollars and other hard currencies. Natural resources, and the military's prolonged war-fighting material reserves, were especially sought after, but apartments, other marketable facilities, and antiques were also in strong demand. The phenomenon created a social stratum called *new Russians*, composed of government insiders and their circles, managers of natural resource–processing facilities, and other lucrative enterprises, speculators, the mafia, and elements of the FSB and military with a strong preference for western consumer goods. Their demand was satisfied in large part through the intermediation of resource processors who used part of the profits from mineral sales to import consumer goods from the West, marketed in Moscow by affiliated retail outlets catering to new Russians. The result was the immediate and conspicuous emergence of a dual economy, with haves living in a dollarized sector and have-nots reduced to barter in a virtual economy.

Box 7.3 Virtual Economy

Virtual economy in the Russian context refers to post-Soviet value-adding activities generated in the remnants of the Soviet physical management system. It can be considered a shadow economy, a parallel economy (to Yeltsin's markets), or even the real economy, depending

---

[13] The *Sberbank* interest rate paid depositors was 90 percent per annum, when the official inflation rate in 1992 was in the vicinity of 2,500 percent per annum.

on definitions of scope and perceptions of size. Its heyday came immediately after the financial crisis of 1998, when most of the economy was
barterized, and can be interpreted as an indicator of transition failure.
As is widely understood, Russia's virtual economy was a degenerate
version of physical systems management with an inferior division of
labor. It was a survival stratagem, not an ideal. Gradual remonetization,
and the petro bubble have drastically reduced its size and scope, but the
phenomenon persists within the military industrial complex and other
sectors with a strong state protectionist presence.

Hyperinflation under these circumstances ebbed and eventually
died a natural death through a tripartite process of dollarization, virtualization, and the partial return of direct taxation as the preferred
mechanism for funding government operations. Having prostrated the
economy, wiped out the population's savings, and blown smoke in the
eyes of those who perceived hyperinflation fighting as optimally managing the order of economic liberalization, the Yeltsin administration
and privateer speculators turned to greener pastures.[14]

As soon as it became clear to the Yeltsin administration that an
increased role for direct taxation was in its interest, speculators within
the government devised a scheme to partly restore fiscal responsibility
that also gave them an opportunity to acquire coveted state assets.[15]

[14] David Lane, "The Evolution of Post-Communist Banking," in David Lane (ed.),
Russian Banking and Prospects, Edward Elgar, Cheltenham, UK, 2002, pp. 9–35.
Satoshi Mizobata, "Bank Sector Restructuring," in Lane (ed.), *Russian Banking
and Prospects*, pp. 36–55. Pekka Sutela, "The Role of Banks in Financing Russian
Economic Growth," *Post-Soviet Geography and Economics*, 39, 2(1998). Pekka
Sutela, *The Road to the Russian Market Economy*, Kikkimora, Helsinki, 1998. Elena
Zhuravskaya, "The First Stage of Banking Reform in Russia is Completed: What
Lies Ahead?" in Jacek Rostowski (ed.), *Banking Reform in Central Europe and the
Former Soviet Union*, CEU Press, Budapest, 1995.

[15] Duncan Allan, "Banks and the Loans-for Shares Auctions," in David Lane, ed.,
Russian Banking and Prospects, pp. 137–60. Heiko Pleines, "Banks and Illegal
Activities," in David Lane, *Russian Banking and Prospects*, pp.119–136. Marshall
Goldman, *The Piratization of Russia: Russian Reform Goes Awry*, Routledge, London, 2003. Allan contends that the loans-for-shares scam grew out of the state's
failed attempts to privatize, rather than as a Muscovite rent-granting operation
designed to secure oligarchic support for Yeltsin's 1996 reelection campaign.
The two interpretations aren't mutually exclusive. Rent-granting has always
involved considerable intrigue and confused objectives. The essential point to
grasp regardless of the details is that the state agreed to transfer the nation's crown
jewels to Yeltsin's cronies for a pittance when it had ample opportunity to protect

The scam was simplicity itself. On March 30, 1995, Vladimir Potanin (president of *Oneksimbank*), speaking on behalf of the Inter-Bank Credit Alliance(MKS) consortium, offered to lend the government money to cover some of the anticipated revenue shortfall from its sputtering privatization program in return for interest and forfeitable shares in companies such as LUKOIL, Chelyabinsk Metallurgical Combine, Norilsk Nickel, SIDANKO, Yukos, and Sibneft, in case of default. After some dickering, the Yeltsin administration agreed to borrow the funds, much of it the state's own deposits to finance the budgetary deficit. This action was portrayed as a testimony to the government's newfound maturity because an increased portion of the budgetary gap was to be funded by loans from the private sector, instead of money emission, a technique likened to the U.S. Federal Reserve's open-market operations. The only difference was the government's consent to transfer the nation's most valuable resource companies to the banks if the state defaulted on its obligations, which it promptly did. Although, the banks had lent the government its own money, and the state had the ability to repay with new emission, or levy special taxes, favored oligarchs like Mikhail Khodorkovsky and Potanin were permitted to abscond with the crown jewels in exchange for bonds needlessly in default, and subsequent share liquidation payments at rigged auctions. What had been billed as a crisis-averting exercise in responsible deficit management was swiftly revealed to be just another privateer rent-granting scam that placed insider welfare above that of the state and the nation.

Box 7.4 Equitable Asset Redistribution

No one seriously contests the claim that most Soviet assets were improperly privatized under Gorbachev and Yeltsin, even when acquirers adhered to the letter of the law. Senior Russian economists also understand that assets must be vested at just prices in the most competent hands to maximize their present discounted value and social welfare.

---

the national interest. Also see Chrystia Freeland, *Sale of the Century: The Inside Story of the Second Russian Revolution*, Little, Brown and Company, London, 2000; Al'fred Kokh, *The Selling of the Soviet Empire. Politics and Economics of Russia's Privatization Programme. Revelations of the Principal Insider*, SPI Books, New York, 1998. Anatoly Chubais, ed., *Privatizatsiya po-rossiiski*, Vagrius, Moscow, 1999.

A strong case therefore can be made both on efficiency and ethical grounds for rescinding Russian privatization and restarting the process afresh. But the vast majority favor letting bygones be bygones because they don't expect the benefits to be worth the disruption. The sentiment is sound, but it also rewards corruption and discourages constructive reform.

The same larcenous behavior was displayed a scant two years later when Yeltsin's financial wizards reversed the ploy by defrauding creditors instead of enriching them, in what is politely described as the financial crisis of 1998, without any disclosure of the government's predatory role. The victim this time around wasn't the Russian people as collective owners of state resource–processing companies; it was foreign bondholders, especially Europeans, who were persuaded by their own greed and a well-orchestrated charm campaign that short-term, high-interest-bearing Russian government securities and bonds floated in the European Union were creditworthy because the state would honor its debts, the government was committed to a stable foreign exchange rate, and residual risks could be hedged with derivatives. Although savvy observers understood full well that foreigners were being baited, that obligations were unlikely to be paid, and insiders would eventually flee the ruble, drastically lowering the foreign exchange rate, the Yeltsin administration did nothing whatsoever to avert the gathering storm. Eurobond sales surged from $1 billion to $16 billion (1996–98), accompanied by the avid foreign acquisition of $20 billion's worth of Russia's State Treasury Obligations (GKO) and Ministry of Finance Bonds (OFZ).[16] Altogether, foreigners held nearly 30 percent of the federal government debt, all of which went into default August 17, 1998, when a flight from rubles

[16] The purchase of government securities by nonresidents began at the beginning of 1996. In the first six months of 1997, net foreign investments amounted to $8.8 billion dollars; in September 1997, they represented nearly one-third of the $60 billion of outstanding State Treasury Obligation, GKO (Gosudarstvennaya kratkosrochnaya obligatsiya) and Ministry of Finance bonds, OFZ (Obligatsii Federal'novo Zaima). Moreover, the state sector raised foreign capital through loans and placements of Eurobonds. Altogether, in 1997 nearly 30 percent of the federal budget deficit was financed from foreign sources. Starting in 1997 foreign investors became more active in the corporate securities market. In the third quarter, they were estimated to control no less than 10 percent of the shares in the Russian stock market, with a capitalization above $100 billion.

drove the ruble down from 16 to 6 cents, or nearly 63 percent.[17] The domestic banking system then virtually collapsed wiping out the saving of most new Russian depositors. This was a crisis caused almost entirely by foreign investment in Russia's sovereign debt, and as such could have been easily prevented had the Yeltsin administration been concerned with the people's welfare instead of personal interests of rent-seekers. Just as before, the government's strategy as rent-granter was to collude with rent-seekers in indulging privilege rather than preventing or optimally managing monetary crises. Because westerners were predisposed to believe that the country was on the high road to normalization, Russian sharps capitalized on their gullibility.

There have been no new financial crises in Russia since 1998 because conditions changed in two fundamental ways. First, the destruction of new Russian wealth together with temporarily diminished ruble purchasing power abroad shifted demand from foreign consumer goods to domestic industrial importables and stimulated exports to the CIS, causing a modest recovery in production and domestic tax collections. Second, the subsequent global rise in natural resource prices, particularly petroleum, filled the treasury's coffers. Russia has run a fiscal surplus (2000–07), with public debt contracting pari *pasu* from 63.3 to 28.1 percent of gross domestic product (GDP).[18] But the mentality hasn't changed. When the natural resource price bubble bursts, some new twist in monetary scamming should be anticipated.

Hyperdepression

The crisis management story for the real economy duplicates the monetary experience. Just like prices, industrial and service sector production in the Soviet Union was positive after World War II. Growth was never spectacular,[19] but the economy was recession free until

---

[17] David Lane and Irene Lavrentieva, "The View from the Ground: Case Studies of Three Major Banks (Sberbank, Uneximbank/Rosbank, Bank of Moscow," in David Lane (ed.), *Russian Banking and Prospects*, pp. 79–115. See Table A4.2 Exchange rates, Russian ruble-U.S. dollar, January 1, 1993, to January 1, 2001, p. 112. The ruble denominated devaluation was from 6.2 on July 1, 1998, to 15.9 on October 1, 1998.

[18] United Nations, *Economic Survey of Europe*, 2005, Table 5.1.1, p. 60.

[19] Steven Rosefielde, "The Riddle of Postwar Russian Economic Growth: Statistics Lied and Were Misconstrued," *Europe-Asia Studies*, vol. 55, No. 3, 2003, pp. 469–81.

Gorbachev's *perestroika* turned sour in 1989. The decline should have raised awareness of potential danger.[20] There was no need for alarm because neither Oscar Lange's authoritative theory of market socialism,[21] nor Deng Xiaoping's marketizing reform provided grounds for anticipating hyperdepression, but the link with *perestroika* should have been studied, and countercyclical measures adopted. Gorbachev's and later Yeltsin's notion of optimal crisis management, however, was to accelerate Muscovite market rent-granting. And the worse matters became, the more adamantly Yeltsin's team opposed constructive intervention. It is easily appreciated why they persevered with privatization and business liberalization given both their declaratory and hidden agendas, but neither motive explains the government's and the West's total disinterest in New Deal–style Keynesian pump priming. It would have been a trivial matter to jump-start recovery given the population's high marginal propensity to consume by partially reinstating state procurement contracts, providing cheap credit to rust-belt industrial firms unable to borrow in the private sector, and initiating public works projects. The multiplier effects should have been prodigious, but neither these nor other conventional stimulatory techniques were employed, on the pretext that pump priming would restore communist physical systems management.

The Yeltsin administration instead was content to tinker with taxes and reduce some barriers to market entry until the economy finally hit rock bottom in 1998, with GDP nearly 50 percent below the 1989 level. Malign neglect wasn't futile. Eventually, rent-grantees and small entrepreneurs learned how to cope constructively with the new environment, prompting a partial recovery. But the improvement achieved in subsequent years should not be conflated with transition to free enterprise or a secure ticket to prosperity. The post-Soviet economic system that emerged as a partial consequence of the state's dereliction of its macroeconomic duties was thoroughly Muscovite. Historical precedent suggests that Russia should be able to grow slowly and fitfully in the tsarist manner, without converging, and perhaps even falling further behind the moving western high frontier. The mismanagement of hyperdepression insofar as it contributed to the misshaping

---

[20] Steven Rosefielde, "Gorbachev's Transition Plan: Strategy for Disaster," *Global Affairs*, Vol. 6, No. 2, 1991, pp. 1–21.

[21] Oskar Lange and Fred Taylor, *On the Economic Theory of Socialism*, University of Minnesota Press, Minneapolis, 1938.

of postcommunist Muscovy thus not only inflicted grave and needless harm on the nation in the short run but impaired its potential.

Unemployment Crisis Management

If there would have been an exception to the Yeltsin administration's callousness, it would have been in its jobs policy. Soviet communism had provided workers with powerful job-rights.[22] Although workers could be dismissed and involuntarily sent on assignment (*komandirovka*), the Bolsheviks after 1928 felt obligated to employ overfully the population through *teleological* planning and managerial bonus incentivization. Workers weren't just kept on the employment rolls to save face. They were assigned real productive tasks, even if they malingered.

This confronted the Yeltsin regime with a dilemma. It could soften its tough love shock therapy by maintaining the facade of full employment, providing funds for wages even though laborers were idle, subsidize wages, put workers on the dole, and create public works projects. Or, it could feed them to the sharks. Its choice was predictable but was partially disguised by the decision of old-line red directors to keep workers on the rolls without pay, waiting for the government to relent. Public awareness of the unfolding calamity was also muted by the government's tactic of reporting only the registered unemployed. Because there was little to be gained by registering, few did, creating a striking anomaly between statistics showing firms operating at less than a third of capacity on the one hand and official unemployment running just a few percent on the other.

The true story wasn't revealed until years later, when *Goskomstat* began applying International Labor Organization survey techniques and then only incompletely. Unemployment instead of being a few percent turned out to be four to five times higher than the registration figures before making allowance for discouraged workers jobless for several years. Fully adjusted estimates reliably derived from Soviet census data and Russian demographic statistics showed that the unemployment rate, including discouraged workers, in 1998 was

---

[22] David Granick, "Soviet Use of Fixed Prices: Hypothesis of a Job-Right Constraint," in Steven Rosefielde, ed., *Economic Welfare and the Economics of Soviet Socialism*, Cambridge University Press, 1981, pp. 85–104.

Table 7.2. *Registered, surveyed, and census-derived estimates of unemployment in the Russian federation (percent of the civilian labor force 1994–2004)*

	Registered	Surveyed	Census
1992	0.8	5.2	–
1993	1.1	6.1	–
1994	2.1	7.8	–
1995	3.2	9.0	–
1996	3.4	10.0	–
1997	2.8	11.2	–
1998	2.7	13.3	21.7
1999	1.7	12.2	–
2000	1.4	9.8	–
2001	1.6	8.7	–
2002	1.8	8.1	–
2003	2.3	8.3	–
2004	2.2	8.0	–

Sources: United Nations, *Economic Survey of Europe*, 2005, No.1, Appendix Table B.7, p. 133, Table 5.2.7, p. 71; United Nations, *Economic Survey of Europe*, 2004, No.1, Table 4.4.2, p. 107; United Nations, *Economic Survey of Europe*, 2003, No.1, Table B.7, p. 229. Steven Rosefielde, "The Civilian Labour Force and Unemployment in the Russian Federation," *Europe–Asia Studies*, 52, 8(2000): 1440.

21.7 percent, not 13.3 percent or 2.7 percent as officially reported (Table 7.2).[23] Additional allowance made for military job seekers discharged from the armed forces, and *ghosting* (dismissed workers still listed as employed) could easily increase the figure to 25 percent, implying a 1 percent job loss for every 2 percent decline in GDP.

Clearly, the Yeltsin administration had just cause to ameliorate the suffering but chose to do nothing. Contemporary western governments with low double-digit employment rates respond with stimulative, retraining, and relief programs, but Russian authorities decided not to intervene at all, either in the 1990s or thereafter. Optimal

---

[23] Steven Rosefielde, "The Civilian Labour Force and Unemployment in the Russian Federation," *Europe-Asia Studies*, 52, 8 (2000), pp.1433–47. Cf. *Monitoring Economic Conditions in the Russian Federation: The Russia Longitudinal Monitoring Survey* 1992–2004, University of North Carolina, May 2005, Table 9, p. 15.

crisis management for them was doing nothing, except eradicating job-right constraints and making labor more docile for rent-seekers.

Barter

The combination of hyperinflation, hyperdepression, and hyperunemployment primitivized the economy, creating still another kind of crisis: barter-driven dislocation. As Adam Smith taught long ago, productivity depends heavily on the division of labor. Output per unit of labor is highest when workers specialize and are assigned to the most profitable tasks. This can be accomplished with barter, but it is difficult to compare apples and oranges. Money prices are better. They enable managers to reduce all aspects of profit maximizing to an easily understood common denominator. Hyperinflation impairs these calculations, and hyperdepression disorganizes interindustrial supplies, chasing producers from monetized markets into fragmented barter circles. This despecialization diminishes factor productivity and consumption possibilities, providing only small consolation by sheltering barters from the prying eye of tax collectors.

Barterization, what Barry Ickes and Clifford Gaddy call the virtual economy, always menaced postcommunist Russia because Soviet-era enterprise managers were accustomed to contracting in physical terms directly with intermediate input suppliers under central planning.[24] When the Soviet control system dissolved, many enterprises looked to these familiar links. The Yeltsin administration should have understood this and anticipated the negative productivity effects but was unswayed with dramatic consequences. George Kleiner and Valerii Makarov estimated that 80 percent of the retail and wholesale industrial goods trade in the late 1990s were bartered.[25] Where Yeltsin's team spoke glowingly about marketization, the reality was barterization.

Barter isn't fatal. It is better than being inert and is reversible. The comparative stability of the Putin years, combined with the

---

[24] Clifford Gaddy and Barry Ickes, "Russia's Virtual Economy," *Foreign Affairs*, 77, 5 (1998): 52–67; Gaddy and Ickes, "An Accounting Model of the Virtual Economy in Russia," *Post-Soviet Geography and Economics*, 40, 3(1999): 78–97; Gaddy and Ickes, *Russia's Virtual Economy*, Brookings Institution Press, Washington, DC, 2002.

[25] Valerii Makarov and Georgii Kleiner, "Barter v ekonomike perekhodnovo perioda: Osobennosti i tendentsii," *Ekonomika i Matematicheskie Metody*, 33, 2(1997): 25–41.

trickle-down effects of the natural resource boom have gradually drawn business back into the monetized market (although the benefit has been dampened by deindustrialization),[26] and further progress can be expected thanks to the Russian people's adaptability, rather than anything remotely resembling wise government policy.

Capital Flight

A high-level official in the Yeltsin government confided years ago that opportunities for colossal theft like those that arose in the post-Soviet years came along only once in a millennium, and he intended to grab his share. However, in the absence of the rule of law, thieves were prey to fellow predators. Gains, ill gotten or not, couldn't be securely kept in domestic banks, or invested, spawning another paradox. While postcommunist Russia under normal conditions should have been a Klondike, affluent citizens hot-wired their money securely abroad.

Capital flight began during the 1980s, even though it was strictly illegal. The ruble was inconvertible, and hard currency acquired domestically could not be exported through official channels. Nonetheless, wealth leaked out like a sieve. Natural resource exporters underreported sales and earnings and kept the difference for themselves in the West. And, it was widely rumored that the Communist Party of the Soviet Union deposited $90 billion in New York, a tale given credibility when the Yeltsin administration unsuccessfully sued for its recovery.

Both Gorbachev and Yeltsin were aware of the problem and understood that depositing wealth abroad reduced domestic investment and consumption but weren't dismayed. Vladimir Zagladin, vice president of the Gorbachev Foundation, explained to Rosefielde in 1992 that capital flight was transitory. In no time at all, he asserted these funds would flood back into Russia to reap prodigious gains. But the reversal didn't even begin to materialize until 2005. Although the amounts remain in dispute, it appears that hundreds of billions of dollars have hemorrhaged out of the country, with only modest counterflows.[27]

[26] Michael Ellman, "Russian Economic Boom: Post-1998," *Economic and Political Weekly*, 39 (2004): 3234–37.

[27] Vladimir Tikhomirov, "Capital Flight from Post-Soviet Russia," *Europe Asia Studies*,49, 4(1997): 591–615; Tikhomirov, "Capital Flight: Causes, Consequences and Counter-Measures," in Klaus Segbers, *Explaining Post-Soviet Patchworks*, Vol. 2, Ashgate, Aldershot, UK, 2001, pp. 251–80; United Nations, *Economic Survey*

The Yukos trial set off a fresh wave of capital flight in 2004,[28] despite offers of partial tax amnesties.[29] Although many owners over the years have chosen to emigrate, reuniting themselves with their money, nothing precludes the possibility that Zagladin may someday be right. And it can be argued on theoretical grounds that free capital flows will be beneficial for Russia's long-term development. Nonetheless, it is also true that no Russian leader from Gorbachev on strove to devise an optimal capital flows policy, preferring to let nature take its course.

Corruption

Muscovite human relations are transgressive. Autocratic rent-granting means that only the ruler has rights, rent-grantees (privateers, oligarchs, *siloviki*) have revocable privileges, and the people are servile. Corruption consequently is endemic from a western perspective because the rights of man aren't protected by the rule of law. Rulers

of Europe, 2005, No. 1, pp. 61–63. There are many definitions of capital flight. The United Nation's broad definition is the difference between the surplus in the balance-of-payments current account and the net accumulation of foreign assets, reflected in an aggregate deficit of the capital and financial accounts. There is also a narrow definition that includes estimates of repatriated export revenues, fictitious import contracts, and errors and omissions in the balance of payments. In absolute terms, the ratio of this measure to the current account surplus decline sharply after the devaluation of the ruble; it then drifted upward after 2001 only to fall again in 2004. A broader coverage along with measurement difficulties may partially explain these movements. A new currency control law enacted in June 2004 envisages a gradual elimination of most capital controls by 2007. Given the net private capital outflow, averaging almost $17 billion annually during the period 1996–2003, Russian residents may have accumulated more than $136 billion abroad. Li Ma, *A Comparative Study of the Russian and Chinese Governments' FDI Policies*, Master's thesis, curriculum in Russian and East European Studies, University of North Carolina, Chapel Hill, 2005.

[28] Peter Gumbrel, "Hurry, While Supplies Last: Despite Fears of Government Meddling, Western Firms Are Buying Russian Businesses at a Record Pace," *Johnson's Russia List*, No. 9128, Article 1, April 24, 2005. According to Russia's Central Bank, capital flight quadrupled last year as worried investors moved their assets offshore. Net capital outflow jumped from $1.9 billion in 2004 to $9.4 billion. Ben Aris, "A Row over Russia's FDI Figures," *Johnson's Russia List*, No. 271, Article 21, December 1, 2006. There was an improvement in 2006. For the first nine months, net FOI was $800 million.

[29] Andrew Hurst, "Putin's Capital Amnesty May Fall on Deaf Ears," *Johnson's Russia List*, No. 9142, Article 4, May 7, 2005. "Pro-Kremlin Consultant Warns That Financial Amnesty Is Not for Oligarchs," *Johnson's Russia List*, No. 9139, Article 9, May 4, 2005. The proposed amnesty for repatriated capital, in return for a 13 percent tax and deposit of funds in Russian banks is not intended for oligarchs.

and rent-grantees aren't restrained by western norms, and ordinary people don't consider themselves bound by formal and informal regulations imposed from above. This didn't prevent tsarist and Soviet economic growth but has always created a potential conflict between the privileged's individual and collective welfare whenever self-seeking got out of hand.

For those who became overnight billionaires or *siloviki*, excessive Muscovite corruption has been worth the trauma, but this isn't so for the majority, and the situation remains in flux. Social welfare could have been vastly improved if the state had exerted leadership, firm discipline, and vigorously prosecuted wrongdoers. The state, however, displayed no interest in plugging the dike, except against political foes.[30] Instead of tolerating spontaneous privatization, voucher privatization fraud, and the loans-for-shares scam, it could have limited asset transfers as Nobel laureate James Buchanan privately advised to those who successfully turned operations around and assured that purchases were made at fair market value. Acquirers who failed would have had their assets confiscated. Likewise, managers should have been prohibited from asset stripping and misappropriating state resources for personal gain. Access to normal managerial rewards should have sufficed and legitimate profit maximizing should have been encouraged. Of course, strict enforcement of the rule of contract law would have improved business gains for the majority of rent-grantees. Although rent-granting is intrinsically inferior to competitive profit maximizing, some rent-granting regimes are more efficient than others. In tolerating extreme corruption, Gorbachev and Yeltsin needlessly created a crisis that aggrandized society's worst elements. Likewise, it should be noted that the state's misuse of foreign assistance was an element of the culture of corruption. Much of the billions of dollars granted Russia during the Yeltsin years by individual countries and international organizations was offered under Graham Allison's concept of the Grand Bargain in which aid was given more or less without safeguards in return for vague promises of transition.[31] All

---

[30] Christopher Cox (Chairman House Policy Committee), *Russia's Road to Corruption*, US House of Representatives, Washington DC, September 2000; Anders Aslund, "Russia's Collapse," *Foreign Affairs*, 78, 5(September/October 1999): 64–77.

[31] Graham Allison and Robert Blackwill, "America's Stake in the Soviet Future," *Foreign Affairs*, 70, 3(Summer 1991), 77–97. Jiri Dienstbier, the foreign minister of Czechoslovakia unveiled a three-year, $16 billion proposal modeled on the Marshall Plan in April 1990 for the benefit of Czechoslovakia, Poland, and

of it disappeared without an audible trail,[32] and none had a visibly positive effect on economic performance or led to a decisive break with Muscovy. A more responsible effort on the Yeltsin's regime part to honor its Grand Bargain obligations would have provided billions of additional assistance, but the government was content to obtain what it could in return for empty promises.[33]

Defense

The crisis in Russia's defense and intelligence establishment was an exception that partly confirmed the rule. Yeltsin had good cause to fear and to punish the security services. Elements of the military and KGB had sought to eliminate him during the abortive coup d'etat against Gorbachev in 1991. Perhaps because he was the ultimate benefactor of the coup, Yeltsin contented himself with being cautiously punitive, adopting a seemingly pragmatic strategy. On the one hand, he cancelled most weapons procurement contracts in 1992, reduced troop size, drastically curtailed funding, compelled many soldiers to forage, and detached important activities from the jurisdiction of the former KGB. On the other hand, he preserved the *genshtab* and the

Hungary. The theme was then picked up by Graham Allison and Robert Blackwill in collaboration with Grigory Yavlinsky who urged a *grand bargain* at the July 1991 G-7 meeting in which the Soviet Union would receive Marshall Plan–scale assistance in return for political pluralization and a coherent economic program for moving rapidly to a market economy. Allison, known for his work on bureaucratic decision making, was assistant secretary of Defense for Policy and Planning (1993–94), where he coordinated strategy and policy toward the states of the former Soviet Union. Blackwill was appointed by President George H. Bush to the post of special assistant to the president for National Security Affairs and senior director for European and Soviet Affairs in 1989. See Steven Rosefielde, "The Grand Bargain: Underwriting Katastroika," *Global Affairs*, 7, 1(Winter 1992): 15–35. Rosefielde, "What Is Wrong with Plans to Aid the CIS?" *Orbis*, 37, 3(Summer 1993): 353–64.

[32] Ron Childress, "The 'Children's Crusade' – Namely the Needless American 'Humanitarian' Assistance to Post-Soviet Russia," paper presented at the American Association for the Advancement of Slavic Studies, Boca Raton, FL, September 1998.

[33] The Japanese official responsible for signing aid checks to Russia informed Rosefielde in 1994 that not a single yen of Japan's G-7 pledge had been disbursed because the Russians hadn't provided suitable guarantees. Steven Rosefielde, "Peace and Prosperity in the Pacific Rim: Optimizing the Benefits of Japanese Assistance to Russia," *Acta Slavica Iaponica*, 12 (1994): 47–61.

Table 7.3. *Output of the Russian defense industry 1991–2003 (index 1991 = 100)*

	Military	Civilian	Total
1991	100	100	100
1992	62.6	96.4	78.7
1993	49.3	82.9	63.6
1994	30.3	51.0	39.1
1995	25.1	39.9	31.4
1996	18.8	28.9	23.1
1997	13.9	28.5	20.1
1998	16.6	28.3	21.7
1999	22.7	36.4	28.8
2000	29.4	43.8	36.1
2001	29.0	49.0	37.7
2002	36.1	51.7	43.7
2003	42.6	58.5	50.7

Source: Institut ekonomiki perekhodnovo perioda, *Rossiiskaya ekonomiia v 2001 gody, tendentsii i perspektivy,* Moscow March 2002, section 2.7. *SIPRI Yearbook 2004*, Table 11C.2. For further details, see Julian Cooper, "The Economics of Russian Defence Policy," paper presented at the conference on Russia under President Vladimir Putin: Towards the Second Term, European University Institute, Florence, April 22–23, 2004.

military industrial complex intact, granted rents to key officials such as Defense Minister Pavel Grachev, allowed senior officers to pilfer prolonged war- fighting reserves, temporized on westernizing military reform, assured the security establishment that they were being treated evenhandedly with the civilian sector, and offered hope that the privileges of the security services and the might of Russia's armed forces would someday be restored.

It was an impressive juggling act. At the same time, defense activities plunged 90 percent from the 1989 level (Table 7.3); the capacity to reconstitute superpower and secret police intervention was preserved as a disincentive to mutiny. But the strategy was hardly optimal from the standpoint of Muscovite national security. Whatever revenge Yeltsin may have sought, while currying critical support within factions of the security services, could have been inflicted with far less damage to the Kremlin's traditional Muscovite agenda.

The shock therapeutic degradation of Russia's intermediate-term national security capabilities, combined with the preservation of a renewed cold war option, was more a dereliction of duty than an ideal reorientation of postcommunist defense policy from either a western rational choice or Muscovite great power perspective. The Yeltsin administration needlessly disregarded its legitimate interest in defending the country's borders and effectively engaging rivals abroad and preserved archaic institutions and obsolescing military industrial production capacities. A better approach would have been to simultaneously downscale and modernize in a sequence that optimized national security benefits throughout all phases of the transformation.[34] Because Muscovite and western security tastes differ, the result of an optimal transformation might not have been entirely to NATO's liking. Yeltsin could have intervened more forcefully in the Balkan wars, suppressed Chechnya, and exerted greater influence in the CIS and throughout the globe. But, correspondingly, Putin's quest to restore Russian superpower might have been blunted. The impetus toward reconstituting a conservative Muscovite authoritarian martial police state is partly a consequence of Yeltsin's mishandling of the post-Soviet defense crisis and must be heavily weighted in any summary assessment of Russia metamorphosis.

Poverty

Muscovy never shed anything except crocodile tears for the common man. Once a course was charted, neither misery nor rational self-interest could stem the tide, until madness ran its course. Yeltsin's shock therapy was no exception. A population assured that those who worked would be fed was abruptly plunged into acute poverty, with 30 to 40 percent living below the official poverty line, computed on the basis of wages or household income.[35] The numbers are difficult to reconcile. According to the CIA's purchasing power parity calculations, Soviet per capita income in 1989 was at the European mean,

---

[34] Steven Rosefielde, *Russia in the 21st Century: The Prodigal Superpower*, Cambridge University Press, Cambridge, 2005.

[35] *Monitoring Economic Conditions in the Russian Federation: The Russia Longitudinal Monitoring Survey 1992–2004*, University of North Carolina, May 2005, Table 10, p. 17.

more than \$23,000 at 2003 prices;[36] yet, the Russian poverty line calculated at the market exchange rate by the *Russia Monitoring Longitudinal Survey* for 2003 was \$1,445 for a household of four.[37] Official data indicate postcommunist consumption only declined 19.5 percent, and exceeded the 1990 level by 2003, offering a favorable impression of living conditions, belied by the premature deaths in the 1990s.[38] Obviously Russian numbers are slippery, sometimes lie, and are deceptive.[39] Nonetheless, the impression of widespread destitution conveyed by the poverty statistic is readily visible beneath the tinsel of downtown Moscow, and throughout the rest of the country, especially in comparison with the West, which progressed from 1990 to 2005, while Russia retrogressed. The official subsistence level, whether computed in rubles or dollars, is paltry even for no-frills Muscovy, and the majority of Russians didn't live much better, until well after the oil bonanza that began in 2002.

[36] Steven Rosefielde, *Efficiency and Russia's Economic Recovery Potential to the Year 2000 and Beyond*, Ashgate, Aldershot, UK, 1998, table S1, pp. xxii–xxiii.

[37] M. Loshkin and Barry Popkin, "The Emerging Underclass in the Russian Federation: Income Dynamics 1992–96," *Economic Development and Cultural Change*, 47 (1999): 803–29; Thomas Mroz and Barry Popkin, "Poverty and the Economic Transition in the Russian Federation," *Economic Development and Cultural Change*, 44 (1995): 1–31; *Monitoring Economic Conditions in the Russian Federation: The Russia Longitudinal Monitoring Survey, 1992–2004*, University of North Carolina, May 2005. See http://www.cpc.unc.edu/projects/rlms/data/stats/html. Tom Mroz: based on these data estimates, the mean and standard deviations of the monthly poverty lines for 2003 as follows:

All Russia mean (std), 3696.99 (2154.48), 18 percent household poverty line
  Regional
2934.19 (1472.53), 13 percent household poverty line
USD Russian mean \$1,445; regional \$1,146 per year, using an exchange rate of 30.69 rubles per dollar.
United Nations, *Economic Survey of Europe*, 2005, No.1, Appendix table B15. The 2003 exchange rate is 30.69. E-mail dated May 23, 2005.

[38] United Nations, *Economic Survey of Europe*, 2005, No.1, Appendix table B.2, p. 129. Real total consumption expenditure in the Russian Federation was 3.8 percent above the 1990 level in 2003. Cf *Monitoring Economic Conditions in the Russian Federation: The Russia Longitudinal Monitoring Survey, 1992–2004*, University of North Carolina, May 2005, table 1, p. 3. These independent survey household data show a maximum 43 percent decline 1992–1998.

[39] Steven Rosefielde, "The Riddle of Postwar Russian Economic Growth: Statistics Lied and Were Misconstrued," *Europe-Asia Studies*, 55, 3(2003): 469–81.

The plight of ordinary people wasn't quite as bleak as these numbers suggest. Service lives of consumer nondurables like clothing were extended as wage income fell. Moreover, most people acquired or continue to reside in their Soviet-era dwellings at nominal expense, and some low-cost (low-quality) public services were available, including medical, educational, municipal transport, and utilities,[40] but the Putin administration passed legislation in 2004 to make pensioners pay full cost for nearly everything.[41] The Soviet social safety net, which was severely frayed during the Yeltsin period, has been shredded,[42] and with it any pretense of being an European Union–style social democracy.

This turn of events should be seen as the culmination of a two-phase Muscovite crisis management process, in which a massive inegalitarian redistribution of income and wealth initially immiserized much of the population, partly ameliorated by the remnants of the Soviet social safety net, to be followed in Putin's second presidential term by a final push, compelling the poor to bear the full burden of rent-granting.[43] The Kremlin denies any such intention, insisting that cash

---

[40] *Monitoring Economic Conditions in the Russian Federation: The Russia Longitudinal Monitoring Survey, 1992–2004*, University of North Carolina, May 2005, table 1, p. 3.

[41] "Why Is Benefit Reform Unpopular?" *Johnson's Russia List*, No. 9033, Article 8, January 19, 2005. On January 1, 2005, a federal law came into force replacing benefits in-kind with cash payments. Over 12 million people are entitled to benefits, but mass protests show they feel aggrieved.

[42] Mark Field and Judyth Twigg, eds., *Russia's Torn Safety Nets: Health and Social Welfare during the Transition*, St. Martin's Press, New York, 2000. Ekspert, "Gray Collars and Unemployed at the Bottom of Russian Social Pyramid," *Johnson's Russia List*, No. 9158, Article 4, May 24, 2004. "The extreme poverty is the lot not so much of Russian retirees, teachers and doctors, but of manual workers and the unemployed in provincial small towns and villages. They account for 24.5 percent of the country's able-bodied population.... Real poverty and despair reign among the so-called gray collar workers doing low-quality manual labor, who account for 14.8 percent of the employable population and earn from 1,500 to 3,500 rubles ($53 to $125) a month, and among the unemployed (9.7 percent), who receive a monthly subsidy of 800 rubles (less than $30)." Cf. Maria Kakturskay, "We Are Slaves of the State," *Johnson's Russia List*, No. 8470, Article 10, November 26, 2004. Academician Dmitri Lvov argues that Russia's workers are being mercilessly exploited. Two-thirds of Russia's revenues come from natural resources exports; but 70 percent of tax revenue comes from the wages of Russian citizens.

[43] Alec Fak, "Moscow Taxpayer Data for Sale on CD-ROM," *Moscow Times*, May 27, 2005, p.7. The gap between the haves and have-nots in Russia is

payments to pensioners will compensate for lost benefits in kind, but few believe it. The Yeltsin administration's response to widespread impoverization of the laborers and pensioners (discouraged workers) was merely to preserve some subsidized basic services, and with a mounting petro-driven economic recovery, the Kremlin sees even less reason for concern.

Democide

The catastrophic effects of post-Soviet immiseration, however, are indelibly engraved in the data on premature deaths. These can be calculated by comparing Russia's population for 1998 estimated by the U.S. Bureau of the Census with the actual figure adjusted for migration and the birth deficit. There should have been 152.8 million people in 1998, but the actual number was only 146.7 million, resulting in a 6.1 million deficit. Natality data revealed a 2.7-million-birth deficit, leaving 3.4 million premature deaths. Although it cannot be proven that all those who died before their time succumbed to the trauma of immiseration, there are no other prime suspects. When all the rationalizations are sifted, it is clear that Yeltsin's mismanagement of the impoverization crisis killed millions, whose graves are testaments to the real nature of Russia's Muscovite *catastroika*. The population deficit (1990–98) isn't as great as the 19.6 million gap caused by Stalin's forced collectivization and Great Terror, but it is startling nonetheless.[44]

Demography

Another essential aspect of Russia's botched postcommunist crisis management with strong human welfare and national security implications is its demographic impact. The hardships of the Yeltsin years are associated with two adverse phenomena, soaring male mortality and sharply declining natality well below replacement rates, portending

understated by tax underreporting. Bootlegged tax data reveal, for example, that Moscow major Yury Luzhkov and Gazprom billionaire Alexei Miller declared 2003 incomes, respectively, of $35,200 and $2,176,000.

[44] Steven Rosefielde, "Premature Deaths: Russia's Radical Economic Transition in Soviet Perspective," *Europe-Asia Studies*, 53, 8(2001): 1159–76.

Table 7.4. *Contemporary Russian vital statistics*

	1990	1991	1992	1993	1994	1995	1996	1997	1998
Birth rate (per 1000 people)	13.4	12.1	10.7	9.4	9.6	9.3	8.9	8.6	8.8
Mortality rate (per 1000 people)	11.2	11.4	12.2	14.5	15.7	15.0	14.2	13.8	13.6
Life Expectancy									
Male	65	63	62	59	58	58	60	61	61
Female	74	74	74	72	71	72	72	73	73
Total fertility	1.89	1.73	1.55	1.39	1.40	1.34	1.28	1.23	1.24

Sources: Goskomstat, *Demographic Yearbook of Russia. Statistical Handbook* (Moscow 1997), Table 2.1, p. 51, Table 2.4, p. 90, Table 2.6, p. 101; Goskomstat, *Demographic Yearbook of Russia. Statistical Handbook* (Moscow, 1998), Table 2.1, p. 50, Table 2.4, p. 89, Table 2.7, p. 101; Goskomstat, *Demographic Handbook of Russia* (Moscow, 1999), Table 2.1, p. 50, Table 2.4, p. 89, Table 2.7, p. 101.

plunging population levels of nearly seven hundred thousand people annually for the next few decades, unless there is compensating in-migration.[45] Table 7.4 presents the essential vital statistics. They confirm that the hardships of Russia's Muscovite transformation sent mortality rates soaring and probably contributed to sharply declining natality and fertility rates. The damage done to the cohorts of the 1990s cannot be undone but may be partially reversible for future generations, despite the development of antinatalist attitudes and risky behavior that has had a severely adverse effect on the population's health and capacities.[46] No doubt the Yeltsin administration could have

[45] Rosefielde, "Premature Deaths," table A2, p. 1173.
[46] Murray Feshbach, "Russia's Demographic and Health Meltdown," Testimony to U.S. Congress, Joint Economic Committee. In *Russia's Uncertain Economic Future*, Joint Economic Committee of Congress, Washington, DC, 2002, pp. 283–306; Feshbach, *The Demographic, Health and Environmental Situation in Russia*, draft report presented at The Future of the Russian State, Liechtenstein Institute on Self-Determination Conference, Triesenberg, Liechtenstein, March 14–17, 2002; Feshbach, *Russia's Health and Demographic Crisis: Policy Implications and Consequences.* Chemical and Biological Arms Control Institute, Washington DC, 2003; Nicholas Eberstadt, "The Future of AIDS," *Foreign Affairs*, 81, 6(2002): 22–45. Eberstadt, *The Demographic Factor as a Constraint on Russian Development: Prospects, Sources and Limits of Russian Power*, National Defense University Press, Washington, DC, 2004; Mark Field, "The Health and Demographic Crisis in Post-Soviet Russia: A Two Phase Development," in Field and Twigg (eds.),

significantly ameliorated both types of demographic harm with an effective antipoverty program and the preservation of the core Soviet public health system. The benefits to Muscovy would have been significant, among other things, strengthening Russian national security potential. But the Kremlin could not bring itself to socially optimize.

Muscovite Governance

Finally, a word needs to be said about the vulnerability of Russian state governance to periodic crisis. Postcommunist Muscovy still hasn't fashioned a secure governance mechanism because power depends more on leadership and intrigue than constitutional rights and the rule of law. Strongmen such as Putin may play factions off successfully and impose a semblance of order, but they are perpetually being tested, are at risk for palace coups, and have only limited ability to influence successors. Yeltsin usurped Gorbachev's power, Putin Yeltsin's, and the final chapter of the Medvedev-Putin diarchy is apt to have a similarly authoritarian outcome.

Conclusion

The saga of Russia's metamorphosis from Reform Communism to Market Muscovy, with its needless miseries is airbrushed by transitologists who conflate aspects of liberalization with optimal crisis management across a spectrum of interrelated issues. Close analysis has revealed that in every instance the response of Russia's leaders to the challenges at hand was inadequate. Russia could have successfully westernized and responsibly managed its public policy, but it didn't.

• The demolition of Soviet institutions followed the West's script, which prescribed the immediate eradication of the Soviet physical management system (shock therapy), its replacement by democratic free enterprise (Washington Consensus), according to Ronald McKinnon's order of economic liberalization (monetary stabilization, market institution building, privatization, democratization).

Russia's Torn Safety Nets, pp. 11–43; Murray Feshbach, "The Russian Military: Population and Health Constraints," in Jan Leijonhielm and Fredrik Westerlund (eds.), *Russian Power Structures FOI*, Swedish Defense Research Agency, Stockholm, January 2008, pp. 111–140.

- This economic advice, rhetorically accepted by the Yeltsin administration, was supposed to cause a short-lived, shallow recession followed by turbocharged growth but was vitiated by revenue misappropriation and asset grabbing instead, culminating in *catastroika*.
- The hyperinflation and hyperdepression that ensued transformed what was supposed to be a trauma-free transition into a tutorial in crisis mismanagement.
- The hyperdepression, including mass involuntary unemployment, was partly left to cure itself, even though Keynesian pump priming could have ameliorated the pain because the Clinton administration feared that government programs might lead to the reestablishment of communism.
- Russian hyperinflation was caused by the Yeltsin administration's reckless money emission, not past Soviet monetary disequilibrium sometimes described as the ruble overhang. State revenues fell drastically in 1992 when the government massively canceled enterprise production contracts, and printing money became an expedient device for paying state bills.
- Enormous fortunes were made by borrowers and lost by savers.
- Hyperinflation barterized (virtualized) most of the economy, except for the dollarized rich.
- It was eventually cured by persuading the Yeltsin administration to borrow funds in the open market instead of printing money and by tightening tax collections.
- Anatoly Chubais's privatization program was supposed to heal *catastroika* but exacerbated it by sanctioning the piratization of Russia's natural resources and by stimulating capital flight.
- The problem wasn't scotched until Putin began reining Yeltsin's oligarchs and direct foreign investment began exceeding domestic capital flight due to the petro bubble.
- Privateering wasn't limited to domestic assets. Insiders in Yeltsin's government promoted the sale of state bonds with unpayable coupons to western governments and individuals and placed themselves in a position to profit when Russia inevitably defaulted. They siphoned funds to themselves initially and sold rubles for dollars just before the August 1998 financial crisis and devaluation.
- Russia's hyperdepression began with Gorbachev's *perestroika*. It was caused by asset-grabbing, enterprise revenue misappropriation, the disorganization of intermediate input supply, and barterization (virtualization).

- Gorbachev's notion of depression fighting was to throw fuel on the fire by quickening the process of asset-grabbing and revenue misappropriation.
- Yeltsin worsened matters by canceling the majority of state contracts and ignoring the consequences. His administration pretended liberalization would automatically restore full capacity utilization and falsely claimed that the unemployment rate was a tenth of the true figure.
- This provided an excuse for shunning Keynesian countercyclical remedies at a time when hyperinflation rendered monetary policy useless.
- The brunt of Yeltsin's malign neglect was borne by the working class. Unemployment rose to 25 percent, wages paid as arrears were ravaged by hyperinflation, life savings were wiped out, and pensions weren't properly indexed.
- The Yeltsin administration's concept of crisis management was to force workers to cope as best they could without government countercyclical policies, public works programs, retraining, or other forms of assistance.
- This same attitude applied to barterization. Monetized business increases market scope (division of labor). Demonetization reverses the process, diminishing factor productivity and GDP. The obvious solution is sound monetary policy. This eventually materialized, but only after the Yeltsin team was chastened by the financial crisis of 1998.
- Capital flight reduces domestic purchasing power and exacerbates depressions. The problem has never been seriously addressed and has only been gradually overcome because of the transitory effects of the petro bubble.
- Corruption impairs productivity, depresses economic activity, and is unjust. Gorbachev, Yeltsin, and Putin encouraged corruption as an aspect of Muscovite rent-granting and did virtually nothing to combat insider malfeasance.
- The same pattern of collusion and neglect applied to poverty and democide.
- Crisis management since 1987 has been primarily a matter of empty rhetoric and abandonment.

PART IV

PUTIN

Putin Timeline

2000

March	Vladimir Putin wins election as president
May	Putin inauguration, reform of the system of governance, including federal prefects to run seven federal districts
June	Summit meeting with President Bill Clinton in Moscow
August	Sinking of the Kursk
December	Meets Fidel Castro in Cuba

2001

February	Putin restores rights of secret police to investigate anonymous denunciations, oligarch Boris Berezovsky gives up stake in ORT television, subsequently goes into exile and receives political asylum in Britain
March	Major cabinet shakeup
April	Private television station NTV taken over by the Kremlin, oligarch Vladimir Gusinsky in exile
June	Summit meeting with President George Bush in Slovenia
July	Friendship Treaty with China
September	Russian pledge to stand by the United States after 9/11

2002

February	BP makes landmark investment in Russian oil
October	Terrorists seize Dubrovka Theater in Moscow, many dead following rescue operation

2003

July	Arrest of Platon Lebedev, start of the Yukos affair

| October | Arrest of Mikhail Khodorkovsky, CEO of Yukos and richest man in Russia |
| December | Duma elections, landslide victory for the party of power |

2004

March	Putin reelected, Mikhail Fradkov prime minister
July	Murder of Paul Klebnikov
September	Beslan hostage crisis, governors no longer to be elected
December	Auction of Yuganskneftegas, main production unit of Yukos

2005

January	Presidential economic advisor Andrei Illarionov fired
February	Nationwide demonstrations against government's reform of social benefits
May	Khodorkovsky sentenced to nine years in prison

2006

January	Controversial law on nongovernmental organizations
March	State visit to China
July	G-8 summit meeting in St. Petersburg
October	Murder of journalist Anna Politkovskaya
November	Death of former KGB-operative Alexander Litvinenko in London, following polonium poisoning

2007

February	Putin delivers hard-line speech in Munich
April	Boris Yeltsin dies of heart attack, Berezovsky repeats threat to overthrow Putin by force
May	Putin compares United States to Third Reich, conflict with Estonia over war memorial
December	Duma election
	Putin endorses Dmitri Medvedev's 2008 presidential candidacy, Medvedev endorses Putin as his future Prime Minister

2008

| March | Presidential election |
| | Reconfiguration of Muscovite governance mechanism |

8

Authoritarian Reconsolidation

Box 8.1 Vladimir Putin

Vladimir Vladimirovich Putin, born October 7, 1952, in Leningrad (now St. Petersburg) served two terms as president of Russia (2000–08), where he engineered its Muscovite authoritarian reconsolidation. He became acting president on December 31, 1999. His mother was a factory worker, and his father was a sailor in the Soviet submarine corp. His paternal grandfather was Lenin's and Stalin's personal cook. Putin graduated from the International Branch of the Law Department of the Leningrad State University in 1975. He was a Communist Party member and KGB recruit, working in the Leningrad regional Directorate, where he first became acquainted with his future first deputy prime minister, Sergei Ivanov. From 1985 to 1990, he was stationed in Dresden, East Germany. He formally resigned from the KGB on August 20, 1991, during the abortive putsch against Gorbachev. In May 1990, Putin was appointed Mayor Sobchak's adviser on international affairs. He then moved to Moscow to assume the position of a deputy chief of the Presidential Property Management Department headed by Pavel Borodin in June 1996. On March 26, 1997, President Boris Yeltsin appointed him deputy chief of the presidential staff, and chief of the Main Control Directorate of the Presidential Property Management Department (until June 1998). During this period, Putin defended his Candidate of Science dissertation in economics on June 27, 1997, large portions of which William King and David Cleland claim were cribbed from their book on *Strategic Planning and Policy*. On July 25, 1998, Yeltsin appointed Putin head of the FSB, and on August 9, 1999, he became one of three first deputy prime ministers. Putin used both these positions to successfully launch his palace coup against Yeltsin, making him president on the eve of the new millennium.

Marxists insist that dialectical materialist forces, not men, govern history, even though the actions of Vladimir Lenin, Joseph Stalin, Mikhail Gorbachev, and Boris Yeltsin belie the claim. In the same sense, our thesis that it has been Muscovy, not westernization, that predominantly explains Russian political economic behavior during the Reform Communist, Market Communist, and postcommunist eras does not preclude the possibility that Russia's future in the decades ahead won't be profoundly shaped by the personalities of its presidents. Gorbachev and Yeltsin were destroyers, unperturbed by the mayhem they caused. Their versions of Muscovy mirrored their character, bombastic, imperious, nihilistic, and dysfunctional. But Vladimir Putin was a man of a very different stamp, closer to Stalin's avuncular public persona than the harebrained schemer Nikita Khrushchev, with profound consequences for the performance and potential of Market Muscovy.

Putin's guiding light since the mid-1990s was to establish himself securely as helmsman of a restored authoritarian martial police state and probe the possibilities. Helter-skelter wasn't his cup of tea. The unruliness of Market Communism and Yeltsin's Market Muscovy were an anathema that he set out to exorcise by borrowing heavily from Stalin's bag of tricks. He kept a low, officious profile but built an effective network of potential supporters by bestowing organizational favors and using entrapment operations (*kompromat*) to compromise rivals.[1] Like Stalin, he mastered the dark art of giving adversaries hope, while using the semblance of due process to teach others that he was implacable. As FSB head, Putin crushed both Boris Berezovsky, Russia's first billionaire, and the media mogul Vladimir Gusinsky. Upon ascending to the presidency, he moved swiftly to subordinate maverick governors to central authority by subjecting them to appointment instead of election.[2] He packed the bureaucracy with active and retired security personnel from the FSB and the

[1] Stephen Blank, "The 18th Brumaire of Vladimir Putin," in Uri Ra'anan (ed.), *Flawed Succession*, Rowman and Littlefield, Lanham, MD, 2006.

[2] Putin introduced Federal prefects appointed directly by the Kremlin as a device for constructing the power vertical (*vertikal vlasti*). His stated intention was to promote a two-party system, excluding third parties, but in the end, the tactic mostly strengthened autocracy. This initiative subsequently was reinforced by the substitution of appointed for elected regional governors, together with the curtailment of religious freedom and NGO activities. And in 2006, he began pressing for the appointment of mayors.

military,[3] altered election rules to effectively eliminate multiparty competition,[4] abused the justice system to bankrupt and imprison Mikhail Khodorkovsky,[5] quelled oligarchic dissidence, squelched the independent media,[6] criticized rival *siloviki*, and reasserted state control (often including ownership) over most of the resource sector and military industrial complex. He became master of rent-granting or, more colorfully, as Grand Prince Vasily III put the matter 500 years before: "All are slaves!"[7]

Again, like Stalin, he was chary of the military, relying more on the secret police than on other branches of the security services, postponing full-scale arms modernization until he had cowed the *genshtab* and appointed his FSB acolyte Sergei Ivanov to Defense Minister's post.[8] But as he gained his footing, supported by a steady economic recovery, an oil windfall, and some trickle-down benefits for a large strata of society, Putin's Muscovy became increasingly pugnacious. Official defense spending rose rapidly,[9] his arms modernization program became more ambitious, and Russia began aggressively fishing

---

[3] For "a detailed survey of the membership of Putin's elite, and the blurred line between liberals" and "*siloviki,*" see Olga Kryshtanovskaya and Stephen White, "Inside the Putin Court: a Research Note," *Europe-Asia Studies*, 57, 7(2005).

[4] Steven Rosefielde and Romana Hlouskova, "Why Russia Is Not a Democracy," *Comparative Strategy*, March 2007.

[5] Stalin too used the facade of due process to mock those he destroyed.

[6] Rosefielde and Hlouskova, "Why Russia Is Not a Democracy."

[7] Michael Cherniavsky, "Khan or Basileus: An Aspect of Russian Medieval Political Theory," in idem (ed.), *The Structure of Russian History: Interpretive Essays*, Random House, New York, p. 73.

[8] Steven Rosefielde, *Russia in the 21st Century: The Prodigal Superpower*, Cambridge University Press, 2005.

[9] Julian Cooper, "The Economics of Russian Defense Policy," paper presented at the conference on Russia under President Vladimir Putin: Towards the Second Term, European University Institute, Florence, April 22–23, 2004. Cooper, "Military Expenditure in the 2005 and 2006 Federal Budgets of the Russian Federation: A Research Note," January 2006; Cooper, "Military Expenditures in the Three-Year Federal Budget of the Russian Federation, 2008–10," Sipri, October 2007, www.sipri.org; Defense spending as a share of GDP using a 1991 base of 100 has risen from a low of 23 in 1998 to 41 in 2006 (budget). The recovery in arms procurement has proceeded after 1998 more dramatically at high double-digit rates. Andrey Frolov, "Russian Defence Procurement in 2007," Moscow Defense Brief, http:mdb.cast.ru/mdb/2–2007/item1/item2/; Defense Minister, "Russia Will Spend 50 Percent More on Weapons in 2006 Than 2005," *Johnson's Russia List*, Vol. 82, April 6, 2006. Steven Rosefielde, "Sputtering toward Fortress Russia," *Problems of Post-Communism*, 53, 5(September–October 2006), pp. 42–50.

in troubled waters from the EU through the Ukraine to Iran, much
as it had during the bad old days of the cold war's first phase. And
it seems there may be truth to persistent allegations, that like Stalin
he bore grudges and targeted enemies like Alexander Litvinenko for
extermination.[10]

The end result can be benignly characterized as a conservative
variant of Market Muscovy with mixed institutions or, more fanci-
fully, as Andrei Shleifer prefers, a normal middle-income system in
patchwork transition to democratic free enterprise.[11] But both are
misleading. The essential significance of Putin is that the cold war is
back, albeit milder (cold peace) than before, that it never really ended
but only shifted footing from Reform Communism to a potentially
more formidable Market Muscovy.

Accordingly, it is important to not just document that Putin's Market Muscovy differs from Yeltsin's because the status of the *siloviki* was
elevated, the state tightened control over its servitors, and the independence of oligarchs was curtailed but to gauge how these changes
altered the system's prospects. Can the superior performance of contemporary Market Muscovy last after recovery is complete?[12] Can
Russia catch up with the West? Can it keep pace with China? History
and systems theory provide clues.

The abrupt shift in Market Muscovy from pandemonium to order
followed a familiar script. Russia's history has been convulsive, oscil-
lating between tumultuous "times of trouble" and bursts of productive energy. In a system bereft of the rule of law, liberalization
fomented turmoil and discipline fostered growth, according to the

---

[10] Stalin infamously killed Leon Trotsky. Putin's alleged targets include Litvinenko,
Anna Politkovakaya, Viktor Yushchenko, Anatoly Chubais, and Yegor Gaidar.
Max Boot, "Don't Play Dead for Putin: What the West Can Do to Help Stop
the Authoritarian President from Garnering Too Much Influence in the World,"
Johnson's Russia List, Article 15, No. 276, December 6, 2006. Erich Folloth
et al., "Following the Litvinenko Trail," *Johnson Russia List*, Article 20, No. 276,
December 6, 2006.

[11] Andrei Shleifer, *A Normal Country: Russia after Communism*, Harvard University
Press, Cambridge, MA, 2005. Cf. Steven Rosefielde, "Russia" An Abnormal
Country," *The European Journal of Comparative Economics*, 2, 1(2005): 3–16.

[12] Although many indicators report that Russia fully reachieved the 1989 levels of
GDP and per capita national income in 2007, IMF data suggest that recovery
won't be complete until 2012. See Bengt-Goran Bergstrand, "Some 'WEO Data'
on Russian Economic Developments," *FOI*, October 16, 2007.

various nuanced economic, political, and sociological interpretations of Alexander Gerschenkron, Alexander Yanov, and Richard Hellie.[13] The first time of trouble (*smuta*) began with Fyodor II's death in 1598, ending with Mikhail Romanov's coronation as tsar in 1613, punctuated with a political and economic collapse reminiscent of Yeltsin's *catastroika*.[14] For a while, when Polish and Swedish armies were making deep inroads into the heartland, it seemed that Muscovy might be obliterated, but the Romanovs rallied against the odds, achieving a complete restoration of the status quo ante,[15] without conceding anything to democracy. Although the boyars who elected the tsar might have used the occasion to impose a Russian Magna Carta, they refrained from doing so, underscoring the tenacity of Muscovite culture.[16] This pattern was repeated thereafter under Peter the Great, Catherine the Great, Alexander II, Nicholas II, and Stalin. Muscovite discipline allowed bold autocrats to consolidate power, overcome adversity, and rouse the nation for great projects. The evidence from the Putin years suggests that Russia could be poised for

---

[13] Alexander Gershenkron, *Economic Backwardness in Historical Perspective,* Harvard University Press, Cambridge, MA, 1962. Alexander Yanov, *The Origins of Autocracy: Ivan the Terrible in Russian History*, University of California Press, Berkeley and Los Angeles, 1981; see especially his presentation of the *political spiral* (on pp. 59–65). Richard Hellie, "The Structure of Modern Russian History: Toward a Dynamic Model," *Russian History*, 4, 1(1977).

[14] It may be worth noting here that there were only three instances in Russian history when the nobility tried to impose restrictions on the autocracy. The first took place during the time of trouble, when a part of the nobility entered into negotiations with the King of Poland. The second consisted of repeated attempts by the Supreme Privy Council, in 1730 to restrain the incoming Empress Anna, and the third being the Decembrist uprising in 1825. On all three occasions, the service state displayed its durability, and the servitors fell back supinely.

[15] The central event of the period may be dated to 1606, when Vasilii Shuiskii's overthrow of the first false Dmitry caused the Muscovite state to literally collapse.

[16] The main proponent of this view is Richard Pipes (most clearly in *Russia under the Old Regime*, Charles Scribner's Sons, New York). The opposite view, challenging the notion of Russian backwardness, is held by Martin Malia who contends that Russia follows the West's past with a fifty-year lag. See Martin Malia, *Russia under Western Eyes: From the Bronze Horseman to the Lenin Mausoleum*, Belknap Press, Cambridge, MA, 1999. This claim conflates westernization with modernization. The first historian to explicitly introduce the concept of path dependence is Richard Hellie, "The Structure of Russian Imperial History," *History and Theory*, Theme issue 44, December 2005, p. 89. For a fuller and more systematic account, see Stefan Hedlund, *Russian Path Dependence*, Routledge, London, 2005.

yet another sustained advance but one less robust than before because of diminishing returns to technology transfer (modernization).[17]

The spadework for Putin was done by Yeltsin. When the FSB chief assumed the presidency in 2000, he was looking at a shipwreck.[18] In addition to hyperdepression and a rapidly declining population, the August 1998 financial crisis left the ruble devalued and the pipeline to foreign credit closed. A miracle was needed to restore discipline, build confidence, spur domestic production, and facilitate technology transfer-driven modernization. It didn't occur, but fate was partly obliging in the forms of the FSB, ruble devaluation, and subsequently an oil price bonanza. The first piece of good fortune connected with ruble devaluation was a terms of trade/inferior good effect.[19] The combination of lost wealth, diminished purchasing power, and sharply higher import prices compelled new Russians to switch from western consumer goods to their low-quality, Soviet-era substitutes,[20] stimulating domestic production and income growth. This together with expanded sales to the Commonwealth of Independent States occasioned by reduced export prices triggered a rebound that moved the economy toward recovery thereafter. Table 8.1 summarizes the trends. It shows the jolt from the terms of trade/inferior economic good effect peaking in 2000, Putin's inaugural year as president, followed by an oscillatory slowdown in GDP, industrial, and investment growth, in

[17]   The Bank of Finland and the OECD are optimistic about GDP growth until 2010, See www.bof.fi/BOFIT, and OECD Economic Surveys, *Russian Federation 2006*, Paris, 2006.

[18]   Andrew Meier, *Black Earth: A Journey through Russia after the Fall,* HarperCollins, London, 2003.

[19]   The increased demand for import substitutes that followed the August 1998 devaluation is characterized here as a terms of trade/inferior good effect because it reflected a sharp fall in wealth and purchasing power as much as a change in the relative price of importables. Even if there had been no change in importable prices, demand for domestic goods probably would have risen because consumers no longer could afford superior western products.

[20]   By the time of the August crash, the Russian ruble had become grossly overvalued. Once the government decided to open the *band* of the ruble corridor, a sharp devaluation was bound to follow. Over the period August–December 1998, the nominal rate of the ruble fell from 6.5 to 20.6 to the dollar. Over 1999, it slid further to 27.0, but then it stabilized, remaining below 30 until the end of 2001 and below 32 throughout 2002. In the course of 2003, it actually began to appreciate, rising to close to 30 by the end of the summer. Measured in real terms appreciation began even earlier, and by the end of 2005, the entire effect of the devaluation had been wiped out.

Table 8.1. *Russian economic growth 1998–2005 (percent per annum)*

	1998	1999	2000	2001	2002	2003	2004	2005
GDP	−5.3	6.4	10.0	5.0	4.3	7.3	7.2	6.4
Industry	−5.2	11.0	11.9	4.9	3.7	8.9	8.3	4.0
Investment	−12.0	5.3	17.4	8.7	2.6	15.0	10.0	12.0

Source: CBR, official statistics.

an environment where Russian industrial output remained well below the Soviet level.

This spurt, buttressed by a reconsolidation of Muscovite state power, reining in Yeltsin's mayhem, and restoring a semblance of commercial order, flagged conspicuously in 2001 and 2002 but soon was reinvigorated by spiraling natural resource prices, and a 57 percent increase in oil output from 6 to 9.4 million bpd, temporarily making Russia the world's leading petro producer. The wealth effect swelled the state treasury and the pockets of the new Russians, sparking a spending spree for luxury imports, domestic services, and selected investment durables. Russia's highways especially in the Moscow region became as congested as Bangkok's by 2007, and residential construction mushroomed. Civilian industrial development, however, seems to be waning, even before the petroleum price spiral eventually peaks, and bursts. The culprit here is often said to be the Dutch disease,[21] an economic malaise caused by the overvaluation of petroleum-rich national currencies. High ruble prices impair the competitiveness of Russia's manufactured exports and encourage overconsumption of imports. But from a larger systemic perspective, the Dutch disease merely compounds the deadening effect of anticompetitive markets, indulgent rent-granting, rampant moral hazard, corruption, state ownership, bureaucratic meddling, government misregulation, and the autarkic tendency, especially in strategic industries sometimes called *Fortress Russia*.[22] As George Kleiner, deputy director of TsEMI put it, Russia's economy is an archipelago with a few islands of natural

[21] Shinichiro Tabata, "The Great Russian Depression of the 1990s: Observations on Causes and Implications," *Post-Soviet Geography and Economics*, 21, 6(2000). Yelena Korop, "Skyrocketing Incomes Threaten Russian Economic Stability," *Johnson's Russia List*, Article 8, No. 276, December 6, 2006.

[22] Mikhail Yuriev, "Krepost' Rossiia kontseptsiia dlia Prezidenta," (Fortress Russia: Strategic Concept for President Putin), *Novaya gazeta*, No. 17, March 15, 2004,

resource–financed prosperity and a multitude of impoverished industrial and agrarian islets, some partially submerged separated by a vast
sea without bridges or other adequate connections.[23] An oil bubble
never sparked sustained superior growth in the past and should not to
do so now.

Some other compensation principle is required to mitigate the
chilling effect of Muscovite inefficiency in any of its various mani-
festations from Reform Communism to Market Muscovy. The preferred solution for Peter the Great, Stalin, and his successors until
1987 was structural militarization, where the Kremlin concentrated
its energies on mass producing weapons in ever greater volumes. This
strategy not only delivered the goods Moscow wanted but did so
self-sufficiently. Another alternative, judging from the Chinese experience under Deng Xiaoping, might be to rely on massive direct foreign investment and technology transfer as a platform for export-led
development and sustained factor productivity growth.[24] No technical
barriers prevent Russia from adopting either strategem or combining
them. Of course, the Kremlin can continue trying to harden property rights and strengthen competition within the limits imposed by
Muscovite privilege. But a clear preference for military modernization remains evident. Sergei Ivanov, former minister of defense for
example announced in June 2006 that Russia would rapidly expand
military industrial production to accelerate economic development.[25]
The main question for the intermediate term seems to be whether
Moscow is willing to divert sufficient resources from the stagnant and
slow-growing components of the civilian sector to match the Soviet
Union's weapons-intensive growth standard and military burden.

http://2004.novayagazeta-ru/nomer/2004/17n7n17n-w4.shtme. Steven Rosefielde, "Russia 2084: The Treadmill of Muscovite Radical Reform," BOFIT
Working Paper, Helsinki, 2005. Aslund Anders Aslund, "Suffering from Oil's
Curse a Matter of Choice," *Johnson's Russia List*, Article 22, No. 276, December
6, 2006.

23 George Kleiner, personal interview, May 16, 2006.
24 Steven Rosefielde, "The Illusion of Westernization in Russia and China," *Comparative Economic Studies*, 49, 2007, pp. 495–513.
25 "Ivanov Says Defense Sector to Become Locomotive of the Economy," ITAR-
TASS, June 14, 2006. "Defense firms will be manufacturing up to 70 percent
of civilian industrial products by the year 2015." Already it accounts for "more
than 70 percent of all science-intensive products made in Russia and more than
half of all research personnel."

Gravity favors a reintensification of structural militarization. While there are always weighty reasons for civilian-intensive growth,[26] the marginal cost of diverting funds to defense is likely to strike future leaders as low compared with the tangible benefit of restoring Russian superpower. There won't be any noticeable penalty for choosing military-led development if discipline can be restored within the military industrial complex[27] because reactivated idle defense industrial capacity will provide high returns, bolstering aggregate economic performance.

The rub, however, as the Soviet experience amply testifies, is that piling on weapons doesn't translate into economic superpower and could be little more than flagrant waste if negated by western and Chinese countermeasures. After the intoxicating effects of the petro bubble pass, Moscow is apt to discover once again that Russia is a squalid superpower capable of being a destructive force, with few tangible material rewards.[28] Democratic free enterprise can provide guns and butter, but Muscovite markets have yet to prove they can do so too. It therefore seems reasonable to surmise that whatever progress is made beneath the statistical fluff in the next few years won't be enough to prevent Russia from sliding further behind the West and the awakening giants in Asia. If Muscovy is to hold its own, it will have to open its economy to direct foreign investment and resist overvaluing its managed currency as Beijing has done or find some other device to offset self-inflicted wounds.

---

[26] Vitaly Shlykov, "Nazad v budushchee, ili Ekonomicheskie uroki kholodnoi voiny," *Rossiia v Global'noe Politike*, 4, 2(March–April 2006): 26–40; Shlykov, "Nevidimaia Mobilizatsii," *Forbes*, No. 3, March 2006, pp. 1–5; Shlykov, "Globalizatsiia voennoi promyshlennosti-imperativ XXI veka," *Otechestvennye zapiski*, No. 5, 2005, pp. 98–115.

[27] The Kremlin's cosmetic enhancement of civilian consumption will conceal the full cost of resource diversion to defense. G. L. Khanin, *Dinamika ekonomicheskovo razvitiya*, Nauka, Novosibirsk, 1991. Khanin, "Ekonomicheskoe razivite Rossii za 1999–2004 gody: predvaritel'naia alternativnaia otsenka sostoiania rossiiskoi ekonomiki i ee analiz," paper presented at the VI World Congress of the International Council for Central and East European Studies, "Europe-Our Common Home?" Berlin, Germany, July 25–30, 2005. Khanin, "Economic Growth and the Mobilization Model," in Michael Ellman (ed.), *Russia's Oil and Natural Gas: Bonanza or Curse?*" Anthem Press, London, 2006, chapter 7.

[28] Steven Rosefielde, "Structural Militarization, War Mobilization Reserves and Russia's Failed Transition," submitted to *Rossiia v Global'noi Politike*, June 2006.

This isn't going to be easy. The Russian impulse is to price dis-
criminate and gouge. The ruble absent the oil bubble is extremely
overvalued,[29] making Russia a high-cost production platform despite
rampant exploitation of Central Asian migrant workers.[30] Foreigners
have no incentive to invest in Russian industrial exportables, even
in new turnkey facilities because factor costs are too high. Russia's
bloated ruble reduces investment returns on its import substitutes.
Likewise, Muscovite insiders aren't thrilled with profit sharing. They
welcome foreign direct investment in high-risk, peripheral operations
but consider lucrative undertakings exclusively theirs.

None of this might matter if domestic entrepreneurs, especially
those flush with petroleum riches, invested heavily in industrial non-
tradeables or were especially productive. Anticompetitiveness, however, is a defining characteristic of lucrative Muscovite markets. Kremlin insiders no more desire to serve as engines of rapid development
than to permit foreigners to do it for them if their privileges are jeopar-
dized, an attitude that precludes effectively using foreign direct investment as a vehicle for technology transfer and sustained modernization.

Ironically, this brings the Kremlin back to its Soviet roots. If domestic entrepreneurs won't, and outsiders can't, then in hoary Muscovite
tradition it behooves the state to fill the civilian industrial gap. This
can be accomplished through public works projects, pipelines, roads,
and other construction of the sort Putin recently trumpeted or by
central planning along the lines favored by the Japan Planning Agency
and MITI after World War II. It is too soon to judge whether the
Kremlin will be content with Putin-type Market Muscovy that under-
performs its neighbors and the West or whether it will try to narrow
the gap supplementing revived structural militarization with centrally
planned public works, industrial subsidies, or even Chinese-style technology transfer. These are Russia's chief alternatives as long as Muscovy
persists.

The rest is macroeconomic policy jockeying, against a background
of tweaked statistics. The issues are substantive involving competitiveness, property rights, rule of law, income and wealth disparities,

[29] Russian natural resources are traded in dollars at world prices. The value of ruble-
traded goods therefore depends mostly on Russia's industrial export capacity,
which is slight (excluding weapons). If the exchange rates were set based on the
Kremlin's low-quality industrial exportables, the ruble would be weak.
[30] "Putin Says up to 15 Million Illegal Migrants in Russia," *Johnson's Russia List*,
Article 20, No. 260, November 17, 2006.

creditworthiness, debt management, international capital flows, exchange rates, price stability, employment, technology, and growth, but their resolution won't cleanse Market Muscovy's defects.

Officially, the Putin years witnessed a succession of economic triumphs. Markets are more efficient, property rights more secure, privatization increased in many sectors, output expanded, inflation was tamed (but is reemerging), unemployment fell, poverty diminished, and international indebtedness became a faded memory, all in stark contrast to the Yeltsin era.

The foreign debt issue underscores how some real improvements were achieved. Toward the end of 2000, Russian premier Mikhail Kasyanov arrived in Germany reiterating Yeltsin's position that new Russian debt assumed after 1991 would be fully serviced, while Soviet obligations would be rolled over. German chancellor Gerhard Schroeder, however, finally had enough. Noting Russia's post-1998 economic momentum, he warned that unless its $42 billion debt to the Paris Club were pared, he would do everything in his power to exclude Russian participation in prestigious western institutions. The message apparently was taken to heart. Since then, the Kremlin has punctiliously serviced its debt, including introducing a stabilization fund in case oil prices fall. The fund now stands at $157 billion,[31] and the Russian Central Bank has accumulated $474 billion in foreign reserves.[32] The International Monetary Fund was paid off in full, and the Paris Club received $10 billion in early repayment. Where Russia's total external debt stood at $130.8 billion in 1999, by September 2007, it had declined to $39.6 billion.

This accomplishment was matched domestically. The petro windfall was used to restore fiscal integrity. The federal budget has been in the black since 2000 and arrears reduced. Through Putin's first term, both wages and pensions were increasingly paid on time and in full, bolstering the president's impressive public approval ratings. Fiscal responsibility also had a beneficial effect on reducing Russia's "virtual economy."[33]

---

[31] Bank of Finland, *BOFIT Russia Statistics,* www.bof.fi/bofit, December 2007. The figures are end year 2007.

[32] Barry Ickes, "Russia's Economy in 2007," November 2007, unpublished manuscript.

[33] Clifford Gaddy and Barry Ickes, "Russia's Virtual Economy," *Foreign Affairs,* 77, 5(1998): 52–67. Gaddy and Ickes, *Russia's Virtual Economy,* Brookings Institution Press, Washington, DC, 2002.

As the economy was gradually remonetized, Russian enterprises substituted money settlements for barter, restoring interest rates as a tool of macroeconomic management. In 2005, Soviet-era in-kind social benefits were transformed into cash payments. As a consequence, most business, government, and private transactions in Russia today are consummated with money or credit, for the first time in nearly three quarters of a century.

There is no gainsaying these fiscal and monetary policy successes. Nor is there any reason to doubt that many business and government institutions are becoming more professional. The Russian economy's footing is sounder than before, and taken together with the ongoing recovery from seventeen years of hyperdepression, post-Yeltsin welfare is indisputably better, even though many still insist that life was superior under communism. The gains however aren't attributable wholly to Putin's autocratic reconsolidation. Without the petro bubble, Russia probably would still be mired in hyperdepression. Putin deserves credit within the Muscovite paradigm for stronger social discipline, especially the containment of helter-skelter plunder. However, the good times for the few are unlikely to portend future prosperity for the many. The Kremlin is retreating from democracy, rule of law, and free enterprise, and the consequences should not be good.[34]

Russia today as Putin once admitted remains a third world country with modest per capita income and extreme inequality. It is an authoritarian martial police state with a narrow economic base, dependent on raw material extraction, particularly petroleum, which accounts for 25–33 percent of GDP, depending on whether fuel transport is included. When mineral prices spike, times are better, and when they plunge, times are worse. More importantly, the Kremlin has never been able to widen the economic base to the global competitive standard with its Muscovite mechanism, so that Russia's tomorrows

---

[34] "Putin's Drive to Restore Russian Power a Source of Concern: Gates," *Johnson's Russia List*, Article 5, No. 276, December 6, 2006; "Nominee Gates Speaks in Testimony of U.S. Warnings about Russian Unreliability," *Johnson's Russia List*, Article 6, No. 276, December 6, 2006. "Unclassified Statement for the Record, Threat Assessment," Senate Select Committee on Intelligence, Director of National Intelligence, John Negroponte, January 11, 2007, *Johnson's Russia List*, Article 35, No. 8, January 12, 2007. Lt. General Michael Maples (Director of the Defense Intelligence Agency) "Current and Projected National Security Threats to the United States," testimony to the Senate Select Committee on Intelligence, January 11, 2007, *Johnson's Russia List*, Article 36, No. 8, January 12, 2007.

always remain well behind the rest of the pack. Although technological progress and diffusion eventually raise most boats, Muscovy's core remains the same. Russia is a third world country not because it shares a common system with other poor nations. It is backward because the Muscovite system impedes and probably precludes catch-up to the West's high frontier. This is a lesson Russians and westerners alike are reluctant to learn. After all is said and done, Putin-type Muscovy is only a better authoritarian mousetrap than Yeltsin's, Stalin's, and Lenin's. As long as it endures, Russia's system won't have the virtues of American democratic free enterprise or European Union social democracy. Despite centuries of wrestling with westernization, the Kremlin has only mastered the West's rhetoric, not its substance. It knows how to falsify, to edit, and to miscompile statistics but shouldn't be able to raise living standards to the West's moving average, nor achieve social justice, empowerment, and freedom. This is the deep reality hidden behind the smoke and mirrors of contemporary Kremlin self-congratulation. A disciplined rent-granting authoritarian martial police state, combining state ownership with contingent private property rights, planning, bureaucracy, oligarchy, and anticompetitive markets can achieve lagged modernization and military superpower, if it doesn't succumb to corruption but is ill suited to fostering national well-being in both absolute and relative senses.[35]

[35] Another way to conceptualize the inefficiency of Putin's Market Muscovy is to examine the sources of its intrinsic dysfunction. The absence of the rule of contract law, combined with patchwork authoritarian discipline, invites fraud, fast money, and speculation. Public productive activities, rent-seeking, and individual transactions are all unusually prone to abuse, including false claims for producing value added. The game rewards the unscrupulous and makes honest business seem a pastime for fools. Winners are conditioned to scheme and are themselves easily scammed because they are preoccupied with making fast money, not investing in the long-term satisfaction their customers. This creates a herd mentality for speculation in real estate, construction, and other tangibles, as well as periodic capital flight that suppresses industrial modernization and global economic integration. The persistent calls for *Fortress Russia*, insularity and self-sufficiency respond to the perceived dysfunction without recognizing that systemic autarky is just another trap as students of North Korea can readily attest. The heart of the matter is Muscovy's rejection of Adam Smith's ethically disciplined invisible hand. Disequilibria in democratic free enterprise are automatically resolved by profit-seeking (Marshallian quantity adjustment mechanism) and open competition (Walrasian price adjustment mechanism). They keep the economy moving along a Pareto optimal path. Muscovite systems of all varieties, lacking the Smithian invisible hand, find themselves perpetually in a wilderness of profligacy and waste. They may stumble from one false path to another but can

- Vladimir Putin was shrewder, more farsighted, methodical, and ruthless than Yeltsin and Gorbachev.
- He reconsolidated Muscovy by reinvigorating the power vertical. He increased the size and broadened the power of the secret police, as well as posting *siloviki* throughout the state bureaucracy, including state-owned enterprises. He suppressed the independent media and encouraged Hitleresque youth movements to press his policies and stifle dissent. He did not shun terror tactics, confiscating the wealth of unruly oligarchs and perhaps assassinating Litvinenko and other oppositionists. And he abolished elected federal governors, contemplated doing the same for mayors, and bent electoral rules to suit himself.
- Putin was chary of the military, relying more on the FSB.
- Putin in Muscovite fashion was cautious and ingratiating when weak and combative when strong, camouflaging his intentions by always sending mixed signals.
- His authoritarian reconsolidation altered the growth potential of the Muscovite model but didn't raise it to the level of democratic free enterprise.
- The petro bubble enhanced the crown's reempowerment, giving Putin an opportunity to emulate Peter the Great, Catherine the Great, Alexander II, and Stalin.
- It may have permitted Russia to recover its prior achieved GDP level by 2007, and could support a sustained growth spurt, but has made the nation vulnerable to crisis when the bubble bursts.
- A growth spurt in contemporary Muscovy could be sustained by rearmament or by emulating China's foreign investment-driven development strategy, but gravity, an overvalued ruble, and reluctance to share lucrative investment opportunities with foreigners favor the first option.
- A liberal transition to democratic free enterprise is a remote possibility.
- Putin-type Market Muscovy is a disciplined, rent-granting, authoritarian martial police state, combining state ownership with contingent private property rights, planning, bureaucracy, oligarchy, and

neither find the right way, nor stay the course if they did. This is the underlying reason the Dutch disease and the resource curses are subsidiary. They only reflect a transitory manifestation of Muscovy's deep pathology. During Soviet times, there was a mania for accumulating strategic reserves and precycling; today it's construction and capital flight, tomorrow perhaps *Fortress Russia*.

anticompetitive markets capable of achieving lagged modernization and military superpower but not superior social welfare.

- It is better than Gorbachev's and Yeltsin's Muscovys to the extent it restored economic order, created a stable platform for modernization, and enhanced Russian security.
- It is worse insofar as it has weakened aspirations for democracy, free enterprise, social justice, and geopolitical self-restraint.

9

Heritage of Neglect

Few in the West today claim that Russia has successfully westernized, or is on the brink of doing so, despite occasional summons to rekindle the dream of 1991. Experts likewise are no longer optimistic that Muscovite modernization will allow the federation to overtake the developed West, as some did during the Soviet era, even though Russia's economic minister predicts that the federation will have the globe's fifth largest GDP (gross domestic product) by 2020.[1] This skepticism reflects the reality of failed transition, the conviction that democratic free enterprise may be best, and more subtly a recognition that the deficiencies of post–Soviet Muscovy could be cumulative.

The risks arising from Russia's heritage of neglect are most apparent in its ailing human capital. The acumen, skill, knowledge, proficiency, adaptability, cooperativeness, longevity and health of its labor force and leadership after decades of Soviet and postcommunist abuse seem impaired, depressing productivity and the quality of life. Human capital productivity deteriorated markedly under Boris Yeltsin, with only a modest rebound thereafter. The federation's educational and health care systems are in shambles, the environment continues to fester, and mortality rates are rising. Moscow has the power to effectuate constructive change but may lack the resolve.

Writing in 2005, the American demographer Nicholas Eberstadt found reason to speak of Russia as *The Sick Man of Europe*, contending that the country was in "the grip of a steadily tightening mesh

---

[1] According to Moscow Russia's GDP will be fifth behind China, America, India, and Japan. The EU isn't recognized as a unitary state. "Russia May Become the World's Fifth Largest Economy by 2020," *Johnson's Russia List*, Vol. 262, Article 3, December 24, 2007.

of serious demographic problems, for which the term 'crisis' is no overstatement."[2] He found that this "crisis is altering the realm of the possible for the country and its people – continuously, directly and adversely."[3] And, even worse, "these constraints stand only to worsen over the years immediately ahead."[4] "Russia is now at the brink of a steep population decline – peacetime hemorrhage framed by a collapse of the birth rate and a catastrophic surge in the death rate."[5]

The onset of this crisis commenced roughly with the collapse of the Soviet Union. At the beginning of 1992, when Boris Yeltsin began his rule the country's population was estimated at 148.7 million. By 2007, the corresponding figure fell to 142 million. In the intervening fifteen years, the population had fallen by almost 7 million people, or 5 percent.

At first sight, these numbers may not appear worrisome. Population declines have beset all the republics of the former Soviet Union, several European Union member states, and are impending in parts of the Asia Pacific region.[6] Closer inspection of the Russian case, however, reveals disturbing patterns. For example, while there are currently 103 Italian deaths for every 100 live births, the worst EU case, the corresponding figure for Russia is 160 deaths per hundred births. The federation is not only facing declining fertility as in the EU but is suffering from exploding mortality, causing demographic shock.

Eberstadt notes that in a society with the type of survival patterns displayed by present-day Russia simple replacement will require women to bear 2.33 children per lifetime on average. In the late Soviet era, from the 1960s until the mid-1980s, that number fluctuated

2   Nicholas Eberstadt, "Russia: The Sick Man of Europe," *The Public Interest*, Winter 2005, p. 1. Nicholas Eberstadt, "The Health Crisis in the USSR," *International Journal of Epidemiology*, December 4, 2006.

3   Eberstadt, Russia, p. 1.

4   Ibid., p. 2. Cf. Mark Field and Judyth Twigg, *Russia's Torn Safety Nets: Health and Social Welfare during the Transition*, St. Martin's Press, New York, 2000.

5   Eberstadt, "Russia," p. 5.

6   Fertility rates, for example, have declined in South Korea from 4.53 in 1970 to 1.22 in 2005, well below the replacement rate of 2.2. The South Korean government has responded aggressively by considering the introduction of a "low fertility tax" aimed at raising funds to assist households with more than two children, expanding childbirth coverage, child care and education subsidies to low-income families. Yoo Soh-jung and Ko Kyoung-tae, "Korea May Introduce Tax to Cope with Low Birthrate, *The Korean Herald*, reprinted in *Asia News Network*, October 17, 2005. Putin introduced Russia's own birth bounty in January 2007.

around two. Then it plummeted, dropping from 2.19 in 1986–87 to 1.17 in 1999. There was a resurgence in the birth rate under Vladimir Putin, but this may merely be a blip because women are becoming increasingly reluctant to become mothers,[7] and sexually transmitted disease combined with high abortion rates are causing increased clinical infertility.

The mortality trend is even more alarming. From the early 1960s to 2003, life expectancy at birth fell by five years for males and close to three years for females. Age-standardized mortality rates rose in the same period by 15 percent for females and 40 percent for males. Female life expectancy today is seventy-two to seventy-three years, while the statistic for men hovers around fifty-eight to fifty-nine, causing an acute gender imbalance aggravated by the fact that male mortality is concentrated in the working-age population. Since 1970 every female cohort between twenty and fifty-eight experienced at least a 30 percent increase in mortality, whereas mortality for men between forty and fifty-nine increased approximately 60 percent, without evoking an adequate government response. The Soviets preferred to hush up matters by severely curtailing the flow of demographic data, rather than adopting appropriate correctives.[8]

Although data from the 1959 and 1970 censuses were promptly published within four years, respectively, in sixteen and seven volumes, journals, and newspapers only published snippets after the census of 1979. A fuller account finally appeared in 1985 but was expurgated and reduced in length to a single volume. One reason for the growing secrecy may have been that the national composition of the USSR was changing detrimentally against the Slavs. Although overall Soviet population growth 1970–79 was about 0.9 percent annually, Russians grew by 0.7 percent and Ukrainians by merely 0.4 percent compared with the Central Asian figure of 2.5 percent. The trend was played out against the background of increasing efforts at russification, and a hardening attitude toward party leaders accused of nationalistic deviations. Given the sensitivity of the nationalities questions, Zvi Gitelman found it "likely that empirical research on nationality questions

---

[7] Lisa Vronskaya, "Motherhood Sliding off Agenda for Russia's Women," *Johnson's Russia List*, Vol. 9263, Article 3, October 10, 2005.

[8] Murray Feshbach, "Between the Lines of the 1979 Soviet Census," *Problems of Communism*, 31, 1(1982); Feshbach, "Population and Labor Forces," in Abram Bergson and Herbert Levine, eds., *The Soviet Economy: Towards the Year 2000*, Allen & Unwin, London, 1983.

is deliberately limited, that the results of studies are carefully screened before publication, and that even certain methods cannot be used by the researchers."[9]

Censors were also motivated by a desire to conceal bad news like falling life expectancy and rising infant mortality. In the first half of the 1980s, the flow of official data dried up and what was made available had little value. With the onset of *glasnost* under Mikhail Gorbachev, this all changed. Insiders and outsiders alike began to seriously consider matters previously taboo.

During the first years of his tenure, *openness (otkritnost)* went hand and hand with social improvements. Most notably, there was a drop in mortality and a rise in life expectancy, partly attributable to the short-term effects of Gorbachev's antialcohol campaign, and partly to a renewed sense of national optimism. But the good times didn't last. Once it became clear that Gorbachev's rule wasn't going to revitalize the system and might hasten its demise, things quickly went from bad to worse.

The 1990s witnessed a substantial deterioration in health standards wrought by shock therapy and other misguided policies.[10] The sky-rocketing mortality was particularly dramatic, and sparked a lively debate, even though some aspects of the *population meltdown* were masked by the net immigration of ethnic Russians from the *near abroad*.[11] Stripped of this distortion, it was clear that while the natural rate of population growth had been 968,000 as late as 1987, it plummeted to negative 900,000 just twelve years latter when Yeltsin exited the Kremlin. The annual rate of population decline on average during this interval was 0.6 percent, and deteriorated thereafter under Putin.

There are many complementary explanations for the abrupt acceleration of negative trends. One is the mounting cumulative effect of environmental degradation affecting the quality of air, water, and

---

[9]   Zvi Gitelman, "Are Nations Emerging in the USSSR?" *Problems of Communism*, 32, 5 (1983). Some observers were also beginning to warn that the nationalities question might actually tear the Soviet Union apart, e.g., Helen Carrère d'Encausse, *Decline of an Empire: The Soviet Socialist Republics in Revolt*, Harper & Row, New York, 1981; and Alexander Motyl, *Will the Non-Russians Rebel? State, Ethnicity and Stability in the USSR*, Cornell University Press, Ithaca, NY, 1987, p. 10.

[10] Michael Ellman, "The Increase in Death and Disease Under 'Katastroika,'" *Cambridge Journal of Economics*, 18, 4(1994).

[11] Murray Feshbach, "Russia's Population Meltdown," *Wilson Quarterly*, 25, 1 (2001).

land. Another was intensifying poverty and social stress, and perhaps the most worrisome from a long-term perspective the spread of epidemic disease, ranging from diphtheria to STD, MDRTB, and HIV/AIDS. The ecological crisis emerged first, but attracted serious political attention slowly.

Boris Komarov, a Soviet author published *Unichtozhenie prirody* (*The Destruction of Nature*) in the West in 1978 but his warnings were brushed aside.[12] According to Soviet ideology, ecological problems were a capitalist phenomenon and could not exist under central planning. As specious as this claim was, many western observers sympathized enough to reject allegations of ecocide as anti-Soviet agitation, until Chernobyl compelled them to face reality.

Although Gorbachev did try at first to cover up, he quickly reversed field when the magnitude of the disaster became apparent. The victims were the principle benefactor but society wasn't placated. Chernobyl became a rallying cry for remedying a wide range of grievances,[13] driven by pent-up discontent. Those aggrieved not only flocked to environmental groups that provided tolerated channels for open protest, they began to engage in nationalist agitation on many issues, including Memorial's revelations of the full extent of the crimes of Stalin's past, and demands for atonement.

There was one group, however, that remained firmly committed to the environmental cause. Sergei Zalygin, editor of *Novyi Mir*, and something of a grand old man of the Soviet cultural intelligentsia, together with many others embarked on a campaign warning of dire consequences if drastic measures weren't taken immediately.

In January 1988, the Central Committee of the Communist Party responded by issuing a decree on environmental *perestroika*, establishing a special commission for the protection of nature, the *Goskompriroda*.[14]

---

[12] Boris Komarov, *Unichtozhenie prirody*, Possev-Verlag, Frankfurt/Main, 1978. Komarov subsequently emigrated to Israel, assumed the name Zeev Wolfson, and as editor of *Environmental Policy Review* became a driving force in the struggle to find out the truth about the degradation of nature in the Soviet Union.

[13] The rapidly emerging environmental movement focused on a variety of causes. In Armenia and Lithuania, it was nuclear power stations. In Estonia, concern was mobilized over Soviet plans for a massive mining of phosphorite to produce mineral fertilizer. In Hungary, a movement was created to block plans for the construction of a hydroelectric dam on the Danube.

[14] *Pravda*, January 17, 1988.

It commissioned two major reports on the state of nature in the first two years, an effort supplemented by *Goskomstat*.[15]

The picture portrayed in these reports was stunning. Bewildered Soviet citizens awoke to a reality marred by *ecological disaster zones*, causing them to ponder how this could be possible. Should they really believe that the nickel smelters in the Siberian city of Norilsk produced more sulfur dioxide emissions than the whole of Italy's industry?[16]

As investigations proceeded, it became evident that the answer was yes; that Norilsk, although extreme in its class, epitomized the consequence of a horrendous economic system that had chosen to wage war against nature. A generation that had accepted Stalin's dictums such as "Nature has committed certain mistakes, which must be corrected," and "We cannot wait for favors from nature; our task is to take from her," discovered that their children had to pay the piper.

The air pollution situation was perhaps the most egregious. Soviet artists had long romanticized massive smokestacks and billowing fumes as icons of socialist progress. Now the population was awakened to the fact that Soviet-style progress had been harmful to their health, not just at the margin but to a colossal extent. Fifty million people in one hundred three cities were informed in 1988 that the air pollutants they breathed regularly exceeded health standards by a factor of at least ten. In sixteen cities, the figures exceeded the norms by fifty times or more. And additional information released in 1989 showed that "thirty-two million people in seventy-three cities were exposed to an unfortunate combination of emissions that created a pollutant *bouquet* especially dangerous for living."[17]

[15] *Sostoyanie priorodnoi sredy v SSSR v 1988g.* Moscow: Goskompriroda, *1988, Sostayanie prirodnoi sredy i prirodookhrannaya deyatelnost v SSSR v 1989 g.*, Moscow: Goskompriroda, 1989, Goskomstat SSSR, *Okhrana okruzhayuschchei sredy i ratsionalnoe ispolsovanie prirodnykh resursov v SSSR*, Finansy i statistika, Moscow, 1989.

[16] D. J. Peterson, *Troubled Lands: The Legacy of Soviet Environmental Destruction*, Westview Press, Boulder, CO, 1993, p. 13.

[17] Ibid., p. 38. See also Brenton M. Barr and Kathleen E. Braden, *The Disappearing Russian Forest: A Dilemma in Soviet Resource Management*, Rowman & Littlefield, 1998. Murray Feshbach, *Ecological Disaster: Cleaning up the Hidden Legacy of the Soviet Regime*, Twentieth Century Fund Project, New York, 1995; Thane Gustafson, *Reform in Soviet Politics: Lessons of Recent Policies on Land and Water*, Cambridge University Press, Cambridge, 1981; Philip R. Pryde, *Environmental Management in the Soviet Union*, Cambridge University Press, New York, 1991, Charles E. Ziegler, *Environmental Policy in the USSR*, Frances Pinter, London, 1987.

The same story was repeated in soil and water resources. Much of the fertile lands in the south had been literally saturated with agrochemicals ranging from ground water table poisoning pesticides such as DDT and hexachlorane (formally prohibited) to mineral fertilizers causing serious damage to the marine environment in the Black Sea. Raw sewage and industrial waste being fed into the mighty Volga River also was responsible for the near extinction of fisheries in the Caspian Sea.

In 1992, the first year of Russia's *transition*, Murray Feshbach and Albert Friendly summed up the legacy of Soviet ecological devastation in a book ominously titled *Ecocide in the USSR: Health and Nature under Siege*. The opening line prefigures the shape of things to come: "When historians finally conduct an autopsy on the Soviet Union and Soviet Communism, they may reach the verdict of death by ecocide."[18]

The precise medical fallout remained difficult to judge. There were no precise epidemiological and toxicological analogues to Soviet-style ecocide. Even if demographic data did not show any immediate links, observers wisely remained wary of delayed effects in future generations, especially so since plentiful regional data on birth defects and mental retardation sounded alarm bells.

Causality was clouded further by serious alcohol and tobacco abuse.[19] Heavy smoking combined with grave atmospheric pollution, compounded by hard drinking surely were detrimental to the nation's health, but efforts at identifying their relative importance proved inconclusive. All that can be said with certainty is that Mikhail Gorbachev's campaign against alcohol abuse appears to have temporarily lowered male mortality rates, and its subsequent reversal restored the status quo ante under Yeltsin, and worsened it during Putin's rule.

Had the Soviet Union endured, enough time would have elapsed by now to reliably quantify the causal links between the environment, smoking and alcohol abuse on one hand, and the country's health on the other. The *catastroika* triggered by the destructive revenue misappropriation, rent-seeking and asset-grabbing of the Yeltsin years blurred causality further by adding income inequality,[20] poverty and torn safety nets to the factors undermining public health.

---

[18] Murray Feshbach and Albert Friendly, Jr., *Ecocide in the USSR: Health and Nature under Siege*, Basic Books, New York, 1992, p. 1.

[19] See further Stephen White, *Russia Goes Dry: Alcohol, State and Society*, Cambridge University Press, Cambridge, 1996.

[20] Current numbers on matters like poverty and income distribution are presented by Goskomstat in its monthly publication *Sotsialno-ekonomicheskoe polozhenie*

Again according to shaky official data, from 1993 to 1995, the poorest 20 percent of the population accounted for less than 6 percent of total incomes, while the richest 20 percent received well over 40 percent. Between 1993 and 1994 alone, the span between the top and bottom 10 percent increased from 11.2 to 15.1 times. One attempt to calculate Russian Gini-coefficients, which is a standard way of measuring income inequality, shows the Russian statistic increasing from 0.260 in 1991 to 0.398 in 1994 and 0.409 in 1995, before slightly reversing.[21]

Box 9.1 Poverty Reduction

All scholars agree that a huge portion of the Russian population was impoverished in the 1990s judged from the American standard and domestic norms. But improvements claimed thereafter are dubious. The dissonance is apparent in repeated surveys that show that the majority of Russians felt worse off in 2007 than under communism against a backdrop of official poverty reduction claims. Until harder scientific studies are forthcoming, it can be crudely surmised that income for a family of four for approximately a quarter of the population in 2003 was in the vicinity of $1,500 per year, a figure that conveys an accurate sense of pain and suffering for Russia's have-nots.[22]

The absolute degree of immiseration is gleaned from the fact that at least 40–45 million people, comprising some 30 percent of the population were driven below the poverty line, in a society that previously claimed to have eliminated destitution. These were the Yeltsin administration's expendable souls, the victims who paid the price for his new Muscovy. Their precise number fluctuated from sixty-four million in

Rossii. For a broader view and a historical perspective, see Jeni Klugman, *Poverty in Russia: Public Policy and Private Responses*, The World Bank, Washington, DC, 1997.

[21] China's Gini coefficient for 2004 was 0.469. See *CIA Factbook: China*. www.cia.gov. The incomes of most wealthy Russians and Chinese are vastly higher than the figures used to compute these estimates. If accurate data were available both Russia and China would probably rank with Brazil in the class of the world's most inegalitarian nations. Their Gini coefficients might well be in the vicinity of 0.6.

[22] Thomas Mroz and Barry Popkin, "Poverty and the Economic Transition in the Russian Federation," *Economic Development and Cultural Change*, 44 (1995): 1–31. *Monitoring Economic Conditions in the Russian Federation: The Russia Longitudinal Monitoring Survey 1992–2004*, University of North Carolina, May 2005. www.cpc.unc.edu/projects/rlms/data/stats/html.

the first quarter of 1999 to *only* 35 million in the fourth quarter of 2001, and their ranks continue to decrease due to the oil bonanza, but their cumulative consequences persist.[23] There can be little doubt that impoverishment contributed importantly to the demographic crisis that began unfolding in the early 1990s. That Russians received only 80 percent of recommended daily caloric intake, 75 percent of proteins, and 50 percent of vitamins in 1993 illustrates the link.

Looking toward the future, there are numerous reasons for concern about Market Muscovy's heritage of neglect. It is a well established fact that increasing inequality hampers growth, and copious empirical evidence showing that Russian developments in the post-Soviet era have been extreme. As Jacques Sapir stresses, the "level of income inequality is not a moral issue, but is instead a concern for the nation's development dynamics."[24] Although, a vast petro dollar inflow has camouflaged these problems, they remain and will take decades to repair under favorable conditions.

Those who counterargue that adverse demographics do not constrain Russia's future growth because immigration from the near abroad and productivity growth will offset the natural decline in population, don't take sufficient account of rising epidemic disease, particularly the emergence of MDRTB and a looming HIV/AIDS catastrophe on the sub-Saharan African scale.[25] Nor do they adequately appreciate the warpedness of Russia's population pyramid. There will be fewer children and able-bodied males, but more old women in the decades ahead, a growth inhibiting burden that will be hard to surmount in an economy still tied to manual labor.

---

[23] For a more detailed argument focused on Russia see Michael Ellman, "The Russian Economy under El'tsin," *Europe-Asia Studies*, 52, 8(2000): 1424–29. Marshall Goldman, "Putin and the Russian Economy: Did he Make a Difference?," *Russia and Eurasia Review*, 1, 1 (2002): 2.

[24] See Torsten Persson and Guido Tabellini, "Is Inequality Harmful for Growth?" *American Economic Review*, 84, 3 (1994). Jacques Sapir, "The Russian Economy: From Rebound to Rebuilding," *Post-Soviet Affairs*, 17, 1(2001): 9. China is an exception to Sapir's rule. See Chapter 14, this volume, for an explanation.

[25] For further insights and discussion, see Nicholas Eberstadt, "Russia: Too Sick to Matter?," *Policy Review*, 95(June–July 1999); Eberstadt, "Russia's Demographic Straightjacket," *SAIS Review*, 24, 2(Summer–Fall 2004), Murray Feshbach, *Russia's Health and Demographic Crises: Policy Implications and Consequences*, Chemical and Biological Arms Control Institute, Washington, DC, 2003; and Steven Rosefielde, "Premature Deaths: Russia's Radical Transition," *Europe-Asia Studies*, 53, 8 (2001): 1159–76.

Another often overlooked impediment is the dilapidated state of Russia's social infrastructure. As the Soviet Union entered its terminal phase, only 29,300 out of 273,000 hamlets and villages, home to nearly one hundred million people, had running water and only seven thousand had sewer systems. One town in ten had a retail store, a healthcare facility or a movie theater, library or other cultural establishment. Chazov, the Soviet Health Minister in 1988 disclosed that two-thirds of all rural district hospitals lacked hot water, while a quarter of all rural hospitals lacked sewage, and that 17 percent had no water at all.[26]

This Third World social infrastructure is hardly conducive to fostering the human capital needed for efficient integration to the global economy. It doesn't encourage improvements in physical health, education, training, and motivation. The deficiencies are pervasive. The quantity and quality of rudimentary health care, modern equipment, pharmaceuticals, maternity wards, and even heating are all inadequate.[27]

Finally, a word is needed about the debasement of Russia's skilled workers, scientists, and engineers. When Gorbachev and Yeltsin chose to abandon the communists' post-Stalin commitment to egalitarianism, universal subsistence and a social safety net the vast majority of the population was cast adrift. Russia needs competent skilled manpower, but the supply is woefully depleted. The fate of its professionals illuminates this deficiency. During the Soviet epoch institutes, academies, and factories were brimming with well-trained skilled workers, scientists, and engineers who somehow managed to make central planning function better than westerners rightly anticipated. In a rational world, Gorbachev, Yeltsin, and Putin would have taken pains to protect and enhance these assets but passively oversaw their deterioration. By denying anything but minimal funding for scientific activity, and industrial modernization, the Kremlin induced the country's technical intelligentsia to leave the country or seek secondary employment outside their fields of expertise.

Ten years after the collapse of the Soviet Union, the academic landscape was blighted. The scene limned by Stephen Blank is revealing.

[26] Feshbach and Friendly, *Ecocide in the USSR*, pp. 54–55.
[27] For a broad assessment, see a collection of papers by a group of prominent experts in a variety of fields contained in NIC, *Russia's Physical and Social Infrastructure: Implications for Future Development*, National Intelligence Council, Washington, DC, 2000 (available at http://www.cia.gov/nic/pubs).

Four thousand scientific research organizations in 2001 received only
a sixth of their former funding. With low pay and meager prospects
discouraging new entrants, the average age of researchers approached
sixty, two years above the male life expectancy. Their ranks had dwin-
dled two-thirds to 910,000, 89 percent senior scientists. Three quarters
of the nation's world-class mathematicians and half of all physicists had
emigrated, and 85 percent of science PhDs were employed abroad. It
is no wonder that Russia's share of the high-tech market is a puny 0.3
percent.[28]

These losses could have been offset by government retaining programs, the emergence of new productive sectors, entrepreneurship,
and the integration of Russian scientists abroad into domestic networks. There were some gains in finance but little else. Most of Russia's
intellectual capital was simply squandered.

The absence of competitive high-tech commercial industries providing alternative employment to Russia's scientists and engineers is
particularly telltale. If the Soviet Union had westernized, given its
scientific legacy, high tech would be a primary growth node in the
new order. Instead of an internal brain drain, transforming knowledge
workers into bodyguards, casino bouncers, taxi drivers, and financial
racketeers, Russia would be moving toward the forefront of today's
scientific and technological revolution.

Summing up the heritage of neglect 1985–2007, we find grounds
for concern. Not only is the Russian population authoritatively forecast fall to between 70 and 110 million by 2050,[29] but the health,
education, skill, and leadership pools are also apt to deteriorate. Where
the United States is expected to be 400 million strong by midcentury,
Russia may well be less than 100 million weak. Given this prospect,
it is more than curious as Eberstadt observes that "neither Russia's
political leadership nor the voting public that sustains it has begun
to face up to the enormous magnitude of the country's demographic
challenges."[30]

- Post-Soviet Market Muscovy has harmed Russia's human capital.
- The wages of abuse and neglect were extreme under Gorbachev's
  and Yeltsin's misrule.

[28] Stephen Blank, "The Material-Technical Foundations of Russian Military
Power," *Ankara Paper* 7, Frank Cass, London, 2003, pp. 25–26.
[29] Feshbach, *Russia's Health and Demographic Crises*, p. 5.
[30] Eberstadt, "Russia," p. 1.

- The damage cannot be easily repaired, and there is no evidence that the Putin administration's efforts were adequate.
- Birth rates have fallen, death rates have surged, and there are only a few signs of sustainable reversals, despite a partial rebound in the birthrate.
- Mortality rates have risen for both genders and all cohorts. The phenomenon isn't explained by an aging population.
- Russia's population has shrunk by nearly 7 million since 1991, despite an influx of Russians from the near abroad (Russians residing outside the Russian federation in Soviet times).
- Environmental degradation (ecocide), substance abuse, infectious diseases, and poverty are the principal consequence of Muscovy's heritage of neglect, and its adverse mortality trends.
- Deteriorating public health, education (including a brain drain), and increasing income equality are conspicuous aspects of Muscovite abandonment. They are all known to impede economic growth and may create a vicious cycle if funds made available by growth aren't allocated to improving Russia's depleted human capital.
- Where the United States is expected to be 400 million strong in 2050 Russia is likely to be 100 million weak.

PART V

ADVANCE AND RETREAT

10

Semblance of Democracy

The concept of democracy always seems to have befuddled the Russians. Vladimir Lenin famously declared that the dictatorship of the proletariat was a million times more democratic than western parliamentary democracy, unfazed by the fact that a dictatorship cannot be democratic. The sentiment was echoed in Joseph Stalin's 1936 and Leonid Brezhnev's 1977 constitutions both of which banned political opposition to Communist Party rule. Circa 1980, democracy for the Kremlin meant Communist Party balloting to determine some policy matters or more often to demonstrate unanimous support for decisions made by senior officials. Important policies were imposed from above by a small coterie, often by the general secretary of the Communist Party or by consensus of the inner party group. Broader party consensus or pluralities sometimes governed lesser decisions, but in no case could it be said that the enlightened will of the people,[1] directly or through freely chosen representatives, ruled. Soviet power was autocratic, not democratic, despite persistent claims to the contrary.

---

[1] The will of the people in the Enlightenment tradition is fully informed and wise within the metaphysical and intellectual limits of bounded rationality, confining misguided emotionalism to the minimum. Governments that thwart enlightened popular sovereignty are undemocratic whether this is accomplished by disenfranchisement, vote rigging, or disinformation and the suppression of economic and social liberties. According to Juan Linz and Alfred Stepan, democracy is defined by free and developed political society (free speech, organization, elections), a well-functioning and impartial bureaucracy, rational legal norms, rule of law, including Lockean constitutionalism, and free markets; Juan Linz and Alfred Stepan, *Problems of Democratic Transition and Consolidation: Southern Europe, South America, and Post-Communist Europe*, Johns Hopkins University Press, Baltimore, 1996.

Mikhail Gorbachev's call for *demokratizatsia* (democratization) should be construed from this perspective as an effort to devolve greater policymaking authority to the lower ranks of the party and encourage broader public participation in Communist Party campaigns rather than as an assault on Soviet autocracy. He was unperturbed by the possibility that shrewd politicians might co-opt his initiative for other ends like destroying the Soviet Union or, even less plausibly, establishing popular sovereignty. Boris Yeltsin sensed the miscalculation and pounced, wresting control of Russia's parliament through the ballot with promises of authentic democratic rule, setting in motion forces leading directly to the Soviet Union's dissolution; however, he found himself confronted with a realization crisis. Now that he was tsar, should he keep his promises by holding a post-Soviet multiparty plebiscite in accordance with majority parliamentary opinion, or should he renege to preserve his authority?

The first test of his priorities arose in 1992–93 over the issue of Deputy Prime Minister Yegor Gaidar's and Anatoly Chubais's (chairman of the Russian State Property Committee) shock therapeutic economic transition program. Yeltsin endorsed and parliament opposed their radical prescriptions. Whatever the technical merits, Yeltsin revealed his true face by insisting that parliament accede to his will, offering only token concessions. Parliament, led by its speaker Ruslan Khasbulatov and supported by Vice-President Alexander Rutskoi, responded in kind, refusing to pass enabling legislation, setting up a classic confrontation that should have been resolved through interbranch compromise. But Yeltsin opted for usurpation. On March 20, 1993, barely more than a year after the founding of the Russian Federation, he declared a state of emergency, asserting that any legislation contravening his presidential decrees had no judicial force. Parliament could do what it wished on peripheral matters, but otherwise had to subordinate itself to the presidency. As in Soviet times, the conflict was played out within a state institutional framework that used voting and majority rule to decide some matters (unanswerable to the people's will), but the final word was the autocrat's.

However, this restoration of the status quo ante 1987 was momentarily forestalled by Valery Zorkin, chairman of the Constitutional Court, who ruled that the president had exceeded his authority. Zorkin and Khasbulatov then offered a zero-option compromise, featuring simultaneous presidential and parliamentary elections over the issue of condominium, that is, dual presidential and parliamentary rule (a harbinger of the Medvedev–Putin diarchy). Yeltsin resisted the referendum, launching a campaign against the bogeyman of communist revanche to curry western support before resuming the offensive. On September 12, 1993, he put forward a constitution of his administration's contrivance, and on September 21, 1993, he signed Executive Order 1400 annulling the powers of the legislature and setting elections for a parliament of a new type. The Supreme Soviet (parliament) responded in kind by impeaching Yeltsin for usurping power and installed Alexander Rutskoi as acting president. Rutskoi annulled Yeltsin's Order 1400, and Yeltsin reciprocated annulling Rutskoi's edict. On September 23, 1993, parliament voted 636 to 2 for Yeltsin's impeachment. According to the Yeltsin government, 70 percent of the regional soviets supported parliament, and demonstrators ringed the White House (parliament building) to protect it. However, when violence flared around the White House and the Ostankino television tower on October 3, 1993, with 143 demonstrators ultimately killed (many by snipers), the military sided with Yeltsin, sending tanks to bombard the White House. The parliamentarians promptly surrendered, with forty-seven arrested. For the next three months, Yeltsin acted as a dictator. He shut down the constitutional court, disbanded the entire national structure of legislatures, and selectively banned nationalist and communist publications, culminating in a rigged referendum on December 12, 1993, that approved his autocratic presidential constitution. The fledgling democracy, which once seemed so promising, thus was nipped in the bud, despite continued hopes and promises of regeneration.[2] Whatever one may think about the comparative merit of Yeltsin's and Rutskoi's programs, the *Fuehrer* principle dominated vox populi.

Prospects for a renewed democratic thrust depended on how political and social forces might alter Yeltsin's resolve to restrict constitutional rights of free political organization, thought, speech, media access, demonstration, and supporting civil liberties, including free enterprise. The 1996 presidential election, originally promised for 1994, confirmed libertarian misgivings. The outcome was never in

---

[2] Peter Reddaway and Dmitri Glinski, *The Tragedy of Russia's Reforms: Market Bolshevism versus Democracy*, U.S. Institute of Peace Press, Washington, DC, 2001; Michael McFaul, *Russia's Unfinished Revolution: Political Change from Gorbachev to Putin*, Cornell University Press, Ithaca, NY, 2001; Lilia Shevstova, *Yeltsin's Russia: Myths and Realities*, Carnegie Endowment for International Peace, Washington, DC, 1999.

doubt. As Stalin once said, "It is enough that the people know there was an election. The people who cast the votes decide nothing. The people who count the votes decide everything."[3] But to be doubly sure, media access was effectively denied Yeltsin's rivals. The democrat Grigory Yavlinsky (former chairman of the State Commission of the USSR for Reform and head of the Yabloko party); Lieutenant General Alexander Lebed (former commander of the 106th Airborne Division), an avowed admirer of Augusto Pinochet, who believed that democracy was bad for Russia; and Communist Party chief Gennady Zyuganov were granted only token air time. The latter finished second with 40 percent of the vote, thirteen percentage points behind Yeltsin. Few believed the election was fair, but more importantly, the voices of liberal democracy received little audible following. Yeltsin, who pretended to speak for democracy, had not only secured his autocratic tenure but fostered an environment in which the alternatives were the authoritarianism of others. The question for the remaining years of the 1990s, therefore, wasn't the incipient flowering of democracy but the possibility of harsher autocracy tied to the resurgence of the military and secret police (FSB).

The threat came from two directions, a palace coup d'etat led by the security services and the possibility that more repressive factions might replace Yeltsin as early as 2000 through the ballot, if he chose to abide by the letter of the 1993 constitution. Although, much remains hidden, it appears that intrigue trumped the ballot box, with the secret police playing a decisive and pernicious role. The essentials seem to be as follows. Although Yeltsin tried to co-opt the Fortress Russia challenge from his right by appointing Alexander Lebed as chairman of his Russian Security Council in 1996 (but removed shortly thereafter over a dispute with Minister of the Interior Anatoly Kulikov), he was forced to rely on the security service because of popular disgruntlement with catastroika and the oligarchs blamed for it. The most visible and significant aspects of the process were Putin's appointments as FSB chief on July 25, 1998, as permanent member of the Security Council of the Russian Federation on October 1, 1998, and as its head on March 29, 1999, which served as stepping-stones toward his palace coup. As FSB head, Putin launched a *kompromat* operation against Yeltsin's daughter,

---

[3] Quotations: Joseph Stalin, http://groups.google.com/group/soc.culture.indian/browse_thread/thread/45da1c184597555a/ 4ffb654d708476c47?Ink=st&q=Joseph+Stalin+counting+votes&rnum=2&ht=en#4ffb654d708476c4.

which he first parlayed into an appointment as acting prime minister on August 9, 1999, and then into the post of acting president after coercing Yeltsin into resigning on December 31, 1999.[4]

This was accomplished by relinquishing his post as FSB chief and switching to the acting prime ministership, which enabled him to be appointed acting president when Yeltsin resigned. In return, Putin signed a federal law on February 12, 2001, shielding Yeltsin and his family from money-laundering charges brought by Russian and Swiss authorities.[5] Edvard Radzinsky claims that former NKVD head Lavrenti Beria poisoned Stalin to gain power March 5, 1953.[6] Yeltsin it seems wisely preferred to step aside before the security services he had empowered liquidated him.

The transfer of power was a stab in the back, not a frontal assault, on the facade of democracy. Putin like his Soviet predecessors retained the fiction that authority flowed from the people through the ballot but moved relentlessly both before and after December 1999 to ensure that power would always flow from the top down, not the bottom up in a process he called the *power vertical (vertikal vlasti)*, a mission accomplished in three steps. First, Putin created a new party of power to represent the Kremlin in the Duma. Although formed only in early fall 1999, before his acting presidency, Unity or alternatively The Bear (Yedinstvo/Medved) made a spectacular run in the December 1999 parliamentary elections, barely losing to the Russian Communist Party. Revealingly, it held its initial party meeting after the election was complete.[7]

Putin with Yeltsin's assistance concurrently repressed opposition. Fatherland/All Russia, led by Moscow Mayor Yuri Luzhkov and former foreign minister Yevgeny Primakov, which seemed on track to presidential victory in late 1999, was persuaded to withdraw after Yeltsin declared Putin heir apparent, leaving the former FSB director virtually unopposed.

---

[4] Stephen Blank, "The 18th Brumaire of Vladimir Putin," in Uri Ra'anan (ed.), *Flawed Succession: Russia's Power Transfer Crisis*, Lexington Books for Rowman and Littlefield, Lanham, MD, pp. 133–70.

[5] *BBC News*, September 13, 2004.

[6] Edvard Radzinsky, *Stalin: The First In-Depth Biography Based on Explosive New Documents from Russia's Secret Archives*. Cf. Abdurahman Avtorkhanov, *The Mystery of Stalin's Death*, Moscow, 1991, and, *Beria*, Moscow, 1977.

[7] The ploy had precedent. Viktor Chernomyrdin promoted "Our Home is Russia" (Nash dom Rossiya) earlier without lasting success.

Analogous pressure and procedural tactics were repeated in the Duma election of 2003, reducing the legislature to a rubber stamp. Unity's victory was so immense that it could change the constitution at will, a result that wasn't lost on perceptive observers like Peter Rutland who noted, "Ironically, the elections mattered because they signaled the demise of competitive democracy in Russia. The election shattered the tripartite structure of Russia's political system (liberals, communists, and traditionalists) that had arisen during Boris Yeltsin's years."[8]
These successes were expanded by cowing potential oligarchic oppositionists in the second phase. Some had set themselves up like grand princes of old, refusing to give obeisance to their tsar, daring the Kremlin to slap them down. Putin didn't hesitate. A series of bills initiated after the Beslan terrorist attacks in September 2004 were railroaded through a pliant Duma, clipping the oligarchs' wings by abolishing gubernatorial elections.[9] The regions were divided into seven federal districts, each controlled by a Kremlin appointed prefect, and the upper house of the Federal Assembly was revamped, with federal appointees displacing ex officio regional representatives. Other bills pruned the powers of local authorities and made it difficult for small parties to run on the ballot,[10] and in 2007, speculation was rife that city mayors soon would become federal appointees too, making it clear that nothing could be further from Putin's thoughts than establishing a Lockean social contract. Nonetheless, western governments before 2004 took these changes in stride, interpreting the power vertical as an effort to restore order after a protracted *smuta*, instead of a Muscovite autocratic consolidation.[11]

[8] Peter Rutland, "Russia in 2003: The Power of One," Transitions Online (http://www.to.cz).

[9] On September 1, 2004, Chechan armed rebels took more than 1,200 school children hostage in the North Ossetian town of Beslan. A gunfight ensued three days later killing 344 civilians, including 186 children. Putin used the event as a pretext for tightening the power vertical. Phillips, *Beslan: The Tragedy of School Number 1,* Granta Books, London, 2007. Jeremy Page, "Putin Plans Raise Specter of Return to One-Party Rule," *The Times* (London), September 25, 2004, p. 22.

[10] Anna Dolgov, "Putin Urges Changes to Centralize Power," *Boston Globe,* September 14, 2004, p. A1; "Russia's Federation Council OK's Bill Amending Election Law," ITAR-TASS, July 13, 2005, available from *Johnson's Russia List,* No. 9199.

[11] Putin's first presidential term can be construed as a period of flux between democratic and authoritarian polarities. See Peter Reddaway, "Will Putin Be Able to Consolidate Power?" *Post-Soviet Affairs,* 17, 1, and Reddaway, "Is Putin's Power More Formal Than Real?" *Post-Soviet Affairs,* 18, 1. "German Ex-Chancellor

This wishful thinking, however, was soon belied when Putin set about repressing the mass media, taking a giant step back toward Soviet-style, constitutionally proscribed political censorship. The Kremlin wrested control of the private TV station NTV from Vladimir Gusinsky and the state ORT TV channel from Boris Berezovsky. Although the attacks were primarily politically motivated, designed to defang Yeltsin and two of his crony oligarchs,[12] it was equally evident that Putin was killing two birds with one stone.[13] Nor was he above taunting. When asked about declining press freedom, in classic KGB black humor he retorted, "Russia has never had a free media, so I don't know what I am supposed to be impeding."[14] His intent was etched in stone in subsequent years by a counterextremism law legitimating the harassment of reporters, a series of high-profile assassinations of wayward journalists transgressing the invisible line[15] and by parallel efforts to further muzzle their employers. In 2006, important newspapers such as *Novaya Gazeta, Nezavisimaya Gazeta,* and *Kommersant*

Schroeder Praises Putin for 'Stability and Reliability,'" *International Herald Tribune,* January 17, 2007; Andrei Shleifer and Daniel Treisman, "A Normal Country," *Foreign Affairs,* March/April 2004; Daniel Treisman, "Putin's Silovarchs," *Orbis,* Winter 2007.

[12] The campaign against Gusinsky began in the summer of 1999, largely over the Yeltsin succession. Gusinsky responded by allowing his media outlets, chiefly the private NTV television network but also the daily *Segodnya* and the weekly *Itogi,* both influential liberal publications, to criticize the war in Chechnya and promote Putin's rivals Luzhkov and Primakov. The peak of the process was marked only days after Putin's presidential inauguration, when the headquarters of Gusinsky's media empire was raided by heavily armed tax police (under FSB control). Following a brief standoff, Gusinsky was arrested and placed in prison for a couple of days, after which he chose to emigrate and give up his media holdings. Meanwhile, Berezovsky was similarly driven by threats of prosecution and imprisonment to abandon his stake in the ORT central state television network, and in the end also to choose voluntary exile in London. He would subsequently claim that Putin had given him a choice of being a political prisoner or a political émigré. Having won political asylum in Great Britain, he would launch a campaign against Putin that rested, inter alia, on accusations that Putin had been involved in the 1999 apartment bombing. Livinenko claims that he was assigned by Putin to kill Berezovsky for this allegation. See Alexander Litvinenko and A. Goldfarb, *Criminal Gang from Lubyanka,* GRANI, New York, 2002.

[13] Putin attempted to conceal his expropriation of oligarch assets by having Kremlin-controlled Gazprom and Lukoil call in Berezovsky's debts.

[14] Paul Jenkins, "Russian Journalism Comes under Fire," *BBC* News, July 2, 2004 (available at http://news.bbc.co.uk).

[15] Steven Rosefielde and Romana Hlouskova, "Why Russia Is Not a Democracy," *Comparative Strategy,* 6, 3, 2007, note 21.

were acquired by Kremlin-friendly companies.[16] The last independent
TV station, REN TV was taken over by the Kremlin-connected bank
Rossiya on April 13, 2007.[17]

Some oligarchs, like their journalist brethren, however, would not
be intimidated. Mikhail Khodorkovsky was the most ambitious and
recalcitrant of the bunch. He used the rhetoric of democracy and individual empowerment in a well-funded campaign to forge an oppo-
sitionist base at home and abroad. Reputed at the time to have a
private fortune of $8 billion, Khodorkovsky postured as a vanguard
figure seeking to transform Russia's rent-seeking tycoons into modern, business school–trained, globalist-minded captains of industry.
At the apex of his power, he appeared poised to strike a deal with
ExxonMobil, assuring America of a steady supply of Russian oil that
threatened the Kremlin's energy monopoly. Although this or a multitude of other factors might have been the straw that broke the camel's
back, it can be reasonably inferred that Putin's bold political response
was preemptive.[18]

On July 2, 2003, Platon Lebedev, chairman of the board of the
financial group MFO Menatep and a major shareholder in Yukos Oil
Company (headed by Russia's wealthiest oligarch, Mikhail Khodorkovsky), was arrested and charged with stealing a 20 percent stake in
Apatit, a company worth $283 million in 1994.[19] Vasily Shakhnovsky,
a billionaire Yukos shareholder, was indicted for tax evasion. Both
events were warning salvos that went unheeded. Then on October
26, 2003, security agents in Novosibirsk stormed Khodorkovsky's
plane. He was hauled off to prison in Moscow, charged with, among
other things, defrauding the state of $5 billion in revenue. Yukos was
forced to pay $6.4 billion in back taxes on July 1, 2004. In Decem-
ber, the government confiscated Yukos's assets for unpaid taxes and

[16] Nikola Krastev, "Freedom House Sees Further Democracy Decline," *RFE/RL*,
      January 17, 2007. According to Russian journalist Rof Shakirov, censorship and
      media propaganda today are comparable to Soviet times. Russia is always pre-
      sented positively, the West negatively. Also the government requires the media to
      disseminate pro-Russian propaganda internationally. "Viewpoint: Soviet Grip on
      Russia Media," *BBC News*, November 26, 2004; Natalia Gorodetskays, "Russia's
      Image Declared Secret," *Kommersant*, July 13, 2005.
[17] "Kremlin-Friendly Bank Takes over Last Independent TV channel," *Johnson's
      Russia List*, Vol. 87, Article 1, April 13, 2007.
[18] Steven Rosefielde, "The Illusion of Transition: Russia's Muscovite Future," *East-
      ern Economic Journal*, 31, 2: 283–96.
[19] Ibid., and Steven Rosefielde, *Russian Economics from Lenin to Putin*, Blackwell,
      London, 2007, p. 175.

transferred them roundabout to Gazprom. And, in May 2005, Khodorkovsky was convicted for a series of economic crimes and sentenced to a nine-year prison term. Unbowed, he has written letters from Gulag describing himself accurately as a political prisoner (although he may be guilty of a multiple of economic crimes), prompting the Kremlin to file additional criminal charges against him in a story still awaiting its end. Years later on May 10, 2007, the remnants of Yukos's assets were disbursed in a closed action to Kremlin insiders.[20]

The message of the Yukos Affair, as it is often called, together with the more than 200 killings of journalists, politicians, and central bankers, [21] Alexander Litvinenko's assassination, Yegor Gaidar's and Viktor Yushchenko's poisonings, and plots against Boris Berezovsky, is that the tsar cannot be provoked without devastating reprisals.[22] Russia's oligarchs now know with certainty that if they challenge Putin, he will confiscate their assets, and they will be imprisoned or killed. This threat has sufficed to quell legitimate political opposition without resorting to a Stalinist reign of terror. Its success enabled Putin to rule as an uncrowned Tsar Vladimir I, adorned with a replica of Vladimir Monomakh's cap, the *Shapka Monomakha*.

The last nail in the coffin of Russian democratization was a crackdown on civil society, that is, the constitutionally protected right of individuals to privately pursue, organize, and politically promote causes of public concern like religion, art, environmental protection, and social services. Repression takes many subtle forms and is difficult to ferret out because the government portrays repressive actions as socially necessary. For example, environmentalists opposing nuclear pollution by the military are repressed for violating national security, not criticizing Moscow's lax ecological management. Nonetheless, Putin's attack on nongovernmental organizations (NGOs) that gathered force in 2004 provides a window into the Kremlin's civic repression strategy.[23] The Putin administration passed legislation in

---

[20] Yukos's assets are being repartitioned. See "Rosneft Wins as Yukos Assets Are Auctioned," *Johnson's Russia List*, Vol. 74, Article 20, March 28, 2007.

[21] David Nowak, "Kremlin Pressed on Killings of Reporters," *Moscow Times*, January 23, 2007.

[22] However, Berezovsky is openly counterplotting to depose Putin. Ian Cobain, Mathew Taylor, and Luke Harding, "I Am Plotting a New Russian Revolution," *Johnson's Russia List*, Vol. 87, Article 16, April 13, 2007.

[23] *Boston Globe*, June 21, 2004. In May 2004, Putin contended that some NGOs were serving "dubious group and commercial interests" rather than the people's needs. Cathy Young, "Bad Old Days Return for Russia's Dissidents," *Boston Globe*, September 14, 2004, p. A11. In January 2006, Putin accused several NGOs

2006 severely curtailing the activities of domestic and foreign NGOs on the Stalinesque pretext that some were havens for foreign spies.[24] NGO offices were raided, and all were compelled to re-register, with many reapplications denied. Those that remain are being intimidated by tight surveillance, hampering operations as intended, and sending a clearly understood message to all individuals and organizations considering opposing the regime social agenda. As with his handling of the oligarchs, Putin deftly applied targeted force to repress the wider community and democratic process.

Likewise, in an all too familiar pattern, the regime organizes and controls puppet civic individuals and groups to intimidate adversaries and provide the illusion of public support. *Idushchem vmeste* (Walking Together), an 80,000 strong quasi-military organization, comparable to the Hitler Youth, is symptomatic. Its members are young, twelve to thirty years of age, fiercely pro–Putin, pro–Russian, and anti–western, and the organization is designed to create a Soviet-style cult of personality around the dear leader.[25]

Nashi (Ours), another red guard youth organization devised and managed by a Kremlin think-tank, according to Vladimir Surkov, the Kremlin chief of staff, is tasked "to defend Russia's youth from the political manipulation of the West."[26] This coded phrase alludes to an alleged western plot fomenting "color" revolutions such as those in Georgia, Ukraine, and Kyrgyzstan pressing the cause of democratization.[27] The regime views *Idushchem vmeste* and *Nashi* as Muscovite troops for shocking and awing friends of democracy.

Putin's three-pronged strategy of democratic suppression – (1) the power vertical, (2) media and oligarchic repression, and (3) stifled

of receiving clandestine payments from British diplomats. "Russian NGO Reject Spy Smear," *BBC News*, January 31, 2006.

[24] "Russian NGO Reject Spy 'Smear'," *BBC News*, January 31, 2006 (available at http://news.bbc.co.uk); "Putin Warning over 'Puppet' NGO's," *BBC News*, January 31, 2006 (available at http://news.bbc.co.uk).

[25] Steven Lee Meyers, "Russian Group Is Offering Values to Fill a Void," *New York Times*, February 16, 2003.

[26] Julian Evans, "How Putin Youth Is Indoctrinated to Foil Revolution," *The Times*, July 18, 2005.

[27] Color revolutions, or flower revolutions, are metaphoric terms for mass, largely nonviolent, democratic movements that erupted in some postcommunist societies in the new millennium. They include the Bulldozer Revolution (Serbia, 2000), the Rose Revolution (Georgia, 2003), the Orange Revolution (Ukraine, 2004), and the Tulip Revolution (Kyrgyzstan, 2005).

civic activism – illuminates the meaning of his managed democracy, a phenomenon that involves neither management nor popular sovereignty.[28] It is Muscovite demagoguery that subdues through *kompromat*, harassment, confiscation, intimidation, imprisonment, and perhaps murder, including liberal politicians Galina Starovoitsova and Sergei Yushenkov; Andrei Kozlov, first deputy chairman of the Central Bank, journalist Anna Politovskaya; and former FSB agent Litvinenko.[29] The gambit is effective. The president has conditioned Russians to anticipate, to decipher, and to obey his veiled commands, while deceiving them into believing that they are independent democratic actors in free Russia. They flocked to join Putin's party. After regional governorships became appointive, all previously elected governors switched to join United Russia.[30]

In doing so, they voluntarily surrendered the possibility of independent opposition outside the power vertical and subjugated themselves to the ruler-through-a-party *apparat* like Soviet cadre before them. As Lenin asserted ninety years ago, citizens should be cogs in a well-ordered Russian society,[31] and Putin resurrected that dream. There are

---

[28] The term *managed democracy* was coined by Vladimir Putin in his second-term inaugural address. Jeremy Page, "Putin Starts Term Vowing to Build a Better Russia: Inaugural Address Omits 'Democracy,'" *Washington Post*, May 8, 2008, p. A8. The term has the same resonance as Putin's earlier "dictatorship of law."

[29] Galina Starovoitsova, co-chairwoman of the Liberal Democratic Russia Party and an undeclared presidential candidate in the 2000 election was gunned down November 1998. Sergei Yushenkov another Liberal Russia party co-chairman was murdered April 2003. His aide Alyona Morozova blamed the FSB. Andrei Kozlov, first deputy Chairman of the Central Bank, known for his anti-money-laundering initiative was shot to death September 2006. Anna Politovskaya, an intrepid correspondent who frequently received death threats for her reportage of the Chechen war, was assassinated on October 7, 2006. Alexander Litvinenko a former FSB agent who claimed he was assigned to kill Boris Berezovsky but disobeyed was poisoned to death in London in November 2006 with radioactive polonium-208. Although the Kremlin denied any responsibility, it was revealed that FSB sharpshooters routinely practiced using targets with Litvinenko's face. See Gary Weiss, "Murder in Russia," *Forbes*, January 30, 2007. David Leppart, Richard Woods, and Mark Franchetti, "The Bastards Got Me," *The Sunday Times*, November 26, 2006.

[30] By early 2006, seventy out of eight-nine regional governors, two-thirds of civil employees, and thousands of prominent personalities had joined the party of power. Those who remained critical came under heavy pressure to join and to change the party from within. Fred Weir, "Ambitious Russians Join the Party," *Christian Science Monitor*, February 15, 2006.

[31] Vladimir Lenin, *State and Revolution*, Moscow, 1918.

no independent legislative chambers, judicial bodies, administrations, regional authorities, or powerful citizens; every person and organization serves the tsar with an increasingly imperial agenda. From the Kremlin's standpoint, this is as it should be, an attitude conveyed in Surkov's latest concept *sovereign democracy*, implying that Russia is not the West and should not be straitjacketed by Enlightenment notions of popular sovereignty.[32] Muscovite autocracy is democratic, if this is how the tsar commands his subjects to see it, and the West, Surkov believes, should respectfully accommodate itself to this version of reality.[33]

The ploy seems to be succeeding because G-7 leaders are usually prepared to acquiesce, believing that Russia's democratic future is foreshadowed in the West's past. It doesn't matter that Freedom House downgraded Russia in 2004 from the status of a "partly free country" to a "not free country"[34] that high western officials periodically voice their displeasure about Russian authoritarianism or that Russian democratic, civil, and economic rights usually have been dead-letter law because hope in the West perennially triumphs over experience, allowing Russia's incipient democracy to be rolled back without meaningful protest.

This disinclination to see the obvious was vividly illustrated by the political theater surrounding Putin's eligibility for a third presidential term in 2008, his appointment of Dmitri Medvedev as United Russia's presidential candidate (Putin's latest party) on December 17, 2007, and Medvedev's immediate designation of Putin as his future prime minister.[35] As a matter of law, Yeltsin's constitution limits presidents

---

[32] George Ilyichev, "Evolution of Putin Aide Surkov's Sovereign Democracy Principle Viewed," *Johnson's Russia List*, Vol. 75, Article 9, March 29, 2007.

[33] "Russian Human Rights Report Highlights Police Violence against Opposition," *Johnson's Russia List*, Vol. 75, Article 5, March 29, 2007; "Public Chamber Acknowledges Crackdown on Independent Media," *Johnson's Russia List*, Vol. 75, Article 7, March 29, 2007; "Clandestines Optimism: Political Parties Pledge to Avoid Protest Demonstrations Kremlin Requests Parties to Sign an Anti-extremism Charter," *Johnson's Russia List*, Vol. 75, Article 10, March 29, 2007; Floreana Fossato, "Russia: Media Decree Targets Internet, Digital TV," *Johnson's Russia List*, Vol. 75, Article 19, March 29, 2007.

[34] http://www.freedomhouse.org. Classification is based on surveys of the electoral process, political pluralism and participation, government functioning, freedom of expression and belief, associational and organizational rights and personal autonomy, and individual rights. The reasons for the downgrade were absence of free and fair decisions, media repression, and harassment of political opposition.

[35] "Reciprocal Appointment: Medvedev Offers Vladimir Putin Post of Prime Minister," *Johnson's Russia List*, Vol. 254, Article 1, December 12, 2007; "Putin

to two terms, but Russians appreciated that like all such provisions it is only binding at the leader's discretion. The maneuver preserves the formality but not the substance of democracy by cunningly sidestepping the two-term constitutional limit on executive tenure. Like Stalin before him, Putin may reconfirm that in Moscow the power of the perceived rent-granting leader is more important than formal titles or the constitution.[36]

Box 10.1 Dmitri Medvedev

Dmitri Anatolevich Medvedev, born September 14, 1965, in Leningrad, holds a Ph.D. in law from Leningrad State University (1990). He was chairman of Gazprom's board of directors and first deputy prime minister of the Russian government since November 14, 2005. On December 17, 2007, he was formally endorsed by United Russia (Putin's ruling party) as its presidential candidate in the March 2008 elections.

On May 7, 2008, Medvedev was elected Russia's third president. He was on Mayor Anatoly Sobchak's entourage, and served under Putin as a legal expert for the Committee for External Relations. When Putin became president in 2000, Medvedev was appointed deputy head of his presidential staff. In November 2005, he was appointed first deputy prime minister and first deputy chairman of the Council for Implementation of Priority National Projects. He is considered a moderate liberal pragmatist and loyalist who poses no obstacle to Putin's future retention of state control in one guise or another.

The process leading to this outcome began in 2005 shortly after Putin's first term ended with media speculation about whether he would seek the presidency in 2008, what role he would play in the new administration, and who might be his successor. The script evolved with events. When the color revolutions erupted, the controlled press claimed that since Putin was the only man capable of coping with the challenge he should stay on until the job was done, however long that might take. Later, when the Ukrainian Orange Revolution went awry, he was hailed for saving Russia from the contagion. When the

---

Accepts the Office of Prime Minister," *Johnson's Russia List*, Vol. 258, Article 5, December 17, 2007.

[36] Anders Aslund argues that Putin is vulnerable to a palace coup by his "closest conspirators from the KGB in St. Petersburg" disgruntled by his choice of Medvedev. See Aslund, "Purge or *Coup?*" *Johnson's Russia List*, Vol. 6, Article 9, January 9, 2008.

petro bubble raised living standards and financed Russia's superpower reemergence, the summons was repeated. And when liberal demonstrators began defiantly protesting government repression in the run-up to the 2007 parliamentary and 2008 presidential elections,[37] the captive media pleaded for Putin to protect society from provocation.[38]

These antics were counterposed throughout with a democratic subplot in which Putin persistently denied desiring a third term, asserted his dedication to democratic process, and promoted rival in-house candidates such as Sergei Ivanov and Dmitri Medvedev.[39] No one consequently could say with certainty whether Putin would or would not remain an autocrat after 2008, any more than it could be proven that democracy was beyond Russia's grasp, or that Russia would become an aggressive superpower.[40] Cultivated ambiguity was the order of the

[37] The media bias in the run-up to the 2007 parliamentary elections was intense, with United Russia and Just Russia receiving most of the airtime. Aleksandra Zaytseva, "Just Russia Shows and Tells," Gazeta.ru, January 17, 2007. The Foundation for Free elections, overseeing the fairness of the last two elections, is headed by a former KGB officer, who believes that KGB officers are "the best informed, best prepared and most sober and democratic" part of Russian society. Arkady Ostrovsky, "Russia Still Has the Attributes of a Democracy, but Managed by the Siloviki, This Could Become Illusory," *The Financial Times*, February 24, 2007.

[38] Toward this end, Putin revived citizen spying, standard practice during communist rule when "agents work in the interest of the state," based on their ideological convictions, that is, today's resurgent nationalism. Paul Starobin and Sabrina Tavernise, "President Putin Cracks Down: Critics Worry He'll Wound Democracy," *Business Week*, http://www.businessweek.com, April 3, 2000. The Russian government has approved a new state education program for the promotion of patriotism and thwarting "attempts at discrediting or devaluing the concept of patriotism in the media and in works of literature or art." "Russia Moves to Inculcate Greater Patriotism," Interfax, June 18, 2005. And a new law prohibits non-Russians and foreigners from offending Russian values, authorities, and symbols. "Russia Visa Risk for 'Disrespect,'" *BBC News*, available at http://news.bbc.co.uk, January 23, 2005.

[39] Sergei Ivanov was Putin's FSB deputy July 1998 through August 1999. In November 1999, Yeltsin appointed him secretary of the Russian Security Council. He became Minister of Defense in March 2001, remaining in the post until February 15, 2007, when he was promoted to first deputy prime minister. Dmitri Medvedev was Putin's chief of staff and chairman of Gazprom's board of directors. On November 14, 2005, he was elevated to first deputy prime minister.

[40] Putin dismisses the idea that Russia is a superpower, while acting with confidence that he knows better. "Putin Touts Resurgent Russia," *RFE/RL*, January 24, 2007. According to the chairman of the Council for Foreign and Defense Policy, Sergei Karaganov asserts that Russia still remains the second-strongest power in the world. Alexander Sargin, "Four Analysts Comment on the Outlook for

day, and it worked. Putin could not be treated as a lame duck, kept all options open, offered hope to those desiring his peaceful exit, and adhered closely enough to the semblance of democratic process to reassure western wishful thinkers.

That he ultimately chose not to run for a third presidential term, switching to the prime ministership instead, does not close the book on either Russian authoritarianism or Putin's executive rule. The details of autocratic governance and succession remain matters of the leader's discretion, with the FSB serving as overseer, arbiter, and administrator of permissible liberties, including most political, economic, social, and civic activities. Whether Medvedev eventually emerges from Putin's shadow is subsidiary. As before, the critical issue continues to be whether the Kremlin is willing to relinquish autocratic Muscovy.[41]

Russian Politics in 2007," *Gazeta*, January 26–28, 2007; Steven Rosefielde, *Russia in the 21st Century: The Prodigal Superpower*, Cambridge University Press, Cambridge, 2005. In this connection, Russia has announced that it will build new intercontinental ballistic missiles, nuclear submarines, and aircraft carriers, as well as improve the army's combat readiness to counter U.S. missile defense negotiations with Poland and the Czech Republic; at the same time, Russia is threatening unilateral withdrawal from the Intermediate-Range Nuclear Forces Treaty of 1987. Vladimir Isachenkov, "Russia May Exit '87 Treaty," *Associated Press*, February 15, 2007. Europe is slowly becoming aware that Russia will use European dependency on Russian oil and gas to exercise significant political control. Recent halts of gas supplies to western Europe during Russia's disputes with Ukraine and Belarus, combined with efforts to create Gaspec, the natural gas analogue of OPEC, underscore the problem. See "Europe: Resisting Assimilation," Stratfor.com, April 2006; Andrea Mihailescu, "Russia Rules Fuel in Much of Europe," *Washington Times*, April 22, 2006.

[41] According to Valery Zorkin, chairman of the Russian Constitutional Court, "Special research has shown that courts are vulnerable to corruption attacks from businessmen. Bribery in courts of law is a most powerful corruption market. Judicial corruption works as part of corruption networks acting on various levels of government and specialize on, for example, hostile takeovers or hindering criminal prosecution." "Russian Judge Admits Widespread Judicial Bribery," *Izvestia*, RIA's Novosti's digest of the Russian press, October 25, 2004. Tamara Morshchakova, a retired Constitutional Court judge asserts, moreover, "Any ruling in any court case can be dictated from outside. This can be done by any state official of any rank – the structure itself does not protect a court against this." Alexander Podrabinek, "The Source of Water Is in the Kremlin," *Novaya Gazeta*, January 15–17, 2007; Paul Goble, "Window on Russia: Is the FSB Assuming the Functions of the KGB's Fifth Chief Directorate?" *Johnson's Russia List*, Vol. 223, Article 22, November 24, 2007. The FSB is pressing to increase harassment of opposition politicians.

It probably isn't. Russia is the only remaining authoritarian great power in Europe. Although it seemed for a moment in December 1991 that Boris Yeltsin would honor his pledge to install popularly sovereign democracy, he didn't. Instead, he forced an authoritarian constitution on the nation against parliament's will in 1993 and never looked back. Vladimir Putin, Yeltsin's former secret police chief and presidential successor, subsequently intrigued his way to power, advancing his former master's hidden authoritarian agenda by more sternly repressing civil rights, political participation, balloting, and parliamentary autonomy. He has orchestrated a post–second-term presidential succession that bodes more of the same.[42] Oppression today isn't as harsh as the bad old Brezhnev years but is heading that way,[43] toward an autocracy where the monarch, whatever his title, is supreme, with or without a ruling party.[44]

---

[42] Putin's former economic advisor Andrei Illarionov contends that there is no economic freedom in Russia because Muscovy is based on favorites – different rules apply to different individuals and companies. Trusted aides such as Viktor Ivanov, for example, were appointed to Aeroflot's board of directors; Sergei Prikhodko was named chairman of Russia's sole nuclear fuel-trading company, TVEL; and Igor Sechin, Vladislav Surkov, and Dmitri Medvedev were assigned chairmanships of state-owned oil and gas companies. "Putin's Aides Elected to Strategic Economic Posts," Mosnews.com, October 25, 2004. The Russian state already controls almost a third of the oil industry, and it is proposed that new offshore gas and oil fields should be reserved to two state companies, Gazprom and Rosneft. Neil Buckley, "Moscow Plans to Reserve New Oilfields for State Giants," *Financial Times*, January 23, 2007.

[43] Steven Rosefielde, "Turmoil in the Kremlin: Sputtering toward Fortress Russia," *Problems of Post-Communism*, 53, 5(September/October 2006): 3–10. "Reciprocal Appointment: Medvedev Offers Putin the Post of Prime Minister," *Johnson's Russia List*, Vol. 254, Article 1, December 12, 2007; "Putin Accepts the offer of Prime Minister, *Johnson's Russia List,* Vol. 258, Article 1, December 17, 2007.

[44] Anders Aslund concurs with our assessment of Russia's "tsarist" authoritarian revanche, but he fails to appreciate the Muscovite character of its markets. He recognizes the phenomenon of rent-seeking but not its historical roots. This causes him to treat market building under Gorbachev, Yeltsin, and Putin as the harbinger of democratic free enterprise in "the not-to-distant future," an attitude we consider wishful thinking and characteristic of his prior advocacy of shock therapy. Similarly, he clings to the idea that Yeltsin was a sincere democrat instead of a Muscovite authoritarian in sheep's clothes. He blames the repression of incipient democracy on Russia's first parliament rather than on Yeltsin's rejection of direct presidential and parliamentary election in 1992 by lamenting that Yeltsin didn't "dissolve the old unrepresentative parliament within half a year after the aborted August 1991 coup." Suppose he had. Would the result in the context of the times have produced a different Yeltsin who relinquished the power of

Box 10.2 Authoritarian Essence

Few democracies closely approximate the popular sovereignty ideal, even in open societies. Principal-agent problems (electorate and representatives), motivated special interests, media mis- and disinformation, and public gullibility rupture the link between the people's informed will and the provision of public services. Democracy can also be fragmented, with weak central governments and partisan paralysis. These imperfections led some to surmise that Russia's democratic claims aren't fundamentally different than those of most inefficient popular regimes. This reasoning conflates inefficiency with authoritarian repression. Russia is an authoritarian state, not a poorly functioning popular representative regime. The people's will is repressed by the power vertical, not the unscrupulous elbowing for advantage by various independent political parties. Likewise, its laws serve Muscovy, not the people. Consequently, citizens of inefficient democracies have more degrees of freedom, more influence, and greater protection from privileged insiders than the Russian populace.

- Muscovite rulers have no difficulty professing democracy by claiming that their actions embody the righteous people's will.
- Many Russian and western intellectuals fail to appreciate that autocrats cannot know the informed popular will if political and civil liberties are curtailed.
- The claim that intraparty balloting reflects the will of the people is specious.
- Gorbachev's democratic reforms were spurious in these senses but had unintended consequences that enabled his vassal Boris Yeltsin to usurp power and destroy the Soviet Union.
- Yeltsin's true intent was revealed when he disbanded parliament and arrested its leaders in 1991, following Lenin's precedent.
- The West extolled Yeltsin as a democrat thereafter without justification.

presidential edicts in favor of parliament rule? Would the West have favored this outcome, if it meant a communist majority? Yeltsin had his chance to construct democracy by decree and chose Muscovy. Anders Aslund, "New Book," *Johnson's Russia List*, Vol. 240, Article 37, November 20, 2007. Also see Aslund, *Russia's Capitalist Revolution: Why Market Reform Succeeded and Democracy Failed*, Peterson Institute for International Economics, Washington, DC, 2007; and Aslund, *How Capitalism Was Built: The Transformation of Central and Eastern Europe, Russia, and Central Asia*, Cambridge University Press, Cambridge, 2007.

- But his autocratic behavior persisted. The 1996 presidential election was rigged, and Yeltsin made no effort to lay the foundations for true representative democracy.
- His position nonetheless was insecure. He alienated the military, and his business cronies were no match for the secret police.
- Vladimir Putin, FSB head, caught Yeltsin's daughter in a *kompromat* operation and through a series of clever maneuvers compelled Yeltsin to cede the presidency.
- Power was usurped by Putin as FSB head, not transferred democratically as might seem to have been the case by the election of 2000, where rivals ceded the field once Yeltsin anointed Putin.
- Vladimir Putin's Unity Party won by a landslide in the 2003 parliamentary elections with the usual chicanery, consolidating the power vertical.
- The process continued in 2004 with a law abolishing gubernatorial elections. Thereafter, governors became presidential appointees.
- The powers of local officials were pruned, and parliament is considering abolishing elected mayors in favor of presidential appointees.
- Muscovite constitution and law are instruments of state power. Private property is supposed to be inalienable, but state appropriation is discretionary, despite a show of due process.
- The Putin administration confiscated the assets of billionaires Boris Berezovsky, Vladimir Gusinsky, and Mikhail Khordokovsky, and BP petroleum lost its Sakhalin petroleum drilling stake.
- Gusinsky and Berezovsky were exiled, and Khordokovsky imprisoned for nine years, which may turn into a life sentence if the state presses various new charges.
- Although, difficult to prove, government complicity is alleged in a wide range of repressive crimes, from the killing of reporters and parliamentarians to the assassination of former FSB agent Alexander Litvinenko with polonium-208.
- Putin vigorously repressed foreign NGOs; he covered his tracks with conciliatory statements one day that he backtracked on the next.
- Like Hitler, Putin organized youth groups such as *Idushchem vmeste* (walking together) to quell opposition.
- The essence of Putin's democratic suppression is a three-pronged strategy strengthening the power vertical, repressing insider opposition (media and oligarchs), and stifling civic activism. The

euphemisms for this authoritarianism are *managed democracy* and *sovereign democracy*.

- Russians have been conditioned to anticipate, to decipher, and to obey the leader's veiled commands.
- Like Lenin, Putin teased the West by claiming that Russian democracy is best.
- Russia remains the only authoritarian great power in Europe.

11

Social Change and Adaptation

The evolution of Russian society since 1980 paralleled incipient democratic developments for a decade and then diverged. While political governance reverted toward Brezhnev-style Muscovy, social change has been multidirectional and complex, reflecting a richer matrix of possibilities.[1] Russia's intelligentsia and rulers have been debating the idea of Russia (the social order that best embodies its national spirit) since the early nineteenth century. The subtext always has been how to reconcile Muscovy's narcissism with reality. This discourse grounded in Russia's *ethos* (beliefs), driven by *pathos* (emotion), and guided by *logos* (rationalization), has taken numerous forms.[2] There were conservative, liberal, slavophil, and socialist variations, each positing an utopia, transmutable into a *kakatopia*, and innumerable composites. One of the Soviet Union's cosmetic triumphs was the proletopian Russian idea that legitimated communist rule and shaped social reality, despite widespread squalor.

---

[1] Politics, economics, and culture are fully integrated in the Enlightenment concept of democratic free enterprise because the Lockean social contract allows individuals to maximize their utility in the conduct of their economic, political, and social activities. This identity is lost if people vote to replace Paretian arrangements with a social contract that benefits the privileged at the expense of the weak. Authoritarians have the option of simulating democratic outcomes with nondemocratic means but never really do so. Consequently, social change in all systems other than enlightened democratic free enterprise typically doesn't parallel transformations of political regimes.

[2] Aristotle identified ethos, pathos, and logos as the three primary elements of rhetoric, treated as speaker, audience, and message by contemporary teachers of English composition. See http://www.public.iastate.edu/~honey1/Rhetoric/. Ethos, pathos, and logos are used here in their root sense of ethnic beliefs, emotional predilections, and rationality.

Soviet society in the benchmark year 1980 was often idealized as classless (propertyless), ruled in the name of the proletariat by Communist Party leaders claiming to be philosopher kings. The Kremlin in this myth was portrayed as upholding Russian *proletopia* by nationalizing the means of production, administering the economy, and suppressing class enemies everywhere, allowing each individual to actualize his or her socialist human potential. As in Karl Marx's early economic and philosophical manuscripts,[3] everyone was supposed to be a Renaissance man/woman, empowered by progressive human rights, and the rule of communist law, efficiently administered by the vanguard of the proletariat, rather than a repressive *state*.

The reality behind the mask defied these categories. Nationalizing productive assets and criminalizing business and entrepreneurship didn't eradicate other forms of material self-seeking, install equal opportunity, or assure justice. Although classes, as Marx conceived them, in proprietary terms ceased to exist, Muscovite hierarchy, rent-granting, rent-seeking, and subjugation continued to govern social relations. The Soviet Union was a society of privileged and disempowered, haves and have-nots concealed behind the pipe dream of *proletopia*. The delusion suited the Kremlin's communist authoritarian martial police state well, but after General Secretary Leonid Brezhnev's death in 1982, *proletopia* soon came under assault with profound consequences for society, the style of Muscovite state rule, and the Russian idea.

Mikhail Gorbachev, a self-proclaimed communist idealist,[4] began the onslaught with his policies of *glasnost* (openness) and *demokratizatsia* (democratization), which quickly revived interest in socialist humanism. At this time, Lenin, as the USSR's founding cult figure was still sacrosanct, but many Soviet intellectuals began rethinking where Bolshevism, Stalinism, and Reform Communism had gone wrong and how Soviet Marxism could be rescued by participatory communitarianism and direct democracy. They were encouraged by Gorbachev's cooperative leasing experiment (*arenda*) and local activism but fretted that private property, even cooperative group ownership, still would be exploitive. Their variant of Russian *proletopia*, compatible

---

[3] Karl Marx, *Economic and Philosophical Manuscripts of 1844*, International Publishers, New York, 1971.

[4] Mikhail Gorbachev, *Perestroika: New Thinking for Our Country and the World*, Harper and Row, New York, 1987.

with some Enlightenment aspirations, and indigenous collectivism (*sobornost*) rejected individual self-seeking, markets, and representative democracy in favor of communalism and participatory democracy, while clinging contradictorily to the Muscovite order.

The brevity of Gorbachev's reign makes it impossible to ascertain whether Soviet society might have changed for the better under the influence of a more communitarian humanist *proletopia*, but the chance, if any, was swiftly mooted by Boris Yeltsin's destruction of communist power. Suddenly, and with little warning, radical social change was thrust on the Russian people willy-nilly by the vagaries of post-Soviet Muscovite culture and high politics without a guiding Russian idea. Russian society, as a result, mutated, but its *logos* is a project still under construction. The Kremlin hasn't decided whether to exclusively embrace the idea of the West; idealize the Muscovite authoritarian martial police state, or craft a composite Russian idea that preserves the prevailing order, while providing a blueprint for a superior future. The only option that seems unthinkable is the universal recriminalization of private property, business, and entrepreneurship.

This is no small matter. For the first time since 1917, businessmen, entrepreneurs, and proprietors of various descriptions have been rehabilitated and are no longer viewed by the authorities as implacable enemies. They are united by a common interest in advancing economic freedom but differ on its scope. Most small and medium-scale businessmen and their intellectual supporters such as German Gref (former Minister of Economic Development and Trade) and Alexei Kudrin (former Finance Minister) favor a laissez-fare social order, while oligarchs addicted to rent-seeking desire only their own empowerment. All enjoy gradually improving stature vis-à-vis workers, collective farmers, administrators, and military conscripts, but the picture regarding the *siloviki,* professionals, intelligentsia, and clergy is mixed and fluid. Of course, rank matters in hierarchical Muscovy. Finding a place in the sun for small businessmen and entrepreneurs of all descriptions is a constant uphill battle, while unscrupulous rent-seeking insiders, by far the strongest element of new propertied class, feel entitled to unearned income, wealth, and privileges. They have not yet found a way to make their advantages hereditary, other than by pressing for longer-tenured leases and freehold property (especially land) but would be pleased to be ennobled if they could.

The oligarchs' main rival for status, wealth, and power in the new autocratic order is the *siloviki*,[5] broadly construed as high-ranking insider members of the security services and military and kindred spirits. Their position initially was tenuous as Yeltsin slashed military and

[5] Stephen Shenfield, "Yet Again on the Siloviki," *Johnson's Russia List*, Article 3, No. 60, March 12, 2007; Shenfield, "'Siloviki': A Complementary Interpretation". Attitudes toward the importance of the *siloviki*, defined as representatives of the 'force structures' active in Russia's government vary. David and Sharon Rivera find that the *siloviki* do not predominate over the business section of the elite. Bettina Renz of King's College London contends that there are no grounds for believing that Putin has systematically promoted *siloviki* as a deliberate strategy aimed at creating a more authoritarian regime. If he had been doing so, Renz argues, there would be more of them in top positions in the presidential administration (PA) and federal ministries. Of forty-seven leading officials in the PA in 2005, only nine had backgrounds in the force structures, and none of these occupied any of the top three positions. Of ten presidential advisers, only two were *siloviki*. In short, the *siloviki* do not constitute a group or faction with the coherence that a word like *militocracy* implies. Ian Bremmer (president of the Eurasia Group) and Samuel Charap (St. Antony's College, Oxford) by contrast consider an emphasis on the importance of the *siloviki* as a Kremlin faction fully justified. They, as do Russian political commentators, employ *siloviki* to mean a Kremlin faction favoring state authority and great power over business priorities, only loosely connected with career background. The faction's general outlook is statist and nationalist, with many members tending toward xenophobia and anti-Semitism. The term doesn't mean that all members of the force structures embrace the *siloviki* agenda. Some such as Sergei Stepashin distance themselves from the faction. Nor does it require that some faction members have different career backgrounds. And Prime Minister Mikhail Fradkov, head of the presidential administration, Sergei Sobyanin, and Putin are independent of factions. Bremmer and Charap identify three factions: (1) free-market oriented liberals associated with German Gref, minister of Economic Development and Trade, and Finance Minister Alexei Kudrin, (2) technocrats such as first deputy prime minister Dmitri Medvedev and Alexei Miller, both Gazprom officials, (3) *siloviki*, including FSB chief Nikolai Patrushev and Putin adviser Viktor Ivanov (responsible for personnel appointments in government agencies and state companies), and Igor Sechin, Rosneft's chairman and deputy head of the presidential administration. The free marketeers are the weakest and the *siloviki* the strongest faction in terms of control over government agencies (defense, FSB, energy, and customs) and its resource base. The hydrocarbons sector dominates Kremlin politics. Defense minister and Deputy Prime Minister Sergei Ivanov is a relatively independent member of the *siloviki*. Bremmer and Charap believe that the faction may not acquire complete dominance but will retain major influence over Russian policy. For one alternative schema, see Arkady Arzamastsev and Svetlana Branitskaya, "The Shadow behind the President," Delovye liudi, January 2004, http://www.dl.mk.ru/article.asp?artid=27730. They claim that the Yeltsin-era "family" is Putin's main opponent.

FSB budgets, but in the late 1990s, the tide turned. The *siloviki* not only gained the ruler's ear but also increasingly staffed the ministries and other government postings. They and their subordinates became the sword, shield, and administrators of Putin's Muscovy and were increasingly regarded as the regime's most reliable ally, in sharp contrast to oligarchs who often proved disloyal, and could be disposed of at little cost. Oligarchs financed some of the president's political operations, and provided valuable economic services, but a competitive modernization would have been better. Consequently, even though Putin played both factions against each other and endorsed the financial technocrat Dmitri Medvedev over former defense chief Sergei Ivanov for the 2008 presidency,[6] the *siloviki* still have the inside track. The situation is mercurial to the extent that the distinction between oligarchs and *siloviki* is becoming blurred as successful members of the security establishment are assigned business tasks in semiprivate corporations like Gazprom. However, *silovarchs* aren't the vanguard of democratic free enterprise as Daniel Treisman hopes.[7] Their culture and loyalties make them the new boyars, devoted and beholden to the realm.

Although the absence of an official governing idea obscures Russia's societal future, experience has clarified some possibilities. It has shown that mass impoverishment isn't an intrinsic feature of post-Soviet Muscovy; oligarchy isn't a turnpike to democractic free enterprise and that oligarchy isn't always an effective counterweight to the *siloviki*. Virulent rent-seeking and asset-grabbing immiserized most Russians for a decade, but their negative effects have been offset by other factors after 1998. Rising living standards in absolute terms driven by modernization, technology transfer, and diffusion now seem likely even if Russia remains an authoritarian martial police state, founded on rent-granting and asset-grabbing, but this doesn't provide a basis for oligarchy overturning Muscovy or popular sovereignty. The state is likely to continue finding an oligarchic presence and demagoguery convenient for its purposes, without being compelled to restructure according to eastern or western ideals.

---

[6] "Reciprocal Appointment: Medvedev Offers Vladimir Putin the post of Prime Minister," *Johnson's Russia List*, Vol. 254, Article 1, December 12, 2007; "Putin Accepts the Office of Prime Minister," *Johnson's Russia List*, Vol. 258, Article 5, December 17, 2007.

[7] Daniel Treisman, "Putin's Silovarchs," *Orbis*, Winter 2007.

Neither Russia's weak nor its strong have been able to craft a
social ideal that commands broad support or even lesser goals safe
from the regime's appropriation. The Kremlin has given liberals sham
democracy and Muscovy-friendly markets; conservatives *Fortress Russia*, and socialists partial renationalization of the natural resource processing sector. And it can continuously alter the mix to deflect dangerous currents. Nor is there any cogent reason to expect that rising living
standards and an emergent middle class will soon prompt Muscovite
rulers to cede the realm. The regime has ample means at its disposal
to depoliticize and co-opt all segments of society, including intellectuals who unlike their nineteenth- and twentieth-century brethren no
longer possess an inspiring vision of a progressive social order.

This doesn't mean that tomorrow will be a carbon copy of today.
The rehabilitation of proprietors, together with the limited empowerment of other stakeholders has created a motley constituency for the
rule of law, and a partial parliamentary counterweight to presidential
authority. The category includes high-level rent-seekers (oligarchs and
siloviki), entrepreneurs, and small businessmen, professionals, administrators, workers, peasants, and civil rights activists of various persuasions. Each desires to be treated fairly but resists relinquishing whatever
power it holds over others, a reluctance increasing up the ladder. Oligarchs and *siloviki* prefer gated communities. Rights and restricted
democracy strengthening their claims are welcome. Everything else
threatens. Reciprocally, those most deprived have the strongest interest
in widening rights and democratic participation, complicating the formation of a mass, popular, middle-class democratic tide. The situation
isn't unique. Democracy in England began gradually with the nobility, opening up to urban proprietors in the nineteenth century before
becoming inclusive in the twentieth century. Nonetheless, it seems
likely that any middle class that might emerge from rising incomes
in Russia splintered by identity politics, won't translate quickly into
a potent movement for universal popular sovereignty and the rule of
law, the essence of authentic democracy.

A petro bubble collapse, renewed hyperdepression, post-Putin political mayhem, or Chinese colonization of the Far East could radically
alter this prognosis turning contemporary Muscovite society topsy-
turvy. These possibilities come with the territory but are too open
ended to warrant elaborate speculation. Suffice it to say, that while
Russia's future isn't closed, no scenario leads in any obvious way to an
eastern or western ideal.

Virtuous Autocracy

However, virtuous authoritarian modernization isn't precluded. The lords of Muscovy can selectively mimic aspects of the West without fully embracing popular sovereignty or its social structure. They have the power to elevate the level of Russian civilization, augment freedom and rights, provide a generous social safety net, dispense compassionate transfers, foster equal opportunity within and across social strata, promote the empowerment of disadvantaged minorities, and champion social justice. Many Muscovite rulers have rhetorically endorsed some or all of these goals during the past quarter millennium and sporadically taken constructive action. The Bolsheviks installed universal free education, basic health care, full employment after 1929 (albeit partly in Gulag), and offered increased opportunities for women and ethnic and religious minorities. They didn't relinquish the authoritarian martial police state for a self-regulating, popularly sovereign society but selectively simulated anything in the West that seemed useful.

Postcommunist authoritarian social modernization has followed the historical Muscovite pattern, but with its own distinctive characteristics. From the outset, the Yeltsin administration distanced itself from communism by jettisoning collective for individual responsibility. During the heyday of asset-grabbing, despite some explicit Russian constitutional guarantees, it disavowed all obligations to the general population, including price-fixing, job rights, state wage and pension payments, and health and education benefits. Later, it phased out housing subsidies, low-cost public transportation, electricity, and access to free recreational facilities, all under the banner of liberalization. The Kremlin claimed that it didn't abandon society. It was merely applying tough love, weaning the people from debilitating state dependency, and nurturing self-reliance, both empowered by the decriminalization of private property, business, and entrepreneurship, as well as new effective rights of assembly, speech, and personal liberty. Setting aside the phenomenon of asset-grabbing and the resulting *catastroika*, Yeltsin's strategy was broadly the same as Deng Xiaoping's, shifting the public burden onto the shoulders of the poor, while touting the virtues of individual responsibility, much as the Victorians had done in Karl Marx's England.[8]

---

[8]   Charles Booth, *Life and Labour of the People of London*, 1891.

Perhaps, like Britain, the harshest aspects of the individual responsibility system will be alleviated by a restored Muscovite social safety net and strengthened rights, which accompanied rising industrial wealth in the West, without the Kremlin having to accept democracy and the rule of law. The evidence thus far isn't encouraging, despite specious rhetorical claims to the contrary. The experience of the Yeltsin years is unequivocal. Collectivist social support continuously spiraled downward without compensatory individually financed health, education, housing, transport, and other human security services. Workers were dismissed or forced into lower value-adding occupations, and human and civil rights were mostly ineffectual, except for those seeking freer lifestyles, including drug addiction and prostitution. Eastern Orthodox Christianity budded, but so did intolerance toward other faiths. Ethnic hatred and xenophobia flared. The condition of most women sharply deteriorated in response to the diminished status of their traditional occupations (teaching, medicine, clerical, commercial service), poverty, increased alcoholism, wrecked families, premature widowhood, and intensified sexual harassment. Many were reduced to sexual commodities, trafficked abroad in the Middle East, Japan, and Europe, or in more fortunate circumstances became internet brides. People did enjoy expanded speech and artistic expression, and they could vote in rigged elections, but only a few benefited significantly.

The economic recovery, which began in 1999, together with Putin's reconsolidation of the Muscovite authoritarian martial police state, has significantly ameliorated some egregious societal misconduct, reduced involuntary unemployment, improved the competitive position of ordinary people, including women, alleviated material suffering, and transformed paper liberties into realities for many, at the same time, it suffocated popular democracy and strengthened state discipline. Later the boom in petroleum and other natural resource prices filled state coffers, providing a no-excuses opportunity to construct a contemporary version of Muscovy with a human face, but it was missed. The Putin administration proved to be long on promises and short on action,[9] a revealing lapse underscoring the importance of westernization. Although modernization can provide elements of a good society, no invisible Muscovite hand can transform promises into reality. Indeed, incentives drive insiders in the opposite direction, toward

[9] OECD Survey, *The Russian Federation 2006*, OECD, Paris, 2007.

strengthening privilege and power at the expense of others. Putin could have replicated the West's health, education, transfer, welfare, and justice systems, but he chose to do very little, even though resulting productivity effects would have advanced the regime's cause.

Identity, Purpose, and Ethics

The Kremlin's mission during the past two decades has been insider empowerment, systems modernization, and bolstered legitimacy. This was Muscovy's agenda under some of the tsars, and the Soviets as well, but ideologies varied. The people always were supposed to serve the state through diligent labor, enhanced skills, material betterment, sacrificing for the greater good when duty called, subject to a complex, tacit, and often unscrupulous ethical code, with identities tied to roles. From this perspective, social behavior has changed less in postcommunist Muscovy than meets the eye. Those at the top still intrigue to stay there. New Russians energetically scramble to advance, and the rest duck and cover. Liberalization hasn't radically transformed the Russian character. Although the upwardly mobile no longer camouflage their self-seeking in the name of *proletopia* and require new skills, their behavior remains familiar. They avidly seek appropriate education and lucrative service jobs, where wages are supplemented by perks, bribes, and networking opportunities, with one significant difference. The rise of business and the decline of ideology have diminished the appeal of scholarship; at the same time, the government has sought to reduce the autonomy and power of the Academy of Sciences.[10] The old intelligentsia and potential new entrants have diverted energy from erudition to service in other fields. Commerce has not only lured many from academia and government but also narrowed intellectual vision. The phenomenon has minuses and pluses. Russian society has become crasser and more pragmatic. It is shallow, corrupt, materialistic, and individually self-seeking but also more capable of commercial value-adding if the system allows.

---

[10] Peter Finn, "Russian Academy of Sciences Reject Demand to Give up Autonomy," *Johnson's Russia List*, Vol. 75, Article 18, March 29, 2007. "Academy Gets New Role," *Johnson's Russia List*, Vol. 241, Article 29, November 21, 2007.

This is the rub. Modernization holds promise everywhere, and sophisticated propaganda doesn't let anyone forget it in Russia as in Hu Jintao's China.[11] Nothing stops authoritarians from posturing as philosopher kings, pretending that the society they installed justly empowers everyone to actualize individual and collective potential or at least improve most people's lot. But there is no self-regulating mechanism compelling Muscovy to realize its modernization potential as the people, or even rulers themselves desire it. Expanded opportunities for all classes, strata, genders, persuasions, ethnic minorities, and religious groups, whatever their scope, aren't sufficient to overcome Muscovite impediments. Russian society is not only adversarial, but also its privileged tend to live for the moment rather than optimize in the intermediate and long runs. They have not and seem unlikely to take the painful steps needed for comprehensive societal empowerment beyond the veneer of progressive change. This is why westernization is so critical. Although western theory and practice have their own deficiencies, they give society more degrees of competitive freedom to dispel the noise of deceptive claims and illusions of progress essential for aligning the supply of public and private goods with welfare-maximizing popular demand.

International Norms

The inadequacies of Russia's societal reconfiguration can be gauged according to universal human and civil norms. Most nations recognize and endorse political and private rights that transcend ideology and culture, even though what is said isn't always meant. These principles enshrined in various international declarations and laws provide a revealing benchmark for weighing Russian social flux since 1980.

---

[11] Hu Jintao and Wen Jiabao launched a Harmonious Society campaign October 11, 2006, at the 6th Plenum of the 16th Central Committee of the Communist Party of China promising a democratic society under the rule of law, based on equality and justice, an honest and caring society, and a stable, vigorous, and orderly society. See Wing Thye Woo, "The Real Challenges to China's High Growth: Institutions, Poverty, Inequality, Environment and Fiscal Balance," *Comparative Economic Studies*, December 2007. For a sobering counterview, see Liang Jing, "Can a Hypocritically Benevolent Government Go on for Long?" *Xin shiji*, March 2007.

Human and civil rights didn't go unnoticed in the Kremlin. Stalin's infamous 1936 Constitution of the USSR pays homage, stipulating that:[12]

Article 3. All power belongs to the working people represented by the Soviets of Working People's Deputies.

Article 4. The socialist system abolishes the exploitation of *man by man*.

Article 10. Citizens have the right to personal ownership of their incomes from work and savings, their dwellings and household goods.

Article 12. Work is a duty. *He who does not work, neither shall he eat*. From each *according to his ability, to each according to his work*.

Article 36. The Supreme Soviet of the USSR is elected for a term of four years.

Article 101. The executive organs of the Soviets of Working People's Deputies are directly accountable both to the Soviets of Working People's Deputies which elected them and to the executive organ of the superior Soviet of Working People's Deputies.

Article 102. Justice is administered by the Supreme Court of the USSR, and its subsidiaries, including People's Courts.

Article 103. Citizens have the right to work, that is are guaranteed the right to employment and payment in accordance with its quantity and quality. The right to work is ensured by the socialist organization of the national economy.

Article 119. Citizens have the right to rest and leisure. The right to rest and leisure is ensured by the reduction of the working day to seven hours, the institution of annual vacations with full pay, and the provision of a wide network of sanatoria, rest homes and clubs.

Article 120. Citizens have the right to maintenance in old age, and also in case of sickness or loss of capacity to work. This right is ensured by the extensive development of social insurance, free medical service, and a wide network of health resorts.

---

[12] 1936 Constitution of the USSR, http://en.wikisource.org/wiki/1936_ Constitution_of_the_USSR. Leonard Schapiro considered the 1936 constitution to be a meaningless propaganda document: "The decision to alter the electoral system from indirect to direct election, from a limited to a universal franchise, and from open to secret voting, was a measure of the confidence of the party in its ability to ensure the return of candidates of its own choice without the restrictions formerly considered necessary," and that " . . . a careful scrutiny of the draft of the new constitution showed that it left the party's supreme position unimpaired, and was therefore worthless as a guarantee of individual rights," Leonard Schapiro, *The Communist Party of the Soviet Union*, 2nd ed., Random House, New York, 1971, pp. 410–11.

Article 121. Citizens have the right to education. This right is ensured by universal, compulsory elementary education; by education, including higher education, being free of charge; by the system of state stipends for the overwhelming majority of students in the universities and colleges; by instruction in schools being conducted in the native language, and by the organization in the factories, state farms, machine and tractor stations and collective farms of free vocational, technical and agronomic training for working people.

Article 122. Women in the USSR are accorded equal rights with men in all spheres of economic, state, cultural, social and political life. The possibility of exercising these rights is ensured to women by granting them an equal right with men to work, payment for work, rest and leisure, social insurance and education, and by protection of the interests of mother and child, pre-maternity and maternity leave with full pay, and by the provision of a wide network of maternity homes, nurseries and kindergartens.

Article 123. Equality of rights of citizens of the USSR, irrespective of their nationality or race, in all spheres of economic, state, cultural, social and political life, is an indefeasible law. Any direct or indirect restriction of the rights of, or, conversely, any establishment of direct or indirect privileges for, citizens on account of their race or nationality, as well as any advocacy of racial or national exclusiveness or hatred and contempt, is punishable by law.

Article 124. In order to ensure to citizens freedom of conscience, the church in the USSR is separated from the state, and the school from the church. Freedom of religious worship and antireligious propaganda is recognized for all citizens.

Article 125. In conformity with the interests of the working people, and in order to strengthen the socialist system, the citizens of the USSR are guaranteed by law:

a. freedom of speech
b. freedom of press
c. freedom of assembly, including the holding of mass meetings
d. freedom of street processions and demonstrations

These civil rights are ensured by placing at the disposal of the working people and their organizations printing presses, stocks of paper, public buildings, the streets, communications facilities, and other material requisites for exercising these rights.

Article 126. Citizens are ensured the right to unite in public organizations: trade unions, cooperative associations, youth organizations, sport and defense organizations, cultural, technical and scientific societies; and the most active and politically conscious citizens in the ranks of the working class and other sections of the working people unite in the Communist Party of the Soviet Union (Bolsheviks), which is the vanguard of the working people in their struggle to strengthen and develop the socialist system and is the leading core of all organizations of the working people, both public and state.

Article 127. Citizens are guaranteed inviolability of the person. No person may be placed under arrest except by decision of a court or with the sanction of a procurator.

Article 128. The inviolability of the homes of citizens and privacy of correspondence are protected by law.

Article 129. The USSR affords the right of asylum to foreign citizens persecuted for defending the interests of working people, or for their scientific activities, or for their struggle for national liberation.

Article 130. It is the duty of every citizen to abide by the Constitution of the Union of Soviet Socialist Republics, to observe the laws, to maintain labor discipline, honestly to perform public duties, and to respect the rules of socialist intercourse.

Article 131. It is the duty of every citizen of the USSR to safeguard and strengthen public, socialist property as the sacred and inviolable foundation of the Soviet system, as the source of the wealth and might of the country, as the source of the prosperous and cultured life of all the working people. Persons committing offenses against public, socialist property are enemies of the people.

Article 132. Universal military service is law. Military service in the Workers' and Peasants' Red Army is an honorable duty of the citizens.

Article 133. To defend the fatherland is the sacred duty of every citizen of the USSR. Treason to the country - violation of the oath of allegiance, desertion to the enemy, impairing the military power of the state, espionage is punishable with all the severity of the law as the most heinous of crimes.

Article 134. Members of all Soviets of Working People's Deputies are chosen by the electors on the basis of universal, direct and equal suffrage by secret ballot.

Article 135. Elections of deputies are universal: all citizens of the USSR who have reached the age of eighteen, irrespective of race or nationality, religion, educational and residential qualifications, social origin, property status or past activities, have the right to vote in the election of deputies and to be elected; with the exception of insane persons and persons who have been convicted by a court of law and who sentences include deprivation of electoral rights.

Article 136. Elections of deputies are equal: each citizen has one vote; all citizens participate in elections on an equal footing.

Article 137. Women have the right to elect and be elected on equal terms with men.

Article 138. Citizens serving in the Red Army have the right to elect and be elected on equal terms with other citizens.

Article 139. Elections of deputies are direct: all Soviets of Working People's Deputies, from rural and city Soviets of Working People's Deputies to the Supreme Soviet of the USSR, inclusive, are elected by citizens by direct vote.

Article 140. Voting at elections of deputies is secret.

Article 141. Candidates for election are nominated according to electoral areas. The right to nominate candidates is secured to public organizations and societies of the working people; Communist Party organizations, trade unions, cooperatives, youth organizations and cultural societies.

Article 142. It is the duty of every deputy to report to his electors on his work and on the work of the Soviet of Working People's Deputies, and he is liable to be recalled at any time in the manner established by law upon decision of a majority of electors.

Although this list of constitutional guarantees omits some modern concerns such as sexual preference, suicide, rights of minors, torture, psychiatric abuses, and involuntary medical experiments, it was exemplary in its day, when constitutions, or supporting statutes in the West, denied many of these protections. The document begins by declaring that all power derives from and is vested in the people, who exert their sovereignty via universal suffrage, assured secret ballots, and regular elections. Even though opposition parties are prohibited by decree, the people can choose representatives from various Communist Party candidates, who are supposed to faithfully provide popular public programs and private consumer goods. To ensure that party representatives heed the people's will, citizens are granted freedom of speech, press, assembly, and demonstration, buttressed by universal free primary education, vocational training, and stipends for university studies. They enjoy freedom of conscience, including both religious and antireligious *propaganda*, and can unite in trade unions, cooperative associations, youth organizations, sports and defense organizations, and cultural, technical, and scientific societies to lead the masses under the guidance of the Communist Party. In pursuing these and other activities, individuals cannot be wrongly arrested or imprisoned nor can their homes be unlawfully entered and their correspondence censored. Moreover, the document makes it clear that the *people* means everyone, including women and national minorities, regardless of race, ethnicity, and religion, except *enemies of the people*, that is, hostile class elements seeking to overthrow popular sovereignty. Violations of these principles are subject to judicial sanctions.

These political safeguards are supplemented with extensive economic rights. Involuntary unemployment is proscribed. Individuals are granted assured employment and job security, with a complementary duty to exercise the right. Labor exploitation is prohibited, a ban enforced by people's representatives obliged to pay fair wages in accordance with skills and length of service. Likewise, as part of the antiexploitation package, Soviet workers are assured proper educational, medical, recreational, vacation, and retirement support, including maternity leaves and benefits. In short, since privilege and all other forms of exploitation are proscribed, Soviet citizens are economically, politically, and socially secure from cradle to grave.

It might seem to follow that if the vanguard of the proletariat diligently suppressed the people's enemies, human and civil rights should have been sacrosanct in the land of the Soviets under Stalin's constitution and the Brezhnev constitution, which replaced it in 1977.[13] But who protected the people from the state? There was no independent rule of law because the Communist Party controlled the judiciary, and there was no venue for political redress because opposition parties were banned. Moreover, how could the Bolsheviks know the will of the people, when there were no markets to evaluate economic preferences, and criticism of communist policies was treated as counterrevolutionary agitation? The answer is simple. An authoritarian state insistent on having its own way, regardless of popular opinion, can neither accurately know nor express the will of the people. It is

---

[13] Brezhnev's constitution dropped the earlier emphasis on workers and peasants, stressing instead the state's role as representative of the "whole people." And it preserved the right of secession, which later played an important role in the dissolution of the Soviet Union. With respect to human and civil rights, Stalin's protections were repeated and expanded with guarantees of privacy, freedom of creative expression, and family security.

an adversary, not a protector making its constitutional guarantees a sham.

We now know that during Stalin's time the Soviet constitution mocked reality.[14] Where it declared the inviolability of political human rights, people had virtually no protection against state oppression. Tens of millions were wrongfully arrested, incarcerated in prisons, and concentration camps (Gulag), exiled, herded into collective farms, stripped of their personal property and civil rights, consigned to forced labor, worked to death, starved, and executed, despite the abolition of capital punishment during peacetime in 1947.[15] Racial and national hatred were rife. Minorities were forcibly relocated to inhospitable places,[16] and Stalin was preparing his own "final solution" for the Jews just before he died in March 5, 1953. Free speech, press, assembly, and demonstration were restricted to communist propaganda, and people were terrorized, arrested, and shot for suspicion of subversive thinking. Democracy was demagoguery, religion repressed, and there were no civil rights superior to communist dictate. Soviet rulers provided educational, medical, recreational, vacation, and retirement support, but they were spartan. Although job rights and wage fixing also were genuine, they were more obligations to labor at subsistence wages than guarantees of economic security.

The gap between constitutional rights and practice today is no longer as glaring as it had been under Stalin, either with respect to the Soviet or to Yeltsin's constitution forcibly imposed on Russia in December 1993.[17] This constitution expanded rights by adding

[14] Steven Rosefielde, *Russian Economics from Lenin to Putin,* Blackwell, London, 2007, chapter 6.

[15] *Vedemosti Verkhovnovo Soveta SSSR,* 1947, No. 17, reprinted in Ministerstvo Yustitsii RSFSR, Ugolovnyi Kodeks RSFSR: Ofitsialnyi tekst s izmeneniyanii na 1 iulia 1950g i s prilozheniem postateino-sistematizirovannykh materialov, Gosudarstvennoe Izdalet'stvo Iuridicheskoi Literatury, Moskva 1950, pp. 140–141. The Presidium of the Supreme Soviet of the USSR commuted the sentences of those already sentenced to death, and those who would otherwise have received the death penalty to twenty-five years corrective-labor in the gulag. Cf. Ger P. Van den Berg, "The Soviet Union and the Death Penalty," *Soviet Studies,* 35, 2(April 1983): 154–74.

[16] Alexander Nekrich, *Punished Peoples: The Deportation and Fate of Soviet Minorities at the End of the Second World War,* Norton, New York, 1978.

[17] Russia's current constitution was crafted by Boris Yeltsin's presidential administration and approved by a referendum in December 1993. It differs from the Brezhnev constitution primarily in its substitution of a strong president for the

prohibitions against environmental degradation, torture, humiliation, forced labor, discrimination on grounds of age, sexual orientation,

Communist Party. Russia as before is declared a popular democracy, with popular sovereignty protected by the judiciary. For the chapter on Rights and Liberties of Man and Citizen, see http://www.departments.bucknell.edu/russia/const/ch2.html. Here is a concise listing of rights and liberties: **Article 17**. Basic rights and liberties recognized by international law are constitutionally guaranteed. They start at birth. Individuals may not violate the rights of others. **Article 19.** All people are equal under the law, regardless of sex, race, nationality, language, origin, property or employment status, residence, attitude toward religion, convictions, and membership of public associations. **Article 20**. Everyone shall have the right to life. Capital punishment may, until its abolition, be instituted by federal law. **Article 21**. Personal dignity is protected by the state. No one shall be tortured, or humiliated. No one may be subjected to medical, scientific or other experiments without his or her free consent. **Article 22**. Everyone has the right to freedom and personal inviolability. Arrest, detention and custody shall be fixed by law. **Article 23**. Everyone shall have the right to privacy, without censorship. **Article 24**. Gathering, storing, using and disseminating private information without consent is prohibited. Individuals have the right to see documents affecting their rights. **Article 26**. Everyone has the right to determine his national identity, use his native language, choose the language of communication, education, training and creative work. **Article 27**. Everyone has the right to freedom of movement, including leaving and returning to the country. **Article 28**. Everyone has the right of freedom of conscience, and religious worship. **Article 29**. Everyone has the right to freedom of thought and speech. Contrary propaganda is prohibited. They have the right to seek, get, transfer, produce and disseminate information. The freedom of the mass media is guaranteed. **Article 30**. Everyone has the right of association in trade union and civil activities. **Article 31**. Everyone has the right to peacefully demonstrate without weapons, and to hold meetings, rallies, demonstrations, marches and pickets. **Article 32**. Citizens have the right to participate in the administration of state directly and through representatives. They have the right to elect and be elected. **Article 33**. Citizens have the right of petition. **Article 34**. Everyone is free to act entrepreneurially, but monopolization is prohibited. **Article 35**. The right of private property is protected, including inheritance. **Article 36**. Citizens have the right to own and use land with terms and procedures determined by federal law. **Article 37**. Work shall be free. Forced labor is prohibited. Everyone has the right to work under conditions meeting safety and hygiene requirements, to non-discriminatory remuneration, at or above the minimum wage. Everyone has job security against unemployment. Collective bargaining and strikes are rights. Everyone has the right to rest and leisure. **Article 38.** Motherhood and childhood and family shall be under state protection. Parents are responsible for childcare, adults for the care of non-employable parents. **Article 39**. Everyone shall be guaranteed social security in old age in case of disease, invalidity, loss of breadwinner, to bring up children. Voluntary social insurance is encouraged. **Article 40.** Everyone has a right to a home. No one will be deprived of a home. Low income citizens and other citizens, who need housing shall be housed free of charge, or for affordable pay from government. **Article 41**. Everyone

and social status; established the principle of presumed innocence; and decriminalized private property, business, and entrepreneurship. Economic, political, and social freedom improved gradually under Nikita Khrushchev and Brezhnev, surged during the Gorbachev and Yeltsin years and shrank thereafter without fully reverting to the post-Stalin norm. Repression in contemporary Russia isn't as intense or pervasive as it was in 1980 and is light-years distant from Stalin's *kakatopia* but remains severe by western standards and is worsening.

The initial advance in Russian human and civil rights occurred under Gorbachev's watch, not his successors. He championed democracy, free speech, communication, and travel in the Soviet period within the parameters of Brezhnev's constitution; legalized leasing, business, and entrepreneurship in defiance of the constitution; and reined in KGB intimidation.[18] Yeltsin deserves credit for constitutionally legalizing freehold property and affirming business rights, for deconsecrating the Communist Party, legalizing organized political opposition, and enlarging the scope of human and civil rights guarantees, as well as further curtailing secret police actions against individual liberties. Both he and Putin also enhanced economic freedom by nurturing market institutions. They promoted price decontrol and deregulation, ruble convertibility, expanded privatization, including land, curtailed leasing in favor of freehold ownership, established stock

shall have the right to health case and medical assistance. State and municipal health care institutions shall be free of charge. **Article 42.** Everyone shall have the right to a favorable environment. **Article 43.** Everyone has the right to education. The accessibility and gratuity of pre-school, general secondary and vocational secondary education in public and municipal educational institutions and enterprises is guaranteed. Everyone has the right to receive free of charge and on a competitive basis higher education in state and municipal institutions. Basic education is mandatory. **Article 44.** Everyone is guaranteed freedom of literary, artistic, scientific, intellectual and other types of creative activity and tuition. Intellectual property is protected by law. **Article 46.** Everyone can protect his liberties in a court of law. **Article 48.** Everyone has the right to legal counsel, free of charge where specified by law. **Article 49.** Everyone charged with a crime shall be considered not guilty until proven otherwise. **Article 50.** No one may be repeatedly convicted for the same offense. **Article 51.** No one shall be obliged to give evidence against himself. **Article 52.** Victims are guaranteed access to justice. **Article 53.** Everyone has the right to compensation by the state for damage. **Article 62.** Foreign citizens and stateless persons shall enjoy the rights of citizens.

[18] In the late 1980s, Rosefielde was told second hand that a detainee had been released because the "boss" (Gorbachev) had instructed the KGB to restrict itself temporarily to collecting incriminating evidence against undesirables.

and commodity markets, encouraged modern banking, opened foreign trade, and accepted direct foreign investment, all buttressed by enabling legislation and reformed judicial oversight. But these gains, which primarily benefited the few at the expense of the many, were offset as time passed by creeping renationalization, tightened state control, the reconfiguration of insider Muscovite privilege toward the *siloviki*, eviscerated democracy, secret police reempowerment, together with increased economic, political, social, and civic repression directed against selected individuals and groups.

Compared with 1980, ordinary people on balance, now enjoy improved personal liberty in lifestyles, travel, thought, speech, occupational, and spatial mobility, as well as access to and influence over product supply but remain disenfranchised, vulnerable to state-condoned victimization, and have partly or wholly lost many former constitutional economic protections, including job security, price and wage fixing, and health, retirement, and recreational access.

An item-by-item comparison of contemporary Russian constitutional rights juxtaposed with their state sanctioned infringement is edifying.[19] It reveals that the constitution is an impotent document intended to gloss social reality rather than assure individual rights and liberties. The degree of social oppression or empowerment in the hoary Muscovite tradition depends on the ruler, not the march of civilization.

1. Individuals may not transgress the rights of others, but Muscovy represses equal opportunity (Article 17, Article 19).
2. Personal dignity is protected, but torture and humiliation are rampant in the military (Article 21).
3. Everyone has the right to privacy without censorship, but the FSB disregards both injunctions allegedly going so far as killing or attempting to kill offending reporters, lawmakers, and oligarchs (Article 23).
4. Individuals and media enjoy free communication, but the media are tightly managed by the Kremlin, and steps are being taken to deter internet dissent (Article 24, Article 29).[20]

[19] See note 15 for a list of human rights guarantees provided in Russia's 1992 constitution.
[20] Floriana Fossato, "Russia: Media Decree Targets Internet, Digital TV," *Johnson's Russia List*, Vol. 75, Article 19, March 29, 2007. "Public Chamber Acknowledges

5. Everyone has freedom of movement, but permission to live in Moscow is controlled (Article 27).
6. Everyone has freedom of conscience, but Eastern Orthodoxy is privileged, and other religious NGOs discouraged (Article 28).
7. Everyone has the right to demonstrate peacefully, but permission is increasingly denied, and defiance violently repressed (Article 31).[21]
8. Citizens are free to elect and be elected, but only the presidential party of the moment counts and eligibility is restricted (Article 32).
9. Citizens have the right to petition, but the Kremlin never listens (Article 33).
10. Monopolization is prohibited but is an intrinsic aspect of rent-granting (Article 34).
11. Private property is sacrosanct but as the Khodorkovsky case makes plain is only so at the state's sufferance (Article 35).
12. Forced labor is prohibited but persists in the Gulag (Article 37).
13. Hazardous working conditions are proscribed but are widespread (Article 37).
14. Wage discrimination is unconstitutional but pervasive (Article 37).
15. Wages must exceed the statutory minimum, except for millions of unprotected migrants (Article 37).
16. Full employment is guaranteed, but unemployment often is high, exceeding 25 percent in the 1990s (Article 37).
17. Everyone has the right to rest and leisure but only in a perfunctory sense (Article 37).
18. Motherhood and childhood and family are under state protection, but the safeguards are thin and weakly enforced (Article 38).
19. Social security is guaranteed but in Yeltsin's time reduced to virtually nothing by hyperinflation (Article 39).
20. Disability security is guaranteed but seldom provided (Article 39).

Crackdown on Independent Media," *Johnson's Russia List,* Vol. 75, Article 7, March 29, 2007.

[21] Alan Cullison and Guy Chazan, "Kremlin's Fears Fuel Brutal Crackdown," *Johnson's Russia List*, Vol. 89, Article 16, April 16, 2007.

21. Everyone has the right to a home, but people are routinely evicted by authorities coveting their property, and homelessness is widespread (Article 40).

22. Everyone has the right to health care, provided free in state and municipal institutions, but the quality of public medical assistance has deteriorated, and payments of all kinds are demanded (Article 41).

23. Everyone has the right to a favorable environment, but Russia's environment continues to be despoiled (Article 42).

24. Everyone has the right to free preschool, secondary, and vocational education, but the educational system is in shambles, and payment is increasingly required (Article 43).

25. Intellectual property is protected in theory but not in practice (Article 44).

26. Everyone can protect his liberties in a court of law, but verdicts depend on state directives, connections, and ability to bribe (Article 46).

27. Everyone shall be considered not guilty until proven otherwise, but the presumption is often perfunctory (Article 49).[22]

The government does not deny that human rights violations are widespread in Russia, including socioeconomic abuses, corruption, police brutality, judicial malpractice, and abridgment of the rights of children, pensioners, soldiers (*dedovshchina*), prisoners, and psychiatric patients,[23] but it isn't perturbed. It portrays them as routine enforcement problems, commonplace in all systems, rather than endemic

---

[22] "Russian Human Rights Report Highlights Police Violence against Opposition," *Johnson's Russia List*, Vol. 75, Article 5, March 29, 2007. "Clandestine Optimism Political Parties Pledge to Avoid Protest Demonstrations, Kremlin Requests Parties to Sign An Anti-Extremism Charter," *Johnson's Russia List*, Vol. 75, Article 10, March 29, 2007.

[23] Robert Coalson, "Russia's Ombudsman Speaks Out," Radio Free Europe, June 2004. http://wwww.rferl.org/featuresarticle/2004/06/00d97e5f-de14-ra35-ae9b-a791f9106124.html. Also, http://en.wikipedia.org/wiki/Human_rights_in_Russia. For more general reading, see David Satter, *Darkness at Dawn: The Rise of the Russian Criminal State*, Yale University Press, New Haven, CT, 2003; Anna Politkovskaya, *Putin's Russia*, Havrill, London, 2004; Jonathan Weiler, *Human Rights in Russia: A Darker Side of Reform*, Lynne Rienner Publishers, Boulder, CO, 2004; Pamela Jordan, *Defending Rights in Russia: Lawyers, the State, and Legal Reform in the Post Soviet Era*, University of British Columbia Press, Vancouver, 2006; Yuri Felshtinsky, Alexander Litvinenko, and Geoffrey Andrews, *Blowing up Russia: Terror from Within*, Encounter Books, London, 2002.

features of Muscovy. Allegations by Amnesty International and others charging discrimination, racism, and murder of ethnic minorities,[24] the killing of forty-four journalists since 1992,[25] and the assassination of lawmakers such as Galina Starovoitsova and Sergei Yushenkov, from the Kremlin's official perspective, demonstrate the need for intensified vigilance, not regime change, leaving little room for hope that Russian society will soon westernize or find alternative means to empower individual liberty.

No matter how the subject is approached from the standpoint of ideas, modernization, or commonly accepted human rights norms, despite Soviet dissolution and the destruction of communism, the more society changes in Russia, the more its oppressive essence stays the same. There have been aspects of social progress, retrogress, and flux since 1980, but no compelling evidence that Muscovy with all its injustices will soon perish from the face of the earth.[26] Indeed, Putin's gradually tightening power vertical indicates that illiberality may worsen.

- Russian society has changed, even though the Kremlin reverted to Muscovite authoritarianism.
- Proletopia has been discredited as the Russian ideal, but no substitute has been found.
- Soviet proletopia was never realized. It was just a dream. The reality was Muscovy in working-class costumes.
- Gorbachev's criticisms of communism's shortcomings sparked a short-lived revival in socialist humanist thought, soon superseded by Yeltsin's Muscovite notion of *democratic* marketization.
- The Kremlin continues to grope toward its defining social idea. Everything except the recriminalization of business seems on the table.
- The relegitimization of business is the hallmark of contemporary Muscovy. It has enhanced businessmen's stature, while intellectuals have become less influential.

---

[24] Amnesty International, Racism Report, http://www.amnesty.org/russia/pdfs/racism_report.pdf.

[25] Committee to Protect Journalists, http://222.cpj.org/killed/killed_archives/stats.html.

[26] "Russia: Civil Society and Human Rights Highlights, October 2007," in *Johnson's Russia List*, Vol. 230, Articles 16, November 24, 2007.

- The two most powerful groupings are oligarchs and *siloviki,* but the power services have the advantage, proven by the emergence of *silovarchs* from the ranks of the *siloviki*, who are both rich and security minded.
- Russian society is in flux, without trending toward any discernible ideal, including Muscotopia.
- Nor is there evidence that social benevolence is Muscovy's priority.
- The state claims that curtailing government support is tough love, but this is window dressing.
- The real income and status of working men and women have diminished.
- Democratic free enterprise's invisible hand is more powerful than Muscovy's in promoting social justice and individual liberty.
- Liberalization hasn't transformed the Russian character.
- Soviet constitutions guaranteed society an extensive and progressive set of liberties and protections, but they were only honored in the breach because no one protected the people from the state.
- Social freedom improved under Khrushchev, Brezhnev, Gorbachev, and Yeltsin but ebbed under Putin.
- Gorbachev, Yeltsin, and Putin deserve credit for some of these gains and blame too for clinging to Muscovy.
- The prognosis is for intensifying Russian social injustice and inegalitarianism, coupled with reduced individual liberties, partially offset by gradually improving material wealth.

12

International Relations

The Soviet defeat of Nazi Germany; Joseph Stalin's postwar expansion in East Europe; the iron curtain; Mao Tse-tung's, Kim Il-song's, and Ho Chi Minh's triumphs in Asia, Castro's victory in Cuba in 1959; and Marxist insurgencies across the globe made it seem that the tide of history was "red" well into the 1970s. Although Nikita Khrushchev spoke of peaceful coexistence in the mid-1950s, the combination of rapid socialist economic modernization and Marxist messianism seemed unstoppable, despite the Polish and Hungarian uprisings of 1956, the Sino-Soviet rift, and the 1968 Prague Spring. The Kremlin's foreign policy during this period was cold war, Muscovite empire building with a communist gloss.

Then suddenly and without warning Soviet communism lost momentum. Economic growth decelerated despite a massive arms buildup that made the USSR a superpower.[1] Neoliberal economic theory gained a toehold in the West, American military prowess recovered from the Vietnam debacle, and global revolutionary fervor subsided so noticeably that Marshal Nikolai Ogarkov, chief of the Soviet General Staff grumbled about an adverse turn in the correlation of forces.[2]

Soviet triumphalism evident in the mid-1970s was displaced just five years later by the specter of domestic economic stagnation and a

---

[1] Steven Rosefielde, *False Science: Underestimating the Soviet Arms Buildup*, Transaction Books, New Brunswick, NJ, 1987.

[2] John Erickson, "Toward 1984: Four Decades of Soviet Military Policy," *Air University Review*, January–February 1984 (http://www.airpower.maxwell.af.mil/airchronicles/aureview/1984/jan). Raymond Garthoff, *Soviet Military Power*, Frederick A. Praeger, New York, 1966. The correlation of forces is a Marxist term for an extended definition of balance of power that includes *soft power* and ideological fervor. Dean Baker, *The United States Since 1980*, Cambridge University Press, Cambridge, 2007.

reversal of international fortune.[3] Moscow responded by intensifying expenditures on technological innovation and defense and proclaiming Mikhail Gorbachev's doctrine of *novoe myshlenie* (new thinking) in 1987.[4] After forty years of confrontation, the Soviet leadership began speaking wistfully about returning to its "common western home," attempting to reconcile opposites or even westernize.[5]

Many observers were electrified. They glimpsed Shangri-la, and urged statesmen to strike while the iron was hot. The fateful decades from 1985 to 2005 were to be a time of exuberant expectations and dashed hopes.

For a few heady years, Gorbachev appeared to be the messiah. He acquiesced to German reunification (October 3, 1990); tolerated the Baltic secessionist movement; terminated the Afghan war (1979–89); reduced financial support for Cuba; signed the Intermediate-Range Nuclear Forces Treaty (INF), withdrawing 1,846 missile systems, including SS20s from Europe in 1987; concluded the Strategic Arms Reduction Treaty (START I) July 1991; and claimed to have cut military spending.[6] However, these substantial gestures were soon eclipsed by the breakup of the Soviet Union into fifteen independent states on December 1991, the liberation of the USSR's East European satellites, Kremlin assistance in denuclearizing the former non-Russian Soviet republics, the disestablishment of the Council for Mutual Economic Assistance (CMEA), the collapse of Moscow's support for international communism, a 90 percent reduction in arms procurement, halving of its armed forces, downsizing nuclear stockpiles, Boris Yeltsin's forbearance in the Kosovo war (1996–99), his acceptance of western transition assistance, and cooperation with the G-7, IMF, World Bank, OECD, US AID, and counterpart EU institutions. These pluses were diminished by some minuses. Despite intense efforts, Japan was unable to secure the return of its northern territories seized by Soviet troops after the conclusion of World War II. There was insubordination in the ranks. General Anatoly Kvashnin, chief of the Russian General Staff, launched military operations against Pristina during the Kosovo

---

[3] Yevdokim Yegorovich Mal'tsev, "Leninist Concepts of the Defense of Socialism," *Strategic Review*, 1975, p. 99.

[4] Mikhail Gorbachev, *Perestroika: New Thinking for Our Country and the World*, Harper and Row, New York, 1987.

[5] Ibid.

[6] Noel Firth and James Noren, *Soviet Defense Spending: A History of CIA Estimates 1950–1990*, Texas A&M University, College Station, 1998.

war without approval or reprimand.[7] And, of course, Yeltsin initiated the First Chechen war (1994–96). Nonetheless, these blemishes
were minor and paled in comparison with the prospect of Russia's
democratic market transition and its prospective incorporation into
the World Trade Organization, NATO, and the European Union.

Box 12.1 Cold War

The cold war was a period of ideology-infused belligerency between
the Soviet Union and the West for territory and influence throughout
the globe, often employing proxy armies, without a formal declaration
of war or large-scale hostilities between uniformed western and eastern
military forces that threatened Armageddon. Its roots can be traced at
least as far back as the Yalta negotiations on the postwar global order
and is often symbolically associated with Winston Churchill's "Iron
Curtain Speech" at Fulton, Missouri, on March 5, 1946. The term was
coined in 1947 by Bernard Baruch and Walter Lippman. The character
of the rivalry, which some believe ended in December 1991 with the
fall of the Soviet Union, varied over the years with a few constants.
Both sides maintained enormous nuclear and conventional armed forces
that could be used to deter or conquer, probed for vulnerabilities, and
were prepared to engage in nuclear brinksmanship in Berlin, Cuba,
and elsewhere when necessary. If the cold war is defined narrowly as
a period of aggressive sparring between superpowers, one representing
capitalism and the other communism, then the interlude is over. But, a
broader definition, replacing communism with Muscovy, can be aptly
applied to characterize Russia's muscular geopolitical assertiveness and
the West's deterrent response. From this perspective, the cold war (cold
peace) never ended. Muscovy temporarily retreated after 1991 to lick its
wounds and returned to the path of predatory confrontation after 2004.

Box 12.2 Military Asset Reallocation and the CIS

Soviet disunion was both a domestic and international event. With the
stroke of a pen, fifteen administrative divisions of the USSR became
independent states, with fragmented armed forces. Large components
of the Soviet defense network and much of the Black Sea fleet fell
outside Moscow's hands, instantaneously making Belarus, Kazakhstan,

---

[7] Stephen Blank, "The General Crisis of the Russian Military," Paper presented at
Putin's Russia: Two Years On, Wilton Park, England, March 11–15, 2002.

and Ukraine potent nuclear powers with combustible possibilities. Fortunately, Moscow's and the West's interests coincided, and they coop-
erated in coaxing the new independent states to transfer their nuclear
weapons to Russia, and after protracted negotiations, the civilian and
military Black Sea fleets were divided between Moscow and Kiev. These
compromises were facilitated by the formation of the Commonwealth
of Independent States (CIS), an association of former republics under
the Kremlin's unified military command. There was and remains a
chance that the CIS can be used as a platform to restore a Soviet-type
reunion, but this doesn't appear imminent. Given the stresses of Soviet
disunion, the peaceful resolution of contested divorce claims was the
era's greatest triumph.

But the bloom was off the rose. The financial crisis of August 1998
marked the beginning of the end. It discredited Yeltsin and set the stage
for the reemergence of Muscovite power institutions, spearheaded
by FSB chief Vladimir Putin.[8] Military spending began recovering in
1999 and surged continuously thereafter.[9] Under his watch, the Second Chechen war was resumed in 1999, and transition derailed. Talk
of EU and NATO accession evaporated. And most importantly, Russia began acting as a *liberal imperial* superpower contesting the West in
the Ukraine, Belarus, Georgia, Moldova, Transdnestria, Iran, Iraq, and
North Korea.[10] It is forging tactical alliances with China and India and
consolidating its influence over the former Soviet Moslem republics.
This renewed assertiveness is certain to intensify as the Kremlin's arms
modernization program shifts into high gear during the next few
years.[11]

[8] Stephen Blank, "The 18th Brumaire of Vladimir Putin," Conference on Succession Crises in Russia, Boston, MA, April 20, 2004; Carolina Vendil Pallin,
Russian Military Reform: A Failed Exercise in Defence Decision Making, FOI, November 2005; Peter Baker and Susan Glasser, *Kremlin Rising: Vladimir Putin's Russia
and the End of Revolution*, Scribner, New York, 2005.
[9] Steven Rosefielde, *Russia in the 21st Century: The Prodigal Superpower*, Cambridge
University Press, Cambridge, 2005; "Defense Minister: Russia Will Spend 50%
More on Weapons in 2006 Than 2005," *Johnson's Russia List*, No. 82, Article 16,
April 6, 2006.
[10] The term *liberal imperialism* was approbatively coined by Anatoly Chubais, co-
leader of the Union of Right Forces, in October 2003. See *Nezavisimaya Gazeta*,
October 1, 2003.
[11] Rosefielde, *Russia in the 21st Century*. Steven Rosefielde, "Russian Rearmament:
Motives, Options and Prospects," in Jan Leijonhielm and Fredrik Westerlund
(eds.), *Russia Power Structures*, FOI, Stockholm, Sweden, January 2008, pp. 63–83.

The resurgence of Russian international pugnaciousness unfolded in two stages. During Putin's first term, the Kremlin dreamed and schemed about Transdnestria, the Balkans, the Caucasus, Central Asia, Iran, the Middle East, India, and China but was severely constrained by its incomplete domestic consolidation and diminished economic prowess. It wheedled, rather than coerced, in pressing for advantage. The petro bubble and reconstitution of the power vertical soon transformed wishes into realities. They facilitated an escalation of Russian international assertiveness from the outset of Putin's second presidency that has steadily accelerated.[12] Where his administration had explored a special relationship with the EU that surrendered some geopolitical aspirations to economic assistance before 2005, Moscow concluded thereafter that confrontation was more profitable. This new attitude is particularly noticeable in its contentious relationship with the EU over the Kremlin's repression of the media, democratic and human rights, rule of law, and market entry, as well as spats with the former Baltic Soviet republics and Poland and its energy machinations.[13] Even small events become heated encounters. When the Estonian government chose to move a Soviet-era war monument, Sergei Ivanov, a first deputy prime minister, urged Russians to boycott Estonia and its goods.[14] An EU-Russian summit at Volzhsky Utyos near Samara May 18, 2007, sought to calm a host of tensions but ended in failure without Germany achieving any of its objectives: the opening of negotiations on a new strategic partnership pact to replace the Russia-EU Partnership and Cooperation Agreement, the lifting of exorbitant overflight fees charged European airlines, and progress on improving energy security.[15]

[12] "Russia: Rebuilding the Iron Curtain," Testimony of David Satter, U.S. House of Representatives, Committee on Foreign Affairs, May 17, 2007, reprinted in *Johnson's Russia List*, Vol. 115, Article 26, May 21, 2007. "What are we seeing today? There is near hysteria in Russia over the removal of the Soviet war memorial from the center of Tallinn . . . , attempts to defend the separatism of Abkhazia and South Ossetia from Georgia . . . , a country that feels itself threatened by plans for a U.S. defensive anti-missile system in Poland and the Czech republic . . . "

[13] Anatoly Tayganok, "The Geopolitical Basin," *Johnson's Russia List*, Vol. 115, Article 38, May 21, 2007.

[14] Erika Niedowski, "Russia Slams the Door on all Things Estonian; War Monument Dispute Escalates into Boycott," *Johnson's Russia List*, Vol.115, Article 35, May 21, 2007.

[15] Hannes Adomeit, "Germany Had No Hope of Saving the Summit," *Johnson's Russia List*, Vol. 115, Article 9, May 21, 2007. The EU is internally divided

Russia also has demanded the creation of an extraterritorial corridor linking Kaliningrad with Pskov through Latvia and Estonia, an issue linked to the thorny question of the right of Russians to backdoor EU citizenship and settlement throughout Europe.[16] It countered Polish

on how best to deal with Russia. Gerhard Schroder, former German chancellor (and head of the shareholders' committee of Nord Stream AG), former French President Jacques Chirac, and Italian Prime Minister Silvio Berlusconi support the broadening of economic, social, and cultural ties with Russia to achieve a long-term strategic partnership and blame America for Putin's assertiveness. They oppose Georgia's and Ukraine's inclusion in an enlarged EU, advocate the renewed ratification of the Treaty on Conventional Armed Forces in Europe (without forcing Russia to withdraw its troops from Georgia and Moldova), and contend that the Kremlin's various transgressions against democracy, civil liberties, and aggression in the Caucauses, Transdnestria, Georgia, and the Ukraine should be disregarded as teething problems. The other camp, which includes conservative governments, the new central and eastern European members of NATO and the EU, and the majority of research institutes and academic specialists working on Russia take a jaundiced view of Putin's Muscovy and counsel treating Moscow as an adversary. Over the past sixteen months, they point to the shut-off of gas or oil to the Ukraine, Moldova and Belarus; the diversion of oil from the Mazeikiu Nafta refinery in Lithuania, the Ventspils port in Latvia, and Tallinn in Estonia to Russian ports; the curtailment of coal deliveries to Estonia; and bans on the import of wine, spirits, mineral water, or other agricultural products from Georgia, Moldova, and Poland. They link these actions to the rising power vertical, increased state control over strategic sectors, and the use of energy as an instrument of foreign policy. And they contend that their misgivings are confirmed by the Nord Stream gas pipeline, Putin's endorsement of GASPEC, recent agreements with Kazakhstan and Turkmenistan on the shipment of Central Asian gas and oil through Russia to Europe, and corresponding deals signed between Gazprom and Germany, Denmark, France, Italy, Hungary, and Slovakia. On the political front, they blame Russia for the so-called frozen conflicts in the former Soviet republics and the tangled situation in Kosovo, its subversion of the color revolutions, indifference to Belorussian President Alexander Lukashenko's repressive policies, its hysterical reaction to the arrest of four Russian military officers in Georgia on suspicion of spying, and the relocation of a Soviet war memorial in Estonia, as well as Putin's recent diatribe against the United States at a security conference in Munich, and the warning issued by General Yury Baluyevsky, head of the armed forces General Staff that Russia could target the U.S. missile shield in Europe, if it were deployed

[16] Yaroslav Bilinsky, "Toward the West: Baltic Realignment and Russia's Reply," *Soviet Legacies*, 28, 1(Spring 2006). "In high diplomacy, the Kaliningrad issue has already been put to rest at the EU-Russian summit of November 11, 2002. A state border delimitation treaty signed with Russia in October 1997 was ratified by the Seimas in October 1999 and by the Russian Duma in May 2003." Nonetheless its latent disruptive potential remains. Cf. Anatol Lieven, "Defusing EU-Russian Tension," *Johnson's Russia List*, Vol. 117, Article 27, May 23, 2007.

ambitions in Lithuania and Ukraine by building an oil pipeline to
Germany that made Warsaw vulnerable to economic disruption.[17]
And it threatened various forms of retaliation if the Baltic states,
Poland, and others permitted America to base antiballistic missiles on
their soil.[18] A similar shift is discernible in Russia's relations with Iran,
Japan, and North Korea. During Putin's first term, Moscow reck-
lessly transferred nuclear technology to Teheran for commercial gain;
indulged Japan's vain hopes for a peace treaty, concluding World War
II; and disregarded Pyongyang. But after 2006, the Kremlin began
playing a complex double game with Teheran and Kim Jong-il that
may have some restraining effect on their nuclear ambitions, treated
Japan as a suppliant, and began fishing in troubled waters by selling
a nuclear power plant to Burma.[19] These actions weren't provoca-
tive in themselves, but mark a way station on the path toward regional
hegemony. Moscow's handling of Ukraine and the former Soviet Central Asian states followed the same trajectory from accommodation to
hegemonic restoration, aimed at driving America from the region and
using its energy card to coerce South and East Asia.

Box 12.3 Natural Resource Superpower

Natural resources can transform large nations into superpowers by
financing armaments and selectively denying rivals market access during periods of anticipated shortage. The Soviet Union was autarkic
until the early 1960s, reserving its resources for domestic military and
civilian purposes, exporting them after Stalin died to finance imports,
with limited political effect in western Europe, the Soviet satellites, and
other targets of opportunity. Its superpower rested primarily in its vast

---

[17] Nord Stream is a planned natural gas pipeline from Russia to Germany partly
constructed under the Baltic Sea from Vyborg to Greifswald, which bypasses
the existing pipeline through Poland. It has been criticized by Poland, Sweden,
the Baltic countries, the United States, and some environmental groups. The
pipeline is seen as a political move by Russia to bypass transit countries (Ukraine,
Slovakia, Czech Republic, Belarus, and Poland). Some fear that the Kremlin
will export political influence by threatening their gas supply, as happened in the
Russia-Ukraine gas dispute in January 2006.

[18] Oleg Shchedrov, "Putin Still Opposes U.S. Missile Shield," *Johnson's Russia List*,
Vol. 118, Article 23, May 24, 2007. After consultations with Washington, Putin
remained adamantly opposed to an American plan to base ten missile interceptors
in Poland and radar in the Czech Republic by 2012.

[19] *The Guardian*, May 18, 2007.

nuclear arsenal (more than 52,000 weapons), and tank armies. As part of the looting of the Yeltsin years, Russia exported enormous quantities of natural resources, helping drive petroleum prices down to $12 per barrel, and privatized most mineral processing companies (but not minerals themselves), while retaining political control through various levers. It maneuvered for long-term gain by negotiating pipeline construction and drilling schemes with rival countries seeking secure supplies. The Kremlin achieved some modest success but not enough to revive superpower nostalgia. The petro bubble occasioned by the American war in Iraq and China's accelerating industrial requirements rapidly altered Moscow's attitude. As natural resources prices rose, especially petroleum and natural gas, the Putin administration saw an opportunity to reactivate its nascent superpower (it may retain as many as 40,000 nuclear weapons, including those requiring reinserted triggers) by rearming and strengthening state control. It renationalized most of the petroleum and natural gas processing and transportation industry, is scheming to create a global gas cartel, and is using its position as a large volume supplier to achieve political leverage over Ukraine, Poland, the Baltic States, EU, Japan, China, and America. These efforts have been largely effective, including blunting America's efforts to obtain natural gas from Central Asia with its Nabucco pipeline under the Caspian Sea. Gas pipeline construction agreements signed May 13 and December 20, 2007, allow Moscow to dominate natural gas deliveries from Turkmenistan and Kazakhstan to Europe and will undoubtedly increase EU dependency on Russia well above 40 percent. Oil pumped west through the Soviet-era Druzhba pipelines – one through Belarus, Poland, and Germany, the other through Belarus, Ukraine, Slovakia, the Czech Republic, and Hungary – once cemented Moscow's grip on its satellites. But it was supplemented December 2001 with a new Baltic (BPS) pipeline carrying crude oil from the West Siberian and Timan-Pechora oil provinces to the newly completed port of Primorsk in the Russian Gulf of Finland, allowing the Kremlin to exert pressure by threatening to suspend petroleum transmission to eastern Europe. The partly constructed Nord Stream gas pipeline, connecting Russia directly to Germany under the Baltic Sea and bypassing the Yamal-Europe II route through Central Europe, will further marginalize Poland, the Baltic States, and Ukraine. Other pipeline projects to Indiga or Murmansk, servicing the American market, are on hold, and the Adria reversal scheme to open up the Adriatic for Russian petroleum exports is proceeding slowly. Regarding the Asia trade, Russia decided in late 2004 to build a pipeline from Angarsk around Lake Baikal to the port of Nakhodka near the Sea of Japan, servicing Japan and perhaps America, instead of a competing scheme to Daqing China. But the deal fell through when Beijing provided funding Japan chose not to match, restoring Daqing as the prime Asian route. Also, about 25 percent of Russia's oil reserves are on Sakhalin Island, providing Moscow with additional means of exporting to the Asian market. The sum and substance of these developments is that Russia now or will soon have the capability of creating petroleum and natural gas dependencies across Europe and Asia and will be in a position to pressure rival recipients for substantial political concessions until the global fuel supply balance improves.

The significance of these changes is best understood as a two-phase challenge to American unipolar power where Moscow first restores the pre-1992 Russia-American superpower condominium and then tries to use the correlation of forces to win the second wave of the cold war (peace). This intention is telegraphed by its strenuous campaign to prevent America from achieving strategic independence,[20] that is, the capacity to carry out conventional military operations with minimal nuclear retaliatory risk by deploying an effective national ballistic missile defense in Alaska and Europe. The Soviets tried to forestall American strategic independence with the now lapsed 1972 Anti-Ballistic Missile (ABM) Treaty, and the Kremlin is mounting a fresh offensive by threatening to withdraw from the 1987 INF treaty.[21] It has suspended onsite CFE inspections,[22] is building a new generation of zigzag ballistic missiles (a multistage ICBM with cruise missile reentry characteristics),[23] and threatening to attack ABM sites in Europe.

[20] Steven Rosefielde and Quinn Mills, *Masters of Illusion: American Leadership in the Media Age*, Cambridge University Press, Cambridge, 2007.

[21] "Putin's Prepared Remarks at 43rd Munich Conference on Security Policy,", *Washington Post,* February 10, 2007; "Russia Warns U.S. of Arms Treaty Pullout," *Washington Post*, February 16, 2007, p. A-20.

[22] "Russia Will End Foreign Inspections Under the CFE – Ivanov," *Johnson's Russia List*, Vol. 117, Article 26, May 23, 2007.

[23] Konstantin Lantratov and Alexandra Gritskova, "Nuclear Achievements," *Johnson's Russia List*, Vol. 122, Article 10, May 30, 2007. "The first successful test launch of the RS-24, a new ICBM with multiple independent warheads, was announced yesterday by the Russian military. Deploying these missiles, each of which can carry several warheads, could enable Russia to maintain strategic parity with the United States." After Russia and the United States abandoned START II, the Russian military announced its intention to produce ground-launched ICBMs with multiple warheads, with a design based on the single-warhead

Should Moscow succeed, Russia potentially will be in a position to severely limit American options in the Middle East and South Asia and might even be able to roll back its presence in Europe.[24] In less than a decade, Russia could reverse the consequences of the Soviet Union's defeat and achieve a stronger position in Europe and the Middle East than during the heyday of the Brezhnev years due in part to its coercive energy politics[25] and German/French antipathy toward American unipolar dominance. Moscow is well placed to capitalize on the EU's vulnerabilities. On the one hand, social democratic pacifism and internal weakness stressed by Russian analysts incline Brussels to accommodate Russian energy pressure and strategic blackmail.[26] EU leaders are upset by the Kremlin's initiative to create GASPEC, a natural gas sister cartel to OPEC that could beggar the continent but have not effectively resisted. On the other hand, the logic of the greater EU project makes Europeans reluctant to ally more closely with the United States. The same sort of contradiction provides fertile soil in

Topol-M missile. Russia has produced no more than ten new Topol-M missiles a year since 1998, no new submarines have been completed yet, and the new sea-launched missile, the Bulava, is plagued with problems (four out of five test launches have failed). Yuri Solomov, director and chief design engineer at the Moscow Institute of Thermal Technology, promised in April 2007 that Russia would have at least 2,000 nuclear warheads by 2011.

[24] "Instead of a unipolar world, where the domination of one superpower has evoked so much apprehension among other countries, we will be faced with a new reality – not 'multipolarity,' which is so dear to so many, but rather growing chaos and a vacuum of governance and security." Council on Foreign and Defense Policy, *The World around Russia: 2017*, Moscow, 2007, p. 6.

[25] "Energy will remain a key factor determining the world's future. However, by the second half of the forecasted period the present acuteness of the energy problem will be partially overcome.... The role of energy and, especially, traditional energy resources, will be reduced for the United States and the European Union. Moscow must take this factor into consideration in order not to be enthralled by the illusion that it can become an 'energy superpower.'" Council on Foreign and Defense Policy, *The World around Russia: 2017*, Moscow, 2007, p. 7. On synfuels cf. Irving Louis Horowitz, "Castro, Corn, and Oil," Foreign Policy Research Institute, May 18, 2007, http://www.fpri.org.

[26] "During the next few years, the European Union will be in a state of prostration. The euphoria from its integration achievements has brought about inflated demands among the EU member countries concerning this organization, while its rapid enlargement in 1995–2006 has caused malfunctions in the pan-European mechanism. Yet, by the middle of the forecasted decade, the integration process may start emerging from its systemic crisis. Economic reforms will be intensified, and the EU may rise above its stagnating development model." *The World around Russia: 2017*, pp. 7–8.

other theaters, especially so if America lapses into another isolationist moment as a consequence of its misadventure in Iraq.

> ## Box 12.4 Arms Control and Disarmament
>
> Arms control and disarmament treaties and processes have been an integral part of Soviet and post-Soviet national security policy. They provide an attractive method of exerting pressure on adversaries to forego, to cut, or to limit the growth of selected dispreferred forces. This permits Moscow to allocate defense funds to other military or civilian uses, while testing the West's resolve by cheating at the margins (for example, the construction of hen house ABM-compatible radars, and antiaircraft missiles with antiballistic missile capabilities, or by using undeclared reloads as first strike weapons). In principle, all parties can play by the same informal rules, but opaque governments have an intrinsic advantage because pacifist factions in the West exert more pressure than their counterparts in Russia (if any) through democratic processes for strict domestic treaty compliance and often disparage claims of Russian circumvention. Russian treaty compliance has varied, as it should from case to case. It honored its INF agreement (Intermediate-Range Nuclear Forces Treaty, signed December 8, 1987, eliminating nuclear and conventional ground-launched and cruise missiles with ranges of 300–3,400 miles) and START I (Strategic Arms Reduction Treaty, ratified July 31, 1991, limiting the USSR and America to 6,000 nuclear warheads atop 1,600 delivery vehicles) but withdrew from START II (signed January 3, 1993, banning multiple independent reentry vehicles [MIRV] on ICBMs) on June 14, 2002, the day after America withdrew from the ABM (Anti-Ballistic Missile Treaty, signed May 26, 1972). It severely stretched the boundaries of the SALT (Strategic Arms Limitation Treaty, signed May 26, 1972, freezing the number of ICBM and SLBM launchers at existing levels) and the ABM agreement. The jury is still out on SORT (Treaty on Offensive Strategic Reductions, signed May 24, 2002, obligating Russia and America to restrict their strategic nuclear arsenals to 1,700–2,200 operationally deployed warheads by 2012). The CFE (Conventional Armed Forces in Europe Treaty, signed November 19, 1990) is under assault because factions within the EU won't ratify until Russia withdraws from Moldova and Georgia. Sergei Ivanov, first deputy prime minister announced that Russia will no longer receive foreign inspections or send notifications on troop movements under the treaty. Interest in both arms control and disarmament waned after the Soviet Union collapsed, deep unilateral troop cuts were made in America, the EU, and Russia, and nuclear weapons

have proliferated. America for its part has decided to let START I lapse in 2009, replacing it with a less formal agreement that eliminates strict verification requirements and weapons limits.* It remains to be seen whether Putin's recent threat to abrogate the INF treaty or the increasing risk of multilateral nuclear exchanges will bring renewed life to this aspect of national security policy.

* Carol Giacomo, "U.S. to Let START Nuclear Treaty Expire," *Johnson's Russia List*, Vol. 117, Article 31, May 23, 2007.

However, Russia is intrinsically weaker in many important aspects than the Soviet Union, and the rest of the world also has changed profoundly since 1991. China's economic and military ascent, together with nuclear proliferation in South Asia and Iran, have undermined the foundations of mutually assured destruction,[27] suggesting that if America abandons its unipolar role, the default option is a nuclear multidominium subject to terrorist destabilization, not a new Russian-American superpower condominium. The incendiary threat of a nuclearized Moslem ummah (formation of a theocratic, pan-Islamic empire) is another twist, as is a rising challenge from China along what for the moment is a quiescent frontier. Vigorously creating and exploiting targets of opportunity in this volatile environment may not be worth the risk.

Russia's internal flaws are equally daunting. Putin's Muscovite economy has downsized and hollowed. The Kremlin lost nearly a third of its Soviet-era territories, 50 percent of its population, and its satellite empire. Industry has contracted, industrial labor skills lost, and the workforce is declining, while the population ages. The economy displays little commercially viable technological innovation and is based on the exchange of natural resources for cheap foreign consumer goods. The strategy may materially support a renewed cold war thrust if America fails to competitively deter, and natural resource prices remain high but will be extremely burdensome. A population less than 18 percent of West's, an inferior economy, an American military technological competition, and the risk of a petro bust (or resource

[27] "East Asia will continue on the path toward becoming a global economic growth center. The region will feature 'soft' integration tendencies, which by the middle of the decade may start acquiring the form of institution." *The World around Russia: 2017*, p. 7.

exhaustion)[28] do not make a promising recipe for a sustainable second-wave cold war victory.

Box 12.5 Russia's Defense Burden

Military spending as a share of GDP is called the *defense burden*. It is often used as an indicator of the level and direction of nations' military capabilities and intentions, even though secrecy makes data suspect, and problems of international comparability abound. For example, during the 1970s and 1980s, the Soviets routinely reported a defense burden of 2.8 percent, until Gorbachev revealed that the official defense budget excluded weapons. The real figure he said was 7.8 percent, while CIA, DIA (Defense Intelligence Agency), and informed Russian sources such as Vitaly Shlykov placed the burden between 15 and 30 percent. The Soviet representative to the United Nations repeatedly challenged America to reduce its defense spending to Soviet-published levels, and RAND economist Abraham Becker recommended that America comply. The particulars of the post-Soviet defense burden have changed but not the guile. Russia continues to publish dishonest statistics that are substantially lower than the real level and direction of the defense burden to misshape foreign perceptions. They are largely successful. Although, official data published by the military industrial complex show double-digit weapons growth, the published burden in 2007 is 2.7 percent, down slightly from the Putin era mean of 3 percent. This allows Sergei Ivanov, first deputy prime minister and former minister of Defense to claim on May 23, 2007, "that Russia isn't the Soviet Union. Russia isn't going to return to an arms race, and our military budget proves that." Seven days later Vladimir Putin accused the United States of triggering a new arms race, rhetoric likely intended to justify an arms modernization drive already under way.*

* Vladimir Isachenkov, "Putin: U.S. Has Triggered New Arms Race," Yahoo! News, May 31, 2007. Vladimir Isachenkov, "Russian Leader Assails U.S. Defenses," *Johnson's Russia List*, Vol. 118, Article 24, May 24, 2007.

Russia's prospects for exercising resurgent superpower are thus mixed. It should be able to gradually exert power over most of the former Soviet republics, including the Baltic states (despite its EU membership), Georgia, Ukraine, Belarus, and Transdnestria, as well

[28] Jacques Sapir, "Oil and Gas in the Capitals," *World Magazine*, Vol. 227, No. 7, July 2006. Bernard Gelb, *Russian Oil and Gas Challenges*, Congressional Research Service, January 3, 2006.

as the Central Asian Moslem regimes. It can meddle in the politics of eastern and central Europe and bend a compliant EU to advantage. The Kremlin's moment as a blue-water naval power in the Asia Pacific is past, unless it can leverage oil piped to Japan and China.[29]

Muscovite expansionist potential, however, is only part of the picture. The Kremlin also faces a set of formidable risks. America is contesting Moscow's sphere of influence in Central Asia; the EU is courting the Ukraine, Georgia, Belarus, Lithuania, Moldova, and Transdnestria as part of its greater Europe project, in an era where Russia can no longer use Marxism to bolster its appeal. The Moslem fundamentalist ummah movement is a challenge all along Russia's southern flank across the spectrum from terrorism to nuclear warfare. And in the longer perspective, the depopulation of the Russian Far East and Siberia create a vacuum that China may find too tempting to resist. There already are numerous reports of Chinese bribing border officials to acquire false Russian citizenship papers and passports.

Muscovite culture in this strategic environment is both a blessing and a curse. It allows the Kremlin to mobilize enormous armed forces for multiple purposes; at the same time, it shackles Moscow to a military posture that may be unsustainable.

Western analysts consider both proclivities unreasonable. They contend that when war threatens, nations preoccupy themselves with balance of power and coalition building, selective "actions that will maximize strategic goals and objectives."[30] Infighting gives way to concerted action. But in tranquil times, when foreign threats are less pressing, organizational and bureaucratic politics come to the fore. Putin, in their view, should not be following the bad Soviet example by building a military with vast predatory potential, and reverting to cold war pugnaciousness when the West doesn't threaten Russia and certainly shouldn't be trying to maintain forces that may not be sustainable. But this is precisely what is being done, underscoring the lesson westerners are reluctant to accept, that Muscovy marches to its own drummer.

It isn't true that the Gorbachev revolution in international relations was thwarted by the Kremlin's failure to reform its post-Soviet military

---

[29] Stephen Blank, "The Great Game Goes to Sea: Naval Rivalries in the Caspian," *Johnson's Russia List*, No. 12, Article 26, January 12, 2006.

[30] Barry Posen, *The Sources of Military Doctrine: France, Britain and Germany Between the World Wars*, Cornell University Press, Ithaca, NY, 1984, p. 60. Cf. Vendil Pallin, *Russian Military Reform*, pp. 35–38.

or because Moscow didn't fully appreciate the virtues of democracy, free enterprise, social justice, globalization, EU enlargement, cooperative engagement, and peace. The leadership understood and desired these ends but not enough to override traditional Muscovite priorities.

Russia's imperial resurgence has not escaped the West's attention, but it has been refracted and obfuscated through America's and the EU's public cultural lenses. Both act as if they believe scolding will suffice, and many in the EU are drawn to appeasement. The U.S. State Department's *Strategic Plan – Fiscal Years 2007–12* sets as its top priority countering Russia's negative behavior, from arms sales to dangerous regimes such as Syria, to political coercion in the Baltic states, Georgia, Ukraine, and Central Asia, by chastising the Putin administration.[31] It also sternly criticized Russia's intensifying authoritarianism in *Supporting Human Rights and Democracy: 2006* (April 2007).

However, Putin has firmly brushed aside all American criticism, contending that Russia is merely expunging the consequences of the United States' bullying, and the Kremlin's ineptitude during the Yeltsin years, an argument that is gaining traction in the EU where quarrels between its eastern members and Moscow are frustrating the resolution of various internal issues. Russian academics, particularly those connected with quasi-governmental institutes, are providing a Soviet-style gloss to these denials; combining a narrative mimicking western liberal mind-sets blaming all the world's ills on the American ruling

---

[31] Sergei Strokan, "Insufferable Strategies: US Lays out Strategic Goals for Next Five Years, Slams Russia in Report," *Johnson's Russia List*, Vol. 90, Article 7, April 17, 2007. The full list includes increasing centralization of power, pressure on nongovernmental organizations and civil society, a growing government presence in the economy and restrictions on media freedom. The only hint of a potent counterstrategy is a toothless promise of assistance for promoting free elections, while expressing hope that Russia can be salvaged as a strategic partner through a wide range of economic, social, scientific, and political ties, including support for Russia's entry into the World Trade Organization. Washington also promises to contest Russian machinations in Georgia and Moldavia, and its misuse of energy to pressure neighboring states. The problem will be addressed by diversifying energy sources, increasing transparency and improving the efficiency of energy usage. The United States proposes to support GUAM an association of Georgia, Ukraine, Azerbaijan, and Moldova as an alternative to the CIS, and to have it ally with Europe and the Euro-Atlantic. "Elsewhere in Eurasia, people cling to the hope kindled by the 'color revolutions of 2002–2005'" (The Putin administration treated this statement as a provocation.) Perhaps the U.S. State Department knows better and is politically constrained, but this doesn't alter the futility of its approach. "The Economist: Georgia in Turmoil," *Johnson's Russia List*, Vol. 238, Article 41, November 24, 2007.

class, airbrushing the Kremlin's transgressions, and positioning Russia
as a progressive leader striving to contain American action within the
rule of international law. After cataloguing trends and dangers threatening the globe during the next decade, they see smooth sailing of the
sort that gives the United States no quarter for independent action.[32]

This forecast not only offers a faulty preview of the shape of things
to come, but it also fosters overreaching. The gulf between ingrained
Muscovite hegemonic aspirations and capabilities is large and likely
to grow during the next quarter century to the detriment of Russia's material well-being and global security. Many perceptive Russian
intellectuals understand the dilemma but are powerless to turn the
Muscovite tide.

- For a time after the Second World War, it seemed to many that the
  tide of history was "red."
- Soviet leaders claimed that Marxist socialism was superior and that
  they had a duty to spread it throughout the world, placing the
  USSR on a collision course with the West. The sparring was called
  the *cold war*.
- This "bloody war for peace and friendship," as Soviets often
  quipped, was mostly a fig leaf for Muscovite imperialism.
- Marshal Ogarkov acknowledged that the red tide ebbed in the late
  1970s.
- By 1980, the Kremlin recognizing the change in the correlation
  of forces began pondering how to realign its international relations
  and defense posture, for the short and long run.
- Gorbachev's doctrine of *novoe myshlenie* (new thinking) was an
  expression of this ferment, although it remains unclear whether
  his charm campaign with the West was a tactic or a break with
  Muscovy.
- The sincerity of his desire to have the USSR return to its "common western home" is supported by his acquiescence to German
  reunification, tolerance of Baltic secessionism, termination of the
  Afghan war, reduced financial aid to Cuba, the signing of the INF
  treaty, and conclusion of START I.
- But rapidly rising weapons procurement pointed to ambivalence or
  a double game.

---

[32] This attitude parallels the World Bank's outlook. See Chapter 13.

- The structure of east-west relations also was profoundly altered by Soviet disunion, the liberation of the USSR's east European satellites, Kremlin assistance in denuclearizing the former non-Russian Soviet republics, the disestablishment of the CMEA, collapse of Moscow's support for international communism, a 90 percent reduction in arms procurement, halving of its armed forces, downsizing nuclear stockpiles, Yeltsin's forbearance in the Kosovo war, and his acceptance of western transition assistance.

- These events appeared to end the cold war and offer the prospect of a new global order, with America as the world's sole superpower.

- The only question was whether Russia was cocooning or had acquiesced to a reduced global stature.

- The turning point was the August 1998 financial crisis that set in motion a series of events rekindling Russia's imperial aspirations and the cold war (cold peace).

- Russia's renewed assertiveness is displayed in the Kremlin's efforts to dominate Ukraine, Belorussia, Moldova, Transdnestria, former Moslem Soviet republics, Iran, Iraq, and North Korea.

- A drive toward full-spectrum, fifth-generation arms modernization confirms these ambitions.

- Russia's imperial revival occurred in two stages. Before the petro bubble, it probed cautiously for advantage. The petro bubble filled the Kremlin with delusions of adequacy and a more assertive foreign policy to match.

- The new attitude is manifest in Moscow's increasingly contentious relationship with the EU over human rights and energy. Russia is also vigorously contesting America's effort to install a ballistic missile defense in Poland, and the Czech Republic.

- Russia has ambitions to harden its control over the CIS, encourage EU appeasement, widen its influence in the Middle East and South Asia, reduce American influence everywhere, and contain China.

- Russia could reverse the consequences of the Soviet Union's defeat in less than a decade.

- Russia is weaker than the Soviet Union. Its territory and population have shrunk by more than 30 and 50 percent, respectively. China and America are stronger than before.

- Russia's industrial sector has hollowed, and its scientific cadre has shrunk.

- Muscovy cannot increase national wealth as rapidly as democratic free enterprise in the long run.

- Muscovy should not win the second round of the cold war.
- And it may not be able to fend off ummah and Chinese incursions along its southern borders.
- The correlation of forces continues trending against Russia, despite a modest reversal wrought by the petro bubble.
- The restoration of the cold war superpower condominium is infeasible because of China and nuclear proliferation.
- Wishful thinking and feckless leadership continue to impair the West's management of east-west relations.
- Russian international security specialists are confident that the Kremlin's international fortunes will steadily increase, despite all difficulties.
- On balance, Russia is likely to outplay the West and be a serious source of international destabilization during the next decade.

PART VI

PROSPECTS

13

Sustainable Growth

A rising tide lifts all boats. Even though international institutions recently have shunned the "T" word (transition) when discussing Russia and non–European Union members of the former Soviet bloc, they have preserved hope by lowering their horizons. Where it once was claimed that post-Soviet workers would cast off their chains, ridding themselves of the authoritarian martial police state, equitably privatizing collective assets, and becoming democratic free enterprisers, many western analysts prefer to forget these unfulfilled promises, concentrating instead on securing sustained economic growth now that Russia has, or soon will recover, the previously achieved Soviet level. By averting their eyes, an unwieldy problem of cultural transformation has been reduced to seemingly manageable dimensions. The approach isn't novel and could succeed in a limited fashion. As shown in Chapter 5, the advantages of relative backwardness enabled the Kremlin to grow modestly during the tsarist and Soviet periods, and it could happen again with or without liberalization. Any complete appraisal of Russia's future therefore has two aspects: the sustainability and merit of Russian GDP growth beyond the peak Soviet level.

Technocrats have little difficulty making a case for sustainable growth, without coming to grips with the deeper problem of inferior Muscovite competitiveness. They argue cogently that growth depends on improvements attainable from technological borrowing and advances in knowledge, other things being equal. Because it is easily demonstrated that Russian know-how is backward, and that global technology has improved steadily for the past 250 years, there is no reason to doubt the Federation's development potential. Russia's living standard should rise from technology transfer and domestic innovation, even if it fails to converge to the global high frontier, or

231

deteriorate gradually relative to the western moving norm. However, this isn't assured because a myriad of factors such as systemic devitalization could countervail sustained growth, as they did in the late 1990s.

International institutions aware that technological progress may not always be enough try to protect their flank with macroeconomic prescriptions (managing aggregate effective demand) and recommendations for structural reform of property rights, market organization, the financial system, and taxation. Without explicitly addressing the Muscovite issue, they assert that Russia can maintain the high rate of economic advance achieved during the recovery years (1998–2006), in the vicinity of 7 percent per annum, despite persistent anticompetitive restraints and rampant corruption. The OECD, for example, contends that "relatively rapid convergence of Russian living standards toward those of developed OECD countries"[1] will continue, if the leadership merely adopts a sound macroeconomic environment and market friendly reforms that include:[2]

1. successful adjustment to permanently high oil prices
2. modulating the speed of real exchange rate appreciation with fiscal policy
3. insulating the economy from terms of trade volatility
4. structural reform
5. reform of public administration
6. empowering citizens
7. enhancing transparency
8. intensified anticorruption efforts
9. legislative change
10. increased use of information and communication technologies (ICT)
11. improved framework conditions for business to realize innovation potential
12. increased responsiveness by the public science sector and domestic intellectual property rights regime (IPR) to business needs
13. more favorable tax regime for private sector research and development (R&D)
14. improved intervention monitoring

[1] OECD Economic Surveys, *Russian Federation 2006*, OECD, Paris, 2006, p. 22. The authors wish to thank William Tompson for sending them an electronic pre-publication version of this document.
[2] Ibid., pp. 11–19.

Table 13.1. *Structural effects of ruble appreciation*

	1990	1995	2000	2004
Industrial Employment Shares				
Total industry	30.3	25.8	22.6	21.5
Manufacturing	–	21.9	18.8	17.7
Nontradable Services	53.4	57.0	60.7	63.9

Source: Federal Service for State Statistics, Central Bank of Russia, Ministry of Finance. OECD, Economic Surveys, *Russian Federation 2005*, OECD, Paris, 2006, Table 2.3.

15. health care reform as part of a larger effort to address Russia's health crisis
16. government identification of the main health care reform priorities
17. reform of the system of mandatory medical insurance

The first three enumerated prescriptions arise from the oil price shock of recent years that has stimulated aggregate effective demand but raised the specter of the Dutch disease. The OECD expects natural resource prices to remain high and sees this as a potential damper on the sustainable rate of growth unless appropriate countermeasures are adopted.

This reflects a judgment about the net result of opposing forces and the assumption that technological progress is faster in manufacturing than in mineral extraction and the nontradable services sector. On the one hand, increased natural resource supply prices in mineral-rich nations such as Russia usually lead to rapid currency appreciation as perceptions of credit risk improve and foreign capital inflows increase, inducing a decline in domestic industry (Table 13.1). Demand for industrial exportables falls because foreign currencies command fewer rubles; the production of domestic industrial importables is pressured by intensified foreign competition;[3] and employment shifts to the low productivity growth, nontradable service sector, all three effects auguring slower growth to the extent that hollowing out diminishes aggregate productivity growth potential.

---

[3] Ibid., p. 80. Enterprise surveys confirm the growing pressure on manufacturers: although foreign competition may have a stimulating effect on domestic productivity, a third of industrial firms now consider it a major obstacle to expansion, as against less that 5 percent in early 1999. S. Tsukhlo, "Promyshlennost," *Rossiiskii byulleten' konynkturnykh oprosov*, 169, June 2006.

Table 13.2. *Petroleum Bubble: Sources of Macroeconomic Stimulation (percent, unless designated otherwise)*

	2001	2002	2003	2004	2005
CPI Inflation	18.6	15.1	12.0	11.7	10.9
Real wage growth	19.9	16.2	10.9	10.6	12.6
Exchange rate					
(rubles per dollar)	29.2	31.3	30.7	28.8	28.3
Real effective exchange rate	77.5	79.6	82.0	88.5	96.2
1998 = 100					
Terms of trade change					
(goods and service)	−5.3	−1.7	7.2	14.8	15.9
Command GDP growth	3.1	4.1	9.9	12.3	12.0
Real GDP growth	5.1	4.7	7.3	7.2	6.4
Real manufacturing growth	–	–	10.3	10.5	5.7
Food	–	–	6.9	4.4	4.4
Textiles		–	1.2	−4.0	−1.5
Wood and wood products	–	–	9.7	8.7	4.5
Chemicals	–	–	5.4	6.6	2.6
Basic metals	–	–	7.2	3.9	5.7
Machinery and equipment	–	–	19.0	21.1	−0.1
Electrical equipment	–	–	43.2	34.5	20.7
Transport equipment	–	–	14.0	11.5	6.0
Gross fixed capital formation	10.2	2.8	13.8	11.3	10.5
Unemployment (ILO-type)	8.8	8.5	7.8	7.9	7.5

Note: Command GDP growth is defined by the OECD as measuring the impact of terms-of-trade shifts on a country's purchasing power, that is, on its ability to command goods and services.

Source: Federal Service for State Statistics, Central Bank of Russia, Ministry of Finance, IMF Expert Group, OECD calculations. OECD Economic Surveys, *Russian Federation 2006*, OECD, Paris, 2006, Table 1.1, p. 23; Table 1.2, p. 24; Table 2.2, p. 80.

On the other hand, the same foreign capital inflows, reinforced by natural resource windfalls, terms of trade driven gains in domestic purchasing power,[4] negative real interest rates,[5] and speculative sentiment spur domestic investment concentrated in the natural resource, metals, chemicals, construction, and nontraded goods sectors,[6] with potentially large spillovers. These forces quantified in Table 13.2, given

[4] Ibid., p. 87.
[5] Ibid., Figure 2.3, p. 90.
[6] Ibid., p. 27.

high involuntary unemployment, spurred by the Keynesian *multiplier* augment aggregate economic activity, and may temporarily accelerate growth. Judging from the OECD's summary appraisal, it is concerned that gains from terms of trade driven aggregate effective demand may be outweighed by the Dutch disease,[7] compounded by "the loss of 'cheap' opportunities to increase production by better utilizing existing resources."[8]

Finer data justify the caution. Table 13.3 shows that market services (typified by low productivity growth) rather than manufacturing and construction have been the dominant contributor to value-added

[7] Ibid., p. 82. The term *Dutch disease* was first coined to describe the decline of the manufacturing sector in the Netherlands (and the rise in unemployment that accompanied it) following the discovery of natural gas in the 1960s. It is broadly understood to denote the harmful economic consequences that may arise in certain conditions from a sudden increase in a country's wealth. See P. Neary 1982, "Booming Sector and De-Industrialization in a Small Open Economy," *Economic Journal* 92, 3(September 1982). W. M. Corden, "Boom Sector and Dutch Disease Economics: Survey and Consolidation," *Oxford Economic Papers*, 26, 3(November 1984). G Ramey. and V. A. Ramey, "Cross-Country Evidence on the Link between Volatility and Growth," *American Economic Review*, 85, 5(December 1995); P. Martin and C. A. Rogers, "Long-term Growth and Short-term Economic Instability," *European Economic Review*, 44 (2000):359–81. P. Krugman, "The Narrow Moving Band, the Dutch Disease, and the Economic Consequences of Mrs. Thatcher: Notes on Trade in the Presence of Dynamic Economies of Scale," *Journal of Development Economics*, 27, 1(February 1987).

[8] OECD (2006), p. 2. According to the OECD author the Balassa-Samuelson effect (Balassa, 1964, and Samuelson, 1964) provides a mechanism for understanding the real appreciation of the currency in the catching-up economy. The real exchange rate is posited to depend only on the difference between (1) the relative productivity of the domestic tradable sector with respect to the domestic non-tradable sector and (2) the relative productivities of the tradable and nontradable sectors abroad. Given that relative productivity gains in the tradable sector are likely to be higher in emerging economies than in developed ones, catching-up countries are expected to have higher inflation in the non-tradable sector and, consequently, higher inflation in the economy. As the Balassa-Samuelson effect is an equilibrium phenomenon, the underlying real appreciation is sustainable and may thus be considered as a benchmark for the real appreciation path. For Russia, Egert (2005) estimates the contribution of the Balassa-Samuelson effect to average CPI inflation at 1.1 percent for 1996–2001. The inflation differential in other studies is limited and suggests a modest Balassa-Samuelson effect on overall inflation in the vicinity of Egert's estimate. See B. Balassa, "The Purchasing Power Parity: A Reappraisal," *Journal of Political Economy*, 72 (December 1964): 6; B. Egert, "Equilibrium Exchange Rates in South-Eastern Europe, Russia, Ukraine and Turkey: Healthy or Dutch-Diseased?" *Economic Systems*, 29 (June 2005): 2. P. Samuelson, "Theoretical Notes on Trade Problems," *Review of Economics and Statistics*, 46 (1964): 2.

Table 13.3. *Contributions to value-added growth (percent)*

	2003	2004	2005
Gross value–added at basic prices	7.4	6.9	6.2
Tradables	2.6	2.0	1.0
Construction	0.7	0.6	0.5
Market services	4.2	3.8	4.3
Nonmarket services and others	−0.1	0.5	0.4

Sources: Federal Service for State Statistics, Central Bank of Russia,
Ministry of Finance. OECD Economic Surveys, *Russian Federation
2006*, Table 1.3, p. 29.

increases (rapidly rising investment and employment, not enhanced
factor productivity), suggesting that the gains from recovery are
attributable more to structural change than to industrial modernization. This finding dovetails with statistics on the composition of GDP
growth. According to the OECD, productivity growth (TFP) compatible with improved capacity utilization in a low physical and human
capital investment environment[9] has been the predominant source of
increased Russian output during the Putin recovery, explaining as
much as 90 percent of the improvement in 2005.[10] Moreover, these
misgivings are compounded by the possibility that increased state ownership,[11] together with the petro bubble has caused speculative misin-
vestment, further reducing growth prospects in the intermediate term.

The OECD's macroeconomic policy recommendations stress this
collection of exchange rate related worries rather than stubbornly
high involuntary unemployment. It urges the Kremlin to sterilize a
larger portion of foreign capital inflows and tighten credit to rein
in excess aggregate effective demand, contain the Dutch disease said
thus far to be mild,[12] reduce inflation, and raise interest rates for

---

[9] *Russian Federation 2006*, Table 1.4, pp. 27, 157.
[10] Ibid., Figure 1.8, p. 43. For Jorgenson type efficiency regressions of TFP growth
     see pp. 183 ff.
[11] Ibid., p. 37. A list of government acquisitions is provided in Table 1.5, p. 38. It
     includes Guta Bank, Mosenergo, Yuganskneftegaz, Tambovyneftegaz, Northgaz,
     Gazprom, Sibneft, and AvtoVaz.
[12] Ibid., p. 85. Although manufacturing has contracted, the decline is characterized
     as less than expected due to the flexibility of Russia's labor market. However, as
     unemployment falls, and the labor market tightens, this flexibility it is feared, will
     evaporate.

the better allocation of loanable funds. The advice implies that if Kremlin authorities adopt disciplined fiscal policy, supplemented with structural reform, improved investment and efficiency will neutralize the growth chilling effects of deindustrialization.

Beyond this, the OECD's remaining fourteen points all concern the possibilities of accelerating productivity growth above the Putin era norm through routine macroeconomic aggregate effective demand management and structural reform unrelated to the sustainability of the petro bubble shock. The latter includes improved industrial governance ranging from innovation and competitiveness incentives to tax and administrative streamlining, assuming that the dynamic gains generated during the recovery phase won't evaporate now that plant and equipment are operating nearer normal capacities. It would seem on the OECD's reckoning that Russia's economic growth tomorrow will be as good or better than today, if Kremlin policymakers are responsible and progress is made fighting crime, improving health, empowering citizens, incentivizing innovation, diffusing advanced technologies, and reforming outdated structures and institutions. Democracy, free enterprise, rule of law, honesty, and social justice in the OECD's narrative, once deemed critical to Russia's intermediate term success no longer seem indispensable for achieving sustained GDP growth and convergence, despite the usual caveats about the need to eradicate authoritarian rent-granting, the rule of men, corruption and inequality in the long run.[13] It is the trans-systemic technocratic elements that are essential: noninflationary full employment aggregate effective demand, together with optimal shock management, resource allocation, productive efficiency, innovation, technology transfer, diffusion, direct foreign investment, finance, product distribution, state

---

[13] Ibid., p. 40. "Recent Russian economic performance corresponds closely to the notion of a *growth acceleration*, as defined by Hausmann et al. (2004). This points to both opportunities and risks for Russia. Hausmann and his colleagues find that most periods of accelerated growth are not sustained over the long term. In particular, they observe that external shocks tend to produce growth accelerations that fizzle out after around seven to eight years. However, they also find that economic reform significantly increases the likelihood that trend growth will remain at a new, higher level following an acceleration. In short, while accelerations appear most often to be triggered by exogenous developments, reforms can be crucial in ensuring that the improvement in growth fundamentals is permanent." Cf. R. Hausmann, L. Pritchett, and D. Rodrik, "Growth Accelerations," Faculty Research Working Papers Series RWP04–030, Harvard University, Kennedy School of Government, July 2004.

Table 13.4. *Fiscal Stance (percent of GDP)*

	2001	2002	2003	2004	2005
Budget balance	3.1	1.4	1.8	4.9	7.7
Conjunctural oil revenue	1.1	1.4	2.8	5.0	9.2
Constant oil price					
budget balance ($20 Ural)	2.1	0	−1.0	−0.1	1.5
Oil-related windfalls	−2.2	−0.2	3.0	3.9	5.1

Source: OECD Economic Surveys, *Russian Federation 2006,* Table 2.4, p. 94.

economic governance, and public programs, including those such as health, education and poverty reduction effecting labor force size, health, and skill.

Pride of place in this laundry list is given to macromanagement large-scale monetary sterilization achieved through the Stabilization Fund of the Russian Federation because of "the weakness of the exchange-rate and interest-rate channels."[14] The fund was established in 2004 following the adoption of amendments of the Budget Code of the Russian Federation in December 2003, for insuring the federal budget against oil price volatility.[15] Budgetary windfalls or *surpluses* arising from high oil prices are automatically accumulated from the natural resource extraction tax and a confiscatory duty on petro exports above a designated price, and the funds may be invested only in foreign government securities. Fund assets cannot be used to balance the Federal budget, unless oil prices fall under $27 per barrel for Urals crude, but sums in excess of 500 billion rubles may be spent for "other purposes," including repayment of foreign debts, and pension fund deficits. In 2005, roughly $49 billion in surplus revenues were channeled into the Stabilization Fund. Approximately $25 billion was retained, $23 billion was used for early debt repayment mainly to the Paris Club to enhance long-term growth,[16] and $1 billion was allocated to cover the Russian Federation's pension deficit. The effects of this fiscal discipline is displayed in Table 13.4.

The Central Bank of Russia (CBR) obviously has done an excellent job managing the petro shock, even though sterilization of dollar

---

[14] *Russian Federation 2006,* p. 76.
[15] Ibid., p. 93.
[16] Ibid., p. 95. On the growth enhancement effect of debt reduction see C. Patillo, H. Poirson, and L. Ricci, "External Debt and Growth," *IMF Working Paper,* 02/69, April 2002.

inflows doesn't dampen windfalls on domestic petroleum sales,[17] other related natural resource windfalls, various circumvention schemes, and the windfall effects of asset appreciation. However, the OECD is perturbed by signs of diminishing resolve.[18] Its primary counsel for facilitating sustained intermediate-term GDP growth in the high oil price environment envisioned, with high inflation and zero real interest rates is to hold the fiscal line; sound advice, but more a political admonition, than a refined macroeconomic strategy.[19]

Moreover, the link between the OECD's macroeconomic policy recommendations and growth is passive. Sterilization doesn't stimulate aggregate economic activity or technological progress, it only prevents inflation from getting out of control, shifting from levels that spur GDP growth to magnitudes that retard it.[20] Transforming recovery into high rates of sustained growth requires active measures, accepting the OECD's position that cheap sources of increased aggregate economic activity have been largely exhausted. The burden here by default lies either in explaining why Muscovy's natural rate of growth is brisk, or showing how government actions are being taken to overcome the dynamic inefficiency of Kremlin rent-granting. The OECD takes the latter tact beginning with a discussion of revised Kremlin programs to improve the quality of public administration, before moving on to innovation policy.

Public administration is said to be pivotal because it is both a source of value-added and a technocratic tool for strengthening productive

---

[17] Ibid., p. 97. But it should be noted that the state captures about 84 percent of the marginal revenue from crude oil and oil products for each one-dollar increase in the price of Urals crude above $25/bbl. It also captures about 42 percent of the additional income from natural gas exports for each additional dollar on the oil price. In 2005, around two-thirds of the increase in revenues from oil, gas and oil product exports was actually sterilized via the Stabilization Fund.

[18] Ibid., p. 96. The OECD is anxious about the CBR's decision to raise the cut-off price for the Stabilization Fund – the oil-price threshold above which surplus revenues flow into the fund – $20 to 27 a barrel, and the practice of increasing fiscal spending via the regular adoption of amendments to the budget law during the course of the year.

[19] Ibid., pp. 98–102. The OECD does elaborate a scheme for improved windfall estimation and related sterilization rules. Surging inflation however suggests that Russia's stabilization efforts are losing their effectiveness, and that inflationary pressures may intensify with the termination of the Stabilization Fund in early 2008. See Shinichiro Tabata, "The Russian Stabilization Fund and Its Successor: Implications for Inflation," *Eurasian Geography and Economics*, 48, No. 6, 2007, pp. 699–712.

[20] On the relationship between inflation and growth, see note 8, this chapter.

relations. It can spur growth by improving internal bureaucratic efficiency with enhanced technique and skills, tightening accountability
and curbing corruption, and in the economy at large by redesign-
ing institutions. The OECD claims despite the burdensome Soviet
legacy that enough progress is being made across the board in changing rather than reducing the state's productive role in the economy,
and thereby lowering business costs, to support high single-digit GDP
growth for the next several years. It recognizes that the reform process
has been fitful but pins its hopes on the government's "new Concept"
for administrative reform 2006–8 promulgated in late 2005.[21]

Soviet public administration we are told was the antithesis of the
Weberian ideal because politics superseded efficient bureaucratic process and jurisdictional lines between hierarchies were blurred.[22] Its
legacy persists and remains the root cause of Russia's administrative
inefficiency. Rectifying the problem and preempting *state capture*,[23]
therefore isn't primarily a matter of downsizing.[24] It requires moving

[21] Ibid. "The precise definition of NPM is rather elusive, for it is more of an
approach than a model as such. It tends to be associated with competition,
performance incentives, open recruitment into middle and upper grades of the
civil service, and more movement into and out of the service."

[22] Ibid., Box 3.1. "The traditional Western model of public bureaucracy, as reflected
in the writings of Max Weber, emphasizes a strict functional/hierarchical division
of labour; the existence of career civil servants as a distinct group, formed on
the basis of competitive recruitment and merit-based promotion; a distinctive
rationality based on legality, impartiality, objectivity and regularity; and a public
service ethos."

[23] Ibid., p. 118.

[24] Ibid., Box 3.2, p. 119. The OECD contends that Russia's civil service isn't
too big despite a 10.9 percent increase in personnel in 2005 alone, driven by a
staggering 28 percent year-on-year increase in the number of people employed in
the federal executive branch. But, almost all the growth reported for 2005 was due
to the inclusion of individuals not previously counted as working in *organs of state
power and local self-management*. If the institutions affected by reclassification are
excluded, then bureaucracy appears to have grown by around 2.1 percent in 2005,
with the federal bureaucracy growing by around 1.5 percent. Altogether, the
number of officials employed in public administration grew by around 33 percent
during 1994–2005, with subnational administrations accounting for most of
the increase. Nevertheless, Russia's public administration appears to employ an
unusually small portion of the labor force when compared with most OECD and
transition countries. Rosstat estimates that Russia in 2004 employed 3.2 federal
administrators per 1,000 population, as against 3.8 in the United States and 5.1 in
Canada and the United Kingdom. This continues the Soviet pattern. The issue
of civil service pay is addressed in Box 3.3, Ibid. It is argued that Russian civil
servants aren't as underpaid as often contended because take-home pay may be
fifteen to twenty times base salary in some cases.

from Gorbachev to Weber, from rapidly increasing corruption to tech-nocratic duty.

The OECD claims that frustration within the presidential adminis-tration regarding the tardy fulfillment of executive orders, confirmed by the World Bank's studies of comparative governance,[25] has mobi-lized Kremlin resolve to modernize Russia's bureaucracy. This deter-mination is complemented by the move to a medium-term budgeting framework, the shift to a performance-oriented budget process,[26] and bureaucratic acceptance of transparency proposals inspired by the New Public Management.

The OECD therefore is guardedly hopeful but acknowledges that the reform of federal bodies is off to a rocky start. Implementation remains spotty,[27] despite an effort to rationalize jurisdictional roles by assigning ministries, services, and agencies, respectively, exclusive authority over policymaking, supervision, and public services. Civil service reform initiated in the Federal Programme for Reforming the State Service of the Russian Federation (2003–5) aimed at transform-ing state service into public service likewise has progressed slowly along conservative lines. However, in late 2005, the cabinet approved an ambitious Concept for administrative reform for 2006–8, along with a detailed timetable for the preparation and implementation of specific measures, reported in Table 13.5.

The virtues of the Concept, according to the OECD, are compre-hensiveness, client-oriented incentives, appreciation of the need for patience, and recognition of the "need for continuous monitoring of the optimal functions of state bodies." But in its view, these goals are unrealistic, and the Kremlin would be well advised to consider:

1. Improving the institutional context within which the bureau-cracy operates
   • Press ahead with reforms aimed at strengthening the rule of law
   • Adopt freedom of information legislation
   • Strengthen parliamentary oversight
2. Empowering citizens vis-à-vis the bureaucracy
   • Ensure open public service standards

---

[25] Ibid., p. 121. The World Economic Forum's *2005 Global Competitiveness Report* dropped Russia from 81 to 91 out of 117 countries with respect to the quality of public institutions.

[26] Ibid., p. 124.

[27] Ibid., pp. 136–37.

Table 13.5. *Administrative reform indicators and targets*

Goal	Indicator	2004	2008	2010
Increasing the quality and accessibility of public services	Degree of public satisfaction with service quality	14	50	70
Reducing bureaucratic interference in private commerce	The cost of overcoming administrative barriers (% business income)	8	5	3
	World Bank governance Indicators (GRICS) for increasing the efficiency and effectiveness of executive bodies			
Government effectiveness		48.1	55	70
Regulatory quality		30.5	60	70

Source: OECD, Economic Surveys: *Russian Federation 2006,* OECD, Paris, 2006, Table 3.2, p. 129.

- • Create an effective nonjudicial mechanism for redressing citizen's grievances
3. Fighting corruption
    - • Expand the range of opportunities for using ICT
    - • Strengthen anticorruption legislation
    - • Adopt *whistleblower protection*
4. Reducing the role of the bureaucracy in commercial affairs
    - • Reduce scope of superfluous regulation
    - • institutionalize regulatory reviews
    - • reduce state ownership
    - • separate state ownership from regulation.

These recommendations are just as impractical in Muscovy as the Kremlin's own Concept. Despite the OECD guarded hopefulness, it provides little reason for believing that Russia will escape the *treadmill of economic reform*[28] or that administrative modernization will transform economic recovery into self-sustaining rapid growth.

[28] Ibid., pp. 129–39. Gertrude Schroeder, "The Soviet Economy on a Treadmill of Reforms," in *Soviet Economy in a Time of Change, Washington, D.C.*: Joint Economic Committee of Congress, pp. 312–66.

The merit of the OECD's forecast by the process of elimination therefore turns squarely on government efforts to promote domestic innovation, technology transfer, and diffusion by strengthening intellectual property rights, competition, the public science sector, special economic zones, and the tax regime for private-sector R&D. This isn't surprising because it is well established that domestic innovation, technology and diffusion are the principle determinants of long-run economic growth,[29] and that recently investment in information and communications technology (ICT), and human capital, combined with more efficient and innovative ways of producing goods and services have been especially important.[30]

The OECD is hopeful because it claims that Russia's innovation potential is greater than most of its peers noting that the country benefits from a substantial science base and a well developed education system in science and technology.[31] Although it is acknowledged that indicators of innovation activity remain disappointing, the imbalance between the public resources devoted to knowledge creation and innovation[32] is construed as disappointingly ineffectual more than as a

[29] P. Donselaar, H. P. G. Erken, and L. Klomp, "R&D and Innovation: Drivers of Productivity Growth," in G. M. Gelauff, L. Klomp, S. E. P. Raes, and T. J. A. Roelandt (eds.), *Fostering Productivity Patterns, Determinants and Policy Implications*, Elsevier, Boston, 2004.

[30] OECD, *The New Economy: Beyond the Hype*, OECD, Paris, 2001; OECD, *The Sources of Economic Growth in OECD Countries*, OECD, Paris, 2003.

[31] *Russian Federation 2006*, pp. 148, 157. Russia has a well-educated workforce, although the quality of higher education appears to have fallen during the 1990s. Tertiary educational attainment is relatively high compared with OECD countries, and Russia produces a far higher proportion of graduates in science and engineering. The number of IT graduates per annum has more than doubled since 1995. However, the country remains a major exporter of researchers, especially in their late twenties and thirties. The limited involvement of higher education institutions in R&D represents a missed opportunity in the university sector. In 2005, HEIs received only about 4.3 percent of budgetary funding for R&D, down from an already low 6.1 percent in 2004.

[32] Ibid., p. 155. The share of technologically new or improved products in industrial sales was just 5.6 percent in 2004, and this share does not exceed 10 percent even for firms engaged in innovation. The share of high value-added goods in manufacturing exports to OECD countries does not exceed 1 percent (0.2 percent for ICT goods) and reaches only 10 percent for high-medium value-added goods. Also, there are very few patents held abroad, and most of them are foreign owned, not Russian. Moreover, only 5 percent of usable models produced during 1992–2002 became objects of commercial agreement. See L. M. Gokhberg, "Russia: A New Innovation System for the New Economy," paper delivered at the First

harbinger of future failure.[33] Moreover, Russia's poor record in developing commercial technology is treated as a fading Soviet legacy of
arrangements that can be reversed, despite the fact that most Russian
R&D is financed by the state, interaction between the state and private R&D sector is limited,[34] the private sector emphasizes imitation
rather than R&D based innovation, many indicators of private innovation activities are declining, and only 30 percent of innovating firms
conduct any R&D at all.[35]

> Global Conference "Innovation Systems and Development Strategies for the
> Third Millennium," Rio de Janeiro, November 2003. A similar picture holds for
> "upstream" or fundamental R&D activity, measured by scientific publications.
> Russian scientists publish only 2.7 percent of the total volume of publications in
> the world's leading scientific journals. But Russia still holds strong positions in
> space research, nuclear power generation and laser technologies, as well as fields
> connected to the exploitation of mineral resources, and areas that do not require
> major capital investment, like mathematics.

[33] Ibid., pp. 148–49. Russia spends more on inputs into knowledge creation than
most countries at similar levels of GDP, but its performance is *mediocre*. It fares
best on international comparative innovation indices when they are weighted
towards inputs into R&D; performs less well on indices that emphasize technical
achievement; and ranks worst on indices emphasizing economic incentives. See
the annex to OECD, *2006 Investment Policy Review of the Russian Federation:
Enhancing Policy Transparency*, OECD, Paris, 2006. Total R&D spending in Russia
amounted to approximately 1.2 percent of GDP in 2004, well below the OECD
average, but more than in most emerging economies. Moreover, R&D intensity
has increased markedly in recent years, recovering from a post-Soviet low of just
over 0.8 percent of GDP. The OECD attributes part of Russia's R&D under
spending compared to the developed nations' norm to its small industrial and
high natural resource base, disregarding the Soviet experience and structural
militarization.

[34] *Russian Federation 2006,* p. 155. Most research personnel in the Russian Academy
of Sciences (RAS) system and in universities have little incentive to worry about
the commercial application of their work.

[35] Ibid., pp. 150–54. Roughly 60 percent of R&D is publicly financed. The ratio
is stable. At first glance, the bulk of R&D appears to be conducted in the business sector, but this reflects the fact that state owned-companies and branches
of research institutes are classified as business entities, and they conduct a large
share of publicly financed innovation activities. Broadening the definition of the
public sphere to include not only state institutes and state unitary enterprise, but
also joint stock companies that are majority state-owned, IET (2006) [*Rossiiskaya
ekonomika v 2005 gody: Tendentsii i perspektivy*, Institute for the Economy in Transition, Moscow, http://www.iet.ru/publication.php?folder-id=44&category-id=
2083] estimates that the state science sector consumes up to 98 percent of budgetary funding for science and represents about 86 percent of the fixed assets of the
science sector. Human resources in R&D are disproportionately large relative to
R&D spending, well above the EU15 average, and labor costs account for about
half of R&D spending. The overwhelming majority of R&D personnel work in

The solution to this impasse is said to lie in better state science policy that improves the framework conditions for business; one that will energize innovation in the private sector, without waiting for the market to empower itself.[36] The OECD contends that "The creation of sound framework conditions for business would appear to be a *sine qua non* for boosting private innovative activities," even though the proposition borders on neoliberal heresy,[37] and is advanced with a conspicuous lack of conviction: "it is important to proceed with a realistic understanding of how far innovation policy can go and what can reasonably be expected."[38]

The framework conditions for turbocharging innovation are familiar: secure property rights, low barriers to market entry, a stable institutional environment, low inflation and low real interest rates (although

the public sphere – 80 percent on the IET's definition. Concerning private R&D activities, the acquisition of patent rights and patent licenses remains marginal, and R&D accounts for only 16 percent of business spending on technological innovation, down from 27 percent in 1995.

[36] *Russian Federation 2006*, p. 158. For research on framework conditions see F. Jaumotte and N. Pain, "Innovation in the Business Sector," Economics Department Working Papers, No. 459, OECD, Paris, 2005, www.oecd.org/dataoecd/49/29/20686301.HTM; OECD, 2006 *Investment Policy Review of the Russian Federation: Enhancing Policy Transparency*, OECD, Paris, 2006; I. Goldberg, "Competitiveness and the Investment Climate in Russia: An Assessment by the World Bank and the Higher School of Economics, Moscow," presented to the 10th annual St. Petersburg International Economic Forum, June 12–14, 2006.

[37] Ibid. The OECD has repeatedly asserted that Russia's market is maturing, which would seem to suggest that the private sector should generate more innovations as times goes by without state hothousing, but adopts the opposite stance here: "Ultimately, a successful innovation policy, in Russia as elsewhere, must provide the right incentives for those engaged in R&D, facilitate contacts between knowledge producers and business, and create an institutional environment that favors the reallocation of resources needed to turn new knowledge into wealth-creating activities." It also contends that state intervention is justified by "information asymmetries involved in innovation and the positive spillovers generated by R&D activities" (p. 148). On spillovers see A. Savvides and M. Zachariadis, "International Technology Diffusion and the Growth of TFP in the Manufacturing Sector of Developing Economies," *Review of Development Economics*, 9, 4(November 2005).

[38] Ibid. Also, "OECD (2005a:15) observes that the empirical evidence regarding the effectiveness of different instruments of innovation policy is mixed. This certainly appears to be true in the Russian case: Yakovlev (2006) reports that 12.6 percent of respondents to an enterprise survey said that they had received state assistance to stimulate innovation in 2004, but such assistance had little impact." Cf. OECD, *Communications Outlook*, OECD, Paris, 2005; and A. Yakovlev, "Mery gosudarstvennoi podderzhki promyshlennosti: masshtaby, adresaty, effektivnost," mimeo, State University – Higher School of Economics, Moscow, July 2006.

its macro strategy calls for higher interest rates),[39] because they enable
businesses to operate with longer time horizons, and reduce risk. A
well-developed financial system including venture capital, absent in
Russia, essential for lowering external financing costs is part of the
package,[40] as is the creation of an attractive environment for foreign direct investment (FDI), including collaborative R&D and innovation. The OECD asserts that there is strong evidence suggesting
that if Russia transforms itself into a magnet for foreign know-how,
with the aid of government science policy, the benefits should be
prodigious,[41] especially in the energy sector where Russian energy
consumption per unit of output is estimated at 2.3 times the world
average.[42] And although the theoretical effect of product market competition on innovation is ambiguous, the correlation is said to be positive.[43] Given weak Russian regional competitiveness, as shown by
Herfindahl–Hirschman indexes in all sectors, enhanced competition
should quicken GDP growth.[44]

Improved intellectual property rights (IPR) provide another
promising venue for stimulating innovation, but here too there are
pluses and minuses. A certain level of protection is needed, but over-
protection risks allowing patent-holders to capture excessive rents at
society's expense. Moreover, research shows that a strict IPR regime
does not always spur R&D spending.[45] Nonetheless, Russia's IPR protection is so weak, despite gains in trademarks and copyrights that it

[39] *Russian Federation 2006*, p. 159.
[40] Ibid. "In Russia, a majority of firms rely on retained earning to finance investment
      and innovation, and surveys almost always report the shortage of own funds and
      the cost of borrowing as the principal barriers to investment and innovation."
      This problem is compounded by a dearth of venture capital.
[41] Ibid. The studies cited supporting this contention are D. Guellec and B. van
      Pottelsberghe de la Potterie, "R&D and Productivity Growth: Panel Data Anal-
      ysis of 16 OECD Countries," *OECD STI Working Paper*, 2004/4 June 2001,
      http://www.oecd.org/findDocument/o.2350,en_2649; P. Hemmings, "Hun-
      garian innovation Policy: What Is the Best Way Forward?" Economics Depart-
      ment Working Papers, No. 445, September 2005.
[42] Ibid., pp. 159–60.
[43] Ibid., p. 60; K. Kozlov and K. Yudaeva, "Imitations and Innovations in a
      Transition Economy," mimeo, Bank of Finland Institute for Economies in
      Transition (BOFIT), October 2004, http://www.bof.fi/bofit/seminar/bofcef05/
      innovations.pdf.
[44] *Russian Federation 2006*, pp. 160–61, especially Figure 4.11.
[45] F. Jaumotte and N. Pain, "From Ideas to Development: The Determinants of
      R&D and Patenting," *Economics Department Working Papers*, No. 457, OECD,
      Paris, 2005, http://www.oecd.org/dataoecd/49/29/20686301.HTM.

can be substantially strengthened with little risk, and great benefit for R&D commercialization.[46] The reduction of assignment and specification (copycatting) problems is especially important because the present IPR regime complicates agent collaboration, inhibiting technology transfer and sometimes creating conflicts of interest. Although, a decree in November 2005 allows state R&D institutions to award IPR to private recipients, studies show that patenting the results of publicly funded research has been disappointing,[47] partly due to technology transfer offices (TTO) demanding more than prudent investors are willing to pay. And most importantly, the significance of the decree should not be exaggerated because IPR enforcement remains weak. Russia ranks 105 of 117 countries in IPR protection.[48]

Specification is also troublesome. Even when IPR are properly assigned, patents are widely disregarded by imitators differentiating their products in trivial ways. The principle of *investive level* is enshrined in Russia law, but not in practice.

The financing of basic research poses another challenge. The 2006 budget envisages the allocation of only 14.6 percent of all civil science funding on a competitive basis, allowing insiders to concentrate on their pet projects instead of socially promising alternatives. The government is trying to increase basic research with little apparent success, while preserving the state's role as principal supplier of basic research, and placing the burden for applied downstream R&D on the private sector. This may be a reasonable strategy, but the OECD worries that government may be too parochial, failing to consult adequately with business, the scientific community and civil society on basic science priorities.[49]

The inefficiency of Russian basic science R&D is partly attributable to institutional structure. Institutes receiving all their funds from the state have inadequate incentives to satisfy consumer demand, and at the same time lack adequate organizational flexibility to respond to customers if this became possible. A new autonomous form is needed to deal with the challenge, but progress has been glacial because

---

[46] Ibid., p. 162. Rospatent, "Godovoi otchet 2004," Federal Service for Intellectual Property, Patents and Trademarks, Moscow, 2005, http://www.fips.ru/rep2001/rep2004/index.htm.

[47] Ibid. OECD, *Science and Innovation Policies: Key Challenges and Opportunities*, OECD, Paris, 2004, p. 81.

[48] Russian Federation 2006, p. 162.

[49] Ibid., p. 164.

Table 13.6. *Organizational transformation of the state science sector, 2005–10*

	2005	2008	2010
Breakdown by sector (percent)			
Academy of Sciences	32.7	31.0	34.4
Applied research sector	48.1	44.3	31.3
Higher education	19.2	24.8	34.4
Breakdown by organization form (percent)			
State unitary enterprises	48.0	2.4	1.3
State institutions	50.0	28.6	25.0
Autonomous state institutions	0	11.9	21.9
Noncommercial autonomous state institutions	0	9.5	15.6
Majority state-owned joint stock companies	2	47.6	36.3
Number of organizations	2,600	2,100	1,600

Source: Ministry of Education and Science. OECD Economic Surveys, *Russian Federation 2006*, Table 4.1, p. 165.

restructuring the state science sector involves not just reorganizing institutions (transforming state unitary enterprises and state institutions into other legal/organizational forms) but consolidation and downsizing. The state science establishment is both too large and too fragmented. The state owns roughly 2,900 R&D organizations, and the number of research institutes has actually risen in recent years, mainly as a result of splits and spin-offs rather than any increase in research capacity. Table 13.6 illustrates the structure of state science sector, and changes envisioned by the government. The OECD is sympathetic to the goal, but cautions that "it would be very risky to force the pace of reorganization and consolidation" because of the reforms' intrinsic complexities.[50]

Science cadres too are part of the problem. The Russian Foundation for Fundamental Research found that roughly 50 to 70 percent of researchers were engaged in real research,[51] and this waste was compounded by poor pay, incentives, and career opportunities for

[50] Ibid., p. 165.
[51] Ibid., pp. 165–66. Other studies suggest that only 40–45 percent of researchers are really productive.

young scientists. Russia is a major exporter of its next generation of researchers, conspicuous in the age profile of the science establishment.

Turning to the private R&D sector, the OECD notes that empirical research into the impact of fiscal support on innovation yields mixed results, with tax relief having a larger effect than direct subsidies.[52] Furthermore, the effectiveness of fiscal instruments is sensitive to framework conditions, and environmental factors like market failure. With these caveats in mind, the OECD advises proceeding slowly and concentrating on reducing fiscal disincentives to R&D with devices such as accelerated depreciation, writing off R&D costs in a single year.[53] It also recommends scrapping the VAT tax break on R&D for research organizations because it provides sectoral, rather than project targeted incentives.

However, this doesn't mean that the OECD is sanguine about targeting in general. It takes a jaundiced attitude toward special economic zones (SEZs), technoparks, science towns, and venture capital (Box 13.1) because the empirical evidence is mixed, there are risks of deadweight losses, a danger of permanent free-riding, and a lack of overarching policy framework,[54] despite the government's strategy for the development of science and innovation to 2015. The OECD understands that private sector venture capital (VC) may play an important role spurring innovation in Russia, but also knows that the industry is still in its infancy. The Russian Venture Capital Association (RVCA) estimates that VC firms invested $427 million in Russian companies in 2003–4, or around 0.04 percent of GDP, most of it dominated by foreigners.[55] And the obstacles to developing VC are

---

[52] Ibid., p. 166. Jaumotte and Pain, "Innovation in the Business Sector," 2005. B. H. Hall and J. Van Reenen, "How Effective Are Fiscal Incentives for R&D? A Review of the Evidence," *Research Policy*, 29 (2000): 4–5. T. J. Kiette, J. Moen, and Z. Griliches, "Do Subsidies to Commercial R&D Reduce Market Failures? Micro-econometric Evaluation Studies," *Research Policy*, 29 (April 2000): 4–5; P. A. David, B. H. Hall, and A. A. Toole, "Is Public R&D a Complement or a Substitute for Private R&D: A Review of Econometric Evidence," *Research Policy*, 29 (April 2000): 4–5.

[53] Ibid., p. 167. A survey found that managers thought the reform had great potential for accelerating R&D. B. Kuznetsov, M. Kuzyk, Yu. Simachev, S. Tsukhlo, and A. Chulok, "Osobennosti sprosa na tekhologicheskie innovatsii i otsenka potential'noi reaktsii rossiiskikh promyshlennykh predpriyatii no vozmoszhnye mekhanizmy stimulirovanie innovatsionnoi aktivnosti(tezisy)," International Department Analytical Centre, Moscow, May 19, 2006.

[54] Ibid.

[55] Ibid., p. 169.

considerable including poor protection for minority shareholders, and the lack of viable exit strategies, due to the underdevelopment of the IPO market and shallow financial markets. The VC industry's heavy dependence on the EBRD and USAID[56] is also telltale.

Box 13.1 Target Innovation Initiatives

Special Economic Zones (SEZ)

The government is creating technical-innovation zones in the Moscow district of Zelenograd (microelectronics), in Dubna, in Moscow Oblast (nuclear physics–based technologies), in Tomsk (new materials), and in St. Petersburg (IT).

Technoparks

The government is planning to create eight technoparks across Russia, including Novosibirsk, Tyumen', Kazan (Tataristan), Sarov (Nizhni Novgorod Oblast), and Obninsk. Two more have been created in the Moscow Oblast designed to be business incubators, and technology transfer centers.

Science Towns

Work is proceeding on constructing more science towns in addition to the ten already in existence. The status entitles them to receive federal funds to develop their science base.

Venture Capital

The following ministries are creating venture capital funds: The Ministry of Economic Development and Trade is organizing ten to twelve regional funds with an initial capitalization of RUB 2.1–2.5 bn, with projects restricted to a few small innovative firms.

The former Ministry of Industry, Science, and Technology lauded a Venture Investment Fund (VIF) in 2000 as a *fund of funds*, but little was done due to lack of resources.

The Ministry of Information Technologies and Communications oversees the Russian Investment Fund for Information and Communications Technologies (RIFICT) established by decree August 2006.

Source: OECD Economic Surveys, *Russian Federation 2006,* Box 4.1, p. 165.

---

[56] Ibid., p. 170.

The OECD's assessment of Russia's R&D effort doesn't seem promising for innovation-driven high GDP growth. It neither identifies magic bullets nor provides compelling evidence that the Kremlin is prepared to replace Ivan the Great with Weber. It clings instead to the hope that because Russia's innovation potential is unusually great, and its leaders pay lip service to progressive reform, the Federation's innovation potential will be tapped by somehow strengthening framework conditions for business, and reforming the public science sector in a stable macroeconomic environment,[57] if its idealistic recommendations catalogued in Box 13.2 are implemented.

Box 13.2 Recommendations on Innovation Policy

1. Improving framework conditions
    - Ensure continued macroeconomic stability.
    - Continue reforms improving the rule of law, the financial system, and the protection of property rights, while reducing the bureaucratic burden on business.
    - Increase competition by reducing barriers to entry, and strengthening competition law enforcement.
    - Facilitate technological cooperation by encouraging foreign direct investment.
    - Eliminate regulatory and infrastructural constraints in the ICT sector.
    - Improve ministerial innovation policy coordination.
2. Strengthening intellectual property rights
    - Improve IPR by increasing penalties for violations, including copycat patents.
    - Increase judicial understanding of IPR issues.
3. Reforming the state science sector
    - Stress project-based financing of state-funded research, increase managerial discretion, and tighten financial discipline.
    - Foster the involvement of the scientific community, business, and civil society in determining the allocation of state R&D funds.
    - Introduce performance-based evaluations.
    - Improve career prospects of young scientists.
    - Reduce the number of direct R&D-funded recipients from the federal budget.

---

[57] OECD (2006), p. 173.

- Rationalize the state science sector.
- Facilitate information exchange between R&D organizations and business.
- Increase the share of public research funding allocated to universities.
4. Promoting private-sector R&D
   - Allow accelerated amortization of R&D expenditures.
   - Keep fiscal R&D incentives simple and universal.
   - Leverage private sector participation.
   - Improve legislative and tax framework for VC firms.
5. Specific innovation-promotion
   - Adopt regular external evaluations of technoparks and special economic zones.
   - Focus evaluations on public goods provision and market failure.
   - Proceed cautiously.
6. Support schemes for innovative start-ups and small innovation firms
   - Adhere to neutral criteria, avoid picking winners.
   - Ensure selection transparency.

Source: OECD Economic Surveys, *Russian Federation 2006*, Box 4.3, pp. 174-75.

No doubt, if Russia transitioned to democratic free enterprise under the rule of law and adopted socially optimal macroeconomic policies, its performance in all regards would converge toward the global high frontier, but because the Federation displays no sign of doing so, the OECD's recommendations are more Polonius's ineffectual counsel of perfection than a practical roadmap.

The same caveat extends to another aspect of its growth support strategy, as Russia leaves the recovery phase, and tries to achieve sustained, high GDP growth. Surprisingly, the issue is public health. Normally, education is showcased as the crucial growth source because of its productivity enhancing knowledge and skill effects. However, dire demographics compelled the OECD to concentrate instead on assessing whether adverse trends can be mitigated with wise state health system reform policies.

The data in Table 13.7 highlight its concerns. They have shown that the economic recovery, which has occurred under Putin's watch, has not yet arrested the acute deterioration in health that commenced in 1990 shortly before the Soviet Union's collapse. A surge in circulatory, respiratory, and infectious diseases, compounded by alcohol poisoning, suicide and murder has sharply reduced life expectancy, especially

Table 13.7. *Selected health and demographic indicators*

	1990	1995	2000	2004
Life expectancy at birth (years)	69.2	64.5	65.2	65.2
Men	63.7	58.1	59.1	58.9
Women	74.3	71.6	72.3	72.3
Death rate (1,000)	11.2	15.0	15.3	16.0
Death from				
circulatory diseases (100/100,000)	137.1	225.0	205.0	249.6
respiratory diseases (100/100,000)	18.9	38.7	35.4	40.8
digestive tract (100/100,000)	15.4	35.7	31.8	49.0
infectious/parasitic disease (/100,000)	11.5	25.0	31.2	33.0
alcohol poisoning (/100,000)	15.6	41.8	34.0	38.5
suicides (/100,000)	33.9	56.4	49.8	42.4
murders (/100,000)	21.4	44.4	38.0	35.6
Tuberculosis cases (/100,000)	34.2	57.8	89.8	83.3
Hepatitis cases (/100,000)	226.7	166.8	183.3	99.1

Data on death rates by cause of death are for the working age population only.

Source: Federal Service of State Statistics. OECD Economic Surveys, *Russian Federation 2006*, Table 5.1, p. 188.

among the working-age population. The share of deaths caused by infectious disease is high for Russia's level of development, and the incidence of tuberculosis and other *poverty-related illnesses* is severe.[58]

Low birthrates compound these adverse trends. Russia's population has been sharply declining since 1990, and the working age population will begin falling around 2007. Since, production function theorists consider employment a principal source of aggregate economic growth, it follows that a shrinking labor force should have an adverse impact. An aging population will aggravate matters further by diverting resources for growth promoting activities to elder health care. And, if the health crisis deepens as many analysts like Murray Feshbach contend,[59] not only will the labor shortage intensify, but the quality of the labor force will deteriorate, depressing productivity, reducing household income and encouraging early exit from the

[58] Ibid., p. 189.
[59] Murray Feshbach, *Russia's Health and Demographic Crises: Policy Implications and Consequences*, Chemical and Biological Arms Control Institute, Washington, DC, 2003.

already diminishing labor force. The OECD doesn't contemplate this scenario, but it is a distinct possibility.

Rather, it assumes that Russian health is already on the mend, and focuses attention on how the public health care system can be reformed to accelerate the process, recognizing inherent limitations. Studies are cited that find little linkage between health and mortality outcomes and access to health care in Russia. In addition, health depends on multiple factors besides medical delivery systems, including the environment, education, road safety, lifestyles, and attitudes toward the future. Still, health care system reform could improve GDP growth prospects by slowing, or reversing Russia's diminishing labor force, and increasing worker quality.

The target of the reform is a Soviet-style integrated, hierarchical, *Semashko* health care system predominantly financed from general government revenues, providing free medical services, where the majority of health personnel are state employees, mixed with post-Soviet private elements. Russia's health care spending is on a par with other middle-income countries and emphasizes epidemic and infectious diseases control at the expense of nonpublic health primary care. Low prestige and poor pay keeps the quality of entrants into the primary care sector low, and encourages informal charges and moonlighting. In principle, the mandatory medical insurance (OMS) system partly financing these arrangements promotes efficiency and choice by enabling patients to choose among competing medical providers. However, it does so ineffectively because funding, competition and microincentives are inadequate.[60]

Despite the intention of reformers, federal and regional budgets still administer about 60 percent of public health expenditure, the remainder allocated through the OMS system. After the introduction of the unified social tax (ESN) in 2001, the OMS system received ESN revenues equal to a 3.6 percent payroll tax, with most monies going to regional OMS funds. This left the system underfunded, and regionally imbalanced because the Federal Fund for Mandatory Medical Insurance (FFOMS) responsible for redistribution, had scant resources. A medical payroll tax cut to 2.8 percent in 2005 further reduced OMS resources, making the health care system more dependent on regional budgetary allocations. Worse still, although there are 300 private insurers, there is little real competition. Individuals have the right to choose, but it is difficult to exercise, and often the choice is made by their

---

[60] Ibid., pp. 190–91.

kickback-seeking employers.[61] Likewise, insurers seldom effectively uphold patients' rights when patient–provider conflicts arise.

The impact of health care reform varies regionally. The majority of public health care institutions are owned and operated by municipalities, but are under the budgetary thumb of regional authorities, causing considerable inequality. The per capita spread between the highest- and lowest-spending regions is eight to one, flouting the constitutional guarantee of equal medical treatment.[62] In principle, the Federal Guaranteed Package Programme should redress the imbalance. The promises are generous, but funding is inadequate, forcing households to fund a good deal of medical care that is supposed to be free. The shortfalls are particularly severe in the provision of high-tech medical procedures, covering about 10 percent of the demand for coronary angiography and heart-valve replacement.[63]

Excessive specialist treatment and hospitalization is another legacy of the Semashko model. Russia has almost twice as many hospital beds per 100,000 population as the European Union, and hospital stays are nearly 50 percent longer.[64] Shifting funds from hospitalization to outpatient primary care would not only be cost effective, but would enhance prevention and early detection. In addition, the development of long-term care facilities would have similar benefits.

This list of woes could be construed as failure, but the OECD prefers to interpret Russia's public health care reform as a half-finished transition that can be completed through the elimination of perverse microincentives, and munificent funding. Moreover, it expects that the *Priority National Project Health* launched in 2005 will help close the gap during 2006–7[65] by channeling 208 billion rubles from federal and regional budgets into health care, spent mostly on increased salaries for primary care physicians, the creation of fifteen new high-tech medical centers and expanded immunization and disease-prevention efforts. The OECD particularly welcomes the focus on primary care and prevention, and the shift from line-item budgetary financing (*smetnoe*) to task performance based compensation. Realization of the Health project if successful is projected to increase demand fulfillment in high-tech medicine from 10 percent to 40 percent within three years. Nonetheless, the OECD cautions "While the project is meant to give

---

[61] Ibid., p. 193.
[62] Ibid., p. 194.
[63] Ibid., p. 195.
[64] Ibid., p. 196.
[65] Ibid., p. 201.

renewed impetus to health care reform, it is far from clear that it will do so. Only limited steps towards greater efficiency or changed incentives are planned. Also the risk of large-scale corruption and waste must be regarded as high." And, it could be added that given the multiple objectives blending equity with efficiency championed by the OECD, ideal outcomes aren't guaranteed even with goodwill, as the west's experience with similar reforms makes abundantly clear. Box 13.3 summarizes the OECD's full set of recommendations for reforming Russia's health care system.

Box 13.3 Recommendations on Health Care Reform

1. **Resolving the mismatch between commitments and resources**
    *   Revise the guaranteed benefits package to bring formal commitments into line with available resources, thereby avoiding perverse incentives.
    *   Create mechanisms to enable citizens to act effectively if commitments aren't met.
    *   Establish a framework for efficient, and transparent review.

2. **Strengthening the OMS system**
    *   End the *two-channel* budget-insurance financing system, making OMS primary.
    *   Create mechanisms for facilitating rational consumer choice.
    *   Strengthen the regulatory framework, encouraging a more active role, while simultaneously fostering competition among regulators.
    *   Encourage regional pilot projects with respect to OMS reform.

3. **Reducing uneconomic hospitalization and specialist care**
    *   Increase primary care investment, including training and integrated care facilities.
    *   Deemphasize cost-reimbursement in favor of volume contracts.
    *   Experiment with fund-holding remuneration for primary care providers encouraging the maintenance of patient health.

4. **Pharmaceuticals provision**
    *   Eliminate inpatient/outpatient distinction for dispensing free medicine and emphasize value-added of expensive drugs. Consider a tier copayment system.
    *   Develop and apply better drug formularies and treatment guidelines.

Source: OECD Economic Surveys, *Russian Federation 2006,* Box 5.1, p. 213.

As with its R&D recommendations, this catalogue is mostly the counsel of perfection. It is the same old Soviet institutional reform prattle in an OECD guise. If Russia weren't Muscovy, then it could be Singapore, eradicating the health care system's adverse effects on the Federation's demography and health. But the Kremlin's problem never has been primarily a matter of faulty comprehension and bad coaching. It always has been addiction to the authoritarian martial police state and rent-granting including agriculture (Box 13.4) that makes OECD style social welfare optimization an obstacle rather than an aid to the fulfillment of Muscovy's real rent-granting agenda.

Box 13.4 Agriculture

Russian economic development has always been impeded by low agrarian productivity. Substantial labor transfers from farms to high value-added industry and services risked famine or made the nation food import dependent. Rapid agrarian productivity growth could have alleviated the constraint but was never achieved.

There are several reasons for this unfortunate state of affairs. Land in old Russia was so plentiful that peasants never developed a sense of proprietorship. Viewing land as communal, they built a system of periodic plot redistribution among households, iron-handedly ruled by village elders.

With the rise of serfdom, landlords found this communal structure useful as a means of administration. They imposed communal obligations that perpetuated both the absence of individual land rights and authoritarian rule, the latter to prevent young able-bodied males from shirking or fleeing.

In the early twentieth century, Prime Minister Pyotr Stolypin made a valiant effort at land reform that gave peasant households a right to receive their share of communal property as hereditary private property. While its feasibility remains controversial to this day, the reform never was adequately tested, interrupted first by World War I and then by the Bolshevik coup d'etat, which nationalized land together with the rest of the means of production.

Joseph Stalin's forced collectivization reimposed serfdom de facto. The consequences would be felt for decades, not only in terms of excess deaths and material destruction, but also in transforming what could have been peasant farming into large scale rural enterprises controlled by the party and security organs.

Following the collapse of the Soviet Union, agrarian private property was created by transforming state and collective farms into joint stock

companies. However, its benefits were diminished by infungible infrastructure and human capital that were suitable for giant enterprises but
not private farming. Roads, water, electricity, storage, and machinery
had to be rebuilt and reallocated. Although farmers can be trained to
be tractor mechanics, it isn't obvious that the process is easily reversible.

Agricultural performance from 1991 onward has reflected these
embedded problems. Following a 44 percent drop in output (1990–
98), Russian agriculture has made a comeback, but the foundations
for recovery remain shaky. Both human and physical capital have been
seriously degraded, the former due to an ongoing exodus by younger
and more productive workers to the cities and the latter due to a lack of
investment. Continuing uncertainties over property rights, the absence
of a functioning land market and urban encroachment have clouded
agrarian decision making and led to a reduction in sown area. Distor-
tions in the price structure also induced a reduction in mineral fertilizer
with a concomitant fall in fertility. There are some grounds for hope,
yet agrarian prospects remain deeply problematic.

This means that Russia's transition from recovery to sustained high
GDP growth, should it occur, requires more than steady-as-you-go
macroeconomic stability and empty promises of fundamental framework change. The OECD is obliged to demonstrate that the authoritarian martial police state will find technocrat surrogates to consumer
sovereign competition for generating rapid technological progress, and
overcoming rent-granting inefficiencies.

This isn't done. The microanalysis provides no evidence suggesting
that Muscovite administration, R&D development, innovation, diffusion, and health care system reform, combined with FDI infused
technology transfer can deliver real GDP growth on a par with or
better than the achieved Soviet level. The OECD might have found
some support for its hopefulness in Putin's arms modernization program but disregarded the planned weapons buildup and military R&D
even though both were principal components of Soviet economic
growth.

The null hypothesis therefore must be that Russian GDP growth
beyond the achieved Soviet output level of 1989 should be lower than
the Gorbachev years because the labor force is declining, immigrant
labor is being discouraged, new fixed capital formation is increasing
relatively slowly, the scientific base has shrunk, and R&D expenditures
have fallen drastically. A strong preference for western brand names

among new Russians, oligarchs, and *siloviki* is a further depressant. This growth retardation should be partly mitigated by improved foreign technology access, lingering benefits of the petro bubble, including a rising tide of FDI, some positive aspects of post–Soviet liberalization, and modest advances in competitiveness. Given Russian economic backwardness, the net result during the Putin-Medvedev years could be moderate GDP growth of a few percent per annum on official measures, and less taking account of the *hidden inflation* Khanin has shown still persists. And, if the petro bubble bursts, the Kremlin surely will experience hard times. The Muscovite authoritarian martial police state is inferior to democratic free enterprise in most regards, and this likely will be reflected in periodic *smuta,* and subpar long-term Russian economic growth that cannot possibly compensate for all Muscovy's inequities, injustices, waste, and corruption.

A careful reading of the fine print demonstrates that despite the OECD's public hopefulness, it understands that Russia's attainment of sustained rapid GDP growth will be an uphill battle. Like the CIA before it in Soviet times, a combination of wishful thinking, political sensibility, and bureaucratic hedging make its assessments inoffensive, and palatable, while providing plausible deniability. Its studies competently inventory technical issues, use sophisticated measurement tools, judiciously include most relevant caveats (except military modernization) and therefore appear persuasively balanced but aren't because the main conclusion doesn't follow from an unbiased weighing of the evidence. The CIA erroneously insisted that the Soviet Union would muddle through, and the OECD's vision of Russian westernization and catch-up is subject to the same pitfalls.

- The OECD predicts that Russia will grow rapidly in a high natural resource price environment.
- Rapid increases in GDP since 1998 are explained by the reactivization of idle capacities, not factor growth or technology transfers.
- The improvement is included in the Solow-Abramowitz growth residual, but should not be interpreted as neutral technological progress.
- The petro bubble has caused ruble appreciation, high inflation and low interest rates.
- Russia has contained the magnitude of these disturbances by imposing natural resource extraction taxes and a confiscatory duty on windfall petroleum export profits.

- The OECD urges Moscow to continue its petro windfall sterilization program.
- The OECD claims that Russia's government sector is growing beneficially because it is becoming more efficient.
- The OECD claims that Russia's state sector is becoming Weberian in accordance with the New Public Management program, without adequate evidence.
- The OECD and the Kremlin contend that Russia has extraordinary commercial potential because of its scientific assets. Although, they didn't pay off in the past, it believes that structural reforms will yield better results.
- Improvements in intellectual property rights are essential, but the IPR regime is weak.
- A host of other specific reforms are sound in theory, but impractical in Muscovy.
- The OECD finds a silver lining in Russia's health care improvement potential because it could stir growth by enhancing human capital, but progress is disappointing.
- Despite the possibilities, Russia's future growth should be below the Soviet benchmark rate because the labor force is declining, immigrant labor is being discouraged, new fixed capital formation is slow, the scientific base has shrunk, and R&D expenditures have fallen.
- Russia may succumb to crisis when the petro bubble bursts.

14

Russia in the Chinese Looking Glass

Hope springs eternal for Russophiles, and in today's world hope may seem justified by the recent successes of authoritarian China. Could a "China card" raise Muscovy's growth prospects above its historical norm? Probably not, but the possibility warrants careful consideration.[1]

China shares many of Muscovy's characteristics and propensities, with a few critical differences that may withstand the test of time. First and foremost, both civilizations are imperial, ruled by omnipotent emperors (Communist Party first secretaries, presidents), with the power of unrestricted informal command (but not totalitarian nanomanagement) over their subjects. Both have laws and judiciaries but not the politically tamper-proof rule of contract law required for well-functioning markets in the West. Both, at least since 1992, grant state enterprise managers extensive custodial rights,[2] and in many

---

[1] The counterview that democracy is an impediment to economic growth has many proponents. See Ashutosh Varshney, "India's Democratic Challenge," *Foreign Affairs*, 86, 2(March/April 2007): 93–106.

[2] In the Chinese case, see "The Regulations on Transforming the Management Mechanism of State-Industrial Enterprises," July 1992. Other reform milestones include: *Open door* policy allowing foreign trade and investment to begin (1978), decision to turn collective farms over to household (1979), township and village enterprise (TVEs) given stronger encouragement (1979), special economic zones created (1980), self-proprietorships (*getihu*) encouraged, of less than eight persons (1984), provisional bankruptcy law passed for state-owned enterprises (1986), contract responsibility system introduced in state-owned enterprises (1987), 1988 beginning of retrenchment of TVEs (1988), stock exchange started in Shenzhen (1990), decision to establish a *socialist market economic system* (1993), company law first introduced (1994), renminbi begins to be convertible on current account (1994), multiple exchange rates ended (1994), shift to contractual terms for state-owned enterprises begins (1997), constitutional amendment passed that

instances proprietary stakes as well. Most state companies are allowed
to engage in for-profit consumer business and act entrepreneurially.
Private enterprise is permitted based on leases of varying duration,[3]
and in Russia, freehold ownership has become widespread. Russia and
China both have formally or informally managed foreign exchange
rates and some state price-fixing, but for the most part, prices are partially competitive in varying degrees. Both permit licensed transactors
to participate in international trade and publicly welcome foreign
direct investment. Both are adept at pirating foreign technologies,
illegally copying trademarked designs, and flouting intellectual property rights. Both have powerful regulatory economic bureaucracies,
employing conventional monetary, fiscal, and administrative policies
to manage aggregate effective demand. Both have social welfare safety
nets and provide barebones social services. Moreover, both are authoritarian with various kinds of subsidiary elective procedures, possess
immense nuclearized military establishments, and use secret police to
discipline and repress opposition to the system and supreme leader.

At this level of abstraction, little appears to explain the immense dis-
parity between Chinese and Russian economic performance during
the last quarter century (Tables 14.1 and 14.2),[4] nor China's superior
recent performance (Tables 13.3 and 14.3). The differences between
their systems and programs however are more illuminating. China

explicitly recognizes private ownership (1999), China accedes to the World Trade
Organization (WTO) 2001, Communist Party endorses role of the private sector,
inviting entrepreneurs to join (2002), decision to *perfect* the socialist market
economic system (2003), constitution amended to guarantee private property
rights. OECD, Economic Surveys, *China*, Vol. 13, September 2005, Paris, p. 29.
[3] There is little freehold property in China. The state is the primary leasor and
consequently remains ultimate owner. This encumbers private proprietary rights
and justifies the claim that China operates today as a form of Langean market
socialism. The OECD, among others, prefers to focus on claimants to residual
income (profit), as the distinguishing characteristic of private property. The scope
of the state sector on this score was only 40.8 percent of the economy in 2003.
The OECD's analysis of Chinese economic performance conceals the leasing
distinction, permitting it to convey the misimpression that China's expanding
private sector is rapidly driving systemic convergence toward full free enterprise
where property rights are market determined, not imposed by the state; OECD,
China, pp. 80–94.
[4] Figures for Russia 1973, 1980, and 1990 in Tables 10.1 and 10.2 refer to the
Soviet Union. This doesn't obscure per capita income comparison because living
standards in the Russian Soviet Federated Socialist Republic were close to the
national mean. However, approximately thirty percent of the decline in Russia's
relative GDP size (1990–2000) is attributable to post-Soviet territorial losses.

Table 14.1. *Comparative size estimates per capita GDP 1973–2000 (America = 100; percent)*

	Russia	China
1973	36.3	5
1980	34.6	5.7
1990	29.6	8
2000	18.3	12.2

Note: The figures for Russia 1973, 1980, 1990 pertain to the USSR. This doesn;t distort the trend because per capita income in the RSFSR was close to the Soviet mean.

Source: Angus Maddison, *The World Economy: Historical Statistics*, OECD, Paris, 2003, pp. 69, 89, 101, 184, 234, and 262.

Table 14.2. *Comparative GDP size estimates 1973–2000 (America = 100; percent)*

	Russia	China
1973	42.8	20.9
1980	40.4	24.7
1990	34.3	36.3
2000	10.0	54.5

Note: The figures for Russia 1973, 1980, and 1990 pertain to the USSR. Approximately 30 percent of the relative decline in Russia's GDP (1990;2000) is attributable to territorial downsizing.

Source: Angus Maddison, *The World Economy: Historical Statistics*, OECD, Paris, 2003, pp. 55–57, 85–86, 98–99, 170, 174, and 176.

Table 14.3. *Recent Chinese economic trends and prospects (percent)*

	1983–88	1998–2003	2003	2004	2005	2006
Real GDP growth	12.1	8.0	9.5	9.5	9.0	9.2
Sources of growth						
labor	1.5	0.3				
capital	5.0	4.9				
residual	5.6	2.8				
of which education	1.0	0.5				
Inflation		1.2	3.9	4.0	4.0	

Source: Data are from national sources. OECD, Economic Surveys, *China*, Vol. 2005/13, September 2005, Paris, pp. 32, 60.

in some important regards is closer to Langean market socialism (or
Soviet NEP) because most of the means of production, including real
estate, remain state owned, with assets leased to state managers and
independent entrepreneurs.[5] China has been much more cautious
about permitting insiders to privatize spontaneously and otherwise
enrich themselves from state assets, no doubt chastened by the chaos
of the Cultural Revolution.[6] Nor has it condoned private capital flight
or tolerated behavior subversive to the party's development program.
Boris Yeltsin had the power to emulate Deng Xiaoping's protection of
the people's wealth against insider asset seizing and his orderly liberalization even after he destroyed communist power, but chose not to
exercise it. Similarly, the Chinese leadership never abandoned Command Communist resource mobilization. Some involuntary unemployment has been accepted as the price for curtailing unprofitable
state enterprises, but monetary and fiscal policy, together with state
civil construction, is dedicated to fostering rapid development in sharp
contrast to the Yeltsin administration, which treated resource demobi-
lization as an unfortunate consequence of crony asset-grabbing. Even
now, the National Projects campaign is mostly empty rhetoric. Also,
with respect to governance, the Confucian foundations of China's
administrative and regulatory bureaucracies, stressing competitive
qualifying examinations and ethical self-restraint for the community's
benefit, seem to provide some counterweight to the venality exhibited
by Russian bureaucrats who treat government posts as rent-seeking
ways of making a living from bribes, with little obligation to provide
worthy service. Corruption in both economies is pandemic, but the
paralysis in Russia is more severe.

China also benefits from a procompetitive commercial culture, willing to satisfy customers and aggressively price discount, whereas Russians treat service as an avoidable burden and price gouge in the spirit
of Gogol's *Dead Souls.*[7] Chinese merchants don't disdain overcharging
the gullible, and the quality of domestic construction and manufactures is shoddy, but these problems are milder when buyers are savvy,
such as in the wholesale export sector. Although Russian construction

[5] Oskar Lange and Fred M. Taylor, *On the Economic Theory of Socialism*, University
of Minnesota Press, Minneapolis, 1938.
[6] Elaine Kurtenbach, "China: 60 Percent of Recent Land Deals Illegal,"
Yahoo!Finance, June 7, 2006. These deals are null and void and perpetrators
will be punished.
[7] Nikolai Gogol, *Dead Souls*, Yale University Press, New Haven, CT, 1966.

contractors ruthlessly exploit itinerant Central Asian workers,[8] there was little scope for using cheap labor as a platform for industrial exports and import substitutes under Yeltsin, and none now that the Putin administration has overvalued the ruble. Moreover, the problem is compounded by Russia's abundant natural resource riches, which allow the privileged to import whatever they choose without concern for deindustrialization, attendant involuntary underemployment, and acute regional inequality.

China's economy also suffers from geographical segmentation between the eastern coastal islands of modernity and its backward hinterland, but rent-granting and rent-seeking in a relatively natural resource–poor setting have not repressed industry nor industrial growth in export and import substitution sectors.[9] China's authoritarian martial police state thrives by promoting value added, (especially in the foreign direct investment intensive export sector), while Russia is content to live as it can from extraction, spillovers, and cheap Chinese consumer goods.

China's pursuit of pro-value-adding industry and commerce furthermore doesn't appear to be severely hampered by structural militarization, mobilization reserves accumulation, and entailed civilian capacities. Although its more than 2 million–strong armed force may be the world's largest,[10] and its military industrial base is regionally strong, the scale of defense activities is substantially smaller than Russia's on a per capita basis.[11] The high opportunity costs of raw material mobilization reserves mitigates against replicating Russia's hoarding, with attendant implications for the scope of war mobilization entailments on civilian production capacities, which might otherwise constrain pro-value-adding industry.

---

[8] Claire Bigg, "Russia: Migrant Workers Struggle to Build Lives amid Poverty, Abuse," *Radio Liberty*, November 8, 2005.

[9] David Zweig and Bi Jianhai, "China's Global Hunt for Energy," *Foreign Affairs*, 84, 5 (September/October 2005): 25–38.

[10] Vladimir Putin stated in December 2003 in a call-in question-and-answer session that the official number of "military personnel and those equal to them in status" in Russia is 4 million, not including the police forces of the Ministry of Interior, which was more than 1 million strong. See Vitaly Shlykov, "The Military Reform and Its Implications for the Modernization of the Russian Armed Forces," in Jan Leijonhielm and Fredrik Westerlund (eds.), *Russian Power Structures*, FOI, Swedish Defense Research Agency Stockholm, January 2008, pp. 50–60.

[11] Office of the Secretary of Defense, *The Military Power of the People's Republic of China 2005*, Annual Report to Congress, 2005.

The crowning element of China's authoritarian systemic success, however, is its aggressive pursuit of technology transfer, not through the industrial espionage Putin practiced as a KGB control in East Germany,[12] but via hands-on direct foreign investment in export industries. The Soviet Union had, and Russia today has, no difficulty innovating commercially useless technologies.[13] Muscovy's problem is applying these intellectual resources profitably. Deng and his successors have partly overcome this impediment by opening enclaves to privately owned and joint state venture foreign direct investment, allowing Chinese nationals to master superior transferred technologies, the products of which have assured markets in the West.[14] It has leveraged these gains by domestic imitation, tied to the global marketing expertise of the overseas Chinese. In doing so, it has enticed direct foreign investors granting them access to cheap resources, especially labor, creating platforms for continuous rapid industrial modernization, supplemented by domestic imitators and indigenous entrepreneurship.[15]

The process can be interpreted in Alexander Gerschenkron's framework as a *missing prerequisite*.[16] Deng Xiaoping discovered that barriers to growth concealed by Mao's misleading GDP growth statistics, associated with the low quality of China's domestic importables could be sidestepped first by enticing foreign direct investment (FDI), and second by harnessing transferred technologies to fuel high value-added export led development. Foreign investors were lured by abundant outsourcing opportunities and cheap labor that made coastal China a low-cost export platform. The more exports soared, the more FDI was attracted (Table 14.4), and the greater the scope for internal transfers. This two-pronged turnpike strategy increased real income doubly by raising the value added of exportables and domestic goods where

---

[12] Ion Mihai Pacepa, "No Peter the Great," *National Review Online*, September 20, 2004.

[13] OECD, *Russian Federation 2006*, Chapter 3. Cf. Jeffrey Sachs and Wing Thye Woo, "Understanding China's Economic Performance," *Journal of Policy Reform*, Vol. 4, No. 1, 2000, pp. 1–50.

[14] Ma Li, *A Comparative Study of The Russian and Chinese Governments' FDI Policies*, Master thesis, curriculum in Russian and East European Studies, University of North Carolina, Chapel Hill, 2005.

[15] David Hale and Lyric Hale, "China Takes Off," *Foreign Affairs*, 42, 6(November/December 2003): 36–53.

[16] On *missing prerequisites*, *relative economic backwardness*, and *catch-up*, see Alexander Gerschenkron, *Economic Backwardness in Historical Perspective*, Harvard University Press, Cambridge, MA, 1962.

Table 14.4. *Foreign direct investment inflows to China (billions of U.S. dollars)*

	2000	2001	2002	2003
Total	40.7	46.9	52.7	53.5
Origin				
Hong Kong	15.5	16.7	17.9	17.7
Taipei	2.3	3.0	4.0	3.4
Singapore	2.2	2.1	2.3	2.1
Percent of GDP	3.8	4.0	4.2	3.8

Source: ECIC database, KPMG (2004) and national governments. OECD, Economic Surveys, *China*, Vol.13, September 2005, Paris, p.36.

conditions permitted. Had China merely cultivated domestic commerce and entrepreneurship without foreign technology transfers its exports and importables value added would have been reduced. The strategy's feasibility hinged on an undervalued foreign exchange rate, repressed wages,[17] and manufacturing tailored to western taste. The leadership deliberately underpriced exports (by undervaluing the renminbi, and overtraded from a static perspective because it felt that the disequilibrium sacrifice was justified by the dynamic benefits of technology transfer and diffusion, which were particularly large due to the value-adding inertia that otherwise would have prevailed in the domestic importables sector. The strategy that flouts key aspects of the Washington Consensus is a sophisticated variant of Mao's resource mobilization that retains wage repression and foreign exchange rate fixing, while discarding autarky and embracing leasing markets within the authoritarian martial police state paradigm. It has proven remarkably robust and is allowing China to become the industrial workshop for the world, with ample labor reserves to continue expansion well into the future, while Russia is content to play its natural resource card.

Beijing's stubborn defense of the undervalued RMB shows that foreign direct-investment-driven, export-oriented industrial modernization is indeed partly a policy ploy.[18] However, it is also essential to recognize that Deng's broader two-pronged strategy wouldn't work effectively in Fortress Russia, even if the Kremlin undervalued the

[17] Wage-fixing in state-owned enterprises, tolerance of adverse labor conditions for migrant workers, and impediments to effective labor organization.

[18] But the real exchange rate is appreciating. In addition, it should be observed that if America jawbones Beijing into substantially appreciating is foreign exchange rate, Deng's two-pronged strategy goes haywire.

ruble because anticompetitive rent-granting dominates market behavior.[19] China's relative success is more than a matter of clever development strategy. It is an artifact of a historically embedded culture, tolerant of commercial and industrial entrepreneurship, stressing responsible Confucian administration, with a government willing to put social prosperity above rent-seekers' parochial interests. China accordingly is well placed to overtake and perhaps overwhelm its not-so-good neighbor in the decades ahead, even as the advantages of relative economic backwardness wane.[20]

It is also well positioned on narrower technical grounds. Its population is growing, new domestic industrial capital formation is brisk, science is improving, transferred know-how is enhancing the effectiveness of domestic research and development, and financial and marketing skills are blossoming. Conventional production function theory therefore points to continued rapid growth driven by labor, capital, and technological progress.[21] Russia, by contrast, as explained in Chapter 13, is likely to grow more slowly because its labor force is declining,[22] immigrant labor is being discouraged, new fixed capital formation is increasing relatively slowly, Russia's scientific base has shrunk, and research and development expenditures have fallen drastically.

Deng's two-pronged catch-up strategy, China's leasing arrangements, movements toward freehold proprietorship, and limited rule of contract law don't make Beijing's authoritarian martial police state benign or superior to democratic free enterprise. China's partially marketized economy, like Russia's, still suffers from rent-granting, rent-seeking, insider-restricted market entry, state ownership, maladministration, bureaucratic corruption, and its own mild form of

[19] For example, Putin has prohibited foreign direct investment in *strategic* industries, which encompasses most large, potentially lucrative undertakings.

[20] Paul Krugman, "The Myth of Asia's Miracle," *Foreign Affairs*, 73, 6(November/December 1994): 62–78. Kent Calder, "China and Japan's Simmering Rivalry," *Foreign Affairs*, 85, 2(March/April 2006): 129–41.

[21] Ibid. Cf. Abram Bergson, "Technological Progress," in Abram Bergson and Hebert Levine (eds.), *The Soviet Economy: Toward the Year 2000*, George Allen & Unwin, London, 1983, pp. 34–78; Gregory Chow, *China's Economic Transformation*, Blackwell, Oxford, 2002; Dwight Perkins, *The Challenges of Chinese Economic Growth*, AEI Press, Washington, DC, 2007. Barry Naughton, *The Chinese Economy: Transitions and Growth,* MIT Press, Cambridge, MA, 2007. For an earlier interpretation see Peter Nolan, *China's Rise, Russia's Fall: Politics, Economics and Planning in the Transition from Stalinism*, Basingstoke, Macmillan, 1995.

[22] Paul Goble, "Window on Eurasia: Moscow Moves to Restrict Abortions to Boost Birthrate," *Johnson's Russia List*, Vol. 230, Article 15, November 24, 2007.

structural militarization. Eventually, as Paul Krugman rightly stresses, there can be no authoritarian miracle for either China or Russia. Nonetheless, as the numbers confirm, Deng's value-added ladder-climbing strategy offers the Kremlin a better development path if *silo-varchs* welcome foreign competitors and if leaders restrain wages and undervalue the ruble. No technical obstacles bar Russia from adopting the Chinese gambit of underpricing industrial exports to expedite technology transfer, but a half-millennium of Muscovite culture makes it unlikely.[23] Russia's long run prospects are blighted because its leaders prefer Muscovy, not because it lacks viable alternatives.

- Russia and China both are authoritarian martial police states.
- Their systems were nearly identical in the essentials from 1949–89, but not their performance since 1980. Opting for *shock therapy*, Russia stagnated and crashed, while China boomed under a grad-ualist regime.
- However, this phase has passed for Russia, without eradicating core commonalities.
- It seems therefore that if Russia identifies the specific causes of China's success, it should be able to emulate them.
- China's relative economic backwardness partly explains its superior growth, but the main reason for its success is a complex value-adding strategy for attracting foreign direct investment within the authoritarian martial police state paradigm that Muscovy finds repugnant.
- Russia can emulate China. Both are imperial nations, ruled by emperors with the power of unrestricted informal command over their subjects. They have laws but not the politically tamper-proof rule of contract law required for well-functioning markets in the West. Both grant state enterprise managers extensive custodial rights, including engaging in for-profit consumer business. Private enterprise is permitted based on leases of various duration, and free-holds are, or promise to, mushroom. China and Russia have managed foreign exchange rates and some state price-fixing. Licensed businessmen may trade internationally. Foreign direct investment

---

[23] Russia is expected to reach China's level of direct foreign investment, 2.7 percent of GDP in 2007, but this investment is concentrated in natural resources, not industry. See "Annual Direct Foreign Investment in Russia Will Reach $50 billion in 3 years," *Johnson's Russia List,* Vol. 239, Article 34, November 15, 2007.

is officially welcomed. Both apply orthodox macroeconomic procedures and have ineffective social safety nets. Moreover, they are authoritarian, with immense nuclearized militaries and secret police tasked to discipline and repress opposition to the system and the supreme leader.

- However, Russia won't emulate key distinctive aspects of the Chinese economic system, including its procommercial competitiveness, value-adding focus, wage repression, exchange rate undervaluation, and profit sharing with foreigners because they are anathemas to Muscovites.
- These attitudes and policies have enabled China to attract direct foreign investment, serve as an outsourcing hub, mass export high value-added manufactures, and diffuse transferred technologies to the importables sector.
- The strategy causes overtrading and imposes opportunity cost losses on excess foreign exchange reserves needed to keep the RMB undervalued, but Beijing appears to understandably feel that the dynamic gains are worth the static costs.
- Russian aversion to this policy package, in the absence of free competition, lashes the Kremlin to a natural resource extraction–driven system that trades petro for cheap Chinese and expensive western imports.
- Russian rent-grantees flourish in Muscovy, but the system necessarily depresses productivity and living standards far below potential.
- Russia would be well advised to emulate Deng's strategy as far as it can, but even if the replication were perfect; its development path would be inferior in the long run.

Conclusion

Russia seizes defeat from the jaws of success! This is the headline of the past twenty years, which seemed to begin so auspiciously with Mikhail Gorbachev's *perestroika*. Having destroyed communism and the Soviet Union in a fit of inadvertence without a civil insurrection or foreign invasion, the Kremlin had a golden opportunity to place Muscovite authoritarianism behind it. However, Boris Yeltsin flinched and Vladimir Putin restored Russia's imperial martial police state. It didn't have to end this way. Things could have been different at every turn. If the Politburo had chosen Grigory Romanov over Gorbachev in March 1984[1] or had the organizers of the August 1991 coup d'etat liquidated Yeltsin, the Soviet Union would have reverted to the Brezhnev mold. If the military had sided with Alexander Rutskoi instead of Yeltsin, parliament would have triumphed over the tsar. If there had been no 9/11, there would have been no petro bubble to pull Putin's chestnuts out of the fire.

Life is strewn with what-ifs. A similar list of contingencies can be prepared for every passage of Russian history since Ivan the Great. What is striking about Muscovy is its unfailing ability to foil westernization. Despite innumerable opportunities, it always finds ways to stay the Muscovite course, rather than transition to democratic free

---

[1] Grigory Vasilevich Romanov was a member of the Politburo and secretariat of the CPSU. In 1985, he was considered Gorbachev's main rival in the succession struggle. Like Putin, his power base was in the Leningrad region. He had reputation for being well versed in economics and a good organizer, and in his capacity as secretary of the Central Committee of the CPSU, he was responsible for industry and the VPK (military-industrial complex). He was one of General Secretary Yuri Andropov's closest collaborators, but after Andropov's death in February 1984, his position was clearly inferior to Gorbachev's.

enterprise, or European Union social democracy. Consequently, not only are its leaders wedded to inefficient rent-granting and bloated militaries, but they also subordinate the rule of law to the rule of men and civil rights to expediency. They know the concepts, laud and enshrine them in Russia's constitutions but never allow them to override autocratic primacy. The welfare of the ruler and his servitors is supreme, and the people are expected to acquiesce, mollified with crumbs and the prospect of national glory.

We also now know that the Muscovite dynasties such as the Romanov tsars and Soviet Communist Party leaders are brittle. They are colossuses, seemingly indestructible but have clay fleet. Their regimes can generate rapid growth for a few decades, but they are always overcome with perilous fatigue. The Romanovs were swept off the throne by a motley group of fanatics and the communists by the Byzantine intrigues of Gorbachev, Yeltsin, and their circles.

Likewise, we learned that Russia's catastrophic hyperdepression – the defining aspect of the Yeltsin years – and the 3.4 million excess deaths it claimed were unnecessary because China managed its market transition without a glitch, and Russia's 1989 living standard may have been recovered by 2007. Whatever gains ultimately accrue from the destruction of communism cannot compensate for these forgotten generations' senseless pain and suffering.

Nonetheless, despite the Kremlin's ham-handedness, aspects of life have changed notably for the better since 1980. Consumer goods, both foreign and domestic, are abundantly supplied in some cities. Moscow's roads are clogged with private cars, and lifestyles are more varied and free. People can travel abroad with few restrictions and the trappings of western commercial culture are ubiquitous. For postcommunist winners and some liberals this is enough, and the resurgence in Russia's international power has solaced others. Putin's 80 percent approval rating, massaged or not, accurately symbolizes the population's willingness to accept Muscovy, despite strong rhetorical support for democracy, civil liberties, social justice, the rule of law, and an anti-imperial foreign policy among the intelligentsia.

The conscience of Russia's rulers, and their commitment to Enlightenment westernization, is imperceptible. Nor do they cherish a coherent Russian idea founded on *sobornost*. Their lot instead has been cast with Muscovy, buttressed by modernization and camouflaged with progressive double-speak.

No one should doubt this strategy's feasibility for the next few years or decades, absent *smuta* or foreign invasion. The wages of sin don't preclude modest, technology-driven material progress or military rearmament. Russia suffers from a different delusion, the belief that domestic adequacy permits it to bear a heavy military burden and sustain an ambitious imperial international agenda in the face of powerful competition from America and China. Some perceptive insiders such as Vitaly Shlykov recognize the error and strive to restrain the impulse but haven't yet carried the day.[2]

Kremlin policies consequently are inferior from all perspectives other than the short-term satisficing of rent-granters and rent-seekers. Russian welfare could be vastly enhanced by adopting democratic free enterprise, paring its armed and security forces, and activating the civil liberties emblazoned in Yeltsin's constitution. Adopting a cooperative international stance would also be a salutory improvement over Moscow's traditional predation. However, Putin's restoration of Russia's imperial martial police state and resumption of the cold war (peace) proves Muscovy's durability;[3] that the twentieth century was really about Muscovy, not communism and that the new millennium may not be different. The West for its part will not accept the reality of Russia's exceptionalism. It persists in chastising and appeasing in lieu of effective policy at considerable peril. Consequently, there is scant reason to doubt that Russian essentials tomorrow will be much like yesterday's, that the Kremlin will be a major player on the global stage, vulnerable to internal rent-seeking subversion, international overreach, and sudden catastrophic collapse.

---

[2] E-mail from Shlykov, May 25, 2007.
[3] Leon Aron, "Putin's Cold War," *Wall Street Journal*, December 26, 2007.

Glossary

adjusted factor costing	A technique for adjusting fiat unit production prices (fiat value-added) to conform with western price formation principles. Soviet ruble prices (fiat values) were factor cost adjusted by stripping nonwage components (retail turnover taxes and profits) and adding imputed interest charges. The resulting adjusted ruble prices had the form of properly constructed value-added prices but not the content because neither wages nor imputed interest charges were competitively determined.
administrative command planning	A summary description of Soviet physical systems management emphasizing the key aspects of state economic management, command and administration. *Khozraschyot* incentivization is subsumed under administration.
adverse selection	A Pareto-inferior choice caused by moral hazards.
agent	Independent for-profit, service provider hired to represent business principals. Agents typically have more autonomy than employees tasked to perform the same jobs.
antiparasite laws	Laws prohibiting able-bodied Soviet citizens from being unemployed or malingering on their jobs. Such individuals were deemed parasites, free riding off the proletariat's labor.
apparatchik	Professional functionary of the Soviet Communist Party or the government. A bureaucrat.
arenda	Leasing of Soviet state property for private business purposes. During NEP, most lessees were private

	individuals. Under Gorbachev, they were mostly cooperatives.
asset grabbing	Insider appropriation or privatization of state assets in an unsettled legal environment. Assets are seized in their entirety.
asset stripping	Selective seizure of valuable enterprise property like furniture and fixtures, or spinning off profitable activities to wholly owned firms at discount, leaving the state with the debt baby. Pieces are stripped, but some of the original asset is preserved.
ASUP	Automatic system of management and planning. Soviet program for constructing a self-regulating computer-based national economic management and planning network.
autarky	National economic self-sufficiency achieved by prohibiting foreign imports and living entirely on domestic resources. More loosely, any regime that severely restricts foreign trade.
authoritarian laissez-faire	An economic system with an authoritarian government that encourages some aspects of free enterprise.
authoritarianism	Political rule by an individual (autocracy) or coterie. More generally, any system where individual autonomy is subordinated, or tightly constrained by dictate, coercion, administration, rules, and management.
autocracy	A political regime where the ruler's commands supersede others' authority and the written law. A dictatorship, even if disguised by various consultative institutions.
Bergson–Arrow–Samuelson welfare standard	An ideal Pareto class set of consumer sovereign, generally competitive economic outcomes, modified by popularly sovereign government programs and transfers (Bergson/Samuelson), subject to the intrinsic inefficiencies of democratic balloting (Arrow), which can serve as a standard of social merit in judging observed economic performance.
blat	The use of network obligations, favors, and bribes to acquire sinecures, privileged access, or consummate business deals in the second economy. The root sense is criminal behavior.

Bolshevik Party	The minority faction of the Marxist Russian Democratic–Labor Party that called itself the majority (Bol'shinstvo) and seized the Russian government in a coup d'etat November 7, 1917, under the leadership of Vladimir Lenin.
Bolshevik Revolution	A misnomer erroneously suggesting that Lenin's coup d'etat was a legitimate mass popular uprising in the name of the proletariat of the future that was replacing Muscovite tsarist autocracy or capitalism with proletarian sovereign democratic socialism. The reality was the old Muscovite authoritarian martial police state in working class garb.
Bolshevik *coup d'etat*	The coup d'etat that brought Lenin's Bolshevik Party to power in 1917.
capital deepening	Improving the embodied technological content and hence the productivity of the capital stock.
capital widening	Increasing the size of the capital stock with machines embodying standard technologies. Capital widening enhances combined factor productivity but not the productivity of the capital stock itself.
capitalism	A loose term for a market economy where owners of real and financial capital are sovereign. The concept is also indiscriminately applied to all market economies based on private ownership of the means of production. Critics portray capitalism as anarchic, internally contradictory, self-destructive, and exploitive. Advocates associate it with perfect competition, personal freedom, democracy, and consumer sovereignty.
catastroika	Catastrophic economic reform. Refers to the hyperdepression caused by Mikhail Gorbachev's failed *perestroika* (radical economic reform).
centralization	Distinguishes tightly disciplined state administrative control regimes where orders are centrally issued from decentralized regimes that allow regional or local entities a degree of autonomy. Many students of political economy seem to erroneously believe that the right administrative mix can produce Pareto quality outcomes.

chto delat   What is to be done? A classic Russian revolutionary battle cry used by Lenin in 1902 and traceable to Nikolai Chernyshevsky's 1862 novel of the same name.

class war   Marxist concept that workers and capitalists were implacable enemies, engaged in a life and death struggle that would inevitably lead to the triumph of socialism.

cold war   Strategic, economic, and ideologic struggle between America and the Soviet Union and their allies, which commenced in 1947 and terminated in 1991. The degree of military preparedness, the threat of armed conflict, tactical probes, and proxy combat short of open superpower conflagration distinguished this rivalrous relationship from ordinary great power engagement. The east–west struggle was partly concealed and perhaps tempered by mutual endorsement of nonbelligerency expressed in slogans like peaceful coexistence and detente.

collectivization   A Soviet policy introduced in the late 1920s under Stalin direction of consolidating land and labor into Communist Party–controlled cooperatives designed to compel peasants to produce for the state, killing those who resisted and exiling agrarian *class enemies* or *kulaks* (fists) to farm the tundra.

Command Communism   Autocratic, physically managed, state-owned natural economy, criminalizing private business and entrepreneurship, and showcasing central planning and *khozraschyot* adopted by Stalin in 1929 and continuing until Khrushchev launched an epoch of reforms in 1955.

command economy   Any economy planned or otherwise based on state dictate instead of markets.

commanding heights   Key industries and economic activities singled out by the Bolsheviks for immediate nationalization, on the premise that their control sufficed to establish socialist economic power. These activities included banking, insurance, petroleum, coal, iron, machine building and foreign trade.

communalism   Social, economic, and political systems designed to promote group well-being by subordinating individual rights and freedom when they cause inequality and disharmony. Worker owned and managed enterprises, kibbutzim, and utopian communism are types of communalism.

communism   An ideal, harmonious, egalitarian society that substitutes communal (community) ownership for private property and eliminates the state. Karl Marx's utopia, elaborated in his *Communist Manifesto* advocates this romantic primitivism. But Lenin's Communist Party turned the concept on its head by adopting the Muscovite authoritarian martial police state as an interim device to *ensure* a coercion-free communitarian future.

Communist Party   A Soviet political organization superseding the Bolshevik Party created by Lenin and assigned to exclusively oversee the state apparatus purportedly to realize Marx's pastoral communist dream.

computopia   An ideal planned economy achieved through perfect computation. Coined by Egon Neuberger.

consumer choice   In economic systems theory parlance, a state where private individual consumer preferences (demand) determine retail purchases but not characteristics, assortments, and volumes of goods and services supplied. Consumer choice in the Soviet context was always associated with forced substitution, and consequently was Pareto inefficient.

consumer   A state where private individual consumer prefer-
sovereignty   ences (demand) determine the characteristics, assortments, and volumes of goods and services supplied. Ideal consumer sovereignty is Pareto efficient.

consumer utility   A Pareto-compatible welfare norm for appraising the
standard   merit of a nation's factor allocation, goods production, and distribution devised by Abram Bergson, making it possible to distinguish economic efficiency from production potential.

convergence   In Sovietology, a hypothesis that capitalist and communist economic systems are destined to converge to a common mixed market and planned welfare state. The notion was fashionable during the 1970s. The post-Soviet variant predicts that economic systems and living standards of all nations will resemble each other, in particular, in America the expectation that living standards of poor nations will rise to

	the level of rich countries due to technology transfer and superior profit opportunities. This assumes that the economic potential of all systems are the same, or that globalization will make them so.
cooperatives	A business organization where labor hires capital, and compensation is tied to membership instead of capital shares. Cooperatives may or may not be egalitarian and involve production, wholesale, and retail operations. They sacrifice some capital efficiency for egalitarianism and mutual support.
correlation of forces	Soviet military strategic concept akin to *balance of power* (*sootnoshenie sil*), which takes into account military capabilities, readiness, and sociopolitical factors such as the class struggle.
Council of Economic Ministers	*Sovet Ministrov SSSR* (1946–91). Postwar successor to the Council of People's Commissars, composed of the heads of various national industries. Joseph Stalin was the first head of the Council of Economic Ministers.
criminalization of private property, business entrepreneurship	Measures taken to achieve Soviet nationalization of the means of production and the establishment of an economy-wide state economic monopoly.
crony capitalism	Strongly regulated capitalist economy operated for the benefit of the ruler's favorites.
culture	Durable attitudes and patterns of behavior approved by communities, which underlie, supplement, shape, and supersede transient public policies and edicts.
cybernetics	The science of feedback mechanisms relevant to the study of economic interactions.
decentralization	The devolution of decision-making authority in the Soviet economic control mechanism from the center to the periphery. See centralization.
dekulakization	Stalin's policy of liquidating the kulaks as a class and destroying their agrarian power. Its main features were mass arrests, exile, and

killings of Russia's marginally better-off peasants. These actions were pendants to forced collectivization.

democracy   Political device for achieving popular sovereignty over the provision of public goods via the ballot. The conceptual counterpart of Pareto optimal consumer sovereignty over private goods. Kenneth Arrow has shown the popular sovereignty in representative democracies cannot be made ideally efficient.

demokratizatsia   Literally, democratization. Gorbachev-era slogan for making communist rule more responsive to popular preferences. Like Lenin's claim that Bolshevik democracy was a million times more democratic than parliamentary democracy in England, the assertion is an oxymoron because the dictatorship of the proletariat precludes popular sovereignty.

dictatorship of law   Putin-era slogan suggesting that the rule of law will replace the rule of men in Russia, tacitly acknowledging that laws will be imposed by the ruler, instead of reflecting popular preferences.

dictatorship of the proletariat   Custodial Bolshevik dictatorship in the name of the proletariat of the future, which Lenin claimed was an essential short-term expedient to forestall counterrevolution.

disequilibrium economy   An economy designed to prevent Walrasian price and Marshallian quantity equilibration to achieve overfull employment and other political economic goals. Disequilibrium economies necessarily cause forced substitutions and therefore are equated by some with *economies of consumer goods shortage*, even though the system as a whole overfully employs its productive assets. Shortage on their reckoning depends primarily on consumers' inability to receive goods with the right characteristics in the desired assortment, not on the absolute magnitude of consumer supplies.

duality theorem   The mathematical demonstration that perfect plans and perfect markets yield identical outcomes if technology, factor endowments, wealth and income distributions, and tastes are the same.

economic system   A set of motivations, mechanisms (markets, gov-
                    ernment, and obligation), institutions, and rules of
                    conduct shaping demand and supply and responding
                    to disequilibrium under conditions of scarcity.

economy of   An economy designed to be in disequilibrium
  shortage   that persistently generates consumer goods deficits
                    because resources are diverted to priority activities
                    such as investment durables and defense. Shortages
                    in such economies are compatible with steady GDP
                    growth.

embodied   Productivity advances generated by new and im-
  technological   proved machinery and equipment (investment dura-
  progress   bles) separate from other kinds of processing gains.

evil empire   Coined by the Reagan administration accusing the
                    Soviet Union of imperialist despotism.

excess deaths   The number of people dying above the actuarially
                    predicted figure from all causes, including disease,
                    catastrophes, accidents, and killings. Synonymous
                    with premature deaths.

extensive growth   Growth generated by capital widening.

fiat prices   Prices arbitrarily fixed by state authorities.

500 days program   *Programma "500 Dnei"* devised by Grigory Yavlin-
                    sky and Stanislav Shatalin in 1989 claiming that
                    the Soviet administrative command planning sys-
                    tems could be transformed into a competitive mar-
                    ket free enterprise regime in 500 days. The goal was
                    aspirational, not scientific.

forced substitution Anticompetitive restrictions that compel people to
                    consume goods they dis-prefer. In the Soviet case,
                    forced substitution was considered an irremediable
                    defect of its economy of shortage.

glasnost   Slogan used by Mikhail Gorbachev, borrowed from
                    tsarism, meaning openness, transparency, candor,
                    and tolerance of free speech. It implied the rejec-
                    tion of the authoritarian culture of lies and deceit
                    (Sovspeak).

glavk   A main department of VSNKh and later of Soviet
                    ministries.

Gosabritrazh   The Soviet state arbitrage agency that adjudicated
                    inter-enterprise contractual disputes in the state sec-
                    tor. Soviet enterprises were legal entities permitted
                    to contract with each other and sue.

Gosbank	Soviet State Bank (*Gosudarstvennyi Bank SSSR*). The central bank tasked to monitor plan-approved inter-enterprise transactions, clear accounts, and provide cash for wages and other authorized purposes. It provided little financial assistance and unlike western commercial banks didn't operate for profit. *Gosbank* was a monopoly from the 1930s to 1987 when Gorbachev created various specialized banks, including *Promstoibank* (USSR Bank of Industrial Construction), *Zhilstroibank* (USSR Bank of Residential Construction), *Agrobank* (USSR Agricultural Bank), *Vneshekonombank* (USSR Foreign Trade Bank), and *Sberbank* (*USSR Savings Bank*).
Goskomstat	Soviet and now Russian State Statistical Committee (*Federal'naya Sluzhba Gosudarstvennoi Statistiki*).
Goskomtsen	State Committee for Prices (*Goskomtsen*) set and revised the majority of all Soviet prices, established regulations for *temporary* prices fixed by enterprise managers for new and improved goods, and negotiated prices for special order goods.
Gossnabsbyt	State Committee for Material-Technical Supply (*Gossnab* for short) was the wholesaling arm of the Soviet procurement system responsible for inter-enterprise supply and distributing final goods to state retail outlets.
Gosplan	Soviet State Planning Agency (*Gosplan* or *Gosudarstvenny Komitet po Planirovaniyu*) was created February 22, 1921, by decree of the Sovnarkom of the RSFSR under the name RSFSR State Planning Commission. It began compiling annual plans (*kontrol'nye tsifry*) in 1925, and five-year plans in 1928.
Gosstandart	Soviet and now Russian state standards bureau.
Gostekhnika	Soviet State Committee for New Technology.
gross domestic product (GDP)	The aggregate value of all marketable goods and services computed at market or official state prices. This measure of aggregate activity excludes income derived from assets held abroad. The GDP is only economically meaningful when prices are competitive (or are shadow equivalents). Otherwise, prices are weak indicators of utilities and opportunity costs.
gross national income	The income paid to primary factors of production for their services computed at market or fiat

prices. Gross national income is only economically meaningful when prices are competitive (or shadow equivalent).

growth retardation · Coined in the 1970s to describe the steady deceleration of Soviet economic growth, attributed to flagging technological progress and a low elasticity of capital labor substitution, both caused by the defects of the physical management system.

Gulag · *Glavnoe Upravlenie Ispravitel'no-Trudovykh Lagerei i Kolonii* (Chief Directorate of Corrective Labor Camp Administration), a complex of World War I–type concentration camps with tsarist antecedents for imprisoning and rehabilitating criminals and those deemed enemies of the people through forced labor. They served as killing fields during much of the Stalin period, and a vast pool of cheap labor for state projects. The legal basis for the system was established June 27, 1929, with corrective labor camps (*Ispravitel'no-trudovye Lageria*) placed under the control of the OGPU (Soviet Secret Police). Gulag was officially liquidated by the MVD on January 25, 1960, but continues under other names.

harmonism · A belief that there exists an ideal state where all human conflicts are reconcilable (like Marx's full communism). The insistence that if threats are placated they will be resolved by reason, or some higher *mystery*.

hidden inflation · Inflation concealed either by Goskomstat's misreporting, or by falsification from below. Many Sovietologists consider spurious innovation to have been the principal source of hidden inflation during the Command Communist period.

hyperinflation · Extraordinarily rapid price inflation, the most drastic cases of which exceed 1,000 percent per annum. Post-Soviet inflation at its worst in the early 1990s was more than 2,500 percent per annum.

idea of the West · The Enlightenment idea that democratic free enterprise, or social democracy, is the most rational and therefore the best way to organize society. Harmonists extend the concept by inferring that if the idea of the West is best, it is also ineluctable. Samuel

Huntington has suggested an expanded list of characteristics, including economic freedom, social justice,
tolerance, diversity, and conflict avoidance. The interpretation of these ideals in practice is often contextual,
subject to dispute, and qualified by subculture, shadow
cultural, and countercultural values.

impoverished   A concept popularized by Charles Wolf, Jr., and
superpower   Henry Rowan suggesting that the defining character-
                    istic of the Soviet Union was the disparity between
                    the nation's living standard and its military might. The
                    concept implied that the USSR's threat potential was
                    constrained by its impoverization.

input-output   An analytic model of a national economy, or activi-
model   ties that maps the flows of primary and intermediate
                    inputs into final goods, assuming fixed coefficients
                    (non-substitutability). The model is computable and
                    useful for national economic forecasting.

institutions   Organizations that set the rules of various kinds of
                    economic conduct.

intensive growth   Growth generated by capital deepening.

invisible hand   Unobserved actions of markets that allocate fac-
                    tors, produce, and distribute goods and services. The
                    Walrasian automatic price and Marshallian quantity
                    adjustment mechanisms are the market's right and left
                    hands.

inspiration   Paul Krugman's term for economic growth driven by
                    technological progress and improved labor skills.

J curve   Economic recovery curve shaped like the letter J,
                    marked by a brief sharp drop and leveling off, followed
                    by a rapid ascent above the previously achieved GDP.
                    The concept was used by transitologists who expected
                    Russia's hyperdepression to be a fleeting prelude to
                    rapid, sustained growth.

job rights   Employment entitlements, benefits, and protections
                    accorded by states or custom to labor. In the Soviet
                    case, David Granick argued that job rights in the
                    Reform Communist period significantly constrained
                    managerial discretion.

khozraschyot   Economic cost accounting. More specifically, the
                    requirement that Soviet enterprises carry out their
                    functions cost effectively, without relying unduly on

state subsidies, with considerable managerial discretion. Akin to *samofinansirovanie*.

kleptocracy
An economic system run by corrupt state officials and their cronies in the private sector. It can be an aspect of a liberal Muscovite system.

kolkhoz
Soviet collective farm where peasant income was a share of net sales (dividend) instead of a fixed wage. Common land was owned by the state. Peasants were permitted small, private plots. The institution was imposed on the peasantry and managed by Communist Party appointees. Farmers preferred their traditional communal arrangements.

kolkhoznik
A *kolkhoz* member.

Kremlin
Moscow fortress that has been the seat of Russian government since the fifteenth century and symbol of the Russian state.

krugovaya poruka
Medieval Russian peasant tradition of mutual obligation and support regarding both tax burdens and group welfare. In Soviet enterprises, it took on the extended meaning of networks supporting members against the state by concealing capacities and swapping favors. The phenomenon is often called *family circle*.

kulak
Literally, tight fisted, referring historically to moderately better off peasants. In Soviet times, a tiny segment of the peasantry classified as class enemies because they were suspected of aspiring to become large property owning capitalist farmers.

Langean market socialism
A socialist economy featuring state ownership of the means of production, a requirement that managers produce to the point where marginal cost equals price, and a price board instructed to continuously adjust prices until markets clear. Oscar Lange purported to prove that this type of market socialism was Pareto efficient, like Meadean social democracy with private ownership but failed to consider the problem of moral hazard where red directors served their own interests first.

law of value
Karl Marx's concept that manufactured goods are or should be exchanged in proportion with their embodied labor input. The hypothesis is an aspect of his labor exploitation theory.

leasing	Rental of property without associated rights of ownership and capital gains.
leisure	Nonwork activities of any type, including pleasure seeking and household maintenance excluded from GDP.
Liberman reform	A proposal advocated by Evsei Liberman to base Soviet enterprise production programs on the maximization of *profitability* instead of the physical volume of output. The notion was vetted in 1962 and partially adopted in the Kosygin reforms of 1965.
liquidation (as a class)	In Soviet Marxist parlance, the eradication of allegedly hostile groups such as the *kulaks* as a social class through resettlement, exile, and assimilation. Mass killings also were employed but weren't a necessary ingredient of the process.
linear programming	Mathematical technique for formulating and solving complex factor allocation, production, and distribution problems where technology exhibits constant returns to scale (is linear).
Lockean social contract	Enlightenment notion that the harmony observed in human relations reflects the existence of an implicit social contract mandating that people refrain from preying on each other and act in accordance with ethical principles like the Golden Rule. The contract is the result of rational choice rather than a manifestation of genetically encoded behavior.
Managed democracy	Euphemism for Putin-style autocratic governance.
Market Communism	A stateless economy with community ownership that creates asset usage rights permitting Paretian utility seeking factor allocation, production, and distribution. The concept was advocated by Mikhail Gorbachev but considered an oxymoron by orthodox Marxian communists.
material balances	Rudimentary Soviet planning technique akin to input-output programming, where a list of materials (factors, raw materials, intermediate inputs) is compiled on a sector-by-sector basis and then allocated to alternative use in a manner

	that tries to ensure that estimated intermediate inputs can actually be produced. The technique is derived from War Communism requisitioning and rationing and provides a formal method for developing alternative production programs.
Meadean social democracy	A Pareto ideal form of EU social democracy with Arrow best social welfare programs.
mechanism	A set of procedures and operations such as markets, administration, and planning used to realize economic ends. A synonym for *systems* but usually describes elements of the composite apparatus.
military industrial complex (VPK)	*Voennyi-promyshlennyi kompleks*, a formal institutional network encompassing the Soviet and Russian *genshtabs*, Ministry of Defense, military enterprises, civilian firms, planners, civil defense organizations, military intelligence, and other security bodies. The scope and cohesiveness of the VPK are principal causes of structural militarization, a characteristic that distinguished them from America's loose military-industrial community of interest. The VPK recently has been renamed OPK, defense industrial complex.
mir	Village authority overseeing peasant communities (*obshchina*) in tsarist Russia.
modernization	Process through which less developed nations acquire the technological characteristics of advance countries. Since technology is separable from culture, societies can modernize without westernizing. The idea of the West implies that nonwesternizing modernization will be less effective and provide lower welfare than Pareto efficient westernization.
moral hazard	Danger that economic self-interest will impel people to place their own material considerations above their moral, professional. and legal obligations.
Muscovy	The Great Princedom of Moscow, successor to Kievan Rus' northern lands, and foundation stone of Russian tsardom. The *Kniazhestvo Moskovskoe* started in the fourteenth century and persisted as the Grand Duchy of Muscovy (*Velikoe Kniazhestvo Moskovskoe*) until the late fourteenth century.

Muscovite model	Authoritarian productive system based on mental frames dating to the post-Mongol rise of Muscovy stressing autocracy, *patrimonialism* (the view that all assets ultimately are the sovereign's), *pomestie* (tenure land grants to supporters, not unlike the revocable property rights of today's oligarchs), *kormlenie* (tax *farming* and rent-seeking), *krugovaya poruka* (network mutual support), *duvan* (plunder), and *slavophilism* (nationalistic preferences), resulting in subjugation and extreme inequality. Liberal variants provide transactors with a significant degree of economic and political autonomy.
Muscovite authoritarian martial police state	Muscovite economic system with a powerful military for imperializing neighboring states and a formidable secret police for internal security control.
nationalization	Transfer of property rights from private entities to the state, sometimes in the name of the people.
natural economy	Economic activities calibrated and executed in physical terms without the intermediation of money including factor allocation, production, and barter distribution.
NEP	New Economic Policy (*Novaya Ekonomicheskaya Politika*). The state administrative and leasing strategies chosen by Lenin to replace War Communism, sometimes called market socialism because of negotiated business relations among various components of the economy including leased private business, state industry and the agrarian sector. The policy began in 1921 and ended in 1929.
nepmen	Tradesmen, peddlers, commercial and industrial leasees, and some private proprietors engaged in business activities among themselves and with the state sector.
NMP	Net material product. Marxist national product concept, similar to GDP, but less comprehensive because
NMP	it excludes *nonproductive* personnel services such as haircuts, leisure transportation, etc.
New Russians	Yeltsin-era term for the garishly affluent (*nouveau riche*) who learned how to thrive under post-Soviet arrangements.

novoe myshlenie	New thinking. Gorbachev-era slogan for applying Enlightenment and humanitarian concepts to the formation of foreign and military policies, superseding cold war power politics.
obshchina	Tsarist-era peasant communities based on collective responsibility and mutual support.
oligarchs	Colloquial term for a small number of super rich dominating Russia's exclusionary markets, who acquired their wealth undeservingly through spontaneous privatization, other forms of asset seizing, asset stripping, presidential largesse, rent-seeking, and a host of criminal activities. They tend to live nonproductively off their assets, transferring their monies to safe havens abroad, underproducing, underinvesting, and suppressing competitive access to their preserves.
OPK	*Oboronnyi-promyshhennyi kompleks*, or defense industrial complex. It is Russia's renamed military industrial complex.
one-man-rule	*Edinonachalie.* Soviet management principle of undivided enterprise authority vested in red directors. Workers and worker councils could have voice but had to obey managerial directives.
order of financial liberalization	Ronald McKinnon's concept that post-Soviet transition should begin with financial stabilization before proceeding with other aspects of privatization and liberalization.
Pareto optimality	Transactions carried to the point where no voluntary transactor can improve his/her utility without another losing. Achieving this condition means that all utilitarian possibilities have been realized. The concept encompasses every aspect of rational choice making for individuals, communities, nations, and the globe.
patrimonialism	Principle of paternal rule. In the Russian historical case, it extends to autocratic ownership of all national property, as well as the power to command and rent-grant.
peaceful coexistence	*Mirovoe sosuchestvovannie.* Khrushchev era Soviet term for cold war adversaries respecting each other's territorial sovereignty and interests. The

	concept implied lower intensity engagement and renunciation of military force as a means of resolving conflicts between ideological rivals.
perekhod	Transition from Soviet administrative command planning to a market economy. This Yeltsin-era term was close in meaning to Gorbachev's concept of *perestroika* but implied a rejection of communism.
perestroika	Radical economic reform. Gorbachev's economic policy adopted in 1987 introducing some liberal market principles into the planned economy without rejecting either socialism or communism.
perspiration	Paul Krugman's term for economic growth generated by capital widening and increased factor input.
physical systems management	The administration, supervision, direction, management, assignment, requisition, rationing, command, incentivization, regulation, and control of factor allocation, production, and distribution in physical terms (or in fiat prices), without the assistance of competitive market profit maximizing and laissez-faire utility seeking. Administrative command planning is a type of physical systems management.
piatiletka	Soviet five-year plan first introduced by Stalin in 1928.
planned chaos	Concept devised by Fredrich von Hayek stressing the detachment of optimal planning from individual utilities and real market values. Planners he asserted may have desired to simulate Pareto optimality and often pretended that they maximized social welfare, but their efforts were chaotic and futile.
planning	In Soviet context, the acquisition and processing of information on input availability, production potential, and national priorities required to physically manage, regulate, administer and govern national factor allocation, production, and distribution. Can be used broadly to include command, administration, and incentivization.
Politburo	*Politicheskoe Biuro* (Political Bureau). The central policymaking and governing body of the Communist Party of the Soviet Union. The party was superior to the state government.
Ponzi scheme	Investment scam devised by the Italian swindler Charles Ponzi, whereby high returns are paid to initial

	participants out of the funds of later investors until the pyramid ultimately collapses.
population deficit	Shortfall between predicted and actual future populations attributable both to variations in natality and mortality. Where concern is for excess mortality alone, the appropriate measure is premature deaths.
piratization	Coined by Marshall Goldman to describe the plunder of the *people's* property by Boris Yeltsin's and Vladimir Putin's oligarchs.
precycling	The recycling of new goods before they are used. A device used by some Soviet enterprises to exaggerate production and delivery of goods to final use without ever producing anything useful.
premature deaths	Deaths occurring before their actuarially expected date. The concept provides a benchmark for assessing whether discontinuities in mortality trends are attributable to natural or political causes. It is synonymous with excess deaths.
privateer	Originally, a private warship authorized by letters of marquee to attack and plunder foreign shipping. Privateering is frequently described as "legal" piracy because it is openly or tacitly approved by the state. The term is used here in an extended sense to include government approved private asset-grabbing and other malfeasance against the "people's" and foreign property.
privatization	Transfer of people's (national), state, collective, or communal property to individuals, not necessarily prior owners, with associated rights of resale and use.
prodrazverstka	Lenin's policy of forced requisitioning of foodstuffs from the peasantry adopted June 1918. It became a hallmark of War Communism and its abolition in March 1921 marks the beginning of NEP.
production potential	Coined by Abram Bergson to distinguish economically from Soviet fiat cost efficient production. Production potential is a supply-side optimum disconnected from consumer utility and demand. Soviet supply efficiency is defined with respect to constrained physically managed production and is not a counterfactual Pareto ideal.

production potential standard	A supply-side standard where the production frontier is generated by planning and false prices as in the Soviet Union. This is a pseudoproduction possibility frontier, that provides measures of pseudosupply efficiency.
predpriyatie	An enterprise.
proletariat	Originally people with no wealth other than the human capital of their sons; transformed by Karl Marx into a synonym for the working class.
purchasing power parity	The valuation of a nation's GDP using the purchase prices of another country, bypassing the foreign exchange rate. The technique entails collecting export prices and matching characteristics of nontradeables so that prices correspond accurately with products.
rationing	The allocation of goods on a quota basis, instead of through competitive sale in the market place.
red director	The state-appointed head of Soviet enterprises tasked to implement plans with no discretionary authority as distinct from managers assigned to maximize goals such as output volumes or profitability.
Reform Communism	Period of post–Stalin economic reforms, 1953–91.
regime change	A change of government that doesn't infringe on national sovereignty.
rent-granting	Awarding the privilege of using state or autocrat rent-generating property to favorites for the grantor's and grantee's mutual benefit.
rent-seeking	Aspiring to acquire the privilege of using state or autocrat rent-generating property for the grantor's and grantee's mutual benefit.
rentier	An individual whose income is derived from economic rents, rather than his labor value-added.
repressed inflation	Price fixing that holds the price level down in the face of excess purchasing power.
requisitioning	Commandeering supplies without compensation.
resource mobilization	Activization of idle factors of production. In the Soviet case, the term implies mustering effort

	above the Paretian norm to a level consistent with a state of wartime emergency.
revolution	A political regime change that ushers in a new economic and social order. The Bolshevik coup d'etat was a regime change with a fresh cast, not a revolution that eradicated the Muscovite socioeconomic system.
rule of law	In economics, the notion that a just society empowers individuals to Pareto maximize utility restricted only by voluntarily negotiated and state-enforced contracts instead of having outcomes dictated by nondemocratic authorities (the rule of men). Courts under the rule of law must be impartial, not instruments of authoritarian administration.
rule of men	In economics, the principle of dictate by the powerful, as distinct from voluntarily negotiated transactions enforced by the rule of law.
ruler sovereignty	Principle of effective demand, where goods and services are supplied to satisfy some powerful entity, or ruler rather than individual consumers.
satisficing	Principle that the good obtained suffices so that there is no need to pursue the best even if search costs are low. Profit and utility equilibria consequently are found at multiple points in a fuzzy set.
science-production associations	Associations of filial Soviet enterprises with shared scientific research and development facilities introduced in the seventies as part of the Kosygin reforms to remedy the separation of technological development from enterprise requirements.
scissors crisis	Name given to the precipitous rise in Soviet industrial terms of trade with the countryside during the early 1920s caused by relatively rapid agricultural rebound from the War Communist hyperdepression. The scissor is formed by plotting terms of trade and its reciprocal on the same graph. The event came to symbolize the danger of following a market path to Soviet industrial socialism.
sebestoimost	Prime cost; the labor, capital, and rental cost of production before white-collar overhead, profit markups, and turnover taxes.

second economy	The informal, parallel Soviet economy where unauthorized goods were produced and traded in the state sector, as well as unreported private services in varying degrees of illegality, which Aron Katsenelinboigen called *colored markets*.
security services	Common term for all branches of the Russian security community.
servitors	Nobles required to provide state service in return for privileges and the retention of their estates. Contemporaries who provide Russia's presidents with services in return for granted rents.
shadow prices	Estimated equilibrium prices computed from the dual of a linear or nonlinear production program. Shadow prices enabled Soviet planners to evaluate *Goskomsten's* fiat prices.
Silovarch	Coined by Daniel Treisman suggesting the tempering of *siloviki* security priorities through their inclusion in oligarchic business activities.
siloviki	A shadowy power clique active in the past three or four years influencing Putin's and Medvedev's personnel appointments.
shock therapy	Radical institutional or systems change undertaken to revitalize the economy. Often used as a term of derision for radical policies that have catastrophic consequences.
social democracy	A variant of the idea of the West in which a socially concerned state manages an otherwise free economy through democratic means to promote social justice. The model is often referred to as the welfare state.
social market economy	Post-Soviet term misportraying Russia's Muscovite market as being responsive to popular needs, suggesting that good aspects of communism have been retained and the bad discarded.
socialism	A loose concept encompassing a wide variety of political and mechanistic arrangements where the state claims to restrict free enterprise in society's interest, with special attention paid to the welfare of workers and the poor.
Sovereign democracy	Euphemism for Putin-style authoritarianism vetted in 2006, claiming that facade democracy is an ingredient of the Russian idea.

Sovietology	The discipline of Soviet studies; broader than Kremlinology, which focuses on domestic and international politics.
sovkhoz	Soviet state farm where land is state owned and farmers are viewed as agrarian workers paid wages instead of sharing net income.
Sovnarkhoz	Council of the National Economy, usually translated as Regional Economic Council (*Sovet Narodnovo Khoziaistva*). Introduced March 1957 by Nikita Khrushchev in an effort to decentralize planning from Moscow to the regions.
spontaneous privatization	Unauthorized privatization of state enterprises by red directors to themselves under the Soviet regime, 1987–91, and in Russia thereafter. This theft of the people's property was often construed by advocates of globalization as a progressive step in Russia's transition to democratic free enterprise.
spurious innovation	Development of products and process that have new or altered characteristics and are assigned higher prices without commensurate increases in value. Spurious innovation is a source of hidden inflation because price increases have no utilitarian justification.
Stolypin reforms	Imperial Russian agrarian reform begun by Prime Minister Peter Stolypin November 1906, establishing the right of unconditional private ownership. Some progress was made before 1917, but tsarist agriculture remained predominantly communal.
storming	In Soviet economic parlance, frenzied effort to meet plan targets just before deadlines.
straightjacket authoritarianism	A term conveying restrictedness of individual liberty in authoritarian societies that verge on, but do not achieve, absolute totalitarian control.
strakh	Russian word for fear that epitomizes the psychological impact of Stalin's terror.
structural militarization	Describes a productive system with a large embedded military-industrial sector capable of persuading government leaders to provide sufficient resources to deal with worst-case security threats.
superpower	Preeminent nuclear states. During the cold war, America and the Soviet Union were considered

superpowers because they possessed more than 90 percent of the planet's nuclear weapons and were said to have rough strategic parity. Some analysts insist that America today is the only superpower because of its economic superiority.

systems directors
Coined by Abram Bergson to describe the high authorities directing the Soviet administrative command planning apparatus.

technological diffusion
The process by which new technologies are transferred from the laboratory into productive service.

tekhpromfinplany
Technical, industrial, and financial plans compiled by the main departments of Soviet industrial ministries from aggregate Gosplans, assigned to enterprises for micro implementation.

the thaw
Title from a novel by Ilya Ehrenburg about the prospects for post-Stalin Soviet liberalization that symbolized the possibilities of peaceful coexistence during the Khrushchev era.

tolkach
Literally a *pusher*, that is, someone assigned by a Soviet enterprise to barter for inputs anywhere within the Soviet system. *Tolkachi* collectively functioned as an informal wholesale network parallel to Gossnab.

totalitarianism
A typology used by political scientists to describe modern states that regulate (control) nearly every aspect of public and private behavior. The distinction between regulation and control is crucial. There are no examples of totalitarian nanocontrol, including Stalin's Russia, only societies that attempt to control nearly every aspect of individual activity.

transition
Literally, a movement from one state or system to another, usually employed to suggest that former planned economies inevitably will be transformed into democratic free enterprise systems, or EU social democracies.

transitologist
Experts who believe that all nations must transform into democratic free enterprise systems, or EU social democracies, and try to assist the process.

treadmill of reform
Used by Gertrude Schroeder to express the futility of Soviet administrative economic reforms.

trudovye kollektivy   Soviet enterprise workers councils serving red directors in an advisory capacity. They were briefly seen as a device for democratizing the workplace during Gorbachev's post-1987 economic reforms.

tsar   Russian title derived from the Latin Caesar meaning autocratic emperor or king. It was the primary title (1547–1721) before becoming subsidiary to Russian autocrat until the end of the Romanov dynasty.

Ummah   In contemporary political usage, a pan-Islamic theocratic state under construction that seeks to restore the governing order of the first Caliphate. Advocates such as Osama bin Laden hope to use the concept to found a mighty empire.

uskorenie   Accelerated GDP growth, a goal showcased in Gorbachev's initial 1985 economic reform package.

value subtracted   Processing that reduces the value of raw materials or intermediate inputs. Some erroneously define value subtracted more broadly to include the production of domestic goods from raw materials that have a higher value abroad. But this phenomenon is mistrading. As long as the domestic value of the fabricate exceeds the domestic raw material cost, value is added, not subtracted.

vanguard of the proletariat   Progressive elements self-tasked with leading the working class in its march to full communism. Lenin claimed that his Bolshevik Party was anointed by history to play this role in the Soviet Union.

visible hand   State directive, administrative, and regulatory economic actions.

virgin lands program   Nikita Khrushchev campaign in 1954 to open up vast tracts of semiarid land for agriculture, which began with a bang but ended badly with diminished soil fertility and erosion. The strategy came to symbolize the shortsightedness and futility of Soviet resource mobilization tactics.

virtual economy   Coined by Clifford Gaddy and Barry Ickes to convey the idea that physical productive management remains the predominant principle governing Russian economic activity after the demise of planning,

	despite the emergence of subsistence and exclusionary markets.
voucher privatization	A scheme advocate by Andrei Shleifer and others, adopted by Boris Yeltsin whereby vouchers for the acquisition of shares in denationalized enterprises were distributed to citizens in recognition of their ownership stake in the Soviet capital stock. The scheme degenerated into a scam when mutual funds acting as intermediaries declared bankruptcy, absconded with the vouchers, and used them as a basis for creating ill-gotten fortunes.
VPK	*Voennyi promyshlennyi kompleks* (Soviet and Russian military industrial complexes).
vrag naroda	Enemy of the people. Used to stigmatize anyone or group that disagreed with the Bolsheviks. Even the mere suspicion of being hostile made people vulnerable to persecution, judicial action, terror, and extermination.
War Communism	A period of Russian civil war between forces loyal to the tsar and the Bolsheviks, as well a series of utopian and expedient attempts to construct a communist society. It can also be construed as a period of Muscovite restoration in proletarian guise.
Washington Consensus	Coined by John Williamson to describe a set of micro- and macroeconomic principles that leading international institutions in Washington, DC, like the International Monetary Fund, and World Bank, believe best serve the cause of economic development and global prosperity. The key elements are free enterprise, financial discipline, and democracy. The Washington Consensus champions liberal globalization, opposes systemic diversity, and believes that only liberal principles are universally applicable regardless of culture or systems.
westernization	The adoption of the ideals of the West, including economic liberty, democracy, social justice, tolerance, diversity, and conflict avoidance by developing and transitioning economies. Westernization is a more demanding concept than modernization, which only entails adopting western technologies.

work   In national income accounting terms, any labor
                        activity that generates marketable value-added, as
                        distinct from nonmarketable activities for own con-
                        sumption.

Yukos Affair   A sequence of events triggered by the arrest of
                        Russian oligarch Mikhail Khodorkovsky that cul-
                        minated in his conviction and imprisonment in
                        2005 for various crimes and the effective renation-
                        alization of his Yukos oil empire. These events are
                        widely viewed as stepping stones in suppressing the
                        post-Soviet transition process and restoring a Mus-
                        covite authoritarian martial, police state.

zastoi   Economic stagnation. Gorbachev's growth acceler-
                        ation campaign was justified by the claim that Soviet
                        GDP halted in 1980, despite *Goskomstat* statistics to
                        the contrary.

Bibliography

Abalkin, Abel, and John Walley. "The Problem of Capital Flight from Russia." *The World Economy* 22, no. 3 (1999): 421–44.

Abouchar, Alan. *The Socialist Price Mechanism*. Durham, NC: Duke University Press, 1977.

Aganbegyan, Abel. *The Economic Challenge of Perestroika*. Bloomington: Indiana University Press, 1988.

Aganbegyan, Abel. *Inside Perestroika: The Future of the Soviet Economy*. New York: Harper and Row, 1989.

Allan, Duncan. "Banks and the Loans-for-Shares Auctions." In David Lane, ed., *Russian Banking and Prospects*. Cheltenham, UK: Edward Elgar, 2002, 137–60.

Amalrik, Andrei. *Will the Soviet Union Survive Until 1984?* New York: Harper and Row, 1970.

Amnesty International, Racism Report. http://www.amnesty.org/russia/pdfs/racism_report.pdf.

Antonov-Ovseenko, Anton. *Beria*. Moscow, 1999.

Arendt, Hannah. *The Origins of Totalitarianism*, Orlando, FL: Harcourt, 1979.

Aris, Ben. "A Row over Russia's FDI Figures." *Johnson's Russia List*, no. 271, Article 21, December 1, 2006.

Arrow, Kenneth. *Social Choice and Individual Values* (2nd edition). New York: Wiley, 1963.

Arrow, Kenneth. "Optimal and Voluntary Income Distribution." In Steven Rosefielde, ed., *Economic Welfare and the Economics of Soviet Socialism*. London: Cambridge University Press, 1981, 267–88.

Arzamastsev, Arkady, and Svetlana Branitskaya. "The Shadow behind the President." *Delovye liudi*, January 2004. http://www.dl.mk.ru/article.asp?artid=27730.

Aslund, Anders. "Heritage of the Gorbachev Era." In *The Former Soviet Union in Transition*. Washington, DC: Joint Economic Committee of Congress, 1993, 184–95.

Aslund, Anders. "Amnesty the Oligarchs." *Moscow Times*, March 14, 2003.

Aslund, Anders. "Russia's Collapse." *Foreign Affairs* 78, no. 5 (1999): 64–77.

Aslund, Anders. *Policy brief #41*.Carnegie Endowment for International Peace, August 2005.

Aslund, Anders. "Suffering from Oil's Curse a Matter of Choice." *Johnson's Russia List*, no. 276, Article 22, December 6, 2006.

Aslund, Anders. *How Capitalism Was Built: The Transformation of Central and Eastern Europe, Russia, and Central Asia*. Cambridge: Cambridge University Press, 2007.

Aslund, Anders. *Russia's Capitalist Revolution: Why Market Reform Succeeded and Democracy Failed*. Washington, DC: Peterson Institute of International Economics, 2007.

Avtorkhanov, Abdurahman. "The Mystery of Stalin's Death." *Novyi Mir*, no. 5 (1991): 194–233.

Bagrinovsky, K. A., and V. S. Prokopova. *Imitatsionnye Sistemy Priniatia Ekonomicheskikh Reshennii*. Moscow: Nauka, 1989.

Baker, Peter, and Susan Glasser. *Kremlin Rising: Vladimir Putin's Russia and the End of Revolution*. New York: Scribner, 2005.

Balassa, Bela. "The Purchasing Power Parity: a Reappraisal." *Journal of Political Economy* 72 (December 1964): 584–96.

Barnathan, Joyce. "Inside the Great Thaw." *Business Week*, August 9, 2004. Reprinted in *Johnson's Russia List*, no. 8320, Article 9, August 7, 2004.

Barr, Brenton M., and Kathleen E. Braden. *The Disappearing Russian Forest: A Dilemma in Soviet Resource Management*. Totowa, NJ: Rowman & Littlefield, 1998

Becker, Abraham. "Gorbachev's Defense-Economic Dilemma." In *Gorbachev's Economic Plans*, vol. 1. Washington, DC: Joint Economic Committee of Congress, 1987.

Becker, Abraham. "Gorbachev's Program for Economic Modernization and Reform: Some Important Political-Military Implications." In *Economic Reforms in the U.S.S.R*. Washington, DC: Joint Economic Committee of Congress, 1987, 95–106.

Beichman, Arnold, and Mikhail Bernstam. *Andropov: New Challenge to the West*. New York: Stein and Day, 1983.

Bergson, Abram. "A Reformulation of Certain Aspects of Welfare Economics," *Quarterly Journal of Economics* 52, no. 1 (1938): 310–34.

Bergson, Abram. "The Concept of Social Welfare." *Quarterly Journal of Economics* 68, no. 2 (May 1954): 233–52.

Bergson, Abram. *The Real National Income of the Soviet Union since 1928*. Cambridge, MA: Cambridge University Press, 1961.

Bergson, Abram. *The Economics of Soviet Planning*. New Haven, CT: Yale University Press, 1964.

Bergson, Abram. "Socialist Economics." In Abram Bergson, *A Survey of Contemporary Economics*. Cambridge, MA: Harvard University Press, 1966, 234–36.

Bergson, Abram. *Essays in Normative Economics*. Cambridge, MA: Harvard University Press, 1966.

Bergson, Abram. "Market Socialism Revisited." *Journal of Political Economy* 75, no. 4 (1967): 655–73.

Bergson, Abram. "Social Choice and Welfare Economics under Representative Government." *Journal of Public Economics* 6, no. 3 (1967): 171–90.

Bergson, Abram. "The Comparative National Incomes of the Soviet Union and the United States." In *Productivity and the Social System – The USSR and the West*. Cambridge, MA: Harvard University Press, 1978, 47–67.

Bergson, Abram. "Technological Progress." In Abram Bergson and Herbert Levine, eds., *The Soviet Economy toward the Year 2000*. London: Allen and Unwin, 1983, 34–78.

Bergson, Abram. "The U.S.S.R. before the Fall: How Poor and Why?" *Journal of Economic Perspectives* 5, no. 4 (1991): 29–44.

Berliner, Joseph. *The Innovation Decision in Soviet Industry*. Cambridge, MA: MIT Press, 1976, 400–27.

Berliner, Joseph. "Planning and Management." In Abram Bergson and Herbert Levine, eds., *The Soviet Economy: Toward the Year 2000*. London: George Allen and Unwin, 1983, 350–90.

Berliner, Joseph. "Organizational Restructuring of the Soviet Economy." In *Gorbachev's Economic Plans*, vol. 1. Washington, DC: Joint Economic Committee of Congress, 1987, 70–83.

Berliner, Joseph. "Prepared Statement." In *Economic Reforms in the U.S.S.R.* Washington, DC: Joint Economic Committee of Congress, 1987, 274–85.

Bertsch, Gary. "U.S. Policy Governing Economic and Technological Relations with the U.S.S.R." In *Gorbachev's Economic Plans*, vol. 2. Washington, DC: Joint Economic Committee of Congress, 1987, 433–47.

Bettleheim, Charles. *Class Struggles in the USSR, Second Period: 1923–1930*. New York: Monthly Review Press, 1978.

Bigg, Claire. "Russia: Migrant Workers Struggle to Build Lives amid Poverty, abuse." *Radio Liberty*, November 8, 2005.

Billington, James. *The Icon and Axe*. New York: Random House, 1970.

Billington, James. *Russia in Search of Itself*. Washington, DC: Woodrow Wilson Center, 2004.

Birman, Igor. *Secret Incomes of the Soviet State Budget*. Boston: Martinus Nijhoff Publishers, 1981.

Birman, Igor. *Ekonomika Nedostach* (The Economy of Shortages). Benson, VT: Chalidze Publishing, 1983.

Birman, Igor. "The Soviet Economy: Alternative Views." *Russia* 12 (1986): 69–71.

Birman, Igor, and Roger Clarke. "Inflation and the Money Supply in the Soviet Economy." *Soviet Studies* 37, no. 4 (1985): 501–2.

Blackwell, Robert. *Gorbachev's Program: Motives and Prospects. Economic Reforms in the U.S.S.R.* Washington, DC: Joint Economic Committee of Congress, 1987, 213–39.

Blackwell, Robert. "Statement." Before the Subcommittee of National Security Economics. Washington, DC: Joint Economic Committee of Congress, September/October 1987 208.

Blackwell, William. *The Beginnings of Russian Industrialization 1800–1860.* Princeton, NJ: Princeton University Press, 1968.

Blank, Stephen. "The General Crisis of the Russian Military." Paper presented at Putin's Russia: Two Years On, Wilton Park, England, March 11–15, 2002.

Blank, Stephen. "The Material-Technical Foundations of Russian Military Power." In *Ankara Paper* 7. London: Frank Cass, 2003, 25–26.

Blank, Stephen. "The 18th Brumaire of Vladimir Putin." In Uri Ra'anan, ed., *Flawed Succession.* Totowa, NJ: Rowman and Littlefield, 2006.

Blank, Stephen. "The Great Game Goes to Sea: Naval Rivalries in the Caspian." *Johnson's Russia List*, no. 12, Article 26, January 12, 2006.

Blough, Roger, Jennifer Muratore, and Steve Berk. "Gorbachev's Policy on the Private Sector: Two Steps Forward, One Step Backward." In *Gorbachev's Economic Plans*, vol. 2. Washington, DC: Joint Economic Committee of Congress, 1987, 261–71.

Bonin, John. "On the Design of Managerial Incentive Structures in a Decentralized Planning Environment." *American Economic Review* 66, no. 4 (1976): 682–87.

Bonin, John, and Wataru Fukuda. "Controlling a Risk-averse, Effort-Selecting Manager in the Soviet Incentive Model." *Journal of Comparative Economics* 11, no. 2 (1987): 221–34.

Boone, Peter, and D. Rodionov. "Rent Seeking in Russia and the CIS." Paper presented at the 10th Anniversary Conference of the EBRD, London, 2001.

Boot, Max. "Don't Play Dead for Putin: What the West Can Do to Help Stop the Authoritarian President from Garnering Too Much Influence in the World." *Johnson's Russia List*, no. 276, Article 15, December 6, 2006.

Booth, Charles. *Life and Labour of the People of London.* London and New York, Macmillan, 1892.

Brada, Josef, and Arthur King. "Is there a J-Curve for Economic Transition from Socialism to Capitalism?" *Economics of Planning* 25, no. 1 (1992): 37–53.

Brainard, Elizabeth. "Reassessing the Standard of Living in the Soviet Union: An Analysis Using Archival and Anthropometric Data." Paper presented at

Abram Bergson Memorial Conference, Davis Center, Harvard University, Cambridge, MA, November 23–24, 2003.

Brainard, Lawrence. "Soviet International Financial Policy: Traditional Formulas or New Innovations?" In *Gorbachev's Economic Plans*, vol. 1. Washington, DC: Joint Economic Committee of Congress, 1987, 100–15.

Calder, Kent. "China and Japan's Simmering Rivalry." *Foreign Affairs* 85, no. 2, (March/April 2006): 129–41.

Central Intelligence Agency. *Handbook of International Economic Statistics*. Washington, DC: The Directorate, 1992.

Central Intelligence Agency and Defense Intelligence Agency. *The Soviet Economy Stumbles Badly in 1989*. Presented to the Technology and National Security Subcommittee of the Joint Economic Committee. Washington, DC: Joint Economic Committee, 1990.

Chang, Gordon. *The Coming Collapse of China*. New York: Random House, 2001.

Chapman, Janet. *Real Wages in the Soviet Union*. Cambridge, MA: Harvard University Press, 1963.

Chapman, Shelia, and Marcella Mulino. "Predicting Russia's Currency and Financial Crises." In David Lane, ed., *Russian Banking and Prospects*. Cheltenham, UK: Edward Elgar, 2002, 137–60.

Cherniavsky, Michael. "Khan or Basileus: An Aspect of Russian Medieval Political Theory." In idem, ed., *The Structure of Russian History: Interpretive Essays*. New York: Random House, 1970.

Childress, Ron. "The 'Children's Crusade' – Namely the Needless American 'Humanitarian' Assistance to Post-Soviet Russia." Paper presented at the American Association for the Advancement of Slavic Studies, Boca Raton, FL, September 1998.

Chubais, Anatoly, ed. *Privatizatsiya po-rossiiski*. Moscow: Vagrius, 1999.

CIA. *Measures of Soviet Gross National Product in 1982 Prices*. Washington, DC: Joint Economic Committee of Congress, November 1990.

"Clandestine Optimism: Political Parties Pledge to Avoid Protest Demonstrations Kremlin Requests Parties to Sign An Anti-Extremism Charter." *Johnson's Russia List*, no. 75, Article 10, March 29, 2007.

Coalson, Robert. "Russia's Ombudsman Speaks Out." *Radio Free Europe*, June 2004. http://wwww.rferl.org/featuresarticle/2004/06/00d97e5f-de14-ra35-ae9b-a791f9106124.htmlhttp://en.wikipedia.org/wiki/Human_rights_in_Russia.

Cocks, Paul. "Soviet Science and Technology Strategy: Borrowing from the Defense Sector." In *Gorbachev's Economic Plans*, vol. 2. Washington, DC: Joint Economic Committee of Congress, 1987, 145–60.

Cohn, Stanley. "Soviet Intensive Economic Development Strategy in Perspective." In *Gorbachev's Economic Plans*, vol. 1. Washington, DC: Joint Economic Committee of Congress, 1987, 10–26.

Colby, William. "Statement." In *Economic Reforms in the U.S.S.R.* Washington, DC: Joint Committee of Congress, 1987, 173–81.

Collier, Irwin. "The Welfare Standard and Soviet Consumers." *Comparative Economics Studies* 47, no. 2 (2005): 333–45.

Committee to Protect Journalists. http://222.cpj.org/killed/killed_archives/stats.html.

Conn, David. "A Comparison of Alternative Incentive Structures for Centrally Planned Economic Systems." *Journal of Comparative Economics* 3, no. 3 (1979): 235–53.

Conn, David. "Effort, Efficiency, and Incentives in Economic Organizations." *Journal of Comparative Economics* 6, no. 3 (1982): 223–34.

Conquest, Robert. *Harvest of Sorrow: Soviet Collectivization and the Terror-Famine.* London: Oxford University Press, 1987.

Conway, Patrick. "Ruble Overhang and Ruble Shortage: Were They the Same Thing." *Journal of Comparative Economics* 24 (1998): 1–24.

Conway, Patrick. "Sustained Inflation in Response to Price Liberalization." *World Bank Policy Research Working Paper* 1368, 1994.

Cooper, Julian. "Technology Transfer between Military and Civilian Ministries." In *Gorbachev's Economic Plans*, vol. 1. Washington, DC: Joint Economic Committee of Congress, 1987, 388–405.

Cooper, Julian. "The Economics of Russian Defense Policy." Paper presented at the conference on Russia under President Vladimir Putin: Towards the Second Term, European University Institute, Florence, April 22–23, 2004.

Corden, W. Max. "Boom Sector and Dutch Disease Economics: Survey and Consolidation." *Oxford Economic Papers* 36, no. 3 (1984): 359–80.

Corden, W. Max, and J. Peter Neary. "Booming Sector and Deindustrialization in a Small Open Economy." *The Economic Journal* 92 (December 1982): 825–48.

Cox, Christopher. *Russia's Road to Corruption.* Washington, DC: U.S. House of Representatives, 2000.

Crisp, Olga. *Studies in the Russian Economy before 1914.* London: Macmillan Press, 1976.

Danilin, Vyacheslav I, Knox Lovell, Ivan Materov, and Steven Rosefielde. "Measuring and Improving Enterprise Efficiency in the Soviet Union." *Economica* 52, no. 206 (1984): 225–34.

Danish Support Committee for Chechnya 2002. "KGB's Terror Bombings in Moscow, Volgodonsk, Buinaksk and Ryazan 1999." http://www.tjetjenien.dk/baggrund/bombs.html.

David, P. A., B. H. Hall, and A. A. Toole. "Is Public R&D a Complement or a Substitute for Private R&D? A Review of Econometric Evidence." *Research Policy* 29 (April 2000): 497–529.

d'Encausse, Helen Carrère. *Decline of an Empire: The Soviet Socialist Republics in Revolt*. New York: Harper & Row, 1981.

"Defense Minister: Russia Will Spend 50% More on Weapons in 2006 than 2005." *Johnson's Russia List*, no. 82, Article 16, April 6, 2006.

Desai, Padma. *Perestroika in Perspective: The Design and Dilemmas of Soviet Reform*. Princeton, NJ: Princeton University Press, 1989.

Desai, Padma. "Perestroika, Prices and the Ruble Problem." *Harriman Institute Forum* 2, no. 11 (1989): 1–8.

Deutch, Shelley. "The Soviet Weapons Industry: An Overview." In *Gorbachev's Economic Plans* 1. Washington, DC: Joint Economic Committee of Congress, 1987, 405–30.

Diamond, Jared. *Collapse: How Societies Choose to Fail or Succeed*. New York: Viking Books, 2005.

Dolgov, Anna. "Putin Urges Changes to Centralize Power." *The Boston Globe*, September 14, 2004, p. A1.

Domar, Evsei. "On the Optimal Compensation of a Socialist Manager." *Quarterly Journal of Economics* 88, no. 1 (1974): 1–19.

Donselaar P., H. P. G. Erken, and L. Klomp. "R&D and Innovation: Drivers of Productivity Growth." In G. M. Gelauff, L. Klomp, S. E. P. Raes, and T. J. A. Roelandt, eds., *Fostering Productivity Patterns, Determinants and Policy Implications*. Boston: Elsevier, 2004.

Dornbusch, Rudiger. "Lessons from Experiences with High Inflation." *World Bank Economic Review* 6 (1992): 13–32.

Duran, James. "Russian Fiscal and Monetary Stabilization: A Tough Road Ahead." In *The Former Soviet Union in Transition*. Washington, DC: Joint Economic Committee of Congress, 1993, 196–217.

Eberstadt, Nicholas. "Russia: Too Sick to Matter?" *Policy Review*, no. 95 (June–July 1999): 3–26.

Eberstadt, Nicholas. "The Future of AIDS." *Foreign Affairs* 81, no. 6 (2002): 22–45.

Eberstadt, Nicholas. "Russia's Demographic Straightjacket." *SAIS Review* 24, no. 2 (Summer–Fall 2004): 9–25.

Eberstadt, Nicholas. *The Demographic Factor as a Constraint on Russian Development: Prospects, Sources, and Limits of Russian Power*. Washington, DC: National Defense University Press, 2004.

Eberstadt, Nicholas. "Russia, The Sick Man of Europe." *The Public Interest*, Winter 2005.

Economicheskaya Gazeta, vol. 41, 1987.

Egert, B. "Equilibrium Exchange Rates in South-Eastern Europe, Russia, Ukraine and Turkey: Healthy or Dutch-Diseased?" *Economic Systems*, 29 (June 2005): 205–41.

Ekspert. "Gray Collars and Unemployed at the Bottom of Russian social Pyramid." *Johnson's Russia List*, no. 9158, Article 4, May 24, 2004.

Ellman, Michael. "The Increase in Death and Disease Under 'Katastroika.'" *Cambridge Journal of Economics* 18, no. 4 (1994): 329–55.

Ellman, Michael. "The Russian Economy under El'tsin." *Europe-Asia Studies* 52, no. 8 (2000): 1424–29.

Ellman, Michael. "Russian Economic Boom: Post-1998." *Economic and Political Weekly* 39 (2004): 3234–37.

Engerman, David. *Modernization from the Other Shore.* Cambridge, MA: Harvard University Press, 2003.

Erickson, John. "Toward 1984: Four Decades of Soviet Military Policy." *Air University Review* (January–February 1984): 31.

Evans, Julian. "How Putin Youth Is Indoctrinated to Foil Revolution." *The Times,* July 18, 2005.

"Evolution of Putin Aide Surkov's Sovereign Democracy Principle Viewed." *Johnson's Russia List,* no. 75, Article 9, March 29, 2007.

Fak, Alec. "Moscow Taxpayer Data for Sale on CD-ROM." *Moscow Times,* May 27, 2005.

Fedorenko, Nikolai. *Optimal Functioning System for a Socialist Economy Progress.* Moscow, 1974.

Felgenhauer, Pavel. "KGB: Big, Bad and Back." *Moscow Times,* March 12, 2003.

Felshtinsky, Yuri, Alexander Litvinenko, and Geoffrey Andrews. *Blowing up Russia: Terror from Within.* London: Gibson Square Books, 2007.

Feshbach, Murray. "Between the Lines of the 1979 Soviet Census." *Population and Development Review* 8, no. 2 (1982): 347–61.

Feshbach, Murray. "Population and Labor Forces." In Abram Bergson and Herbert Levine, eds., *The Soviet Economy: Towards the Year 2000.* London: Allen & Unwin, 1983.

Feshbach, Murray. "Crisis Call by Gorbachev." In *Economic Reforms in the U.S.S.R.* Washington, DC: Joint Economic Committee of Congress, 1987, 63–89.

Feshbach, Murray. "Prepared Statement." In *Economic Reforms in the U.S.S.R.* Washington, DC: Joint Economic Committee of Congress, 1987, 63–90.

Feshbach, Murray. "Soviet Military Health Issues." In *Gorbachev's Economic Plans,* vol. 1. Washington, DC: Joint Economic Committee of Congress, 1987, 462–80.

Feshbach, Murray. "Environmental Calamities: Widespread and Costly." In *The Former Soviet Union in Transition,* vol. 2. Washington, DC: Joint Economic Committee of Congress, 1993, 577–96.

Feshbach, Murray. *Ecological Disaster: Cleaning up the Hidden Legacy of the Soviet Regime.* New York: The Twentieth Century Fund Project, 1995.

Feshbach, Murray. "Russia's Population Meltdown." *Wilson Quarterly* 25, no. 1 (2001): 15–21.

Feshbach, Murray. *The Demographic, Health and Environmental Situation in Russia.* Draft report presented at The Future of the Russian State, Liechtenstein

Institute on Self-Determination conference, Triesenberg, Liechtenstein, March 14–17, 2002.

Feshbach, Murray. "Russia's Demographic and Health Meltdown." In *Russia's Uncertain Economic Future*. Washington, DC: Joint Economic Committee of Congress, 2002, 283–306.

Feshbach, Murray. *Russia's Health and Demographic Crisis: Policy Implications and Consequences*. Washington, DC: Chemical and Biological Arms Control Institute, 2003.

Feshbach, Murray. "The Russian Military: Population and Health Constraints," in Jan Leijonhielm and Fredrik Westerlund, eds., *Russia Power Structures*, FOI, Swedish Defense Research Agency, Stockholm, January 2008, 111–40.

Feshbach, Murray, and Albert Friendly Jr. *Ecocide in the USSR: Health and Nature under Siege*. New York: Basic Books, 1992, 54–55.

Field, Mark. "The Health and Demographic Crisis in Post-Soviet Russia: A Two Phase Development." In Field and Twigg, eds., *Russia's Torn Safety Nets*. New York: St. Martin's Press, 2000, 11–43.

Field, Mark, and Judyth Twigg. *Russia's Torn Safety Nets: Health and Social Welfare during the Transition*. New York: St. Martin's Press, 2000.

Finn, Peter. "Russian Academy of Sciences Reject Demand to Gwelip Autonomy." *Johnson's Russia List*, NO. 75, Article 18, March 29, 2007.

Firth, Donald, and James Noren. *Soviet Defense Spending: A History of the CIA Estimates 1950–1990*. College Station: Texas A&M University Press, 1998.

Fleishman, Jeffrey. "Russia Pulls the Migrant Welcome Mat." *Johnson's Russia List*, no. 44, Article 21, February 22, 2007.

Folloth, Erich et al. "Following the Litvinenko Trail." *Johnson Russia List*, no. 276, Article 20, December 6, 2006.

Fossato, Floreana. "Russia: Media Decree Targets Internet, Digital TV." *Johnson's Russia List*, no. 75, Article 19, March 29, 2007.

Gaddy, Clifford, and Barry Ickes. "Russia's Virtual Economy." *Foreign Affairs* 77, no. 5 (1998): 52–67.

Gaddy, Clifford, and Barry Ickes. "An Accounting Model of the Virtual Economy in Russia." *Post-Soviet Geography and Economics* 40, no. 3 (1999): 78–97.

Gaddy, Clifford, and Barry Ickes. *Russia's Virtual Economy*. Washington, DC: Brookings Institution Press, 2002.

Garthoff, Raymond. *Soviet Military Power*. New York: Frederick A. Praeger, 1966.

Gerschenkron, Alexander. "The Rate of Growth of Industrial Growth in Russia since 1885." *Journal of Economic History* 7-S (1947): 144–74.

Gerschenkron, Alexander. *Economic Backwardness in Historical Perspective*. Cambridge, MA: Harvard University Press, 1962.

Gitelman, Zvi. "Are Nations Emerging in the USSR?" *Problems of Commu-nism* 32, no. 5 (1983): 35–47.

Gleason, Abbott,. *After Totalitarianism*. London: Oxford University Press, 1995.

Gogol, Nikolai. *Dead Souls*. New Haven, CT: Yale University Press, 1966.

Gokhberg, L. M. "Russia: A New Innovation System for the New Econ-omy." Paper delivered at the First Global Conference Innovation Systems and Development Strategies for the Third Millennium, Rio de Janeiro, November 2003.

Goldberg, I. "Competitiveness and the Investment Climate in Russia: An Assessment by the World Bank and the Higher School of Economics, Moscow." Presented to the 10th annual St. Petersburg International Eco-nomic Forum, June 2006.

Goldman, Marshall. "Gorbachev and Perestroika." In *Economic Reforms in the U.S.S.R.* Washington, DC: Joint Economic Committee of Congress, 1987, 47–58.

Goldman, Marshall. "Putin and the Russian Economy: Did He Make a Difference?" *Russia and Eurasia Review* 1, no. 1 (2002): 2.

Goldman, Marshall. *The Piratization of Russia: Russian Reform Goes Awry*. London: Routledge, 2003.

Goldman, Marshall. "Putin and the Oligarchs." *Foreign Affairs* 83, no. 6 (2004): 33–44.

Goldman, Marshall. *What Went Wrong with Perestroika*. New York: Norton, 1991.

Goldsmith, Raymond. "The Economic Growth of Tsarist Russia 1860–1913." *Economic Development and Cultural Change* 9 (1961): 441–75.

Golitsyn, Anatoly. *New Lies for Old*. New York: Mead & Company, 1984.

Golitsyn, Anatoly. *The Perestroika Deception: The World's Slide towards the "Sec-ond October Revolution."* London & New York: Edward Harle, 1995.

Goodman, Ann, Margaret Hughes, and Gertrude Schroeder. "Raising the Efficiency of Soviet Farm Labor: Problems and Prospects." In *Gorbachev's Economic Plans*, vol. 2. Washington, DC: Joint Economic Committee of Congress, 1995, 100–25.

Goodman, Seymour. E. "The Prospective Impacts of Computing: Selected Economic-Industrial-Strategic Issues." In *Gorbachev's Economic Plans*, vol. 2. Washington, DC: Joint Economic Committee of Congress, 1987, 176–84.

Gorbachev, Mikhail. *Perestoika i Novoe Myshlenie*. Moscow: Politicheskie Lit-eratury, 1987.

Gorbachev, Mikhail. *Perestroika: New Thinking for Our Country and the World*. New York: Harper and Row, 1987.

Goskomstat. *Demographic Yearbook of Russia. Statistical Handbook*. Moscow: Goskomstat, 1997.

Goskomstat. *Demographic Yearbook of Russia. Statistical Handbook.* Moscow: Goskomstat, 1998.

Goskomstat. *Demographic Handbook of Russia.* Moscow: Goskomstat, 1999.

Goskomstat SSSR. *Okhrana okruzhayuschchei sredy i ratsionalnoe ispolzovanie prirodnykh resursov v SSSR.* Moscow: Finansy i statistika, 1989.

Graham, Allison, and Robert Blackwell. "America's Stake in the Soviet Future." *Foreign Affairs* 70, no. 3 (1991): 77–97.

Graham, Thomas. "AEI Conference Remarks." In *Johnson's Russia List*, no. 9270, Article 2, October 14, 2005.

Granick, David. "The Ministry as a Maximizing Unit in Soviet Industry." *Journal of Comparative Economics* 4, no. 3 (1980): 255–73.

Granick, David. "Soviet Use of Fixed Prices: Hypothesis of a Job-Right Constraint." In Steven Rosefielde, ed., *Economic Welfare and the Economics of Soviet Socialism.* Cambridge: New York, Cambridge University Press, 1981, 85–104.

Gray, Kenneth. "Reform and Resource Allocation in Soviet Agriculture." In *Gorbachev's Economic Plans*, vol. 2. Washington, DC: Joint Economic Committee of Congress, 1987, 9–25.

Gregory, Paul. "Economic Growth and Structural Change in Tsarist Russia: A Case of Modern Economic Growth." *Soviet Studies* 3 (1972): 418–34.

Gregory, Paul. "Russian Industrialization: A Survey of the Western Literature." *Jahrbucher fur die Geschichte Osteuropas* (December 1976).

Gregory, Paul. "Russian National Income in 1913 – Some Insights into Russian Economic Development." *Quarterly Journal of Economics* (August 1976): 445–59.

Gregory, Paul. "Russian Living Standards during the Industrialization Era." *Review of Income and Wealth* 26 (1980): 87–103.

Gregory, Paul. *Russian National Income, 1885–1913.* Cambridge: Cambridge University Press, 1983.

Gregory, Paul. *Before Command: The Russian Economy from Emancipation to Stalin.* Princeton, NJ: Princeton University Press, 1994.

Gregory, Paul, ed. *Behind the Facade of Stalin's Command Economy.* Princeton NJ: Princeton University Press, 2002.

Gregory, Paul. *The Political Economy of Stalinism: Evidence from the Soviet Secret Archives.* London: Cambridge University Press, 2003.

Grossman, Gregory. "Roots of Gorbachev's Problems: Private Income and Outlay in the Late 1970s." In *Gorbachev's Economic Plans*, vol. 1. Washington, DC: Joint Economic Committee of Congress, 1987, 213–30.

Guellec, D., and B. van Pottelsberghe dela Potterie. "R&D and Productivity Growth: Panel Data Analysis of 16 OECD Countries." OECD STI Working Paper 2004/4, June 2001, http://www.oecd.org/findDocument/o.2350,en_2649.

Gumbrel, Peter. "Hurry, While Supplies Last: Despite Fears of Government Meddling, Western Firms are Buying Russian Businesses at a Record Pace." *Johnson's Russia List*, no. 9128, Article 1, April 24, 2005.

Gustafson, Thane. *Reform in Soviet Politics: Lessons of Recent Policies on Land and Water*. Cambridge: Cambridge University Press, 1981.

Hale, David, and Lyric Hale. "China Takes Off." *Foreign Affairs* 42, no. 6 (November/December 2003): 36–53.

Hall, B. H., and J. Van Reenen. "How Effective Are Fiscal Incentives for R&D? A Review of the Evidence." *Research Policy* 29 (2000): 449–69.

Harrison, Mark. "Command and Collapse: The Fundamental Problem of Command in a Partially Centralized Economy." Paper presented at the Abram Bergson Memorial Conference, Harvard University, November 2003.

Hausmann, R., L. Pritchett, and D. Rodrik. "Growth Accelerations." *Journal of Economic Growth* 10, no. 4 (2005): 303–29.

Hayek, Fredrich A. von. *Collectivist Economic Planning: Critical Studies on the Possibilities of Socialism*. London: George Routledge & Sons, 1935.

Hayek, Fredrich A. von. "Socialist Calculation: The Competitive Solution." *Economica* 7 (1940): 125–49.

Hedenskanz, Konnander, et al. *Russia as a Great Power*. New York: Routledge, 2005.

Hedlund, Stefan. *Russian Path Dependence*. London: Routledge, 2005.

Hellie, Richard. "The Structure of Modern Russian History: Toward a Dynamic Model." *Russian History* 4, no. 1 (1977): 1–22.

Hellie, Richard. "The Structure of Russian Imperial History." *History and Theory*, Theme Issue 44 (2005): 89.

Hellman, Joel. "Winners Take All: The Politics of Partial Reform in Post-Communist Nations." *World Politics* 50, no. 2 (1998): 203–34.

Hemmings, P. "Hungarian innovation Policy: What Is the Best Way Forward?" *Economics Department Working Paper*, no. 445, September 2005.

Hewett, Ed, Bryan Roberts, and Jan Vanous. "On the Feasibility of Key Targets in the Soviet Twelfth Five Year Plan (1986–90)." In *Gorbachev's Economic Plans*, vol. 1. Washington, DC: Joint Economic Committee of Congress, 1987, 27–53.

Hewett, Ed. "The June 1987 Plenum and Economic Reform in the USSR." In *Economic Reform in the U.S.S. R.* Washington, DC: Joint Economic Committee of Congress, 1987, 290–302.

Hewett, Ed. "The New Soviet Plan." *Foreign Affairs* 69, no. 5 (1990).

Hlouskova, Romana. "Golitsyn, KGB, and the Velvet Revolution." Unpublished paper, December 2003.

Holmstrom, Bengt. "Design of Incentive Schemes and the New Soviet Incentive Model." *European Economic Review* 17, no. 2 (1982): 188–248.

Holzman, Franklyn. "Are the Soviets Really Outspending the U.S. on Defense?" *International Security* 4, no. 4 (1982): 78–101.

Hough, Jerry. "Prepared Statement." In *Economic Reforms in the U.S.S.R.* Washington, DC: Joint Economic Committee of Congress, 1987, 426–44.

Hough, Jerry. "*Statement.*" Before the Subcommittee of National Security Economics. Washington, DC: Joint Economic Committee of Congress, 1987, 420–21.

Hough, Jerry. *Opening up the Soviet Economy.* Washington, DC: Brookings, 1988.

Howard, David. *Disequilibrium Model in a Controlled Economy.* Lexington, MA: Lexington Books, 1979, 139–48.

Hui, Qin. "Fin de Siede China." *The Chinese Economy* 38, no. 5 (September–October, 2005): 3–54.

Huntington, Samuel. "The West: Unique, Not Universal." *Foreign Affairs* 75, no. 6 (1996): 28–46.

Huntington, Samuel. *The Clash of Civilizations and the Remaking of World Order.* New York: Simon & Schuster, 1996.

Hurst, Andrew. "Putin's Capital Amnesty May Fall on Deaf Ears." *Johnson's Russia List*, no. 9142, Article 4, May 7, 2005.

IET. *Rossiiskaya ekonomika v 2005 gody: Tendentsii i perspektivy.* Moscow: Institute for the Economy in Transition, 2006, http://www.iet.ru/publication.php?folder-id=44&category-id=2083.

Ilyichev, George. "Evolution of Putin Aide Surkov's Sovereign Democracy Principle Viewed." *Johnson's Russia* List, no. 75, Article 9, March 29, 2007.

Institut ekonomiki perekhodnogo perioda. *Rossiiskaya ekonomiia v 2001 gody, tendentsiii perspektivy.* Moscow: Institut ekonomiki perekhodnogo perioda, 2002, section 2.7.

Ireland, N., and Peter Law. "Incentive and Efficiency in the Kosygin Reform." *Journal of Comparative Economics* 4, no. 1 (1980): 33–39.

"Ivanov Says Defense Sector to Become Locomotive of the Economy." ITAR-TASS, June 14, 2006.

Jaumotte, F., and N. Pain. "Innovation in the Business Sector." *Economics Department Working Paper*, no. 459, OECD, Paris, 2005, http://www.oecd.org/datataoecd/49/29/20686301.HTM.

Jaumotte, F., and N. Pain. "From Ideas to Development: The Determinants of R&D and Patenting." *Economics Department Working Paper*, no. 457, OECD, Paris, 2005, http://www.oecd.org/dataoecd/49/29/20686301.HTM.

Jenkins, Paul. "Russian Journalism Comes Under Fire." *BBC* News, July 2, 2004, http://news.bbc.co.uk.

Jing, Liang. "Can a Hypocritically Benevolent Government Go on for Long?" *Xin shiji*, March 2007.

Jing, Liang. "Property Law, Seed of Prosperity or Landmine of Disruption." *Radio Free Asia*, April 3, 2007, http://www.ncn.org/asp/zwginfo/da.asp?D=71214@ad=4/3/2007.

Johnson, Juliet. *A Fistful of Rubles*. Ithaca, NY: Cornell University Press, 2000.

Jordan, Pamela. *Defending Rights in Russia: Lawyers, the State, and Legal reform in the Post Soviet Era*. Vancouver: UBC Press, 2006.

Judy, Richard. "Information, Control, and Soviet Economic Management." In John Hardt et al., eds., *Mathematics and Computers in Soviet Economic Planning*. New Haven, CT: Yale University Press, 1967, 1–67.

Judy, Richard. "The Soviet Information Revolution: Some Prospects and Comparisons." In *Gorbachev's Economic Plans*, vol. 2. Washington, DC: Joint Economic Committee of Congress, 1987, 161–75.

Kakturskaya, Maria. "We Are Slaves of the State." *Johnson's Russia List*, no. 8470, Article 10, November 26, 2004.

Katsenlinboigen, Aron. *Studies in Soviet Planning*. New York: M. E. Sharpe, 1978, 165–202.

Keenan, Edward. "Muscovite Political Folkways." *Russian Review* 46, no. 2, (1987): 199–209.

Keidel, Albert. "China's Social Unrest: The Story Behind the Stories." *Policy Brief*, no. 48, Carnegie Endowment for International Peace, September 2005.

Keren, Michael, I. Miller, and J. Thornton. "The Ratchet Effect: A Dynamic Managerial Incentive Model of Soviet Enterprise." *Journal of Comparative Economics* 7, no. 4 (1982): 347–67.

Khanin, Girsh Itsykovich. *Dinamika ekonomicheskovo razvitiya*. Novosibirsk: Nauka, 1991.

Khanin, Girsh Itsykovich. "Ekonomicheskoe razvitie Rossii za 1999–2004 gody: predvaritel'naia al'ternativnaia otsenka sostoiania rossiiskoi ekonomiki i ee analiz." Paper presented to the Sixth World Congress of the International Council for Central and East European Studies "Europe – Our Common Home?" Berlin, July 25–30, 2005.

Khanin, Girsh Itsykovich. "Economic Growth and the Mobilization Model," in Michael Ellman, ed., *Russia's Oil and Natural Gas: Bonanza or Curse?* Anthem Press, London, 2006, chapter 7.

Khrushcheva, Nina. "Vova the Dread." *Wall Street Journal*, March 4, 2005. Reprinted in *Johnson's Russia List*, no. 9077, Article 14, March 4, 2005.

Kingkade, W. Ward. "Demographic Trends in the Soviet Union." In *Gorbachev's Economic Plans*, vol. 1. Washington, DC: Joint Economic Committee of Congress, 1987, 166–86.

Kingston-Mann, Ester. *In Search of the True West: Culture, Economics and Problems of Russian Development*. Princeton, NJ: Princeton University Press, 1998.

Kissinger, Henry, Lawrence Summers, and Charles Kupchan. *Renewing the Atlantic Partnership: Independent Task Force Report.* The Council on Foreign Relations, 2004.

Klein, Lawrence, and Daniel Bond. "The Soviet Bloc in the World Economy." In *Gorbachev's Economic Plans,* vol. 1. Washington, DC: Joint Economic Committee of Congress, 1987, 84–99.

Klette, T. J., J. Moen, and Z. Griliches. "Do Subsidies to Commercial R&D Reduce Market Failures? Micro-Econometric Evaluation Studies." *Research Policy* 29 (2000): 471–95.

Klugman, Jeni. *Poverty in Russia: Public Policy and Private Responses.* Washington, DC: The World Bank, 1997.

Knight, Amy. *Spies without Cloaks: The KGB's Successors.* Princeton, NJ: Princeton University Press, 1996.

Knight, Amy. "A Modern Crime and Punishment: Who Killed Russia's Leading Liberal?" *The Globe and Mail,* April 23, 2003. Reprinted in *Johnson's Russia List,* no. 7153, article 12, April 24, 2003.

Kokh, Al'fred. *The Selling of the Soviet Empire. Politics and Economics of Russia's Privatization Programme. Revelations of the Principal Insider.* New York: SPI Books, 1998.

Komarov, Boris. *Unichtozhenie prirody.* Frankfurt/Main: Possev-Verlag, 1978.

Komsomolskaya Pravda, September 29, 1990.

Koopmans, Tjalling, and Michael Montias, "On the Description and Comparison of Economic Systems," in A. Eckstein, ed., *Comparison of Economic Systems.* Berkeley: University of California Press, 1971, 27–78.

Korop, Yelena. "Skyrocketing Incomes Threaten Russian Economic Stability." *Johnson's Russia List,* no. 276, Article 8, December 6, 2006.

Kosygin, A. "Ob uluchshenii upravleniia promyshlennostiu sovershenstvovanii planirovania i usilennia ekonomicheskovo stimulirovanii promyshennovo proizvodstva" (On Improving Industrial Management, Perfect Planning and Increasing Economic Incentives for Industrial Production). Pravda, September 28, 1965.

Kovalev, Vladimir. "Group Says to Restore Novgorod Republic." *Johnson's Russia List,* no. 9107, March 30, 2005.

Kozlov, K., and K. Yudaeva. "Imitations and Innovations in a Transition Economy." Bank of Finland Institute for Economies in Transition (BOFIT), October 2004, http://www.bof.fi/bofit/seminar/bofcef05/innovations.pdf.

Krastev, Nikola. "Freedom House Sees Further Democracy Decline." *RFE/RL,* January 17, 2007.

Kreshover, Douglas. "Gorbachev and the Economy: The Developing Gameplan." In *Gorbachev's Economic Plans,* vol. 1. Washington, DC: Joint Economic Committee of Congress, 1987, 54–69.

Kroll, Heidi. "Decentralization and Pre-contract Dispute in Soviet Industry." *Soviet Economy* 2 (1986): 51–71.

Krueger, Anne. "The Political Economy of Rent–Seeking Society," *American Economic Review* 64, no. 3 (1974): 291–303.

Krugman, Paul. "The Narrow Moving Band, the Dutch Disease, and the Economic Consequences of Mrs. Thatcher: Notes on Trade in the Presence of Dynamic Economies of Scale." *Journal of Development Economics* 27, no. 1 (1987): 41–55.

Krugman, Paul. "The Myth of Asia's Miracle." *Foreign Affairs* 73, no. 6 (November/December 1994): 62–78.

Krugman, Paul. "Whatever Happened to the Asian Miracle." January 1998, http://web.mit.edu/krugman/www/perspire.htm.

Kryshtanovskaya, Olga, and Stephen White. "Inside the Putin Court: a Research Note." *Europe-Asia Studies* 57, no. 7 (2005): 1065–75.

Kurtenbach, Elaine. "China: 60 Percent of Recent Land Deals Illegal." *Yahoo!Finance*, June 7, 2006.

Kurtzweg, Laurie. "Trends in Soviet Gross National Product" In *Gorbachev's Economic Plans*, vol. 1. Washington, DC: Joint Economic Committee of Congress, 1987, 126–65.

Kushnirsky, F. I. "The Role of Industrial Modernization in Soviet Economic Planning." In *Gorbachev's Economic Plans*, vol. 1. Washington, DC: Joint Economic Committee of Congress, 1987, 257–73.

Kuznetsov, B., M. Kuzyk, Yu. Simachev, S. Tsukhlo, and A. Chulok. "Osobennosti sprosa na tekhologicheskie innovatsii i otsenka potential'noi reaktsii rossiiskikh promyshlennykh predpriyatii no vozmoszhnye mekhanizmy stimulirovanie innovatsionnoi aktivnosti." (Tezisy). Moscow: International Department Analytical Centre, May 19, 2006.

Kuznetsov, S. A., V. L. Makarov, and V. D. Marshak. *Informasionnaia Baza, Perspektivnovo Planirovannia v OASU*. Moscow: Ekonomika, 1982.

Lane, David. "The Evolution of Post-Communist Banking." In David Lane, ed., *Russian Banking and Prospects*. Cheltenham, UK: Edward Elgar, 2002, 9–35.

Lane, David, and Irene Lavrentieva. "The View from the Ground: Case Studies of Three Major Banks (Sberbank, Uneximbank/Rosbank, Bank of Moscow)." In David Lane, ed., *Russian Banking and Prospects*. Cheltenham, UK: Edward Elgar, 2002, 79–115.

Lange, Oskar, and Fred Taylor. *On the Economic Theory of Socialism*. Minneapolis: University of Minnesota Press, 1938.

Laskova, I., *"A Russian Defense Reform: Current Trends,"* November 2006, http://www.StrategicStudiesInstitute.army.mil.

Ledeneva, A., *How Russia Really Works: The Informal Practices that Shaped Post-Soviet Politics and Business*, Ithaca, NY: Cornell University Press, 2006.

Lee, William. "The ABM Treaty Charade: A Study in Elite Illusion and Delusion." *Journal of Social, Political, and Economic Studies*, Monograph 25 (1997): 97–105.

Leggett, Robert. "Soviet Investment Policy: The Key to Gorbachev's Program for Revitalizing the Soviet Economy." In *Gorbachev's Economic Plans*, vol. 1. Washington, DC: Joint Economic Committee of Congress, 1987, 236–56.

Lenin, Vladimir. *State and Revolution*. London: Penguin Classics, 1993.

Liang, J. "Property Law, Seed of Prosperity or Landmine of Disruption," *Radio Free Asia*, April 3, 2007, http://www.ncn.org/asp/zwginfo/da/asp?ID=71214@ed-4/3/2007.

Liberman, Evsei. *Economic Methods and the Effectiveness of Production*. White Plains, NY: International Arts and Science Press, 1972.

Linz, Juan, and Alfred Stepan. *Problems of Democratic Transition and Consolidation: Southern Europe, South America, and Post-communist Europe*. Baltimore: John Hopkins University Press, 1996.

Litvinenko, Alexander, and A. Goldfarb. *Criminal Gang from Lubyanka*. New York: GRANI, 2002.

Loshkin, M., and Barry Popkin. "The Emerging Underclass in the Russian Federation: Income Dynamics 1992–96." *Economic Development and Cultural Change* 47 (1999): 803–29.

Ma, Li. *A Comparative Study of The Russian and Chinese Governments' FDI Policies*, Master's thesis, curriculum in Russian and East European Studies, University of North Carolina, Chapel Hill, 2005.

Ma, Ying. "China's Stubborn Anti-Democracy." *Policy Review* (February/March, 2007). http://www.hoover.org/publications/policyreview/.

Maddison, Angus. *The World Economy, Historical Statistics*. Paris: OECD, 2003.

Magat, W., and M. Loeb. "Success Indicators in the Soviet Union: The Problem of Incentives and Efficient Allocation." *American Economic Review* 68, no. 1 (1978): 173–81.

Makarov, Valerii, and Georgii Kleiner. "Barter v ekonomike perekhodnovo perioda: Osobennosti i tendentsii." *Ekonomika i Matematicheskie Metody* 33, no. 2 (1997): 25–41.

Maier, Hans. *Totalitarianism and Political Religions: Concepts for the Comparison of Dictatorships - Theory and History of Interpretations*, Vol. 3. Abingdon: Routledge, 2008.

Malia, Martin. *Russia under Western Eyes: From the Bronze Horseman to the Lenin Mausoleum*. Cambridge, MA: Belknap Press, 1999.

Mal'tsev, Yevdokim Yegorovich. "Leninist Concepts of the Defense of Socialism." *Strategic Review* (Winter 1975): 99.

Maples, Michael. "Current and Projected National Security Threats to the United States." *Johnson's Russia List*, no. 8, Article 36, January 12, 2007.

Marshall, Andrew. "Commentary." In *Gorbachev's Economic Plans*, vol. 1. Washington, DC: Joint Economic Committee of Congress, 1987, 482–84.

Martin, P., and C. A. Rogers. "Long-term Growth and Short-term Economic Instability." *European Economic Review* 44 (2000): 359–81.

Marx, Karl. *Economic and Philosophical Manuscripts of 1844.* New York: International Publishers, 1971.

Matlock, Jack F., Jr. *Reagan and Gorbachev: How the Cold War Ended.* New York: Random House, 2004.

Matosich, Bonnie. "Estimating Soviet Military Hardware Purchases: The 'Residual' Approach." In *Gorbachev's Economic Plans*, vol. 1. Washington, DC: Joint Economic Committee of Congress, 1987, 404–30.

McConnell, J. Michael. "Annual Threat Assessment of the Director of National Intelligence for the Senate Arms Services Committee." Washington, DC, February 2007.

McFaul, Michael. *Russia's Unfinished Revolution: Political Change from Gorbachev to Putin.* Ithaca, NY: Cornell University Press, 2001.

McFaul, Petrov, et al. *Between Dictatorship and Democracy: Russian Post-Communist Political Reform.* Washington, DC: Carnegie Endowment, 2004.

McHenry, William. "The Integration of Management Information Systems in Soviet Enterprises." In *Gorbachev's Economic Plans*, vol. 1. Washington, DC: Joint Economic Committee of Congress, 1987, 185–99.

McIntyre, Joan. "Soviet Efforts to Revamp the Foreign Trade Sector." In *Gorbachev's Economic Plans*, vol. 2. Washington, DC: Joint Economic Committee of Congress, 1987, 489–503.

McKinnon, Ronald. *The Order of Economic Liberalization: Financial Control in the Transition to a Market Economy.* Baltimore: John Hopkins University Press, 1991.

Meier, Andrew. *Black Earth: A Journey through Russia after the Fall.* London: HarperCollins, 2003.

Meyers, Steven Lee. "Russian Group Is Offering Values to Fill a Void." *The New York Times*, February 16, 2003.

Mises, Ludwig von. *Socialism.* London: Jonathan Cape, 1936.

Mizobata, Satoshi. "Bank Sector Restructuring." In David Lane, ed., *Russian Banking and Prospects.* Cheltenham, UK: Edward Elgar, 2002, 36–55.

Mosse, W. E. *Perestroika under the Tsars.* London: I. B. Taurus & Co, 1992.

Motyl, Alexander. *Will the Non-Russians Rebel? State, Ethnicity, and Stability in the USSR.* Ithaca, NY: Cornell University Press, 1987.

Mroz, Thomas, and Barry Popkin. "Poverty and the Economic Transition in the Russian Federation." *Economic Development and Cultural Change* 44 (1995): 1–31.

Mustard, Allan, and Christopher Goldthwait. "Food Availability in the former Soviet Union: A Summary Report of Three Missions Led by the

U.S. Department of Agriculture." In *The Former Soviet Union in Transition*, vol. 2. Washington, DC: Joint Economic Committee of Congress, 1993, 506–13.

Narodnoe khoziastvo SSSR. Moscow: Finansy i statistika, 1987.

Narodnoe khoziastvo SSSR. Moscow: Finansy i statistika, 1990.

Narodnoe khoziastvo Rossiiskoi Federatsii. Moscow: Finansy i statistika, 1992.

Naughton, Barry. *The Chinese Economy, Transitions, and Growth*. Cambridge, MA: MIT Press, 2007.

Negroponte, John. "Unclassified Statement for the Record, Threat Assessment." *Johnson's Russia List*, no. 8, Article 35, January 12, 2007.

Nekrich, Alexander. *Punished Peoples: The Deportation and Fate of Soviet Minorities at the End of the Second World War*. New York: Norton, 1978.

NIC. *Russia's Physical and Social Infrastructure: Implications for Future Development*. Washington, DC: National Intelligence Council, 2000.

"Nominee Gates Speaks in Testimony of U.S. Warnings about Russian Unreliability." *Johnson's Russia List*, no. 276, Article 6, December 6, 2006.

Noren, James, and Laurie Kurtzweg. "The Soviet Union Unravels: 1985–91." In *The Former Soviet Union in Transition*, vol. 1. Washington, DC: Joint Economic Committee of Congress, 1993, 31–33.

North, Douglass, and Robert Thomas. *The Rise of the Western World*. London: Cambridge University Press, 1972.

Nove, Alec. *An Economic History of the U.S.S.R.* London: Penguin, 1982.

Nye, Joseph, and Whitey Macmillan. *How Should America Respond to Gorbachev's Challenge? A Report of the Task Force on Soviet New Thinking*. New York: Institute for East-West Security Studies, 1987.

OECD. *The New Economy: Beyond the Hype*. Paris: OECD, 2001.

OECD. *The Sources of Economic Growth in OECD Countries*. Paris: OECD, 2003.

OECD. *Science and Innovation Policies: Key Challenges and Opportunities*. Paris: OECD, 2004.

OECD. *Communications Outlook*. Paris: OECD, 2005.

OECD. *Economic Surveys, China*, vol. 13. Paris: OECD, 2005.

OECD. *Economic Surveys: Russian Federation 2005*. Paris: OECD, 2005.

OECD. *Economic Surveys: Russian Federation 2006*. Paris: OECD, 2006.

OECD. *2006 Investment Policy Review of the Russian Federation: Enhancing Policy Transparency*. Paris: OECD, 2006.

Office of the Secretary of Defense. *The Military Power of the Peoples Republic of China 2005*. Annual Report to Congress, 2005.

Olson, Mancur. *Power and Prosperity: Outgrowing Capitalist and Communist Dictatorships*. New York: Basic Books, 2000.

Pacepa, Ion Mihai. "No Peter the Great." *National Review Online*, September 20, 2004.

Page, Jeremy. "Putin Plans Raise Specter of Return to One-Party Rule." *The Times* (London), September 25, 2004, p. 22.

Pallin, Carolina Vendil. Russian *Military Reform: A Failed Exercise in Defence Decision Making.* Stockholm, FOI Scientific Report FOI-R–1777-SE, November 2005.

Pareto, Vilfredo. *Manuel d'economie politique.* Paris, 1909.

Patillo, C., H. Poirson, and L. Ricci. "External Debt and Growth." In T. Addison, H. Hansen, and F. Tarp, eds., *Debt Relief for Poor Countries.* Basingstoke: Palgrave Macmillan for UNUWIDER, 2004.

Pei, Minxin. *China's Trapped Transition.* Cambridge, MA: Harvard University Press, 2006.

Penelope, Doolittle, and Margaret Hughes. "Gorbachev's Agricultural Policy: Building on the Brezhnev Food Program." In *Gorbachev's Economic Plans*, vol. 2. Washington, DC: Joint Economic Committee of Congress, November 23, 1987, 26–44.

Perkins, Dwight. *The Challenges of China's Growth.* Washington, DC: AEI Press, 2007.

Persson, Torsten, and Guido Tabellini. "Is Inequality Harmful for Growth?" *American Economic Review* 84, no. 3 (1994): 600–21.

Phillips, Tim. *Beslan: The Tragedy of School Number 1.* London: Granta Books, 2007.

Prtukhov, Vladimir, and Georgy Ilyichev. "A Bit of Turmoil on Red Square." *Johnson's Russia List*, no. 8335, Article 1, August 20, 2004.

Pipes, Richard. *Russia under the Old Regime.* New York: Charles Scribner's Sons, 1974.

Pipes, Richard. *Property and Freedom.* New York: Alfred A. Knopf, 1999.

Pipes, Richard. "Flight from Freedom: What Russians Think and Want." *Foreign Affairs* 83, no. 3 (2004): 9–15.

Pipes, Richard. "Inside Reagan's Bid for Détente." *Johnson's Russia List*, no. 8337, Article 12, August 22, 2004.

Pleines, Heiko. "Banks and Illegal Activities." In David Lane, ed., *Russian Banking and Prospects.* Cheltenham, UK: Edward Elgar, 2002, 119–36.

Plots of August: 13 Years Later." *Johnson's Russia List*, no. 8342, Article 15, August 25, 2004.

Polischuk, Leonid, and Alexei Savvatev. "Spontaneous (non) Emergence of Property Rights." *Economics of Transition* 12, no. 1 (2004): 103–27.

Politkovskaya, Anna. *Putin's Russia.* London: Havrill, 2004.

Popov, G. *Elektronnye mashiny i upravlenie ekonomiki.* Moscow, 1963.

Popov, Vladimir, and Nikolai Shmelev. *The Turning Point: Revitalizing the Soviet Economy.* New York: Doubleday, 1989.

Posen, Barry. *The Sources of Military Doctrine: France, Britain and Germany between the World Wars.* Ithaca, NY: Cornell University Press, 1984.

Pryde, Philip R. *Environmental Management in the Soviet Union*. New York: Cambridge University Press, 1991.

"Public Chamber Acknowledges Crackdown On Independent Media." *Johnson's Russia List* no. 75, Article 7, March 29, 2007.

Pugachev, V. F. "Voprosy optimal'novo planirovanniia narodnovo khoziaistvo s pomoshch'iu edinoi gosudarstvennoi seti vychislitel'nykh tsentrov." *Voprosy ekonomiki*, no. 7 (1964): 103.

"Putin Says up to 15 Million Illegal Migrants in Russia." *Johnson's Russia List*, no. 260, Article 20, November 17, 2006.

"Putin's Drive to Restore Russian Power a source of Concern: Gates." *Johnson's Russia List*, no. 276, Article 5, December 6, 2006.

"Putin Warning over 'Puppet' NGO's." *BBC News*, January 31, 2006, http://news.bbc.co.uk.

Radzinsky, Edvard. *Stalin: The First In-Depth Biography Based on Explosive New Documents from Russia's Secret Archives*. New York: Anchor Books, 1997.

Ramey, G., and V. A. Ramey. "Cross-Country Evidence on the Link Between Volatility and Growth." *American Economic Review* 85, no. 5 (1995): 1138–51.

Rapawy, Stephen. "Labor Force and Employment in the U.S.S.R." In *Gorbachev's Economic Plans*, vol. 1. Washington, DC: Joint Economic Committee of Congress, 1987, 187–212.

Reddaway, Peter. "Will Putin Be Able to Consolidate Power?" *Post-Soviet Affairs* 17, no. 1 (2001): 23–24.

Reddaway, Peter. "Is Putin's Power More Formal than Real?" *Post-Soviet Affairs* 18, no. 1 (2002): 21–40.

Reddaway, Peter, and Dmitri Glinski. *Tragedy of Russia's Reforms: Market Bolshevism against Democracy*. Washington, DC: U.S. Institute of Peace, 2001.

Rice, Condoleezza. "Soviet Foreign and Defense Policy Under Gorbachev." In *Economic Reforms in the U.S.S.R.* Washington, DC: Joint Economic Committee of Congress, 1987, 135–44.

Rice, Condoleezza, Stephen Hadley, and Robert Zelikow. *The National Security Strategy of the United States*, National Security Council, September 17, 2002.

Robbins, Lionel Charles, and Baron Robbins. *An Essay on the Nature and Significance of Economic Science*. London: Macmillan, 1932.

Rosefielde, Steven. *The Transformation of the 1966 Soviet Input-Output Table from Producers to Adjusted Factor Cost Values*. Washington, DC: G. E. Tempo, 1975.

Rosefielde, Steven. "Book Review of Birman, Secret Incomes of the Soviet State Budget." *Journal of Economic Literature* 21 (1983): 1018–19.

Rosefielde, Steven. "Regulated Market Socialism: The Semi-Competitive Soviet Solution." *Soviet Union/Union Sovietique* 13, Part 1 (1986): 1–21.

Rosefielde, Steven. *False Science: Underestimating the Soviet Arms Buildup*. New Brunswick, NJ: Transaction Press, 1987, chapter 11.

Rosefielde, Steven "The Soviet Economy in Crisis: Birman's Cumulative Disequilibrium Hypotheses." *Soviet Studies* 40, no. 2 (1988): 222–44.

Rosefielde, Steven. "Ruble Convertibility: Promise or Threat." In Simon Serfaty, ed., *The Future of U.S.–Soviet Relations: Twenty American Initiatives for a New Agenda*. Baltimore: Johns Hopkins University Press, 1989.

Rosefielde, Steven. "State Directed Market Socialism: The Enigma of Gorbachev's Radical Industrial Reforms." *Soviet Union/Union Sovietique* 16 (1989): 1–22.

Rosefielde, Steven. "Is the Economy as Bad as the Soviets Say?" *Orbis* 34, no. 4 (1990): 509–27.

Rosefielde, Steven. "Soviet Market Socialism: An Evolutionary Perspective." *Research on the Soviet Union and Eastern Europe* 1 (1990): 23–43.

Rosefielde, Steven. "Market Communism at the Brink." *Global Affairs* V, no. 2 (1990): 95–108.

Rosefielde, Steven. "Democratic Market Communism: Gorbachev's Design for Utopia." *Shogaku-Ronshu (Fukushima Journal of Commerce, Economics and Economic History)* 59, no. 3 (1991): 15–23.

Rosefielde, Steven. "Gorbachev's Transition Plan: Strategy for Disaster." *Global Affairs* 6, no. 2 (1991): 1–21.

Rosefielde, Steven. "Les limites du liberalisme economique sovietique: la perestroika va-t-elle passer a la trappe?" (The Limits of Soviet Economic Liberalism: Perestroika in Limbo). *Revue D'Etudes Comparatives Est-Ouest* 22, no. 2 (1991): 59–70.

Rosefielde, Steven. "The New Soviet Foreign Trade Mechanism: East West Trade Expansion Possibilities under Perestroika." In Eric Stubbs, ed., *Soviet Foreign Economic Policy and International Security*. Armonk, NY: M. E. Sharpe, 1991, 75–86.

Rosefielde, Steven. "The Grand Bargain: Underwriting Katastroika." *Global Affairs* 7, no. 1 (1992): 15–35.

Rosefielde, Steven. "What Is Wrong with Plans to Aid the CIS?" *Orbis* 37, no. 3 (1993): 353–64.

Rosefielde, Steven. "Peace and Prosperity in the Pacific Rim: Optimizing the Benefits of Japanese Assistance to Russia." *Acta Slavica Iaponica* 12 (1994): 47–61.

Rosefielde, Steven. "Stalinism in Post-Communist Perspective: New Evidence on Killings, Forced Labour and Economic Growth in the 1930s." *Europe-Asia Studies* 48, no. 6 (1996): 959–87.

Rosefielde, Steven. *Efficiency and Russia's Economic Recovery Potential to the Year 2000 and Beyond*. Aldershot, UK: Ashgate, 1998.

Rosefielde, Steven. "The Civilian Labour Force and Unemployment in the Russian Federation." *Europe-Asia Studies* 52, no. 8 (2000): 1433–47.

Rosefielde, Steven. "Premature Deaths: Russia's Radical Economic Transition in Soviet Perspective." *Europe-Asia Studies* 53, no. 8 (2001): 1159–76.

Rosefielde, Steven. *Comparative Economic Systems: Culture, Wealth and Power in the 21st Century*. London: Blackwell, 2002.

Rosefielde, Steven. "The Riddle of Postwar Russian Economic Growth: Statistics Lied and Were Misconstrued." *Europe-Asia Studies* 55, no. 3 (2003): 469–81.

Rosefielde, Steven. "An Abnormal Country." *The European Journal of Comparative Economics* 2, no. 1 (2005): 3–16.

Rosefielde, Steven. *Monitoring Economic Conditions in the Russian Federation: The Russia Longitudinal Monitoring Survey* 1992–2004. University of North Carolina, May 2005, 15.

Rosefielde, Steven. *Russia in the 21st Century: The Prodigal Superpower*. Cambridge: Cambridge University Press, 2005.

Rosefielde, Steven. "Tea Leaves and Productivity: Bergsonian Norms for Gauging the Soviet Future." *Comparative Economic Studies* 47, no. 2 (2005): 259–73.

Rosefielde, Steven. "Russia 2084: The Treadmill of Muscovite Radical Reform." *BOFIT Working Paper*, Helsinki, 2005.

Rosefielde, Steven. "The Illusion of Transition: Russia's Muscovite Future." *Eastern Economic Journal* 31, no. 2, 2005, 283–96.

Rosefielde, Steven. *Russian Economics from Lenin to Putin*. London: Blackwell, 2007.

Rosefielde, Steven. "Structural Militarization, War Mobilization Reserves and Russia's Failed Transition." Submitted to *Rossiia v Global'noi Politike*, June 2006.

Rosefielde, Steven. "Turmoil in the Kremlin: Sputtering toward Fortress Russia." *Problems of Post-Communism* 53, no. 5 (September/October 2006): 3–10.

Rosefielde, Steven. "The Illusion of Westernization in Russia and China." *Comparative Economic Studies*, 49 (2007): 495–513.

Rosefielde, Steven. "Russian Rearmament: Motives, Options and Prospects," in Jan Leijonhielm and Fredrik Westerlund, eds., *Russian Power Structures*, FOI, Swedish Defense Research Agency, Stockholm, January 2008, 63–83.

Rosefielde, Steven, and Romana Hlouskova. "Why Russia Is Not a Democracy," *Comparative Strategy*, 6, no. 3, 2007, 215–29.

Rosefielde, Steven, and Quinn Mills. *Masters of Illusion: American Leadership in a New Age*. Cambridge: Cambridge University Press, 2007.

Rosefielde, Steven, and R. W. Pfouts, "Economic Optimization and Technical Efficiency in Soviet Enterprises Jointly Regulated by Plans and Incentives," *European Economic Review* 32, no. 6 (1988): 1285–99.

Rosefielde, Steven, and R. W. Pfouts. "Reform and the Defense Sector."
Kommunist, no. 15 (1989): 65–66.

"Rosneft Wins as Yukos Assets Are Auctioned." *Johnson's Russian List*, no.
74, Article 20, March 28, 2007.

Rospatent. "Godovoi otchet 2004." Moscow: Federal Service for Intellectual
Property, Patents and Trademarks, 2004, http://www.fips.ru/rep2001/
rep2004/index.htm.

"Russia 2000." November 2, 1999, http://www.Stratfor.com. *Johnson's Russia List*, November 3, 1999, 13. *Russian Federation 2006.*

"Russian Human Rights Report Highlights Police Violence against Opposition." *Johnson's Russia List*, no. 75, Article 5, March 29, 2007.

"Russian NGO Reject Spy 'Smear.'" *BBC News*, January, bbc.co.uk.

"Russian Ministry Publishes U.S.-Russian WTO Agreement." *Johnson's
Russia List*, no. 262, article 6, November 21, 2006.

"Russia's Federation Council Ok's Bill Amending Election Law." *ITAR-
TASS*, July 13, 2005.

Rutland, Peter. "Russia in 2003: The Power of One." *Transitions Online*,
http://www.to.cz.

Ryzhkov, Nikolai. "O gosudarstvennom plane ekonomicheskovo i sot-
sial'novo razvitiia SSSR na 1986–1990 gody (On the State Plan of the
Economic and Social Development of the USSR during 1986–90). *Pravda*,
June 19, 1986, 1–3.

Sachs, Jeffrey, and Wing Thye Woo. "Understanding China's Economic
Performance." *Journal of Policy Reform* 4, no. 1 (2000): 1–50.

Samuelson, Paul. "Theoretical Notes on Trade Problems." *Review of Economics
and Statistics* 46, (1964): 145–154.

Samuelson, Paul. "Reaffirming the Existence of a 'Reasonable' Bergson-
Samuelson Social Welfare Function." *Economica* 44 (1977): 81–88.

Samuelson, Paul. "Bergsonian Welfare Economics." In Steven Rosefielde,
ed., *Economic Welfare and the Economics of Soviet Socialism*. Cambridge: Cambridge University Press, 1981, 223–66.

Sapir, Jacques. "The Russian Economy: From Rebound to Rebuilding."
Post-Soviet Affairs 17, no. 1 (2001): 9.

Satter, David. *Darkness at Dawn: The Rise of the Russian Criminal State*. New
Haven, CT: Yale University Press, 2003.

Savvides, A., and M. Zachariadis. "International Technology Diffusion
and the Growth of TFP in the Manufacturing Sector of Developing
Economies." *Review of Development Economics* 9, (2005): 482–501.

Schapiro, Leonard. *The Communist Party of the Soviet Union*, 2nd ed. New
York: Random House, 1971.

Schroeder, Gertrude. "The Soviet Economy on a Treadmill of Reforms." In *Soviet Economy in a Time of Change*. Washington, DC: Joint Economic Committee of Congress, 1979, 312–66.

Schroeder, Gertrude. "Soviet Economic 'Reform' Decrees: More Steps on the Treadmill." In *The Soviet Economy in the 1980s: Problems and Prospects*, vol. 1. Washington, DC: Joint Economic Committee of the Congress of the United States, 1982, 79–84.

Schroeder, Gertrude. "Anatomy of Gorbachev's Economic Reforms." *Soviet Economy* 3, no. 3 (1987): 219–41.

Schroeder, Gertrude. "Organizations and Hierarchies: The Perennial Search for Solutions." *Comparative Economic Studies* (1987): 7–28.

Schroeder, Gertrude. "Prepared Statement." In *Economic Reforms in the U.S.S.R.* Washington, DC: Joint Economic Committee of Congress, 1987, 307–26.

Schroeder, Gertrude. "U.S.S.R.: Toward the Service Economy at a Snail's Pace." In *Gorbachev's Economic Plans*, vol. 2. Washington, DC: Joint Economic Committee of the Congress of the United States, 1987, 240–60.

Schroeder, Gertrude. "Post-Soviet Economic Reforms in Perspective." In the *Former Soviet Union in Transition*, vol. 1. Washington, DC: Joint Economic Committee of the Congress of the United States, 1992, 47–80.

Shatalin, Stanislav. *Transition to the Market: 500 Days*. Moscow: Arkhangelskoe, 1990.

Shelton, Judy. *The Coming Soviet Crash: Gorbachev's Desperate Pursuit of Credit in Western Financial Markets*. New York: The Free Press, 1989.

Shenfield, Stephen. "Yet Again on the Siloviki." *Johnson's Russia List*, no. 60, Article 3, March 12, 2007.

Sheviakov, A. I., and A. I. Kiruta. *Modelirovanie Sbalansirovanosti I Soglasovaniia Planovykh Proizvodstvennykh Ob"edinenii I Modeli Planirovania ikh Deiatel'nosti*. Moscow: Nauka, 1984.

Shevstova, Lilia. *Yeltsin's Russia: Myths and Realities*. Washington, DC: Carnegie Endowment for International Peace, 1999.

Shleifer, Andrei. *A Normal Country: Russia after Communism*. Cambridge, MA: Harvard University Press, 2005.

Shleifer, Andrei, and Daniel Treisman. "A Normal Country." *Foreign Affairs* 83, no. 2 (2004): 20–39.

Shlykov, Vitaly. "Chto Pogubilo Sovetskii Soiuz? Amerikanskaia Razvedka o Sovetskikh Voennykh Raskhodakh" (What Destroyed the Soviet Union? American Intelligence Estimates of Soviet Military Expenditures). *Voenny Vestnik*, no. 8, 2001.

Shlykov, Vitaly. "Russian Defence Industrial Complex after 9-11." Paper presented at the Russian Security Policy and the War on Terrorism conference, U.S. Naval Postgraduate School, Monterey, CA, June 2003.

Shlykov, Vitaly. "Globalizatsiia voennoi promyshlennosti-imperativ XXI veka." *Otechestvennye zapiski*, no. 5 (2005): 98–115.

Shlykov, Vitaly. "Nazad v budushchee, ili Ekonomicheskie uroki kholodnoi voiny." *Rossiia v Global'noe Politike* 4, no. 2 (2006): 26–40.

Shlykov, Vitaly. "Nevidimaia Mobilizatsii." *Forbes*, no. 3, March 2006, 1–5.

Shlykov, Vitaly. "The Military Reform and Its Implications for the Modernization of the Russian Armed Forces," in Jan Leijonhielm and Fredrik Westerlund, eds., *Russian Power Structures*, FOI, Swedish Defense Research Agency, Stockholm, January 2008, 50–60.

Simons, Thomas. "Prepared Statement." In *Economic Reforms in the U.S.S.R.* Washington, DC: Joint Economic Committee of Congress, 1987, 351–69.

Sostoyanie priorodnoi sredy v SSSR v 1988g. Moscow: Goskompriroda, 1988.

Sostayanie prirodnoi sredy i prirodookhrannaya deyatelnost v SSSR v 1989g. Moscow: Goskompriroda, 1989.

Stern, Jonathan. "Soviet Oil and Gas Production and Exports to the West: A Framework for Analysis and Forecasting." In *Gorbachev's Economic Plans*, vol. 1. Washington, DC: Joint Economic Committee of Congress, 1987, 500–13.

Stiglitz, Joseph. *Globalization and Its Discontents*. New York: W. W. Norton, 2002.

Stroganov, Yuri. "Oleg Shenin: It's a Pity Yeltsin's Wasn't Arrested." *Johnson's Russia List*, no. 8333, Article 9, August 19, 2004.

Sutela, Pekka. *The Road to the Russian Market Economy*. Helsinki: Kikkimora, 1998.

Sutela, Pekka. "The Role of Banks in Financing Russian Economic Growth." *Post-Soviet Geography and Economics* 39, no. 2 (1998): 96–124.

Teague, Elizabeth. "Gorbachev's 'Human Factor' Policies." In *Gorbachev's Economic Plans*, vol. 2. Washington, DC: Joint Economic Committee of Congress, 1987, 224–39.

Tabata, Shinichiro. "The Great Russian Depression of the 1990s: Observations on Causes and Implications." *Post-Soviet Geography and Economics* 21, no. 6 (2000): 389–98.

Tanner, Murray. "China Rethinks Unrest." *The Washington Quarterly* 27, no. 3 (Summer 2004): 137–56.

Tikhomirov, Vladimir. "Capital Flight from Post-Soviet Russia." *Europe-Asia Studies* 49, no. 4 (1997): 591–615.

Tikhomirov, Vladimir. "Capital flight: Causes, Consequences and Counter-Measures." In Klaus Segbers, *Explaining Post-Soviet Patchworks* 2. Aldershot, UK: Ashgate, 2001, 251–80.

Toda, Yasushi. "Catching-up and Convergence: The Standard of Living and the Consumption Pattern of the Russians and the Japanese in 1913 and 1975–1976." Paper presented at the 10th World Congress of the International Economic History Association, Leuven, 1990.

Treisman, Daniel. "Putin's Silovarchs." *Orbis*, Winter 2007, 141–153.

Treml, Vladimir. "Gorbachev's Anti-Drinking Campaign: A 'Noble Experiment' or a Costly Exercise in Futility?" In *Gorbachev's Economic Plans*, vol. 2. Washington, DC: Joint Economic Committee of Congress, 1987.

Trenin, Dmitri. "Russia Leaves the West." *Foreign Affairs* 85, no. 4 (July/August 2006): 87–96.

"Triumphant Vengeance: Philosopher Zinoview Considers that the West Regained Its Power Thanks to Russia's Defeat." *Pravda*, June 30, 2004, reprinted in *Johnson's Russia List*, no. 8276, Article 15, July 1, 2004.

Tsukhlo, S. "Promyshlennost." *Rossiiskii byulleten' konyukturnykh oprosov*, 169, June 2006.

Ugolovnyi Kodeks RSFSR: Ofitsialnyi tekst s izmeneniyanii na 1 iulia 1950g i s prilozheniem postateino-sistematizirovannykh materialov. Moskow: Gosudarstvennoe Izdalet'stvo Iuridicheskoi Literatury, 1950.

United Nations. *Economic Survey of Europe 2005, No. 1*. New York: United Nations, 2005.

Van Den Berg, Ger. P. "The Soviet Union and the Death Penalty." *Soviet Studies* 35, no. 2 (April 1983): 154–74.

Varshney, Ashutosh. "India's Democratic Challenge." *Foreign Affairs* 86, no. 2 (March/April 2007): 93–106.

Vedemosti Verkhovnovo Soveta SSSR, no. 17, reprinted in Ministerstvo Yustitsii RSFSR, 1947.

Vronskaya, Lisa. "Motherhood Sliding off Agenda for Russia's Women." *Johnson's Russia List*, vol. 9263, Article 3, October 10, 2005.

Weber, Max. *Wirtschaft und Gesellschaft*, vol. 1. Tubingen: Mohr, 1981, 133.

Weiler, Jonathan. *Human Rights in Russia: A Darker Side of Reform*. Boulder, CO: Lynne Rienner Publishers, 2004.

Weir, Fred. "Ambitious Russians Join the Party." *Christian Science Monitor*, February 15, 2006.

Weitzman, Martin. "Iterative Multi-Level Planning with Production Targets." *Econometrica* 38 (1970): 50–65.

Weitzman, Martin. "Prices versus Quantities." *Review of Economic Studies* 41 (1974): 477–91.

Weitzman, Martin. "The New Soviet Incentive Model." *Bell Journal of Economics* 7 (1976): 251–57.

Wertman, Patricia. "The External Financial Position of the Former Soviet Union: From Riches to Rags?" In *The Former Soviet Union in Transition*, vol. 1. Washington, DC: Joint Economic Committee of Congress, 1993, 389–404.

White, Stephen. *Russia Goes Dry: Alcohol, State and Society*. Cambridge: Cambridge University Press, 1996.

"Why Is Benefit Reform Unpopular?" *Johnson's Russia List*, no. 9033, Article 8, January 19, 2005.

Wigg, David. "Prepared Statement." In *Economic Reforms in the U.S.S.R.* Washington, DC: Joint Economic Committee of Congress, 1987, 15–30.

Williamson, John. "Democracy and the 'Washington Consensus.'" World Development 21, no. 8 (1993): 1329–36.

Wohlstetter, Albert. "Racing Forward or Ambling Back." In Robert Conquest et al., *Defending America*. New York: Basic Books, 1977, 110–68.

Wolf, Charles, Jr., and Henry Rowen. *The Impoverished Superpower: Perestroika and the Soviet Military Burden*. San Francisco: Institute for Contemporary Studies, 1990.

Woo, Wing Thye. "The Real Challenges to China's High Growth: Institutions, Poverty, Inequality, Environment and Fiscal Balance." *Comparative Economic Studies*, December 2007.

World Bank Report. *From Transition to Development: Poverty Reduction and Economic Management Unit Europe and Central Asia Region*, April 2004, http://www.worldbank.org.ru.

Yakovlev, Alexander. *A Century of Violence in Soviet Russia*. New Haven, CT: Yale University Press, 2002.

Yakovlev, A. "*Mery gosudarstvennoi podderzhki promyshlennosti: masshtaby, adresaty, effektivnost.*" Moscow: State University – Higher School of Economics, 2006.

Yanov, Alexander. *The Origins of Autocracy: Ivan the Terrible in Russian History.* Berkeley and Los Angeles: University of California Press, 1991.

Yoo, Soh-jung, and Ko Kyoung-tae. "Korea May Introduce Tax to Cope with Low Birthrate." *The Korean Herald*. Reprinted in *Asia News Network*, October 17, 2005.

Yuriev, Mikhail. "Krepost' Rossiia kontseptsiia dlia Presidenta." (Fortress Russia: Strategic Concept for President Putin) *Novaya gazeta*, no. 17, March 15, 2004.

Zaleski, Eugene. *Planning Reforms in the Soviet Union 1962–1966.* Chapel Hill: University of North Carolina Press, 1967, 141–83.

Zhuravskaya, Elena. "The First Stage of Banking Reform in Russia Is Completed: What Lies Ahead?" In Jacek Rostowski, ed., *Banking Reform in Central Europe and the Former Soviet Union*. Budapest: CEU Press, 1995.

Ziegler, Charles E. *Environmental Policy in the USSR.* London: Frances Pinter, 1987.

Zweig, David, and Bi Jianhai. "China's Global Hunt for Energy." *Foreign Affairs* 84, no. 5 (September/October 2005): 25–38.

1936 Constitution of the USSR, http://en.wikisource.org/wiki/1936_Constitution_of_the_USSR.

Index

500 days program, 36, 69–70, 282. *See
    also* Shatalin, Stanislav
food, 162, 234t
    program for, 41
forced substitution, 17, 27, 89–90, 282
foreign bondholders, 117–18, 134
foreign debt, 149
foreign direct investment (FDI), 246
    for China, 266–7, 269
foreign investment, 117–18, 148, 246
    for China, 266–7, 269
    in venture capital, 249
foreigners, 200
"The Former Soviet Union in Transition,"
    Vol. 1, 74
Fortress Russia, 145, 151–2
free enterprise theory, 109. *See also*
    democratic free enterprise
freedom. *See also* constitution;
    economic freedom
    of information, 241
    religious, 199
Freedom House, 180
Friendly, Albert, 160
FSB. *See* secret police
Fukuyama, Francis, 19, 23
Fyodor I, 23n12

G-7
    appeal to, 49
    grand bargain at, 125n31
    on transition, 3
G-8, 138
Gaddy, Clifford, 122
Gaidar, Yegor, 170
Gaspec, 182n40, 215n15, 220
Gazprom (gas industry), 48, 215n15
GDP. *See* gross domestic product
Geary, R. S., 87
Geary-Khamis approach, 87
gender
    in development, 162
    life expectancy and, 132t, 156–7,
        253t
genshtab, 52, 62, 101
German reunification, 66–7, 71, 212
gerontocracy, 42
Gerschenkron, Alexander, 4, 9, 143,
    266

ghosting (dismissed workers still listed as
    employed), 121
Gilelman, Zvi, 156–7
GKChP. *See* State Emergency
    Committee
GKO. *See* State Treasury Obligations
glasnost (openness), 61, 66, 157, 189. *See
    also otkritnost*
    for depression, 1
    western public culture on, 56–7
glavk (administrative departments), 46,
    97, 282
GNP. *See* gross national product
Gogol, Nikolai, 264
golden rule, 15n18
    rule of contract/criminal law v., 15
Goldman, Emma, 5
Golitsyn, Anatoly, 60n12
Gorbachev, Mikhail Sergeyevich. *See
    also* coup d'etat
    Baltic states and, 70–1
    Bolsheviks v., 47
    Communist Party and, 45n16
    for cooperatives, 47
    correlation of forces and, 62, 64
    for democratization, 52
    for economic growth, 42
    expectations for, 53–4
    GKChP against, 68n22, 76
    as hero, 63
    for human/civil rights, 205
    liberalization of, 42
    on Market Communism, 34, 39–40
    as *mineralny sekretar,* 45
    at Murmansk, 45–6
    for new thinking, 52, 58, 212
    on ownership, 98
    against physical systems management,
        62–3
    against popular sovereignty, 67
    power elite and, 44–5
    for privateers, 49, 51–2
    with Reagan, 35–6
    reality of, 64
    reforms of, 43n15, 45–7, 49, 75
    for Shatalin plan, 69–70
    Stalin v., 54
    summary of, 40
    timelines on, 35–7, 74–5

TFP. *See* productivity growth
the thaw, 297
timelines
    on Gorbachev, 35–7, 74–5
    of Putin, 137–8
    for Yeltsin, 93–4
Tiutchev, Fyodor, 102
tobacco abuse, 160
tolkachy (pushers), 29, 39
totalitarianism, 297
town and village enterprise (TVEs), 261
trafficking, 195
transition, 297
    imminence of, 10
Transition to the Market, 69
transitologist, 297
    on liberalization, 133
treadmill of economic reform, 242
treadmill of reform, 41, 297
treaties, 21n8. *See also specific treaties*
Treaty on Offensive Strategic
        Reductions (SORT), 221
Treisman, Daniel, 192
Trotsky, Leon, 142n10
trudovye kollektivy (enterprise worker
        councils), 38–9, 49–50, 298
trust, 19
tsar, 11–12, 298. *See also specific tsars*
TTO. *See* technology transfer offices
Tugan-Baranovsky, Mikhail, xxii
turnover tax (value-added tax), 113
TVEs. *See* town and village enterprise

ukaz, 12–13
Ummah (Moslem fundamentalists), 222,
        224, 298
unemployment, 135, 234t, 236n12. *See
        also* workers
    in China, 264
    statistics on, 120–1
unemployment crisis management,
        120–2
unified social tax (ESN), 254
Union of Soviet Socialist Republics
        (USSR)
    correlation of forces against, 30
    Socialists for, 56
United Nations, 123n27
United Russia, 179

United States (U.S.), 18. *See also* arms
        race; Bush, George; Central
        Intelligence Agency; cold war;
        democracy; Reagan, Ronald; the
        West
U.S. *See* United States
U.S. Bureau of the Census, 131
USAID, 250
USSR. *See* Union of Soviet Socialist
        Republics
USSR/Russia, GDP for, 86t, 87t
USSR/Russia per capita, GDP for, 86t,
        88t
USSR/U.S.
    GDP for, 87t, 88t
    GDP per capita for, 87t
    PPP for, 89n15, 90t

value subtracted, 298
value-added growth, 236t
vanguard of the proletariat, 298
Vasily III, 141
VC. *See* venture capital
veche (popular assembly), 106n8
venture capital (VC), 250
    foreign investment in, 249
Venture Investment Fund (VIF), 250
Vertyachikh, Alexander, 106n8
VIF. *See* Venture Investment Fund
violence, 171. *See also* repression; secret
        police; terrorism; war
virgin lands program, 298
virtual economy, 114–15, 134, 298–9
    barterization as, 122
visible hand, 298
voucher privatization, 110, 125, 299
vozhd (leader), 11
VPK. *See* military industrial complex
vrag naroda (enemy of the people), 24
    market leasing socialism v., 31, 299

wages
    in China, 267
    enterprise wage funds and, 112
Walesa, Lech, 71
Walking Together *(Idushchem vmeste),*
        178
war. *See also* cold war; 'Star Wars'
    class, 20–1, 84, 278